Bread and salt

Bread and salt

A social and economic history of food and drink in Russia

****

R.E.F. SMITH

and

DAVID CHRISTIAN

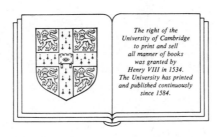

The right of the
University of Cambridge
to print and sell
all manner of books
was granted by
Henry VIII in 1534.
The University has printed
and published continuously
since 1584.

CAMBRIDGE UNIVERSITY PRESS

Cambridge

London   New York   New Rochelle
Melbourne   Sydney

Published by the Press Syndicate of the University of Cambridge
The Pitt Building, Trumpington Street, Cambridge CB2 IRP
32 East 57th Street, New York, NY 10022, USA
296 Beaconsfield Parade, Middle Park, Melbourne 3206, Australia

First published 1984

Printed in Great Britain by the University Press, Cambridge

Library of Congress catalogue card number: 83–18812

British Library Cataloguing in Publication Data
Smith, R.E.F.
Bread and salt: a social and economic history of food and drink in Russia
1. Food–History   2. Cookery, Russian–History
I. Title   II. Christian, David
641.3′00947   Tx85

ISBN 0 521 25812X

Churches, ikons, crosses, bells,
Painted whores and garlic smells,
Vice and vodka every place –
This is Moscow's daily face.

> Quoted in Olearius, *Travels*, 1647.

Ils mangent & boivent fort mal.

> Foy de la Neuville, *Relation curieuse et
> nouvelle de Moscovie*, 1699.

The Diet of Russia is exceedingly good, and, in my Opinion, this Place is very fit for an Epicure; for, in short, Eating and Drinking take up a Third Part of their Time.

Elizabeth Justice, *A Voyage to Russia*, 1739.

We must begin by stating the first premise of all human existence and, therefore, of all history, the premise, namely, that man must be in a position to live in order to be able to 'make history'. But life involves before everything else eating and drinking.

Karl Marx, *The German Ideology*, 1845–6.

Contents

Illustrations

Plates

Figures

Maps

Tables

Acknowledgements

We are grateful to all those colleagues and friends who have contributed greatly to this work by discussion and criticism. In particular, R.H. Hilton, D.J.L. Johnson and Maureen Perrie made many helpful suggestions on various aspects of the early chapters. V.L. Ménage was generous in his efforts to elucidate the origins of the term *kabak*. The late A.E. Pennington made most helpful comments on the seventeenth-century material; it is sad not to be able to thank her again. Part of the introduction was the basis for a paper presented to *IIème Colloque International du Centre d'Etudes Médiévales de Nice*, on the theme 'Manger et Boire au Moyen Age', in October 1982. Earlier versions of chapter 3 appeared in *Peasants in History: Essays in Honour of Daniel Thorner* (Calcutta, OUP, 1980) and of chapter 6 in *Petits Propos Culinaires*, no. 4.

David Christian would like to thank Macquarie University and the Australian Research Grants Committee for financial support during two periods of study leave in England and Finland.

We would also like to thank the British Library and the Royal Library, Copenhagen, for permission to reproduce illustrations.

R.E.F. SMITH
DAVID CHRISTIAN

Abbreviations

AAE
Akty sobrannye v bibliotekakh i arkhivakh Rossiiskoi imperii arkheograficheskoyu ekspeditsieyu, Arkheograficheskaya Komissiya (4 vols., SPB., 1836).

AFZ
Akty feodal'nogo zemlevladeniya i khozyaistva XIV–XVI vekov (3 vols., M., 1951–61).

AI
Akty istoricheskie (5 vols., SPB., 1841–2).

Arkhiv IT v R
Arkhiv istorii truda v Rossii.

ARG
Akty Russkogo gusudarstva 1505–1526gg. (M., 1975)

ASEI
Akty sotsial'no-ekonomicheskoi istorii severo-vostochnoi Rusi kontsa XIV-nachala XVI v. (3 vols., M., 1952–64).

AYu
Akty otnosyashchiesya do yuridicheskago byta drevnei Rusi (3 vols., SPB., 1857–84).

BSE
Bol'shaya Sovetskaya entsiklopediya

ChtOIDR
Chteniya v Obshchestve istorii i drevnostei rossiiskikh pri Moskovskom universitete (264 vols., 1846–1918).

DAI
Dopolneniya k Aktam istoricheskim (12 vols., SPB., 1846–72).

EzhAI
Ezhegodnik po agrarnoi istorii Vostochnoi Evropy

GVNiP
Gramoty Velikogo Novgoroda i Pskova, M.-L., 1949.

IAO
Imperatorskago (Moskovskago) arkheologicheskago obshchestva

IKDR
Istoriya Kul'tury Drevnei Rusi, Domongol'skii period (2 vols., M.-L., 1948–51).

IZ
Istoricheskie zapiski, M. (fasc. 1ff, 1937ff).

KS
Kratkie soobshcheniya o dokladakh i polyevykh issledovaniyakh (M.-L., 1939f).

LZAK
Letopis' zanyatii Arkheograficheskoi komissii (SPB. etc., 1864f).

MIA
Materialy i issledovaniya po arkheologii SSSR (M.-L., 1941f).

MISKh
Materialy po istorii sel'skogo khozyaistva i krest'

	yanstva SSSR (vols. III, M., 1959f). Continuation of following.
MIZ	*Materialy po istorii zemledeliya SSSR* (2 vols., M., 1952–6). Continued as *MISKh*.
NIL	*Novgorodskaya pervaya letopis' starshego i i mladshego izvodov*, ed. A.N. Nasonov (M., 1950).
OIDR	*Obshchestvo istorii i drevnostei rossiiskikh.*
ORK	*Ocherki russkoi kul'tury: ORK* XIII–XV*vv*. (2 parts, M., 1970), *ORK* XVI*v*. (2 parts, M., 1977), ORK XVII*v*. (2 parts, M., 1979).
ORSA	*Otdelenie russkoi i slavyanskoi arkheologii.*
Pam Ryaz	*Pamyatniki russkoi pis'mennosti*, XV–XVI*vv*, *Ryazanskii krai*, ed. S.I. Kotkov (M., 1978).
PiB	*Pis'ma i bumagi Imperatora Petra Velikogo.* (vols. I–VII, SPB., 1887–1918; VIIIf M., 1948f).
PL	*Pskovskie letopisi*
PRP	*Pamyatniki russkogo pravda*, 8 fasc. (M., 1956–63).
PSRL	*Polnoe sobranie russkikh letopisei* (SPB., L., 1841f).
PSZ	*Polnoe sobranie zakonov Rossiiskoi Imperii.*
PVL	*Povest' vremenykh let*, ed., V.P. Adrianova-Peretts, D.S. Likhachev (2 vols., M., 1950).
RANION	*Rossiiskaya assotsiatsiya nauchnoissledovatel'skikh institutov obshchestvennykh nauk*
RIB	*Russkaya istoricheskaya biblioteka* (39 vols., SPB., 1872–1927).
RIZh	*Russkii istoricheskii zhurnal*
SGGD	*Sobranie gosudarstvennykh gramot i dogovorov.*
SGKE	*Sbornik gramot Kollegii ekonomii* (2 vols., Peterburg, 1922–9).
TrGIM	*Trudy gosudarstvennogo istoricheskogo muzeya* (M., 1935f).
TrVEO	*Trudy Vol'no-ekonomicheskago obshchestva* (280 vols., SPB., 1765–1915).
ZhMVD	*Zhurnal Ministerstva vnutrennykh del* (SPB., 1829–62).
ZORSA	*Zapiski Otdeleniya russkoi i slavyanskoi arkheologii Imperatorskago russkago arkheologicheskago obshchestva* (13 vols., SPB. etc., 1851–1918).

Note on units

The publisher suggested that, throughout the text, modern equivalents be restricted to metric units. For those who are not familiar with this system, the following table of equivalents may be helpful.

Weight

1 pud = 16.38 kg = 36.11 lb
1 pound (Russian = 410 g = 14.44 oz)

Length
1 versta = 1.067 km = 0.663 mile
1 sazhen = 2.134 m = 7 feet

Area
1 desyatina = 1.0925 ha = 2.7 acre
1 chet = $\frac{1}{2}$ desyatina

The chetvert or chet was also used as a grain measure. Until the early seventeenth century the chet contained 4 puds of rye or $2\frac{1}{2}$ puds of oats.

Introduction

This book is a study of some of the social and economic implications of eating and drinking in Russia before 1900. It is not about Russian cuisine, nor a detailed excursion into the curious anthropology of Eastern Europe, though at times it touches both. We treat eating and drinking as social activities which involve the economics of production, storage and distribution. These aspects in their turn involve both social controls and state taxation. Approached in this way the subject illuminates many aspects of Russian history and culture.

Our concern is with agrarian Russia prior to the rapid industrialisation in the late nineteenth century. The twentieth century is a separate matter, governed as it is by different rules of production, methods of storage and distribution.[1]

In all pre-industrial societies food was (and is) a far more vital concern for both the individual household and the state than it is in industrial societies today. At the national level, agricultural produce accounted for 50% of Russian national income in 1870 and 44% even as late as 1913.[2] In industrial societies scientific agriculture, extensive trade networks, refrigeration and chemical preservatives have made problems of food supply seem merely technical; in pre-industrial and early industrial societies food was *the* vital concern. Further, foodstuffs in such societies generally contributed the bulk of society's 'surplus' production, and were therefore the major element in exchanges and the fiscal systems. The chapters which follow give many examples of the age-old struggle between state and peasant for control of the foodstuffs produced by the peasant, and of the way in which this struggle affected social and economic conditions.

For all its importance, the historical study of food is in practice

[1] There is, in any event, an excellent study on the twentieth century: Basile Kerblay, 'L'évolution de l'alimentation rurale en Russie (1886–1960)', *Annales: Economies, Sociétés, Civilisations* (September–October, 1962), 885–913.

[2] R.W. Goldsmith, 'The Economic Growth of Tsarist Russia', *Economic Development and Cultural Change*, IX (1960–1), 444–5.

extremely difficult to tackle systematically. There are a number of pioneering works in the field, but as yet there exists no clear methodology and no general agreement even on the basic questions that need to be asked. In 1961, as part of a larger project on material life, *Annales* launched a long-term symposium on the subject of *alimentation*. Yet fourteen years later the historical study of food had still not advanced very far.[3]

These difficulties mean that it is unrealistic to attempt any precise quantitative study. We have chosen rather to illustrate the wide implications of eating and drinking for Russian history by looking at some selected topics. This is a first attempt at a broad survey of some, mainly social and economic, aspects of food and drink in Russian history. Section one, dealing with what may be loosely called the pre-modern period, surveys the importance of grain and flour products, of gathering, of the salt industry and of drink in early Russia. This extends into the late seventeenth century. Section two focusses on the increasingly important part played by the state, particularly clear from the early seventeenth century, in regulating food and drink for both social and financial purposes. Section three discusses peasant diets before the massive changes of the late nineteenth-century industrialisation, but already under the impact of the growth of town population, of markets and of the railway network. Chapters 1–6 have been written by R.E.F. Smith and 7–9 by David Christian, but we are jointly responsible for the book as a whole. We hope that our different emphases and approaches, partly the results of different types of data, will stimulate further work. A survey of the history of Russian diet may be of interest in itself; but we hope also that it will help to adjust some ideas about European patterns by making some East European materials more widely available and stressing the changes which could occur within the grain dominated pre-industrial dietary regime.

[3]'Pour l'histoire de l'alimentation: quelques remarques de méthode', *Annales: Economies, Sociétés, Civilisations*, II–III (March–June, 1975), 431. English translation in *Food and Drink*, ed. R. Forster and O. Ranum (The Johns Hopkins University Press, Baltimore and London, 1979), 1–16.

PART I

****

The early diet

I

※※

Farming and gathering:
grain and game

The forest was the natural environment that the East Slavs colonised and it is often thought that the gathering of forest products, together with hunting and fishing, was the first form of economic activity in the area which is now European Russia. In fact, this is by no means certain. It is much more probable that farming by means of slash and burn techniques was the technology which mediated the Slavonic penetration of the forest zone. Such farming was, of course, accompanied by gathering; this combination is enshrined in the Russian term for hospitality (*khleb-sol'*, literally 'bread-salt'). Bread and salt, then, had important symbolic significance, a significance which does not appear to have specifically Christian roots. The two elements of the term represent essential items in Russian diet, but also signify two types of economy: farming and gathering. Both continued not only through the late colonisation of the East European plain, but into modern times.

The grains grown on the closes and fields burnt and cleared in the forests were winter-sown rye (the basic grain for human consumption) and spring-sown oats (for consumption by man and horse), with barley and millet of less importance for much of the area. There was relatively little wheat; its scarcity added to its status value: in 1471 in Novgorod 'the barleymen rose against the wheatmen'. From the thirteenth–fourteenth centuries on, buckwheat was a minor, but gradually increasingly important, item among the grains grown.[1]

Hemp and flax seeds were also used as foodstuffs. They were used in dishes with peas, for instance, or gave oil which was either an element in various dishes or the medium in which they were cooked.[2] Vegetable oils such as these were of especial importance during fasts, when animal fats were forbidden by the Orthodox church.

Grain was consumed in a great variety of ways, as would be ex-

---

[1] Dal', *Tolkovyi slovar'*, vol. I, 1353, s.v. *zhito*. Smith, *Peasant Farming in Muscovy* (Cambridge, 1977), 32–5.
[2] *Ibid.*, 39–40.

pected, since it formed by far the greatest part of the diet. Whole grain was used for gruels (*kashi*, *kashitsy*) and related dishes both savoury and sweet, some of which, such as frumenty, had ritual significance, and this perhaps hints at their antiquity. As late as 1636 priests complained that

On the seventh Thursday after Easter, lord, the women and maids gather under trees, under birches and, as it were, bring sacrifices, pasties and gruel and omelettes, and bowing to the birches they begin to sing, weaving satanic songs, going and clapping hands, and acting in every way like devils, sitting down, they eat what they have brought.[3]

Groats, the hulled or pounded but not ground grain, was used for a range of similar gruels, pottages and porridge, and also fools (*kiseli*). Flour was the basis for a great variety of bread and pastry, but it was usually leavened. Pancakes, fritters and pies were all common and made with risen dough. Bread was usually made from rye flour. In the seventeenth century an English doctor recorded that the tsar's bread 'is made of Rye, which the Russian esteem a stronger nourishment than Wheat'.[4] This, presumably, was the tsar's everyday diet. The flour could be of different grades according to fineness. This varied according to the milling and also the subsequent treatment: coarse flour was put through a sieve (*resheto*), but fine flour was bolted (*sitnaya*). The finest wheat flour (*krupichataya*), used at the tsar's ceremonial feasts and on other special occasions, was 20% of the original amount of grain; white flour was 23% and the rest 35%.[5] Rolls made from wheat were a delicacy and came in a number of shapes and types; they were sold at markets, particularly in the larger towns. Wheat was also used to produce the communion bread; this, too, was leavened. Unleavened noodles (*lapsha*) and pastry used, like ravioli, to enclose some mixture (*pel'meni*), seem to be sixteenth-century loans, allegedly, from the Tatars, but probably such items had long been general among the non-Slav mid-Volga peoples.

Grain and grain products formed the basis of a number of other items of diet. Apart from their contribution as thickeners in some soups, perhaps their main additional use was as the raw material for a range of drinks which varied from the non-alcoholic kvas ('a Liquor one degree below our small Beer'), the everyday drink, to light beer (*braga*) and fully fermented strong beer.[6]

[3]*ChtOIDR* (1902), book 2, miscellany, 28–9.
[4]Collins, *The Present State of Russia*, 57.
[5]*Domostroi po spisku Imp. OIDR*, 152, includes a regulation on this.
[6]Collins, *The Present State of Russia*, 13.

гоⷮⷤⷤⷤⷤⷤшⷨⷡⷡⷡⷡⷡⷡⷤⷤⷡⷤⷤⷤⷤⷤⷡⷡⷡⷡ

1 Convulsions from ergotism, sixteenth century.
A manuscript illustration showing figures in the foreground suffering convulsions. The inscription reads: 'That autumn, on 14 September, the convulsions disease started among the people and in the winter there was a great famine.'

A diet based overwhelmingly on grain and foodstuffs derived from it involved certain dangers. If the grain crop failed, dearth or famine inevitably followed; people fled elsewhere, or social disturbance and epidemic disease were likely to appear. There are numerous references to this in the early Russian chronicles.[7] In the winter of 1187–8 in Novgorod there was a dearth: 'they bought grain at two nogatas and a barrel (*kad'*) of rye at six grivnas; but by God's mercy there was no disturbance amongst the people', as evidently might have been expected.[8] There was widespread exposure to the risk of ergotism and similar diseases caused by the consumption of mildewed grain. There are references to ergotism in many saints' lives from various parts of Russia, and these outbreaks were often associated with famine, as in 1422.[9] The disease was, evidently, largely a lower class phenomenon.[10]

Cultivated crops also included vegetables and fruits, not always used in ways to which we are accustomed. Early in the seventeenth century an Englishman wrote that '*Garlicke* and *Onions*, must besauce many of my words, as then it did the most parte of their dishes.'[11] Later writers confirm this. 'They generally prepare their food with garlic and onion, so all their rooms and houses, including the sumptuous chambers of the Grand Prince's palace in the Kremlin, give off an odor offensive to us Germans.'[12] 'The victor's palm among the fruits the Russians favour and value goes to the onion and garlick.'[13] It seems unlikely that these crops were a speciality of monastic and boyar cooking, as has been suggested, and only later became items of general consumption.[14] Common people ate garlic raw with bread. The Danish envoy to Russia in 1709 recorded that garlic was 'not only used to flavour all dishes, but they also eat it raw throughout the day'.[15] Garlic was the Russians' third doctor (the first two were the bath and vodka).

Turnips, especially in northern Russia, were important, largely occupying the place in diet later held by the potato. We do not know when the phrase originated, but 'cheaper than a boiled turnip' suggests how readily and cheaply available they were. Carrots, beetroot and radishes were also common; radishes were sometimes cut and dried,

[7]For example, to take only the Novgorod chronicle, see *NIL*, 21 (1127), 22 (1128), 54–5 (1215–16), 69–70 (1230–1), 91 (1303). See also Kahan, 'Natural calamities', *Jahrbücher*, 16, 365f.
[8]*NIL*, 39. Note also events in 1169–70, 1314–15, 1455.
[9]Bogoyavlenskii, *Drevnerusskoe vrachevanie*, 176–8, 257–9; Alexander, *Bubonic Plague*, 15–16.
[10]Bogoyavlenskii, *Drevnerusskoe vrachevanie*, 113, 178.
[11]*Sir Thomas Smithes Voiage and Entertainment in Rushia* (London, 1605).
[12]*The Travels of Olearius in Seventeenth-century Russia* (Stanford, 1967).
[13]Reitenfels, 'Skazaniya' in *ChtOIDR* (1906), book 3, 155.
[14]Vdovina in *Ocherki russkoi kul'tury XVII veka*, part 1, 226.
[15]Just, cited in Mel'gunova, *Russkii byt*, 86.

then pounded into a flour which was then made into a sweet (*mazyu-n'ya*).[16] Peas were fairly common, but pulses in general do not seem to have been important in the diet. Cabbage, on the other hand, was greatly used, especially in soups, and was pickled in vast quantities. Cucumbers, too, were commonly pickled. Olearius, in the 1630s, therefore, was probably in part correct in claiming that the Russian's daily food consists of 'groats, beets, cabbages, cucumbers, and fresh or salt fish'.[17] Elsewhere he commented favourably on the pies, caviare and mead, but he failed to appreciate the great variety of bread and other pastry. At the end of the seventeenth century another foreigner gave a differing, but not totally dissimilar account. 'They eat and drink very badly, their most usual nourishment being only cucumbers and Astrakhan melons, which they pickle in water in summer, flour and salt.'[18] Presumably many grain constituents in the diet, common to both eastern and western parts of Europe, were omitted from consideration.

Melons, some grown locally, some imported from the south, were available in Moscow. Apple orchards were known from the twelfth century.[19] Pears, cherries and plums were also used.[20] Lemons, preserved in salt, were imported. Lemon rinds, wheaten rolls, apples, nuts were listed as snacks or appetisers at the early seventeenth-century court.[21] For the most part, too, spices were imported; they became commoner in the sixteenth–seventeenth centuries, perhaps as a result of Tatar tastes spreading after the defeat of the Kazan' Khanate in the mid-sixteenth century. Imports, however, often also came from the West through Archangel. Pepper, ginger and cloves were supplemented later by saffron and coriander.[22]

Gathering, unlike farming seems in the main to have been the means of providing raw materials rather than food, but this may be a distortion of reality by documents often concerned with rents in kind or marketed produce.[23] Many of the foodstuffs gathered were fragile, not easily transported without damage when fresh, and so were best consumed on the spot or processed in some way in order to preserve them. Berries and fungi of all sorts are in this category. Berries preserved with

---

[16]Vdovina, *ORK XVIIv.*, part 1, 227.
[17]*Travels*, 155. But Collins, *The Present State of Russia*, 13 suggests a similar diet, though without fish, was that of fast days.
[18]Foy de la Neuville, *Rélation curieuse et nouvelle de Moscovie* (The Hague, 1699), 182–3.
[19]Artsikhovskii, in *ORK XIII–XVvv.*, part 1, 299.
[20]Margeret, *Estat de l'Empire de Russie et Grande Duché de Moscovie* (Paris, 1607), 2v., noted there were few pears and plums.
[21]Peyerle, Ustryalov, *Skazaniya*, 59.
[22]Kurts, *Sochinenie Kil'burgera, passim*.
[23]Smith, *Peasant Farming*, 47–56.

honey or dried strings of fungi were transportable. Fungi in the seventeenth century were 'the poor man's food, the rich man's dainties' and
it was estimated that a thousand cartloads a year were preserved in
brine in Moscow alone.[24] Some plants are also likely to have been
consumed locally: nettles, sorrel, goose-foot, ground-elder are known
to have been used.[25] Nuts would withstand handling better. Honey
from wild bees was used to prepare a sort of sweet from berries, which
was dried in the sun into a kind of jelly or pastille.[26] The sugared
cranberries sometimes to be found in Soviet shops seem to be a descen-
dant of this.

The most important items of food gathered, however, were fish and
game. These were important sources of protein; in fact, they may well
have been virtually the only source of animal protein for most people:
with the adoption of Christianity fish became very important, because
the church decreed between 192 and 216 fast days in different years.
Fasts were strict and seem to have been truly observed.[27] Even the tsar'
during Lent 'eats but three meals a week, *viz.* on *Thursday, Saturday,
Sunday*; for the rest he takes a piece of brown bread and salt, a pickled
Mushroom or Cucumber and drinks a cup of small beer'.[28]

A great range of fish was taken from the rivers and lakes of Russia
from early times.[29]

In all Europe there cannot be better or more diverse kinds of freshwater fish,
of which there are a great number, that is to say the sturgeon, the beluga, the
catrina [sc. *osetrina*, i.e. *nisetru*], the *belaya ryba* which means 'white fish' is
bigger than the salmon, the sterlet and all those kinds that we have in France,
except for trout, and very cheap, as are also other kinds of food.[30]

Salmon, sturgeons and other noble fish were perhaps not available to
all, but pike-perch, pike, bream, white-fish and smelts were probably
common. Sixteenth-century documents mention at least thirty-five
different kinds of fish.[31] Those not consumed fresh were mostly salted;
some were smoked, while others were packed in ice. Dried fish was
grated to make a flour for adding to soups. By the late sixteenth

[24]Collins, *The Present State of Russia*, 138–9.
[25]A recent Russian work, A.K. Koshcheev, *Dikorastushchie s"edobnye rasteniya v nashem pitanii* (Moscow, 1980), lists almost a hundred wild plants still used as food.
[26]V. Peskov gives an account of present-day gathering of wild honey in Bashkiriya in *Komsomol-'skaya pravda* (6 Dec. 81). I am grateful to M.J. Berry for calling my attention to this item.
[27]Olearius, *Travels*, 269–71. Cp. Margaret, *Estat*, 11v.–12; Collins, *The Present State of Russia*, 13; Foy de la Neuville, *Rélation curieuse*, 201.
[28]Collins, *The Present State of Russia*, 122.
[29]Smith, *Origins*, 40–2; *Peasant Farming*, 60–6.
[30]Margeret, *Estat*, 3.
[31]Gorskaya, in *ORK XVIv.*, part 1: 223.

century fish-ponds had been developed at some monasteries and other wealthy estates.[32] For the tsar's table, and no doubt for some other very rich consumers, boats with perforated holds were used to transport live fish. In the late seventeenth century the tsar's expenditure on fish was enormous, more than 100,000 rubles a year.[33] Foreigners were impressed by, and sometimes misinterpreted, the Russian taste for fish ripened in brine. 'In Moscow they use coarse salt fish, which sometimes stinks, because they are thrifty with the salt. Nevertheless, they like to eat it.'[34] Snacks such as these contributed both to the Russian addiction to drink and to an enormous consumption of salt.

Game was plentiful and may even have supplied the greater part of the meat consumed.[35] In the early seventeenth century, according to a French mercenary, there were still

... all manner of venison and animals which are found in France, but for the boar. For of stags, does and roe deer there is a plenty in the east and in the south in the lands of Tatary and between Kazan' and Astrakhan', and there are many elans which they call the great beast: throughout Russia rabbits are very rare; pheasants, partridge, thrushes, blackbirds, quail and larks are found in great quantity, as well as numberless other game, but woodcocks are seen but little, though in August and September there are many cranes; wild swans, geese and duck in winter, but I have seen no storks, except one only which was all black.[36]

The omission of any mention of hare is strange.

The fact that game was there, however, did not necessarily mean it was available to eat. Three points seem worth making in regard to this. One: the documentary evidence shows that the distribution of animal species changed as a result of man's activities in the forest; in particular, the larger animals and those demanding an undisturbed environment were increasingly restricted in distribution even before the great changes of the seventeenth and eighteenth centuries.[37] Pollution is not a modern problem.

Two: the mass of peasants were deprived of access to large game as a source of protein even before changes in the distribution of such species had taken place. As estate boundaries came together, at least nominally, in the fifteenth and sixteenth centuries, lords sometimes claimed hunt-

---

[32]Smith, *Peasant Farming*, 138.
[33]Kotošixin, *O Rossii*, 116.
[34]Olearius, *Travels*, 155–6. Cp. Collins, *The Present State of Russia*, 31; Foy de la Neuville, *Rélation curieuse*, 201.
[35]Smith, *Peasant Farming*, 66–70.
[36]Margeret, *Estat*, 3.
[37]See the works of S.V. Kirikov.

ing rights. Peasants were in practice largely restricted to taking small game. Larger animals, whether used as food or not, were reserved for the pleasure of hunting. A sixteenth-century visitor to Moscow observed that 'an incredible number of wild goats and horses abound in the fields adjacent to the town, but no one is allowed to take them either with nets or dogs; the sovereign grants permission for this pleasure only to those closest to him or to foreign ambassadors'.[38] Such restrictions, at least around Moscow, increased with the elaborate development of the tsar's hunt in the seventeenth century.

Three: powerful voices, however, were raised against nets and snares in which animals and birds were killed without their being bled. 'And of those who live in villages do some eat squirrel or anything else? This is evil, but more evil than that is the flesh of a strangled animal; it would be better to eat squirrel and beaver rather than the flesh of a strangled animal.'[39] The Orthodox Church was concerned about moral, not economic pollution. Vermin, such as squirrel, were not to be eaten; beaver and horsemeat were also unclean. This attitude derived ultimately from the Jewish food laws found in Leviticus, but mediated by the decree of the Jerusalem council recorded in Acts xv. In the West, however, the fourfold prohibition imposed on Christians (idols, fornication, things strangled and blood) sometimes appeared as a threefold one, omitting the third item.[40] In this threefold form, 'blood' is then most naturally interpreted as 'murder' and the decree becomes a purely moral injunction not connected with dietary laws. Even when the fourfold version subsequently became accepted in the West, for practical purposes it was ignored and the earlier tradition maintained.[41] The Orthodox, however, kept their dietary purity and long continued to accuse the Western church of lapsing by eating 'things strangled and carrion'.[42]

The church council of 1551, for example, prohibited the consumption by cleric or layman of blood and of things strangled and urged the tsar' to send his instruction round 'all towns and market-places that things strangled, grouse and hares, should not be sold and Orthodox Christians should not buy or eat such things at all'.[43] Some, it was complained, 'for the satisfaction of their belly, by some craft, make the

[38]Cited, without source, in Rabinovich and Latysheva, *Iz zhizni drevnei Moskvy*, 161.
[39]Kirik to Bishop Nifont (before 1156), in *Ruskiya dostopamyatnosti*, part 1 (Moscow, 1815), 100.
[40]Tertullian, *De pudicitia*, xii.
[41]I am most grateful to the late Professor H.F.D. Sparks for guidance on this difference between Russia and the West.
[42]Sreznevskii, *Materialy dlya slovarya drevnerusskago yazyka*, iii, 1144 (fourteenth century).
[43]*Stoglav*, ch. 91, question 1, 260; cp. question 32, 55.

blood of each animal into a dish which they call sausage and so eat the blood'. Such black puddings were also prohibited. The prohibitions seem to have had little effect. In 1636 priests were still complaining that 'every sort of illegal act has increased: Hellenic nonsense and rubbish and devilish games, and, lord, they eat the flesh of strangled animals and in the markets, alas, they sell strangled animals, geese, ducks, grouse and hares which are not proper for Orthodox Christians to eat'.[44]

As late as the end of the seventeenth century such prohibitions were noted and commented on by foreigners.

It is to be observed, that the *Muscovites* retain to this Day some Remnants of the *Mosaick* Law; For, though they do not abhor Swine's Flesh, yet they will not touch a Squirrel, Coney, or Hare. But, which is the oddest of all, They hold it *Pagan*, or *Unclean*, to eat Veal; but not Lamb: For what Reason, neither they, nor anybody else, know.[45]

Earlier in the century Collins had explained that 'That which is *Pogano* (or unclean) may not be eaten at any time; as Horse-flesh, Mares milk, Asses milk, Hares, Squirrels, Coneys, Elks: *Theriaca* or Treacle is *Pogano*, because it has Vipers flesh in it.'[46] At about the same date a Frenchman who served in Russia wrote that 'they eat no veal because of a consideration it is improper to name, nor pigeon because of superstition, since the Holy Spirit is represented by that figure'.[47] Earlier in the seventeenth century, however, another Frenchman had observed that 'no veal is eaten in Russia, this being against their religion'.[48] Olearius, on the other hand, noted that veal was good.[49] Thus, it was not a lack of meat-bearing animals but institutional, especially religious constraints that limited the meats allowed in Russian diet.

Apart from some items consumed raw, these products of both farming and gathering were cooked, either when fresh or after they had been preserved, by freezing in winter, by brining, smoking or drying, for example. Cooking involved the use of heat from a stove; the stages in the development of stoves might provide a rough chronological framework for some changes in diet. Unfortunately, little appears to be known about the history of stoves in Russia and less about cooking methods. In the tenth century stoves, apparently, were semi-spherical

[44]*ChtOIDR* (1902), book 2, miscellany, 30.
[45]Crull, *Antient and Present State of Muscovy*, vol. I, 322. (*sc.* 222).
[46]Collins, *The Present State of Russia*, 14.
[47]Foy de la Neuville, *Rélation curieuse*, 183. See also Collins, *The Present State of Russia*, 14, 60; Reitenfels, 'Skazaniya', 154.
[48]Margeret, *Estat*, 4.
[49]*Travels*, 156.

2 Reapers fed by angels, sixteenth century.
The main cauldron suspended over the open fire is made of metal strips
riveted together. Food is brought to the reapers in a container of vertical strips
which is suspended from a light yoke. The object near the centre of the table
might be a pie. 'And the Angels fed them with most abundant food', is part of
the inscription below.

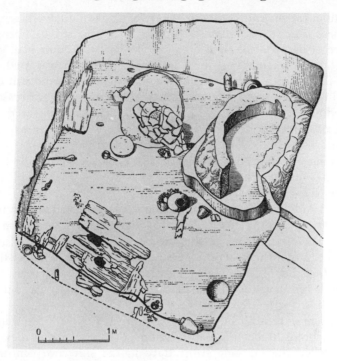

3 Reconstruction of a Kievan stove.
Semi-dugout excavated in Kiev by M.K. Karger.
The stove stands on an earth platform. The fire does not appear to be confined
within a semi-spherical structure, but to be more like an open fire surrounded
by a low wall.

constructions, three or four feet across with a hole in the top through
which the smoke came; there was no chimney, but the hole may have
been covered with a board when not in use.[50] Such structures were of
clay daubed over a frame of withies which burnt away when the stove
was fired, thus producing a sort of hollow insulating material. It seems
possible that, if this interpretation of the archaeological evidence is
correct, vessels placed over the smoke-hole in such stoves were used for
frying and boiling. This is important because it implies a quite different
cooking method from that practised with the large traditional Russian
stove in which a single opening originally served both for stoking and

[50]N.N. Voronin, in *Istoriya Kul'tury drevnei Rusi* (2 vols., Moscow; Leningrad, 1948–51), vol. I,
214–15, illustrations on pp. 205 and 206; Karger, 'Zemlyanka kievskogo khudozhnika XIIIv.',
KS, 11, 5–15. Zasurtsev, *MIA* no. 65, 272.

as an outlet for the smoke. Baking, however, would have taken place, as in these later stoves, in the hot ashes inside the stove. There is no evidence of flat, pancake-like bread cooked on the outer wall of such stoves; this is presumably so because leavened dough was used. In the thirteenth–fifteenth centuries the majority of stoves were still domed and built of clay; early in this period stone-built stoves occasionally occurred and towards the end of it some brick ones appeared.[51] The remains of domed stoves found in Novgorod 'were almost exclusively stone and clay'.[52] To protect such stoves from decay as a result of damp being drawn up from the earth floor, they were usually built on a raised base of solid timber.[53]

When the cube-shaped 'Russian' stove developed is not exactly known.[54] An illustration of around 1600 shows such a stove in use (see plate 4). It appears to be considerably taller than it is wide; the stoke-hole is a fairly tall arch, not the almost semi-circular entry found in some other stoves, and there is a pair of vents above. The fact that the man loading the stove is only slightly stooping implies that, as in some nineteenth-century stoves, the platform on which it was built was quite high (0.7–1 metre last century).[55]

In the late sixteenth century the flat-topped stove appeared in some rich households 'under the name Dutch'.[56] Glazed stove tiles apparently reached the Ukraine from Italy in the sixteenth century and thence reached central Russia. Such tiles were made in Moscow, Velikii Ustyug, Kaluga, Chernigov and the Poltava area in the seventeenth century; this suggests that such stoves were then well-established. Tiles from Saxony and Holland were imported during the reign of Peter the Great.[57] Tiled, flat-topped stoves of the sixteenth century have been excavated in Moscow, but they were for heating reception rooms in rich houses only; probably they did not always have a chimney.[58] The sixteenth–seventeenth century space-heating stoves had solid bases to carry their great weight.[59] Such Dutch stoves, found mainly in reception rooms, were penetrating into the countryside from the towns in

[51]Rabinovich, *ORK XIII–XVvv.*, 2 parts (Moscow, 1970), part 1, 266–7.
[52]Zasurtsev, *MIA*, 65, 272.
[53]*Ibid.*
[54]Gromov, *ORK XVIv.*, part 1, 199.
[55]*Khozyaistvo i byt*, 139.
[56]Brokgauz–Efron, 46 (XIIIA), 541. On German stoves, see N. Nagel, *Kachelöfen des 15. bis 17. Jahrhunderts* (Darmstadt, 1955). Ovsyannikov, *Russkie izraztsy*, 14, claims late fifteenth-century stove tiles have been found in Novgorod.
[57]Evdokimov, 'Starinnye krasnoborskie pechi', 129.
[58]Rabinovich, *O drevnei Moskve*, 243.
[59]Levko, *Vitebskie izraztsy*, 13.

4 Preparing flour, baking, sixteenth century.
Sergius, for his efforts, was chosen abbot. 'Every day he performed the liturgy standing and himself baked the communion loaves, pounded and ground the wheat, sifted the flour, mixed the dough and soured it.' The miniature shows the sifting of grain, its milling and hulling, the preparation of dough and baking.

the second half of the nineteenth century.[60] Common people, too, evidently had, and probably cooked with, stoves. Chancellor stated that 'they have floores wherein in the morning they make a fire, and the same fire doth either moderately warm or make very hot the whole house', but 'floores' here is evidently a misprint for 'stooves'.[61]

A Lithuanian gentleman in Moscow with the Poles in 1610 recorded in his diary the wedding-feasts of well-known people who entertained their guests 'to numerous dishes in the form of broths, serving them in dishes whitened on both sides and set on skillets so that they might very conveniently be heated on the coals'.[62] This might describe either the use of a type of range or of round-bottomed pots set in the Russian stove, though on skillets, not directly in the ash.

In the seventeenth century, certainly, the semi-spherical stoves were no longer encountered.[63] Olearius noted that 'in winter they sleep on flat-topped stoves, like bake-ovens, as the non-German people in Livonia do'.[64] But though rich townsmen sometimes had solid, tiled stoves of western type, and with chimneys, the majority of peasant dwellings continued to be heated 'blackly', as the Russian phrase has it; there was no chimney.[65]

In the rooms of baron V.V. Golovin, during the reign of Peter the Great's daughter, Elizabeth, there were four stoves, with a servant each.

Before tea they usually came into the house; Vorob'eva opened the doors to the hall and said:

> Heed you now and hearken:
> Look upon the stove here;
> Light it up and stoke it,
> Do not go and leave it.
> Sootless let the room be;
> Stinkless let the smoke be.
> Firmly keep you to it
> See to it and watch it
> Come with caution and with care
> Come with purity and prayer.

The stove-men replied by making the sign of the cross and crying Amen; then they threw the firewood from their backs loudly onto the floor; two went up

[60]A.S. Bezhkovich *et al.*, *Khozyaistvo i byt russkikh krest'yan* (Moscow, 1959), 142.
[61]Chancellor, in Hakluyt, *Principall Navigations*, vol. I, 292.
[62]Maskiewicz, *Pamiętniki*, 60.
[63]Gromov, *ORK XVIv.*, part I, 200. Gromov, however, ascribes the transition to 'somewhere on the boundary between the fifteenth and sixteenth centuries'.
[64]*Travels*, 155. Cp. Crull, *Antient and Present State*, vol. I, 162.
[65]Gromov, *ORK XVIIv.*, part I, 189.

to the attic to open the chimneys at a command from the two below who opened the dampers, said aloud a prayer to Jesus, put the wood in the stove and instantly lit it.[66]

This ceremony conveys something of the rituals and importance associated with fire-lighting even in the household of a great, though admittedly eccentric, nobleman in mid-eighteenth century Russia.

Fortunately for our concerns, towards the end of the eighteenth century, some Japanese were shipwrecked off Kamchatka and one of them has left an account of Russia. This includes a description of stoves, by then with chimneys, and also a brief reference to cooking methods. The stoves described were between six and eight feet high (1.8–2.4 m) and six or seven feet long (1.8–2.1 m), thickly plastered with clay and decorated with blue glazed tiles. 'Poor people have stoves which are only whitewashed', he added.[67] Approximately in the middle of the stove was a partition with a semi-circular opening in the lower part; 'the fire is beyond this partition; above they cover it in two or three layers. Before the partition they arrange a wooden pipe to let the smoke out . . . the pipe is made of thick boards like our water conduits, is whitewashed and fixed to the stove so that its end sticks out high above the roof.'[68] An iron plate inserted across the chimney acted as a damper. He also noted that, though at first he and the other Japanese suffocated from the heat and suffered giddiness, they became accustomed to it in time. Apart from these remarks on space heating, he commented on the use of stoves for cooking.

Simple people prepare their food morning and evening as follows: they put grain and other products into pots, place them before the hearth, close the pipe, as explained above, and it quickly cooks . . . The nobles have a different sort of fire in the kitchen. The base is made of stones, an iron grid is set above it on which they put frying pans and saucepans.[69]

These travellers' tales can be supplemented by some archaeological and documentary material. Examination of the remains of a seventeenth-century dwelling house in Pskov has shown that its stoves with a chimney had four to six interior vertical tubes, built up from nesting ceramic semi-circles, which helped convey the heat to the solid bulk of the stove and linked with the chimney.[70] Other semi-circular ceramic

---

[66]Cited in Mel'gunova, *Russkii byt*, 362.

[67]Katsuragawa, *Kratkie vesti*, 176.

[68]*Ibid.* Such wooden smoke-stacks *(dymnitsy)* were still found in the nineteenth century; *Khozyaistvo i byt*, 140–1.

[69]Katsuragava, *Kratkie vesti*, 177.

[70]Spegal'skii, *KS*, 113, 74–7. Finds of sixteenth-century circular pottery may perhaps have been misinterpreted as chimneys, e.g. Rabinovich, *O drevnei Moskve*, 243.

Table 1.1. *Allowances in grain etc.*

	Rye (chets)	Oats (chets)	Wheat (chets)	Malt (chets)	Salt (puds)	
1 *1506*						
Priest	15	15			5	a
deacon	10	10			3	
host-maker	6	6			1	
17 monks and nuns (each)	1 *okov*	1 *okov*				
2 *1519*						
Widow	20	20	4	6		
3 *1545–6*						
Widow	10	6	1 *kad'*	1 *kad'*	1 *lub*	b
4 *1551*						
Cross-maker	4	4			1	c
5 *1556*						
10 Gunners (each)	12 *korob'ya*	12 *korob'ya*			2	d
6 *1560–1*						
Widow	13	7	2	4	1 *lub*	e
7 *1619*						
50 post-horse men (each)	12					f
8 Early 17th century and 1623						
Officer i/c						
100 men						g
50	7					h
10	6½					i
other ranks	6	6				j
9 *1679*						
200 musketeers:						
officers i/c						
50 men	4	4				k
10	3½	3½				
other ranks	3	3				
10 *1681*						
musketeers						l
officers i/c						
50 men						
10	6	6				
other ranks						
exiles						
11 *1682*						
gunners and garrison men	2	2				m

units with a flat decorated surface were used to face the arch of the stoke-hole. Stoves such as these were composed mainly of stone rubble held in place by small bricks (those found in Pskov were 22 × 12 × 3.5 cm) and some iron fastenings. A Pskov document of 1658/9 specified only three hundred bricks, but seven cartloads of clay and seven of stone rubble for a stove.[71] Repairs to space-heating stoves in royal apartments towards the end of the seventeenth century also specify large quantities of clay and rubble.[72] Such stoves sometimes had two stoke-holes and were either tiled or sometimes painted.[73] There are rare references to cooking stoves. On 16 February 1682 there was an order 'to repair anew fourteen cooking stoves in the Bread establishment and the tenement that belonged to boyar Semen Luk'yanovich Streshnev, to lay and make good the floors, and make two new

Notes to Table 1.1. (contd.)
[a] 2 chets of wheat and 1 pud of salt were additionally granted for the communion bread.
[b] Plus $\frac{1}{2}$ chet hemp, $\frac{1}{2}$ chet peas, 1 chet buckwheat.
[c] Plus $\frac{1}{4}$ chet hemp, $\frac{1}{4}$ chet peas, $\frac{1}{4}$ chet groats, $\frac{1}{4}$ chet oatmeal (*tolokno*).
[d] Plus 1 r. a year, or money equivalent at local prices. Gatemen, blacksmiths, carpenters, etc. at the same rates.
[e] Plus 1 chet hemp, 1 chet peas, 1 chet oatmeal, $\frac{1}{2}$ chet hulled oats, $\frac{1}{2}$ chet buckwheat.
[f] Plus 20 r. Now 7 r. and no grain.
[g] 10 r.
[h] $2\frac{1}{2}$ r. (1623 $3\frac{1}{2}$ r.)
[i] $2\frac{1}{4}$ r. (1623 $3\frac{1}{4}$ r.)
[j] 2 r. (1623 3 r.)
[k] Or 10 altyns per pair (*yuft'*); i.e. 1 chet each of rye and oats.
[l] Pay, respectively: $3\frac{1}{2}$ r., 3 r. 8 alt. 2 d., 3 r. and 2 r.
[m] Plus 2 chets barley.
Sources:
1 *ARG*, no. 15 (March 1506).
2 *ARG*, no. 179 (21 December 1519).
3 *AFZ*, II, no. 186 (1545–6).
4 *Kniga Klyuchei i dolgovaya kniga Iosifo-Volokolamskogo monastyrya*, 46.
5 *DAI*, I, no. 90 (13 and 26 January 1566).
6 *AFZ*, II, no. 283 (1560–1).
7 *AI*, III, no. 78 (July 1619).
8 *AAE*, III, no. 148.
9 *AI*, V, no. 35 (1679).
10 *DAI*, X, no. 20 (1681).
11 *DAI*, X, no. 36 (1682).

[71] Spegal'skii, *KS*, 113, 74.
[72] Zabelin, *Domashnii byt russkikh tsarei*, vol. I, 660–1, 663, 744.
[73] *Ibid.*, 634, 657.

stoves and two new hearths'.[74] Thus, by the late seventeenth century both the Russian stove and open fires of some sort were being used for cooking.

These two forms of heating differ in the utensils suitable for use with them and in the type of cooking possible. The stove is in general a slow cooker; once the flame has died down, pots may be set in the deep layer of ash and left all day or overnight to produce porridges, stews and so on. Bread, too, would be set directly in the stove. This type of cooking is by means of heat which is slowly declining in temperature. The open fire can be more readily controlled and the temperature can be made to rise even after the flat-bottomed pans have been set over it. It is interesting that these differences can be observed in Russian terminology. The word for a frying pan (*skovoroda*) occurs in a number of Slav languages; it presumably goes back to very early times when cooking took place over an open fire. Such pans must originally have been of earthenware. There was also a term for a ceramic frying pan (*latka* or *ladka*), or a flat-bottomed dish with straight sides, which has continued to have that meaning. All such pans could have continued to be used once the fire was contained in a domed stove with a hole in the top. The word for all types of pot used in flat-topped stoves (*gorshok*) derives from the term for a furnace (*gor''n*) and is differentiated in a number of folk sayings from the all-purpose cauldron used over an open fire (*kotel*): 'The pot doesn't quarrel with the cauldron' etc.[75] The pot was the most common cooking container.[76] Most people had 'not more than three or four earthen pots and as many clay and wooden dishes'.[77] When, by the late seventeenth century, an open fire with a grid above it – a sort of early range – appeared, new utensils soon followed. These were flat-bottomed ceramic or metal casseroles or saucepans (*kastryulya*, *kastryul'ka*), the term for which is a West European loan first attested in Peter the Great's Marine Regulations of 1720.[78] In terms of the stove or range, therefore, the eighteenth century marks a new stage.

Such changes, of course, were not immediately disseminated throughout Russia or its society; survivals of some of the earlier forms of stove were to be found even in the early twentieth century. Nevertheless, we may, as a crude first approximation, suggest that the period

[74]Zabelin, *Domashnii byt russkikh tsarei*, vol. I, 630. Streshnev had been exiled as a result of being accused of sorcery under Aleksei Mikhailovich: Solov'ev, *Istoriya Rossii* (15 vols., Moscow, 1959–66), vol. VII, 135.

[75]See Dal', *Tolkovyi slovar'*, *s.v. gorshok*.

[76]Smirnova, *MIA*, 55, 232.

[77]Olearius, *Travels*, 155.

[78]*PSZ* 6, 55, no. 3485.

until about 1600 was the period of the domed stove; the seventeenth century was that of the flat-topped stove; and, from the eighteenth century, ranges and western-style equipment gradually spread throughout society.

Foods based on grains were evidently basic to Russian diet. The description of military provisions as 'bread, beer and sops (*vologa*), as for a feast' does not sound very elaborate.[79] *Vologa* indicated any moist dish such as porridges, thick soups or mashes; it might, thus, be either food or drink, but all such items mentioned were derived from grain. Such pottages, as well as gruels, both savoury and sweet, pasties and many types of bread and, less commonly, rolls, were cooked in stoves, whatever their type. Pottages, gruels and stews could be left to cook slowly throughout the working day or overnight. Whatever the supplements used, grain and its products were dominant. This impression can be supported in a number of ways. Table 1.1 summarises allowances granted to individuals in a variety of social and economic situations. There are grants to church or monastic officials and dependents (numbers 1, 4), provision made for surviving widows by will (2, 3, 6), grants to servitors (7) and the military (5, 8–11). On the basis of this material it is not easy to establish precise consumption norms, but it looks as if three chets of rye and two or three chets of other grains was the minimum required for each adult.[80] Allowances of more than six chets may be accounted for as a result of high status (perhaps requiring maintenance of servants) or onerous conditions. The main point, however, is that grain, whatever the precise amount involved, was always present in quantity. Money was paid additionally to soldiers, but the ration of grain was still crucial.

We will see, too, that in the early seventeenth century, and possibly a little before then, efforts were made in Moscow to control the price and quality of a range of bread products on sale in the city.[81] This shows that bakers were producing for the Moscow market. Indeed, a partial census of Moscow in 1638 showed about 600 people engaged in the food trades; the majority were in trades based on grain. They included 76 wheat-roll men and 2 women, 53 bread men and 1 woman and 35 pie-men.[82] There were at least an additional 56 in other grain-based trades, apart from 79 in trades dealing with grain-based drinks (see Table 1.2[83]). Some partially comparable evidence for 1723 is also

[79]*P2L*, 60 (1480).
[80]See also Smith, *Peasant Farming*, 88.
[81]Chapter 4 below.
[82]Belyaev, 'Rospisnoi spisok', XVIII–XXIII.
[83]Belyaev, 'Rospisnoi spisok', XVIII–XXIII; Kafengauz, *MIZ*, I, 475.

Table 1.2. *Grain-based tradespeople, Moscow 1638, 1723*

Making or dealing in:	1638			1723^a
	Men	Women	Totals	Totals
Flour	24			
Corn (*zhito*)	20			
Groats	4			
Buckwheat				26
			48	
Wheat-rolls	76	2		245
Saikas				55
Bread	53	1		85 (incl. loaves)
Pies	35			25
Pancakes	24	1		25
Gingerbread	6			9
Frumenty	1			
Rusks	1			
Fools				10
			200	480^b
Kvas	38			
Malt	30			
Beer	10			
Wort (*suslo*)	1			
			79	
			327	Plus 1 master miller (a foreigner) and 10 millers.

Notes:
^{a} Objects of trade were indicated for 510 of 757 registered traders.
^{b} Plus 15 dealing in 'foodstuffs'.
Source: Belyaev, 'Rospisnoi spisok', XVIII–XXIII; Kafengauz, *MIZ*, I, 475.

given and shows a considerable increase in numbers, even though corn chandlers and brewers are not mentioned. The increase in the numbers of dealers in wheat-rolls is particularly striking.

Evidently, the homely everyday diet of bread, porridge and pastry was supplemented by purchases of rarer and tastier items in the relatively few towns. Similarly, in sixteenth-century Novgorod there had been 241 wheat-roll men, but 121 bread men and 67 pie-men (as well as various other flour-based trades).[84] In the 1590s in Kaluga, how-

[84]Pronshtein, *Velikii Novgorod v XVIv.*, 246–51.

5 Catching a whale in the White Sea, 1760.
An item from *Moscow News* for Friday, 21 July 1760, reporting the catching of a whale in the White Sea.

ever, there were 13 wheat-roll men and 30 bread men.[85] The pattern there was probably closer to the average consumption of most people because Kaluga was so much smaller than Moscow or Novgorod.

The register of food issued in the household of the Patriarch Adrian at the very end of the seventeenth century specifies the rations sent each Saturday to those working outside. On Easter Saturday, 15 April 1699,

The week's allowance was sent to the kitchen garden monk who is at Presnya and the two workmen; to the monk, for the month, half a beluga; to the workmen, for the week, half a small sturgeon [*chalbush*]; and to the monk and the workmen a small measure of smelts each, 2 pounds of butter, a mug of hempseed oil, a chetverik of oatmeal, 3 monastery loaves.[86]

[85]Volkov, *Istoriya SSSR* (1972), 4, 204–6.
[86]*Raskhodnaya kniga*, 173–4.

Similar entries continue until September when, presumably, work on
the kitchen garden ceased. Early in May the groom on the pasture was
sent 'bread, a small measure of smelts, a chetverik of buckwheat, a
quarter of a small sturgeon'.[87] In July, when there were two grooms at
the pasture, they received 'a loaf each'; similarly in August the various
servants evidently supervising the mowing each received 'a week's
loaf'.[88] Loaves, then, seem to be the basic food, supplemented by grits
for porridge and something to go with the bread, in this case usually
smelts.

Overall, then, early Russian diet (like the diet in later times) was
largely based on grain and grain products with little meat, but a range
of vegetables, and supplements from hunting, fishing and gathering.
Much food was preserved, perhaps originally because of isolated, small
settlements and the long and severe winters, but this necessity became a
virtue and Russians had established a preference for pickled, brined and
other soured products long before the eighteenth century. Salt was,
thus, important, especially in fish brines, and this had far-reaching
effects which will be dealt with in later chapters. There seem to have
been relatively few changes in the general diet in this period. In the
sixteenth century some unleavened pastry items appeared; in large
towns professional bakers were selling special items. The wealthy had a
wider variety of native foodstuffs at their disposal than the common
people; this was increasingly supplemented throughout the seventeenth
century by imported spices, wines, sugar and sweetmeats. The development of new cooking equipment, both stoves and vessels, at least in
part also imported, contributed to some eighteenth-century developments. The growth of imports was in large part a result of increased
state power over these centuries. This was a fundamental change which
resulted in attempts to control and extract revenue from some elements
in Russian diet, especially drink, once the colonisation of the East
European forest zone had resulted in increased population densities.

[87] *Ibid.*, 236.
[88] *Ibid.*, 267, 271.

2

❋❋

Salt: a major extractive industry

The largest non-agricultural activity in Russia before the industrial developments under Peter the Great was salt winning. This was a specialised extractive industry with a number of forms. It provided an element in the diet not readily available in the areas of early Russian colonisation. Much more important than its direct contribution to the diet, however, was its indirect one: it was much used as a preservative for such important supplements to the grain-based foods as fish and cabbage, as well as many other foodstuffs.

Salt is often considered essential for both human and animal consumption, though, according to some scholars, it is in fact an addiction, the earliest human narcotic; a diet containing meat is likely to provide all the salt the body requires, only an entirely vegetarian diet might be deficient.[1] Animals consume more salt than humans; a cow takes about 100 g, a horse about 50 g a day, but human adults only 12–15 g a day, 4.4 to 5.5 kg (10–12 lb) a year. This figure for human culinary consumption is often exceeded for household consumption, which includes salt expended on such items as brine pickles; this has been calculated as 7.5 kg ($16\frac{1}{2}$ lb) a year.[2] There are, of course, wide variations.

In Russia salt was not only used for great quantities of brine pickles (needed as a store for the long winters), but also for curing fish and meat, in crafts and trades such as the tawing of hides and as a mordant in dyeing textiles. In a version of the early Russian law, *Russkaya pravda*, which may date from the late eleventh century, a scale of supplies was laid down for an official (*virnik*); this included a measure (*golvazhen'*) of salt a day.[3] Unfortunately, it is not known what this measure amounted to; the term used suggests it may have been cone-shaped.[4] In late nineteenth-century Russia one estimate for domestic

[1] Multhauf, *Neptune's gift*, 3–4.
[2] Nenquin, *Salt*, 140; Multhauf, *Neptune's gift*, 3–4, 6, 240, 249.
[3] *PRP*, I, 75–6, 109.
[4] *Ibid.*, 143.

6 Boiling brine, sixteenth century. A view through the walls of a building showing the suspended iron pan surrounded by flames and with salt crystallising in heaps. In the background monks dig with long-handled spades and a pick-like implement.

consumption of salt was 5.2 kg a year; a soldier's ration was then 7.2 kg.[5] Peasant consumption, however, was sometimes much higher; one example was 11.4 kg a year.[6] Probably the predominantly vegetarian nature of the diet and the need for winter stocks of food account for such high levels of domestic consumption.

The three most important modes of obtaining salt have all been present in Russia, but to different degrees at different periods. Rock salt (*kolomyya*) was obtained at Udech and Kolomyya, near Galich on the Dnestr, and was traded, before the Mongol invasions of the thirteenth century, into what was to become Russia.[7] In 1164 300 salt traders are said to have drowned in the flooded Dnestr.[8] Local princes distributed the salt obtained or the right to mine it to their retinues.[9] Secondly, crystallised sea and lake salt was obtained in the south from

[5]Gomilevskii, *Sol'*, 139, 141, 143, 146.
[6]*Ibid.*, 143.
[7]Aristov, *Promyshlennost'*, 68–9; Rybakov, *Remeslo*, 571; Grinchenko, *Slovar'*, vol. II, 271.
[8]*PSRL*, II, 524.
[9]*PSRL*, II, 789 (1240).

the Crimea and the mouth of the Volga near Astrakhan', where there were salt lakes and deposits of salt resulting from natural evaporation. Such salt, too, had been traded into Slav territory from such lakes in the Crimea in the thirteenth century.[10]

Thirdly, the most important mode of winning salt in Russia for many centuries was to crystallise it from brine obtained either from sea water (as in some locations on the White Sea) or, more commonly, from underground sources.[11] The earliest reference to this evaporation process appears to be a Novgorod charter of 1136/7.[12] The bishop was to have 'at the sea a measure (*puz*) from each iron pan and boiling vat (*ot chrena i ot salgy*)'.[13]

The origin of this industry is not known in detail. The essential development was from evaporating sea water or surface brine deposits in small vessels (perhaps called *salgi*; the precise meaning of this term is not known) to sinking wells and pipes to tap underground sources of brine for evaporation. This had taken place perhaps around the middle of the fourteenth century, a time when there were great changes in European salt production in general. This change to drilling for brine was one of many technical innovations in the second half of the fourteenth century.[14]

Establishing a brine-evaporating salt-works (*varnitsa*) involved arduous and sometimes lengthy work. A number of plants were indicators of salt soils: marsh samphire, sea wormwood and others.[15] Once a likely source of brine had been discovered drilling had to start. By the late sixteenth century the technique was well-established and considerable depths were then being reached. A detailed account of deep drilling is given in a late sixteenth-century document from Tot'ma and this may represent a further stage in technical development.[16] First, two forked posts, forty or fifty feet (10–15 m) high, and a cross-beam were set up; beneath this beam a well was dug until the water-table was reached, then drilling commenced.[17] Depending on soil conditions,

[10] *The Journey of William of Rubruck* (Hakluyt Society, second series), vol. IV, 52.

[11] Zaozerskaya, *U istokov*, 110; Savich, *Solovetskaya votchina*, 94.

[12] *Drevnerusskie knyazheskie ustavy*, 148.

[13] According to Kolominskii, 'Torgovlya', 1, the *puz* became the *chetverik* (about 3 pecks or 26 litres); early this century in the Archangel dialect it was 2 chetveriks; see Aristov, *Promyshlennost'*, 70. Kamentseva and Ustyugov, *Russkaya metrologiya*, 48, state that the *puz* weighed up to 108 lb in the sixteenth-seventeenth centuries.

[14] Rybakov, *Remeslo*, 575, 595.

[15] Gomilevskii, *Sol'*, 29.

[16] Prozorovskii, 'Starinnoe opisanie solevarennogo snaryada', *IAO*, VI, section 1, fasc. 3, 233–55; Kolominskii, 'Torgovlya', 37–42; Ustyugov, *Solevarennaya promyshlennost'*, 34–40.

[17] On Western drilling equipment of relatively advanced type from 1420 and later see Conrad, *Technikgeschichte*, 38, 298–301. In China drilling for brine was practised from about AD 400.

the wooden drilling tube, tipped with iron, sank about two to ten inches (5–10 m) a day. In 1641 a merchant stated that 'where the soil is softer, in those places the pipes are done in about three or four months, sometimes in half a year, sometimes more. But in places where the soil is stony, there they go on a long time – for about three or four years'.[18] This implies depths of 100 to 200 feet (30–60 m). The process might, evidently, take up to seven or eight years.[19] Depths attained 450 feet (137 m) or more in the late seventeenth century. Such deep drilling was referred to as Perm' or Balakhna style, evidently because it was best, or first, established in those locations.[20] In addition to sinking the pipes, a well (*kolodets*) or pit (*lari*) to store the brine, and the salt-boiling shop itself had to be built, as well as a store and, since locations were often remote, accommodation for workers. Such structures were basically comparable with the wooden buildings usual for that time. The pan (*chren* or *tsren*) was made of as many as two hundred iron plates, each several feet long and a few inches wide. They were fastened together by folding the ends around one another and fixing them with nails and fasteners; up to a hundredweight of the latter alone were required for a vessel which sometimes was as much as 25 feet (7.6 m) across.[21] Pan size at Staraya Rusa apparently grew to about 240 sq. feet (22 sq. m) by the seventeenth century, but this was only a third the size of pans at the Perm' salines and of some belonging to the Solovki monastery.[22]

Although this evidence is from the sixteenth and seventeenth centuries, the terminology does not differ from the earlier period. It seems unlikely that there had been any substantial change in technique since the mid-fourteenth century, except in the depths reached by drilling and the increased size of pans.

Some scholars regard the techniques as simple, which is basically true, and so suggest that the establishment of a salt-works did not involve considerable expenditure.[23] The latter view seems mistaken. The time needed to discover a potential source and to drill down to it was usually considerable. Men and equipment had to be maintained for this period with no returns and with no certainty that there would be

[18]Cited by Ustyugov, *Solevarennaya promyshlennost'*, 34. Vvedenskii, *Dom Stroganovykh*, 165, says 'up to 2–5 years'.

[19]Zaozerskaya, *U istokov*, 166; Kolominskii, 'Torgovlya', 43.

[20]Zaozerskaya, *U istokov*, 79.

[21]Savich, *Solovetskaya votchina*, 101. Cp. Zaozerskaya, *U istokov*, 144; Ustyugov, *Solevarennaya promyshlennost'*, 38. Ustyugov gives a plate length of 27–30 cm, but this is evidently incommensurate with his other statements.

[22]Zaozerskaya, *U istokov*, 83.

[23]Aristov, *Promyshlennost'*, 73; Savich, *Solovetskaya votchina*, 101.

any even in the future. In seventeenth-century Tot'ma the sinking of a new bore-well for brine cost 800 rubles.[24] In 1693 a Sol' Kama merchant stated that he had

. . . cleared the forest and, for the brine pipes, hired pipe-men and annual labourers and gave them big advances and set up a house for those pipe-masters and labourers at that empty place, seeing that that empty place was suitable for the brine-boiling trade; that cost me, your slave, about five hundred rubles or more for pipe-men and pipe labourers and all sorts of equipment for that place and in clearing the forest.[25]

For the late 1680s in this area, the annual subsistence minimum for a worker has been estimated at 3 rubles 65 kopeks to 4 rubles 63 kopeks.[26] The investment required, therefore, was considerable in both time and money.

The cost of an iron pan, the central item of equipment, varied from 20 to 60 rubles; an old one might be bought for 15 rubles.[27] Some in the second half of the sixteenth century cost even less.[28] For comparison, in the late sixteenth century a cow could often be bought for a ruble or less and the grain allowance for a family (two adults, two children) for a year probably cost little more than three rubles.[29] In the mid-fifteenth century such a pan has been valued at two sokhas for the purposes of an irregular tax (*chernyi bor*); it had, thus, been equated with a plough (*plug*) or a boat (*lod'ya*), two blacksmiths or eight horseless men.[30] Pans had to be repaired quite often. Salt rapidly corroded them. Sometimes they had to undergo major repairs which might take 140–50 iron plates which would cost eight to eight-and-a-half rubles. These and other material costs, together with pay for the blacksmith and hammer-men, meant that a major repair amounted to about 40 or 60 rubles. The pans lasted only a year or eighteen months and then had to be replaced.[31] The pipes carrying the brine also had to be repaired from time to time and sometimes replaced; repairs cost more than a ruble, but relaying the pipes, as much as 30 rubles.[32] A smithy was essential to cope with repairs and maintain production at a salt-works. It seems clear, therefore, that both initial outlays and running costs were considerable.

[24]Zaozerskaya, *U istokov*, 166.
[25]Cited in Vvedenskii, *Dom Stroganovykh*, 167.
[26]Ustyugov, *Solevarennaya promyshlennost'*, 238.
[27]Savich, *Solovetskaya votchina*, 101; presumably this refers to the sixteenth or seventeenth centuries.
[28]Man'kov, *Tseny*, 71.
[29]Man'kov, *Tseny*, 122–33; 104–11; Smith, *Peasant farming*, 88.
[30]*GVNiP*, no. 21.
[31]Ustyugov, *Solevarennaya promyshlennost'*, 226.
[32]Savich, *Solovetskaya votchina*, 101.

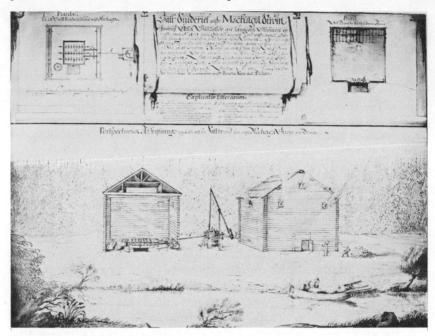

7 A salt-works on the Mshaga, 1674. The main picture shows men between the jumbled heap of timber for fuel on the right and the entrance to the boiling house which, to conserve heat, has a wicket-door in the gate. Steam and smoke escape from small hatch openings high in the walls. There are no windows. Between the houses is a well or reservoir for brine, surrounded by a platform reached by a short ladder. A counterbalanced crane enables brine to be tipped into channels which feed troughs in the houses on either side. The salt produced is sacked and carried away by boat.

Above the picture diagrams show the works in plan and profile. The pan in this works, unlike that shown on p. 28, is suspended by iron bands from a low frame of poles. In the floor in front of the pan is an ash-pit. In the original the detail is fine enough to show various items in use at the pan: the troughs and internal channels conveying brine to the pan, a tub, hoe-like rakers etc.

Perhaps the greatest problem, however (apart from finding a source of brine with a relatively high concentration of salt), was ensuring an adequate fuel supply. A one-pan salt-works in the sixteenth century used 600 fathoms of timber in a year.[33] The instruction to the peasants obliged them

[33] *AAE*, I, no. 268 (1564). The fathom (*sazhen'*) was a stack of firewood about 7 ft (2 m) long and high; the logs were about 30 in (80 cm) long.

Map 1 Main locations involved in the salt industry in Russia before the eighteenth century

... to heat the iron-pan, winter and summer, a hundred and sixty nights, and you have cut firewood for the pan, for the winter and the summer firings, six hundred fathoms for the year and have stocked up firewood for the year and you have not cut firewood for other future years; if anyone begins, contrary to our regulation, to fire additional nights, or cut excess firewood, or cut wood for the future, we order the salt from those additional nights and the excess firewood to be taken by the monastery, and a penalty, which we shall indicate, to be imposed.

The cutting, carting, or floating, and stacking of firewood was sometimes a labour-rent imposed on local peasants, but at salt-works of monasteries and merchants it seems frequently to have been done by hired labour.

The demand for salt, then, was evidently sufficient to lead to the growth of an industry in early Russia which required considerable inputs of time, money, labour and organisational effort. By the fifteenth century salt was being won at a number of locations extending across northern and central European Russia. The history of the industry involved both changes in location and development of techniques; it impinged on the economic, social and even, at times, the political history of Russia. Let us now look at some of the more important locations of the industry in order to trace some of these changes and see something of how this humble condiment had a part in the development of Russia. We will first survey briefly the salines of the White Sea area where sea brine was sometimes used as the raw material, then locations across central European Russia where brine was extracted from the soil. Finally, we will look at the immense surface salt workings of the deposits in the Lower Volga area and glance at Siberia.

THE WHITE SEA

Individual winning of salt appears to have existed in the White Sea area from ancient times; probably the Finns were active in salt extraction before the Slav colonisation of this area.[34] The abundance of fish caught in the region may have stimulated a demand for salt as a preservative. In the fifteenth century, when monasteries had been established there and, later, actively acquired salt-works, these were usually designated by the name of their former owners.[35] Among these,

---

[34] Ostroumov, 'Drevnerusskie solevarennye tovarishchestva', *Ustoi*, (1882), 5, 66.
[35] Savich, *Solovetskaya votchina*, 94.

evidently, were state peasants in the sixteenth century.[36] Any such original extraction of salt, however, seems likely to have been on a small scale until the new techniques of drilling had been introduced and sea water largely replaced by brine as the source material.

According to the *Life* of the founders of Solovki monastery, the monks in the later fifteenth century 'drew water from the sea and, boiling it, made salt and sold it to the traders and took from them every sort of thing for the needs of the monastery'.[37] It is clear, however, that not all salt-works located by the sea used sea water; at Nenoksa a brine spring was being exploited in the fifteenth century.[38] It is at that time that we have the first evidence for the Solovki monastery acquiring an interest in such works.

The Solovki monastery repeatedly claimed that

From of old Solovki monastery has had no eternal heritable estates; they feed themselves from their own labours; from the beginning of the life of the venerable Zosima and Savvatii, the wonder-workers, they have boiled salt by the sea . . . The salt that they boil with their labours they carry in boats on the Dvina past the town of Archangel to Kholmogory, and from Kholmogory in vessels past Ustyug Vclikii and Tot'ma to Vologda, and at Vologda they sell it; and with those salt monies at Vologda and at Ustyug they buy every sort of provision of grain and goods for the supply of the monastery.[39]

Another route active in the sixteenth century ran from the western shores of the White Sea and the Onega Gulf through Turchasov and Kargopol'.[40] The salt trade of this monastery based on islands in the White Sea was dependent on grain, the essential foodstuff, and other goods produced in the central regions. Its workers 'drink and eat from the monastery's store'; they lived 'on the monastery's bread'.[41] Before 1592 the monastery, which then had enormous salt-workings in the White Sea area, had a standard ration calculated per pan: 200 chets of rye, 10 of barley, 30 of oats, 5 of boiled groats, 5 of oat flour, 1 measure of peas, 1 measure of hemp seed (for oil), $\frac{1}{2}$ a measure of buckwheat, 5 puds of oil, as well as 50 rubles.[42] This would be adequate for an

[36]*Ibid.*, 95.
[37]*Ibid.*, 94.
[38]Zaozerskaya, *U istokov*, 99.
[39]Cited, without indication of source, in Savich, *Solovetskaya votchina*, 93.
[40]Ostroumov, 'Drevnerusskie solevarennye tovarishchestva', *Ustoi* (1882), 5, 62; Zaozerskaya, *U istokov*, 100.
[41]Savich, *Solovetskaya votchina*, 111, 114. Workers sometimes bought food for themselves in this area: Zaozerskaya, *U istokov*, 144.
[42]Savich, *ibid.*, 115.

absolute maximum of 20 families.[43] The individual salt-works was, evidently, quite small in terms of its immediate labour need.

Solovki monastery, like others in the area, had only gradually come to play a major part in salt production and trade. In 1530 the monastery rented a salt-works in Nenoksa for twenty years.[44] Other works owned by individuals were acquired in other ways. In 1572 the monastery took a seventh share in a new salt-works at Velikii mesta (lit. 'Grand Places') as collateral security for a loan; the debtor declared that 'if I do not pay the money on time, then this deed to that seventh share of the iron pan with its hoops is a firm deed of purchase with no right to repurchase'.[45] By this time, the intervention of monasteries, supported by the state, both hindered the development of the local industry and so contributed to its difficulties that it was often easy to acquire shares in salt-works. Natural disasters and state demands combined to ruin a local industry faced with competition from monasteries which had adequate resources. By the 1590s entire volosts were in the hands of Solovki monastery.[46] By 1600 other monasteries, such as St Nicholas of Korel' and the Saviour of Priluka, had a firm foothold in the industry.[47] Although the peasant industry was relatively simple and lacked the resources available to the monasteries, its output around 1560 in the Northern Dvina area has been estimated at 400,000 puds (more than 6.8 mln kg).[48]

Some of the complexities of the joint ownership of rights in salt-works is demonstrated by what has to be called a deed of sale.

Now I, Shestoi [i.e. 'Sextus'], son of Fefilat Proskurnin, have sold to the monk Varsonofei of the St. Nicholas of Korel' monastery an eighth part of a twelfth in the New salt-works at Velikie mesta which comes from Yakov Veprev; and in that eighth part a third [is to go] to the St. Nicholas monk, and another third to my father, Fefilat, and to Grigorii Zavertkin, half each; the third third to my father, Fefilat, and Grigorii Zavertkin with his fellows; they are to divide that third third into eleven sections, through the Klimshin salt-works from the sixteenth share; and I, Shestoi, have sold my share in those two-thirds [i.e. his one-third] to the monk Varsonofei; I held it through my purchase deeds and the share list.[49]

These complicated arrangements seem to mean that this one, but very

[43]See Rozhkov, *Sel'skoe khozyaistvo*, 261; Smith, *Peasant Farming*, 88.
[44]Savich, *Solovetskaya votchina*, 97.
[45]*Ibid.*, 98.
[46]Zaozerskaya, *U istokov*, 105.
[47]*Ibid.*, 113.
[48]Kopanev, *Krest'yanstvo*, 174–5.
[49]*SGKE*, I, no. 271 (13 September 1583).

rich, source of brine and salt was ultimately divided, notionally, into 3,160 units (1/11 of 1/3 of 1/8 of 1/12). Such sub-divisions and the intermingled partnerships involved in them demonstrate not only the wealth of some salt-works; they show: first, the need for a share list; secondly, the continuing active participation of substantial peasant families, some old-established dynasties, in the salt trade and, thirdly and lastly, the immense opportunities afforded monasteries and wealthy individuals from other parts to participate in salt-works and, sometimes, to acquire control of them piecemeal.

Towards the end of the sixteenth century output was apparently about 80–100 thousand puds (1.3–1.7 mln kg) a year for Solovki monastery alone.[50] This was the largest producer in the area, but it was not the only one. During the Time of Troubles, especially when the White Sea volosts were under attack, production, of course, fell; the decline, however, seems to have been short-lived. By the 1620s new salt-works were being developed.[51] At the end of the 1660s the monastery had twenty undertakings with fifty-four salt-works. This seems to have been the high-point; towards the mid-seventeenth century trade in salt lost much of its attractiveness in the centre which was receiving enormous quantities of salt from Astrakhan', Perm' and Balakhna.[52] In 1672 the monastery was allowed tax exemption on 130 thousand puds (2 mln kg) of salt a year.[53] A decline is particularly noticeable from the mid-1680s and by the early eighteenth century many of the pans were no longer operating.[54] Fuel supplies were certainly a major difficulty; but transport of timber from more distant forest might have been possible had labour been available at prices low enough to enable the White Sea workings to compete with the massive supplies from Sol' Kama and Astrakhan' on the central Russian market. In fact, of the 54 Solovki salt-works in the late 1660s, half appear to have been working in the early eighteenth century. Of the 27 which were not, 11 were in disuse or 'rotted', but the reason is not stated; 1 was closed because of shortage of supplies for the iron pan, 3 had been destroyed by Swedish invaders; in 8 cases shortage of grain, often in conjunction with lack of fuel, is given as the reason for closure; in only 4 cases is shortage of fuel given as the sole reason for their ceasing to operate. [55] It seems, therefore, as if the fundamental problem to main-

---

[50]Savich, *Solovetskaya votchina*, 116–30.
[51]*Ibid.*, 115.
[52]Zaozerskaya, *U istokov*, 137.
[53]*AI*, IV, no. 228.
[54]Savich, *Solovetskaya votchina*, 116.
[55]Savich, *ibid.*, 116–33.

tain the salt-workings in the White Sea area was to provide grain to support the necessary labour in the adverse conditions of this region.

Apart from a steward, each saline had monastic servitors (*slugi*) who had food and clothing from the monastery; from the early sixteenth century on there is evidence for servants (*sluzhebniki*) as well. These contracted to work for a certain period, sometimes a year, for a set wage as cooks, cow-herds, laundry-men and so on. The hired work people (*rabotnye lyudi*) were both long-term and those taken on temporarily (*prikhozhie*). At its 20 salt-works in 1669 the Solovki monastery had 827 long-term work people (plus 1,485 members of their families) and 266–86 temporary workmen; all these men were supplied with food and the long-term work people with clothing as well.[56] Although there was a certain very limited amount of arable land at some of the salines, every single salt-works had to have grain and other foodstuffs from the monastery; these supplies had to be obtained by purchase through a network of agents and contractors operating in Vologda, Yaroslavl', Ustyug, Kostroma and other areas.[57] Salt was sold, mainly in Vologda, at three times its price at Kholmogory.[58] The proceeds were used for the purchasing programme which started from the beginning of September; the supplies obtained were taken back to the monastery on the boats which had brought the salt. In 1667 the right of peasants to acquire grain by barter or purchase in Kholmogory and at Archangel was reaffirmed 'because in those maritime [Solovki] monastery places grain does not grow and there are no tilled lands'.[59]

The price of salt sometimes fell, but in general throughout the sixteenth century it remained high relative to that of grain; weight for weight, salt cost more than rye, the basic grain, though at Kholmogory, where grain had to be imported from more southerly regions, grain cost considerably more than salt in crisis years.[60] It was this relativity which allowed the great development of the White Sea salt industry through the sixteenth and much of the seventeenth centuries. The provisioning of the industry came from grain grown over wide areas of central European Russia and as long as its price was low relative to that of the salt produced from brines of low salinity the industry could flourish. In the late seventeenth century, however, the situation changed and the two commodities were of a similar price (see

[56] *Ibid.*, 110–11.
[57] *Ibid.*, 114–15, 154–5.
[58] Zaozerskaya, *U istokov*, 100–1.
[59] *AI*, IV, no. 198.
[60] Man'kov, *Tseny*, 67.

Table 2.1. *Prices of rye and salt (dengas/pud)*

	1551		1576		1587		1600		1674	
	rye	salt	rye	salt	rye	salt	rye	salt	rye	salt
Kholmogory	5	6	5	9½	11	7				
Vologda					12	13	7	11	18–27	18–24[a]
Moscow				27	8	28	7	18	20–23	40[b]

Notes:
[a] rye 1673, salt 1673–4.
[b] 'the very best salt', probably not from the White Sea area.
Sources:
Man'kov, *Tseny*, 69; Savich, *Solovetskaya votchina*, 149, 157; Kurts, *Sochinenie Kil'burgera*, 177.

Table 2.1[61]). This made the industry uneconomical. Table 2.2 shows the income from salt sales and expenditure on purchase of rye for Solovki monastery. There were, of course, other grains and many other provisions, both foodstuffs, textiles and other equipment which had to be purchased, but rye was the bulkiest item and the essential foodstuff. Although the price of rye fell after the high prices around mid-century, the monastery's income from salt sales fell so much that in 1691–2 the amount spent on buying rye was almost twice the income from salt. Without a credit system to tide it over such a crisis even a monastery as powerful as Solovki could not continue to provide an adequate supply of foodstuffs for its work force.

CENTRAL EUROPEAN RUSSIA

Salt extraction also took place from early times in a broad belt across central European Russia; from the Pskov region in the west, along the valleys of the Sukhona and Vychegda (tributaries of the Northern Dvina), in the regions of the Upper and Middle Volga, to the Kama in the east.

The Pskov–Novgorod region

In 1363 or 1364 two salt-works were mentioned at a location of Rokha or Rukha near Pskov, but, according to the chronicle, they were

[61] Man'kov, *Tseny*, 69; Savich, *Solovetskaya votchina*, 149, 157; Kurts, *Sochinenie Kil'burgera*, 177.

Table 2.2. Salt sales and rye purchases (Solovki monastery)

	1 Sales of salt at Vologda (puds)	2 Price obtained (a) per pud		2 (b) total			3 Purchases of rye (a) chets	3 (b) puds	3 (a) price per chet		4 Price paid (b) Total			4 (c) price per pud		5 Rye purchases as % of salt sales 4(b)/2(b)
		alt.	d.	r.	alt.	d.			alt.	d.	r.	alt.	d.	alt.	d.	
1589	71,654	2	5	6,256	3	3	4,472	17,888	13	4½	1,844	23	2	3	3	30
1598	92,990	1	5	5,206	10	1	4,900	19,600	7	4½	1,139	8	2	2	0	22
1594	—															
1639	120,736	3	3	12,889	25	3½	5,050	30,300	27		4,090	16	4	4	3	32
late 1660s																
1667	140,730	5	1	21,984	7	2½	5,429	32,574	1r. 2 to	3	5,836	5	5	6	0	27
1668	83,210	5	4	14,065	14	4½	3,618	21,708 to	27	2	4,451	26	0	4	3	20
									36	5	3,997	29	4	6	1	28–21
									27		2,930	19	2	4	3	
1680s																
1685–6	99,210	2	2	6,999	26	5	4,139	33,112	16		1,986	24	0	2	0	28–36
									20		2,483	13	2	2	3	
1688–9	98,281	2	3	7,128	14	2½	5,703	45,624	17	4	3,022	19	4	2	1	42–39
									16	2	2,794	15	4	2	0	
1689–90	121,139	3	1	11,575	24	4½	7,034	56,272	11		2,321	7	2	1	2¼	20–1
									11	4	2,461	30	0	1	2¾	
1690–91	48,515	2	5	4,241	30	5½	8,162	65,296	11		2,693	15	2	1	2¼	64–87
									15		3,672	30	0	1	5½	
1691–2	15,492	2	5	1,316	27	2	6,109	48,872	13	2	2,443	20	0	1	4	186

Source: Savich, *Solovetskaya votchina*, 148–9, 155–7.

unsuccessful and were abandoned.[62] This entry in the Pskov chronicle suggests the importance then attached to such undertakings and the large inputs required by the new technique; it also implies that drilling for brine was a novelty.[63] At Rusa, later called Staraya Rusa, near Novgorod, the brine was of only 1.36% or 1.75% salinity.[64] The great advantage here was that brine was then available at the surface. This resulted in relatively easy conditions for starting salt-boiling without some of the initial outlays essential elsewhere. A consequence was that local peasants of no great wealth were able to engage in the trade. The majority of, if not all, tenements engaged in the salt industry.[65] Obligations were met in measures of salt. Princely grants were made to the fishermen at Staraya Rusa in the fifteenth century; they were freed from the obligation to pay a local salt tax (a hundredth) and were 'to engage in the Rusa trade, to boil salt'.[66] A similar, but more detailed, grant a generation later refers to four generations of these salt-working fishermen.[67] This not only takes us back probably to the beginning of the fifteenth century, but also stresses the association between salt and fish. But the lack of salt in Russia in the fourteenth and fifteenth centuries created a great demand and led to salt being imported from the Livonian towns.[68] Doubtless, this demand both justified the industry at Staraya Rusa and made working even such weak brines profitable. Later, perhaps in the sixteenth century, the Pskov area, presumably including Staraya Rusa, exported salt abroad despite this being prohibited.[69] At the same time changes in the techniques, organisation and external circumstances resulted in hundreds of small-scale producers being ruined.

A register of 1607 shows 174 salt-works in use, but 26 not in use and 309 'places' of salt-works empty from of old and recently.[70] Of the salt-works then operating, the overwhelming majority, 150, were still held by men of the artisan quarter. The area suffered badly from Swedish attacks in 1609 and 1617, however, and a decline ensued, much salt then being produced in the area outside the town. There appears to have been a certain recovery in the 1640s, but by this time enterprising traders from other towns had arrived and were competing

[62]*PL*, I (1363); *PL*, II (1364).
[63]Bernadskii, *Novgorod i Novgorodskaya zemlya*, 142.
[64]Gomilevskii, *Sol'*, 78; Ustyugov, *Solevarennaya promyshlennost'*, 311.
[65]Bernadskii, *Novgorod i Novgorodskaya zemlya*, 137–8.
[66]*ASEI*, III, no. 13 (*c.* 1456–61).
[67]*ASEI*, III, no. 21 (1484–1505).
[68]Khoroshkevich, *Torgovlya*, 262.
[69]*AAE*, III, nos. 136 (1623), 195 (*c.* 1630).
[70]Zaozerskaya, *U istokov*, 71.

with the local men of the artisan quarter. They included some names which became well-known, Venevitov, for example. In the period after the Time of Troubles, Parfen Venevitov from Murom, one of a family which became members of the merchant guild, was allowed tax exemption for four years in 1636 to build four salt-works.[71] In 1623 he had been appointed an official dealing with the customs and other matters, including the drink-shops in Pskov.[72] This overlapping concern with the excise on drink and with salt is not unique; it suggests another form of the grain–salt link. It was this dynasty of salt-men who had much to do with the growth of the salt industry at Sol' Kama from the 1660s.[73] This became their main concern, but they did not abandon the works at Staraya Rusa.

Newcomers such as these, arriving in Staraya Rusa in the 1630s, brought in techniques of deep drilling and larger pans from the experience of the Balakhna and Perm' salines.[74] Few men of the artisan quarter had at their disposal resources adequate for the new techniques, so the statement of the military commander (*voevoda*) in 1650 that the former Staraya Rusa system of salt-works had been entirely superseded implies considerable changes. The fact that Perm' type pans now had an area of up to 72 sq. metres was important, since such changes resulted in almost doubling output per pan in the mid-seventeenth century to 4–5 thousand puds a year.[75] By 1662 the 52 salt-works may have achieved an annual output in the range 200–260 thousand puds.[76] Yet the documents show not a single case of an ordinary salt-boiler directly becoming a large-scale producer; the initial outlay was beyond his means and the low salinity of the Staraya Rusa brines provided particular difficulties.[77] Output levels of some salt-works in the late seventeenth century were in the range 5–10 thousand puds.[78] These wide variations are reflected in the categories of tax liability of 45 salt makers in 1682: 12 paid 12–32 eighth shares (the unit of account); 16, 4–8; and 17, $1\frac{1}{2}$–3.[79] By 1705, when a state salt monopoly was introduced, 45 individual salt-boilers delivered salt to the treasury as follows:

[71] *RIB*, v, no. 6, 14.
[72] *AAE*, iii, no. 143.
[73] Ustyugov, *Solevarennaya promyshlennost'*, 75–7.
[74] Zaozerskaya, *U istokov*, 79–80.
[75] *Ibid.*, 80.
[76] *Ibid.*, 83.
[77] *Ibid.*, 82–3.
[78] *Ibid.*, 85.
[79] *Ibid.*, 87.

3	10–27 thousand puds	
8	6–9	
13	3–5	1 salt-works or
17	1–2	a share in one
4	< 1	

This implies that the relatively small-scale boilers of the artisan quarter continued to be an important element in Staraya Rusa. The high price of their salt, caused mainly by high expenditure of the fuel owing to the low salinity of the brines, and the competition of cheaper salt from other areas, put limits on the development of the trade. As some larger entrepreneurs moved to locations in other parts of the country, the smaller men of the artisan quarter in part took their places, sometimes forming companies to share the burdens they had undertaken.[80]

The Vychegda and Sukhona regions

At Sol' Vychegda the brine was of 2.5% salinity and was, ultimately, obtained from depths as great as 170 metres.[81] Initially, however, at the end of the fifteenth century, brine may have been scooped directly from a salt lake without even the use of pipes.[82] This was evidently a peasant industry; there was then no artisan quarter there. Nevertheless, the Stroganovs, who were to contribute so much to the development of the salt industry (and the expansion of the Russians into Siberia), appeared at Sol' Vychegda before 1497 when Fedor Lukich Stroganov died.[83] From the 1520s members of the family were acquiring shares in the local industry, as were monasteries: the Saviour of Priluka and the Presentation of the Blessed Virgin. The Stroganovs had 10 salt-works by 1550 and 14 in 1587. The sixteenth century was evidently the time when the industry flourished, though the total number of salt-works remains unknown; estimates suggest numbers from less than 50 to 90.[84] There seem to be no estimates of total annual output. That of up to 400,000 puds for the 14 Stroganov works (more than 28,000 puds each) seems excessively high.[85] The seventeenth century output of the two salt-works belonging to the Saviour of Priluka monastery is stated to have varied between 3,000 and 10,000 puds, i.e. 1,500 and 5,000

[80] *Ibid.*, 89–90.
[81] Ustyugov, *Solevarennaya promyshlennost'*, 311.
[82] Zaozerskaya, *U istokov*, 153.
[83] *Ibid.*, 154.
[84] Ostroumov, *Ustoi* (1882), nos. 9–10, 141.
[85] Cited in Zaozerskaya, *U istokov*, 155.

each.[86] Even these figures, however, may be high as averages. The outputs listed for certain years between 1618 and 1679 varied between 1,046 and 10,737 for the two works.[87] The average for the 29 seasons listed was 5,818 puds. We have excluded the years from 1681 onwards, not one of which achieved an output of 6,000 puds for the two works; if we include the additional 12 surviving items for the years to 1697, the average falls to 5,146 puds. The evidence suggests that output varied greatly from year to year, as did the length of the season, and that average output of each of these two salt-works, which used brine from the Stroganov pipes, was around 2,500–3,000 puds a year. The output of the 14 Stroganov works, therefore, may have been nearer 40,000 rather than 400,000 puds a year.

Sol' Vychegda suffered a set-back from the Polish–Lithuanian invasions of 1613 which inflicted much damage on the artisan quarter of the town and scattered its population.[88] In addition, in the words of a petition of 1627, 'the best people were written off with their salt industries . . . and do not pay any of your, the Sovereign's, taxes along with the men of the artisan quarter', i.e. the rich entrepreneurs sought exemption from inscription on the ordinary tax lists of the townspeople.[89] By the 1620s the Stroganovs considered Sol' Vychegda as 'poor industries; in three days and three nights only about fifty puds or less are produced'; for want of brine 'in some years full boilings occur, but in others they are not full, but for themselves'. They reckoned the annual output at 'almost three thousand puds' and with the proceeds from this they paid their taxes and other obligations.[90] Stroganov concern was now focussed on the Perm' area with its richer resources of brine, even though they remained powerful merchants and landowners at Sol' Vychegda. In the late seventeenth century three members of the family were paying 1,192 rubles directly to Moscow for their holdings although only one had any salt-works.[91]

The market-place had 54 stalls in 1627 and there was a square where 'trading people set up with bread and wheat rolls on sledges, and peasants from the uezd with carts with every sort of grain, and hay and firewood and every sort of good'.[92] Despite this lively picture of trade in the necessities of life, the artisan quarter was in decay and the petitioners ascribed this to an edict from Moscow allowing spirits and

---

[86]Prokof'eva, *Votchinnoe khozyaistvo*, 52.

[87]*Ibid.*, 53–5.

[88]Zaozerskaya, *U istokov*, 156.

[89]*Ibid.*, 154.

[90]Zaozerskaya, *U istokov*, 155.

[91]*Ibid.*, 161.

[92]*Ibid.*, 157.

beer to be sold on credit. The townspeople claimed that 'many small people of the artisan quarter at Sol' have drunk all they had at the drink shops . . . and have lost their enterprises'; they became dependant on the 'best people', especially the Stroganovs, and suffered when these turned their attention to other locations.[93] Salt-making, like other hot jobs, was thirsty work, of course, but it also seems that control of alcoholic supplies, particularly spirits, was a ready means of recruiting and retaining labour, and that this was reinforced by indebtedness for drink.

The decline of the Sol' Vychegda industry has been ascribed mainly to the weakness of its brines and the small total stock of brine.[94] However, little seems to be known about the costs of production and selling price of the salt produced. This, too, may have been important, if other salines were able to compete on the basis of higher salinity or proximity to the main markets. In the seventeenth century the immense resources of Astrakhan' and other Lower Volga lake salt had become available on a mass scale.

At Yarensk, upstream of Sol' Vychegda, salinity was 6–8%; this brine, stronger than elsewhere in the north, was taken from depths of 182 metres. This could only be done as a result of the achievement of deep drilling; hence, the area only became a major producer in the seventeenth century. The Pankrat'evs, merchants who originated from the Galich artisan quarter, were the initiators, founding the Seregova works in 1637.[95] In 1646 there was only one salt-works with five houses which had only two permanent inhabitants, but accommodated the seasonal workers. In 1674 there were five works and an output of 133,000 puds (2.1 mln kg). In 1678 there were six works and a seventh under construction; output reached 191,000 puds (3.1 mln kg). In 1698 there were thirteen salt-works which produced 310,000 puds (5 mln kg), mostly exported to Vologda.[96] Considerable quantities of supplies, especially metal, were required each year, including imported materials. In 1673, for instance, the list of requirements included '200 large German sheets for the iron pans; 100 puds of Swedish iron'.[97] Firewood had to be bought; even in 1674 12,000 fathoms were used; at its height the works used, perhaps, 30,000 fathoms.[98]

Labour was mostly hired 'for the day and for the month', 90 such

[93]*Ibid.*, 158.
[94]*Ibid.*, 161.
[95]Ustyugov, *Solevarennaya promyshlennost'*, 6–7, 13; Ostroumov, *Ustoi* (1882), nos. 9–10, 141.
[96]Bakhrushin, *Nauchnye trudy*, vol. II, 247; Geiman, *LZAK*, xxxv, 17; Ustyugov, *Solevarennaya promyshlennost'*, 306.
[97]Geiman, *LZAK*, xxxv, 19–20.
[98]*Ibid.*, 21.

men in 1678; there were also permanent workers, such as 1 pipe-man, 4 smiths, 6 salt-boilers, 1 leather-worker, 1 ship-maker and 10 others (probably less skilled).[99] Pay was at least partly in salt and the workers were fed by the employer. Pankrat'ev had arable land and livestock for this purpose, looked after mainly by slaves, including prisoners of war. Apart from hired labour, there were also serfs. At the end of the seventeenth century three volosts of peasants dependant on the sovereign were obliged to supply firewood to the works compulsorily.[100] There was a rapid decline subsequently; by 1702 only two works were in use and output had fallen to 100,000 puds (1.6 mln kg) or less. The main reason was lack of cash for current expenditures.[101] The steward stressed that 'any year better off for money we buy more firewood and make salt for 14 barges (*doshchanniki*), but any year when the money sent hinders the buying of firewood, then with great loss we scarcely make salt for 10 barges'.[102]

At Tot'ma, on the Sukhona, the brine had a salinity of 3.5% but was raised from depths as great as 500 to 630 feet (152–192 m).[103] Deep drilling, in fact, may have been developed at this location; a text-book on the technique is generally accepted as emanating from Tot'ma in the late sixteenth century.[104] In the 1550s, Feodosii, founder of the Saviour of Priluka monastery, appealed to Ivan IV, claiming that the monks 'feed themselves, cut firewood and sell it at the saline; but there is nothing with which they can feed themselves apart from that firewood, so they are in great need'.[105] The monks were granted the right to develop salt-works. The grant mentions that if the brine is of good quality, 5,000 puds of salt a year is produced; if medium, 4,000, and 3,000, if of poor quality. Soon after this the monastery had 6 pipes, 4 salt-works and 2 shops selling salt in Tot'ma.[106] Total output at Tot'ma has been estimated at 300,000–500,000 puds in this period.[107] This implies between 75 and 125 salt-works altogether, if with average quality brine; it seems a high estimate in terms of what little is known for the sixteenth century and of the much more detailed information available for the seventeenth century.

The powerful and experienced entrepreneurs, the Stroganovs, ap-

[99]Bakhrushin, *Nauchnye trudy*, vol. II, 248.
[100]Geiman in *Ocherki istorii SSSR XVII vek*.
[101]Geiman, *LZAK*, xxxv, 17.
[102]Cited *ibid.*, 24. Such barges could carry 1,000 puds.
[103]Ustyugov, *Solevarennaya promyshlennost'*, 34, 311.
[104]See p. 29 above.
[105]Cited by Ostroumov, in *Ustoi* (1882), nos. 9–10, 137.
[106]*Ibid.*, 138.
[107]*Ibid.*

peared in Tot'ma in the mid-sixteenth century; at the same period, in
1555, the Saviour of Priluka monastery received its grant to develop
salt-works. Such competitors with resources adequate to undertake the
new technique of deep drilling challenged the smaller-scale operations
of the men of the artisan quarter, who often shared their holdings,
sometimes with the newcomers. Probably as a consequence of these
developments at least 56 works ceased operating between 1570 and
1600. In 1619 there were only 7 monastic salt-works operating; the 3 or
4 works of the Saviour of Priluka in that year produced about 8,000
puds.[108] If all 16 salt-works then operative had similar outputs, the
total would not have exceeded 40,000 puds. The Saviour of Priluka
itself achieved outputs estimated at more than 33,000 puds in 1624/5
and 31,000 in 1638/9, but output varied greatly and these were exceptional years. In 1634/5 sales of salt amounted to well over 70,000 puds,
but this may have included salt produced elsewhere.[109] We do not
know, then, whether the total Tot'ma output in 1619 was of the order
of a tenth what it had been in the 1550s. This seems unlikely, even
though a survey in the 1620s showed that there had been '43 pipes of
men of the artisan quarter, but the men of the artisan quarter and the
volost' peasants said that they did not remember whose those pipes
were; the pipes were disused for a hundred years or more'.[110]

A fire in 1646 destroyed at least seven salt-works and contributed to
the changes taking place in the pattern of ownership. The men of the
artisan quarter and peasants were increasingly displaced by the monasteries and by merchants from other parts, especially Moscow.[111] Some
of these rich entrepreneurs bought or otherwise acquired land; 'land
and the populated hamlet was a valuable item for the large-scale men
in the industry and they to some extent became landowners'.[112] Salt
winning was the stimulus to their entrepreneurial activity and the basis
of their wealth. It had an impact, too, on some local peasants; 'enterprise in industry, even an extractive one, involved the appearance of a
new means of livelihood for the local peasants and, on the other hand,
their break with the old means; this was a significant process in the
prehistory of capital'.[113] Yet the mid-seventeenth century may have
been the high point for Tot'ma; in the second half of the century, as a
trade and industrial centre, it underwent a period of stabilisation linked

---

[108]Zaozerskaya, *U istokov*, 164; Prokof'eva, *Votchinnoe khozyaistvo*, 50. This calculation assumes
190 puds a *poluvar'*, as estimated by Prokof'eva, *ibid.*, 47.
[109]*Tamozhennye knigi*, I, 489–92; Ostroumov, 'Tovarishchestva', *Ustoi* (1882), nos. 9–10, 139.
[110]Cited in Ustyugov, *Solevarennaya promyshlennost'*, 6.
[111]Zaozerskaya, *U istokov*, 168.
[112]*Ibid.*, 171.
[113]*Ibid.*, 174.

with the fact that the appearance of Astrakhan' and Perm' salt reduced the stream of purchasers to the northern areas of the country.[114] To some extent, therefore, entrepreneurs may at that time have been seeking alternatives to the Tot'ma salt industry.

In 1674, according to a foreigner in Russia, Tot'ma produced 'much salt as white as that from Luneburg'.[115] An occasional drink was, evidently, an aid to this continuing production. The head of the treasury salt industry at Tot'ma was asked about an expenditure of 1 ruble 3 altyns 2 dengas at Easter 1673 and replied that 'for that money spirits were bought for the work people; spirits are bought in the industry, for the work people to celebrate the festival at the salt-works, so that they cause no harm in the saline'.[116] There were other links between salt and drink at Tot'ma in the late seventeenth and early eighteenth century. The wealthy merchant Vasilii Grudtsyn continued to engage in trade and contracts after he entered the salt industry and had a number of salt-works on the Ledenga. Among sums due from him in 1705 was one of 4,600 rubles for a shortfall in spirits he should have delivered.[117] He, too, acquired land and peasants who provided a basis for his dependant work force.

Some salt production continued at Tot'ma throughout the late seventeenth and first half of the eighteenth centuries, but its scale is unknown.[118] It seems to have been declining. A survey in 1687 disclosed more than 100 pipes abandoned for many years, 27 not in use, and only 5 pipes and one brine well being used.[119] Evidently there was also some small outflow of labour to the developing, and competing, industry at Sol' Kama.[120]

The Upper Volga area

From the fourteenth century on there are documentary references to salt winning towards the central regions of what was to be the Moscow state. A boyar, Semen Fedorovich Morozov, gave the Trinity monastery of St Sergius 'half my salt-works and half the well at Sol' Galich in

---

[114]Prokof'eva, *Votchinnoe khozyaistvo*, 68.

[115]Kurts, *Sochinenie Kil'burgera*, 110.

[116]Cited in Ustyugov, *Solevarennaya promyshlennost'*, 238. On Easter and drink see pp. 91, 103, 152 below.

[117]Zaozerskaya, *U istokov*, 169–70.

[118]Ostroumov, *Ustoi* (1882), nos. 9–10, 140.

[119]Kolominskii, 'Torgovlya', 5.

[120]Ustyugov, *Solevarennaya promyshlennost'*, 19.

the Podol [the lower town] which my salt-boiler worked for me, with all its customary dues'.[121]

Concern for the great quantities of firewood needed is shown by a copied Trinity monastery list of amounts at Sol' Galich in 1476/7.[122] A few years earlier the monastery had had difficulties with the local officials who had 'forbidden the Trinity salt-boiler to hire anyone for firewood, and, thus, the wood stayed in the forest; and their salt-works, allegedly, are thereby without wood; and your [i.e. the official's] people have assaulted the boilers at the salt-works and broken two of the monastery's iron-pans and burnt those pans'.[123] The Grand Prince ordered his officer not to oppress the monastery.

In fact, there is much evidence to show princely support of and encouragement for monastic salt-works. The Grand Prince had his own salt-boiler at Sol' Galich.[124] There may have been some competition between prince and monastery, but in general the surviving documents (from monastic archives) show a series of rights granted by princes together with some exemptions, sometimes for specified periods, from quit-rents, taxes and a multiplicity of trading imposts.[125] The earliest of these privileges included the right 'to establish a salt-works . . . and if any people come to that salt-works to boil salt for the archimandrite and the brethren, those people are not subject to my tribute and the salt-works are not liable to any customary dues nor to the volost head's commune payment either, nor to any customary dues'.[126] Apart from such privileges, princes also made donations of salt-works to monasteries.[127] In the fifteenth century there is also some equivocal evidence for private holdings of salt-works. A monk gave the Moscow St Simon monastery his 'salt-works with its iron pan at Rostov'.[128] The monk, however, may not have been an individual owner in reality; he was also a salt-boiler and steward of the Trinity monastery of St Sergius at Sol' Galich; he is mentioned in at least eight other charters, mostly of the 1440s and 1450s, in connection with Sol' Pereyaslavl', Sol' Galich and Kostroma.[129] His 'gift', of course, may well have been part of a deal between the two monasteries. The high

---

[121] *ASEI*, I, no. 3 (before 25 September 1392).

[122] *ASEI*, I, no. 454.

[123] *ASEI*, I, no. 361 (1467–74).

[124] *ASEI*, I, no. 225 (15 August 1449).

[125] *ASEI*, I, nos. 237 (1450), 245 (1453), 248 (1453–5), 320 (1462–6), 491 (1481 with confirmations to 1506), 502 (1483), II, no. 351 (1451); III, nos. 195 (1463–78), 207 (1478), 481 (1405–15). *AFZ*, I, no. 264 (1473–84).

[126] *ASEI*, III, no. 481 (1405–15).

[127] *ASEI*, III, no. 236 (1450); II, no. 455 (*c.* 1451–64).

[128] *ASEI*, II, no. 344 (1445–53).

[129] *ASEI*, I, nos. 83, 102, 103, 116, 214, 361, 590, 592.

value of salt-works is also shown by frequent references to shares of a
half, a quarter or an eighth in such enterprises.[130] The Trinity monastery acquired an eighth of a salt-works from Esip Savel'evich.[131] He
was evidently a peasant of some local importance; he witnessed a
document and was 'with his fellows', a good-man and old-established
peasant, on behalf of a monastery in a land dispute.[132] The phrase
'with his fellows' indicates he was acting on behalf of a peasant commune or partnership; we have here, then, either individual or communal peasant participation.

At Sol' Galich the Trinity monastery of St Sergius continued to
extract salt throughout the sixteenth and seventeenth centuries. In 1649
the monastery's authorities claimed that 'until now our monks have
supplied the whole monastery from those salt-works'; this was, of
course, untrue. They appealed against an order to sell the works arising
from a decree that only traders of the artisan quarter were to have such
works.

But, they claim that in those salt-works of theirs, the monastery has expended
much money on firewood and every sort of equipment for the future industry, and much money has lain idle in salt taken by enterprising traders on the
side, and in what has been taken as debts for supplies for the works and in
accordance with the debt-contracts; payments are not much in a year or in
two. Money and provisions have been given to the work people at the salt-
works and they work that off over many years, but there is no money
payment from those workmen.[133]

In the late seventeenth century, then, the monastery was selling salt, as
well as meeting its own needs; it also displayed the uncertain attitude to
hired labour characteristic of Russia at the time, when what might be
regarded as hired wage-labour was often treated as a category of debt-
serf or slave.

Salt winning at Nerekhta, south of the Upper Volga, is known from
the fourteenth century, though the amount of information is small.[134]
In the fifteenth century the metropolitan and the Trinity monastery of
St Sergius had salt-works in the region which used both free and
dependent labour.[135] A Grand Prince made a grant to the Trinity
monastery about their salt-works at Nerekhta:

---

[130]*ASEI*, I, nos. 64, 65, 68 (all 1428–32).
[131]*ASEI*, I, nos. 67 and 68 (1428–32).
[132]*ASEI*, I, nos. 159 (*c.* 1430s–1450s); 340 (*c.* 1464–78). He may also be the Osip Savel'evich
    mentioned in a purchase deed; *GVNiP*, no. 248 (fifteenth century).
[133]Shumakov, *Sotnitsy*, no. II (25 May 1649, with confirmation in 1680).
[134]Ostroumov, in *Ustoi* (1882), nos. 5, 70–1, 78.
[135]*Ibid.*, 93; nos. 9–10, 141.

If any salt-boiler goes from those salt-works to sell salt, or sends [anyone] with monastery salt for sale, two trips down and up the Volga in summer, or to Varok to buy iron pans, and twice in winter with fifty loads, they are not liable to [various customs imposts] *myt* and *tamga* or *vosmnichee* or *kostki* or any other customary dues, apart from church customary dues, in all my, the Grand Prince's, estate, in all towns.[136]

At Bol'shie Soli ('Large Salts') and Malye Soli ('Small Salts') in the same area in 1518–20 a survey disclosed 31 empty salt-works places, two of which were the metropolitan's.[137] At the end of the sixteenth century there were nineteen works mostly belonging to local people on a shared basis.[138] A survey of 1591/2 showed only twelve tenements in the artisan quarter so development evidently occurred after this.[139] We again find hints of links between salt, drink and taxation: there were warehouses for salt, drink-shops and the customs house located by the thirty-three stalls.[140] There was great destruction from the military activities in 1609 and the town had evidently not recovered by 1628. Around the middle of the century there were four, evidently large, salt-works, but the last surviving works closed in 1699; salt was then imported from Balakhna and Elton.[141] The salt lakes in the south were now more securely in Russian hands as a result of Peter the Great's military activities.

Sol' Kama

At Sol' Kama, still further east, the salinity of the brine was very high, 12-15%, and brine was found at depths of 210–80 feet (64–85 m), not nearly as deep as at many other locations.[142] The salt-works extended over a considerable area in the region along the Kama, the Zyryanka and the Lenva. There is a tradition that the earliest salt-working here took place in the early fifteenth century; the earliest documentary evidence, however, is a survey of 1579.[143] Table 2.3 summarises the data on the number of salt-works.[144]

Initially, in the town, the men of the artisan quarter dominated the industry; they held all sixteen works in 1579, but no one man held more than two works. Even in the quarter itself outsiders came to play

[136]*ASEI*, I, no. 202 (1447–55).
[137]*AFZ*, I, no. 168.
[138]Ostroumov, in *Ustoi* (1882), nos. 5, 142.
[139]Zaozerskaya, *U istokov*, 20.
[140]*Ibid.*, 21.
[141]*Ibid.*, 23.
[142]Ustyugov, *Solevarennaya promyshlennost'*, 34.
[143]*Ibid.*, 41.
[144]Ustyugov, *Solevarennaya promyshlennost'*, 138.

Table 2.3. *Number of salt-works, Sol' Kama*

	Artisan quarter	Pyskorka monastery	Zyryanka	Lenva	Stroganovs	Total
1579	16	1			27 (13)	44
1623–4	35	1	2		23 (6)[a]	61
1634–5	52	3	10		28	93
	fire 1635					
1644–7	27	8	12		31	78
1685	58	10	39	20	78	205
	fire 1688					
	fire 1695					
1696		23	44	44	78	189 minimum
1697		25	4		162	191 minimum
1700–8	46	23			162	231 minimum

Notes: Figures in brackets are works known not to be in use.
[a] Ustyugov, *Solevarennaya promyshlennost'*, p. 135, gives 21, not 23 works.

an increasing part, especially after the fire of 1635 destroyed more than half the salt-works in the town. Further disastrous fires in the course of the seventeenth century ruined the small and middling owners and resulted in a concentration of the industry in fewer hands. The industry outside the town was also developed by those with greater resources; for example, a monastery (whose works were later taken over by the state) and great merchant families such as the Stroganovs, who acquired the Lenva works and those of the treasury towards the end of the century. By around 1700 two families owned the majority of works in the town and the Stroganovs were dominant in the uezd. 'Thus, the road taken by the salt industry of Sol' Kama from the 1570s to the eighteenth century was signposted by the seizure of the entire uezd salt industry by feudal lords and the creation of a large-scale industry in the artisan quarter.'[145]

Firewood was both obtained locally and was floated down the Kama from the Cherdyn' region. The Pyskorka monastery considered, in 1696/7, that 'each salt-works burnt 12 fathoms of wood' at a firing.[146] There was an annual demand per works of 3,608 fathoms which indicates that this saline was firing on 300 days a year. The usual Sol' Kama season of 22 notional 'weeks' of 12 days each, 264 days in all, would require 3,168 fathoms. The wood should be cut 'from good, big, solid

145 *Ibid.*, 143.
146 Cited in Ustyugov, *Solevarennaya promyshlennost'*, 248.

wood . . . each piece to be cut an arshin or four and a half spans', i.e. 710–812 mm.[147] It was supplied by peasants who contracted to cut, float and stack a specified quantity for an agreed price. The customer was normally responsible for catching the loose floating logs and hauling them up any side water and to the bank. For the early part of the seventeenth century the price of local firewood seems to have been 10 kopeks or so a fathom, but by the mid-1680s, this had risen to 15 kopeks. The clearing of forest for hayfields was then used as a means of obtaining local wood more cheaply.[148]

Although the Cherdyn' timber floated down the Kama was mostly pine (which was more highly valued than the local fir), the prices paid for it were similar to, or even less than, those for the local wood. The contractors, however, seem to have had their money in advance instead of part in advance and the remainder on completion. The Cherdyn' peasants also cut and floated timber to Sol' Kama without any contract; there was evidently a ready sale either in the town or in the surrounding district.[149] In addition, some consumers sent their work people into the Cherdyn' forests to cut timber and this led to conflicts, clashes and complaints. The Cherdyn' peasants had the right to cut and float timber without payment of any dues other than the tax on sales; others, however, were liable to pay a customary forest due of 20 dengas per 100 fathoms of firewood, per 100 beams and per fathom length of any boats built.[150] The Cherdyn' people appealed to Moscow in 1677 to prohibit the intrusions of outsiders. In reply they were

. . . ordered to withdraw their petition about the forests until a survey is carried out; the people of Usol'e [i.e. Sol' Kama] are ordered to go to those forests and cut firewood and pay to the Great Sovereign's treasury the customary forest due from the firewood and every timber as before, so that there shall be no reduction in the dues collected by the Great Sovereign's treasury. To this end the Cherdyn' people, making a contract for firewood, are not to supply it at a high price so that salt shall not be dear.[151]

Government concern for state income and the avoidance of any increase in the price of salt was evidently not the only element in this decision. It was ironic that the Cherdyn' people had to appeal to the office in which the clerk, Yakov Kirillov, like his father before him, owned salt-works in Sol' Kama; it was he who signed the memoran-

---

[147]Cited, *ibid.*, 249.
[148]*Ibid.*, 250.
[149]*Ibid.*, 251.
[150]*Ibid.*, 253.
[151]Cited, *ibid.*, 255–6.

dum to Cherdyn'.[152] This overlap between bureaucracy and entrepreneurial activity no doubt contributed greatly to the scale of the abuses suffered by the people of Cherdyn'. In 1697 the people sent a petition that

. . . stewards from other towns, of the man of repute, Grigorii Dmitrievich Stroganov, and people of Usol'e and of other towns, gathering many work gangs and looking to that, about three thousand and more persons, wandering people, ride into Cherdyn' uezd every year across the recorded boundary . . . along the rivers Kama and Vishera and around the fields they cut firewood for the salt-works and for every sort of structure and float it to their salt workings . . . And the work people come out into the Cherdyn' hamlets in gangs for their work – they beat the peasants and burn them with fire and torture them to death for their property, seize their wives and daughters; they engage in brigandage along the rivers, plunder and torment the trading people who pass and do them to death.[153]

The fact that payment was made to those cutting and supplying wood does not mean that they were always freely working for wages. More often the payment, or the advance, was treated as a debt, which then had to be worked off in the terms of the contract. The peasants had little choice but to engage in by-trades. With little opportunity to win a livelihood from their infertile land, the peasants were at the mercy of the powerful owners of the salt-workings; they were sometimes, as on the Stroganov estates, obliged to cut firewood as a form of labour rent, or they virtually became debt-serfs when they engaged in by-trades.

Each salt-works required ten to twenty men for the actual production process; the total number required when the industry was developing, from the mid-seventeenth century, was too great to be found locally. There was an influx of workers, mainly from the northern maritime area throughout the century, and especially from the 1660s when the White Sea industry was in decline; this continued despite the tax reform of 1679 which, by making the tenement the tax-liable unit, increased the tax burden for many newcomers who held tenements.[154] Some work people lived with the salt-boilers; these included some who were hired on an annual basis, others who were debt-serfs. The majority of work people, however, held tenements in the artisan quarter.[155] Others had their tenements on the land of the larger owners; some lived in their establishments either as debt-serfs, on a limited term

---

[152]The Kirillovs served in the Novgorod Office 1677–80 (Bogoyavlenskii, *Prikaznye sud'i XVII veka*, 95). They served in other central offices as well and were last noted in 1682.
[153]Cited in Ustyugov, *Solevarennaya promyshlennost'*, 254.
[154]*Ibid.*, 146, 148, 189, 193.
[155]*Ibid.*, 202.

contract or on a yearly wage.[156] The work force included Polish prisoners of war, as well as purchased Tatars, Khanty, Mari and Kalmyks, some of them newly converted to Orthodoxy.[157] Finally, many temporary workers were hired from the poor of the artisan quarter of the town.

The skilled workers, such as pipe-layers and blacksmiths, were paid an annual wage. Those directly engaged in the evaporation process were paid according to the number of 'weeks' (twelve-day periods) worked. Amounts varied from 25 rubles a year for a master pipe-layer to 3 rubles for a man to carry the sacks.[158] Expenditures on food have been calculated at 2.15 to 3.13 rubles a year.[159] Clothing amounted to an additional ruble-and-a-half. It therefore seems that only those with wages above the minimum or having their own holding were in a position to maintain themselves and their families. The amount of cultivated land, however, declined in the seventeenth century (Table 2.4).[160]

Moreover, the area was not particularly fertile. It was, therefore, largely dependent on imports, mainly from Vyatka, despite high transport costs and other difficulties, and, from the 1670s, from Kungur in the Western Urals.[161] Work people were sometimes paid in grain, not money, and the Pyskorka monastery hired many 'on the monastery's grain', i.e. supplying them with food. Such facts indicate the need for caution in interpreting all references to hire and wages.

There were certainly some supplements to any pay. In 1640 a merchant owning a saline on the Zyryanka was allowed to import duty-free from Nizhnii Novgorod 50 buckets of spirits a year 'as succour for the work people'.[162] The Pyskorka monastery bought 200 buckets of spirits at the pot-house in Sol' Kama in 1696/7 and over 100 in 1698/9, presumably for treating work people engaged in particularly arduous work, or to celebrate the start of firing a pan or, perhaps, as a general 'sweetener'. At the Resurrection monastery, for instance, the workers were given one or two buckets of beer on lighting up, three if a new salt-works was being commissioned. Festivals were also celebrated in this way, and sometimes wheaten rolls were also distributed. Evidently, too, money was on occasions given for beer.[163]

[156] *Ibid.*, 203.
[157] *Ibid.*, 204–5.
[158] *Ibid.*, 230–5.
[159] *Ibid.*, 236–7.
[160] Ustyugov, *Solevarennaya promyshlennost'*, 272.
[161] *Ibid.*, 272; Preobrazhenskii, *Ocherki kolonizatsii*, 114–16.
[162] Ustyugov, *Solevarennaya promyshlennost'*, 238.
[163] *Ibid.*, 238–40.

Table 2.4. *Cultivated land, seventeenth century*

	Arable land (chets in one field)	Tenements	Arable land per tenement (chets in one field)
1623/4	2,149	718	3.0
1707/9	929	1,319	0.7

Source: Ustyugov, *Solevarennaya promyshlennost'*, 272.

The wage relationship between worker and employer (and this applied to the majority of the hired work people) meant that they were not formally dependants and were free to move if dissatisfied.

The men of the artisan quarter and the labourers of Sol' Kama, and the peasants of the uezd, working in the salt industry remained tax-liable. This was their 'trade'; from the income they fed themselves and paid the state tax . . . The impoverishment and ruin of a considerable part of the men in the artisan quarter, and of the peasants in the maritime regions, separated them from the means of production and made them either flee to new places or seek earnings by selling their labour power. These were new features in the social history of the Russian 17th century state, the initial stage in the process of primary accumulation and elements in the evolution of capitalist relations.[164]

Even so, there were still considerable traces of relations of dependence and it remains uncertain what proportion of the work force at Sol' Kama were independent wage labourers.

The Mid-Volga

At the great bend of the Volga at Samara, Nadei Sveteshnikov was granted an extensive territory in 1631. It was an area unsettled and undefended, completely open to the nomads of the steppes.[165] Salt production started here in 1640; by 1646 there were eight salt-works, six of them operative (two on the steppes were destroyed by nomads).[166] The workers were hired by contract for a set period; four of them were to boil salt and to be paid 40 dengas for every 100 puds; two made and repaired the iron pans for which they received 30 rubles a year; others had 3 rubles for the winter; sawyers who cut firewood had 4 rubles for the winter; a pipe-man received 30 rubles a year; all of

[164]*Ibid.*, 241.
[165]Bakhrushin, *Nauchnye trudy*, vol. II, 232.
[166]*Ibid.*, 234–5.

them 'ate and drank his, Nadeino's', supplies. The pay for the specialists appears to be quite high. For comparison, a junior boyar on service in Siberia rarely received more than 15–20 rubles a year, plus a grain allowance; watchmen and other hired men at state institutions had 4 rubles and an allowance of grain.[167] Presumably high rates of pay were needed to induce the specialist workers to come to this remote and dangerous place. The ordinary work people included peasants who had been transferred, not always willingly, from Sveteshnikov's other estates.[168] Altogether, in 1646 there were 108 men, apart from clergy, and these included 33 armed men to keep the fort which had been built for protection. There were 30 peasants, 28 labourers who paid labour rent at the works, 13 work people. Both the labourers and the peasants were often held in dependance by debt to Sveteshnikov; the peasants, however, worked the land in order to provide a local supply of foodstuffs; by 1660 this was, at least in part, in the form of labour rent. At this time, fourteen years after Nadei Sveteshnikov's death under flogging for a debt to the treasury, there were 112 tenements; 101 of these were now labourer ones and there was a total of 158 men. Later it seems that some natives, Chuvash and Mordva, joined the settlement, probably to avoid the heavy taxation they escaped on conversion to Orthodoxy.[169] According to Kilburger in 1674 this saline was producing 'so much salt that the inhabitants all around there can be supplied with it'.[170] In this frontier area there was timber for fuel, but a considerable proportion of the work force had to be devoted to defence and a local agriculture had to be established for maintenance.

THE SOUTH AND SIBERIA

Towards the mouths of the Volga and Astrakhan' there are more than 2,000 salt lakes. The largest of these is Elton, about 170 miles northwards of Astrakhan'; it has an area of up to 54,000 acres; Baskunchak lies about 50 miles to the south and has an area about half that of Elton.[171] About 1900, the output from Elton alone amounted to 12–15 mln puds (195–245 mln kg) annually.[172] Baskunchak then produced about $14\frac{1}{2}$ mln puds.[173] This area, east of the Volga, was not

[167] *Ibid.*, 236.
[168] *Ibid.*, 243–4.
[169] *Ibid.*, 236–46.
[170] Kurts, *Sochinenie Kil'burgera*, 110.
[171] Semenov, *Rossiya*, vol. VI, 39.
[172] *Ibid.*
[173] *Ibid.*, 528.

firmly in Russian hands even in the seventeenth century, but was continually exposed to nomad incursions; this, and the lack of cultivation in the area, hindered the full exploitation of these exceptionally rich sources.

In the fifteenth century Barbaro had noted that, near Astrakhan', much salt was taken 'from the sea' and that 'every year people from Moscow come on their boats to Astrakhan' for salt'.[174] Contarini, in the 1470s, commented that in the region of Astrakhan' there was a huge salt lake; 'they say that it provides so much salt that it could supply the greater part of the world. Almost all Russia uses this salt and it is of excellent quality.'[175]

In 1558, two years after the capture of Astrakhan' and at the time of a famine in the area, Jenkinson regarded it as dead for trade and unlikely to develop.[176] Arthur Edwards, another Englishman in the employ of the Muscovy Company, took quite a different view about ten years later. 'There passe downe Volga every Summer, 500. boats great & smal, from all the upper parts of the river, whereof some be of 500. tunne. They go for Minerall salt and for Sturgeon.'[177] If we arbitrarily assume that half the boats noted by Edwards went for salt and their average tonnage was 250, they would take 62,500 tons or 3,875 thousand puds in a single trip. It seems not unreasonable to assume another 1 mln puds or so would be used to salt fish and caviare and to be exported southwards. On such assumptions, then, the output of Astrakhan' might have been 4–5 mln puds a year even in the second half of the sixteenth century; nothing appears to be known of the amount of earlier output.

Whether the acquisition of the Lower Volga by the Russians at this time resulted in an increased amount of cheaper salt from this area remains unknown. A generation after Jenkinson's pessimistic view, Giles Fletcher remarked simply that 'At Astrakhan' salt is made naturally by the sea water that casteth it up into great hills, and so it is digged down and carried away by the merchants and other that will fetch it from thence. They pay to the emperor for acknowledgment or custom three pence Russe upon every hundredweight.'[178] Nevertheless, it appears that even in the sixteenth century, despite the enormous developments which had taken place in salt getting, supplies were not fully satisfying demand.

---

[174]'Viaggio allo Tana', section 53.
[175]'Viaggio in Persia', section 19; Skrzhinskaya identifies the lake as Baskunchak, but this does not seem certain.
[176]In Morgan and Coote, *Early Voyages and Travels*, vol. I, 58–9.
[177]In Hakluyt, *Principal Navigations*, vol. III, 71.
[178]*Of the Russe Commonwealth*, chapter 3.

This unsatisfied demand, aided by access to richer but remoter sources and the decline of some of the older centres of production, was the main stimulus to the changes which took place in the seventeenth century. In any event, in 1606 Margeret noted that Astrakhan' carried 'a very lively trade, more lively than all other Russian towns, and supplies almost all Russia with salt and salt fish'.[179] Olearius, who was in Russia in the 1630s, mentioned three lakes situated about 6 and 20 miles west of Astrakhan'.

This wasteland furnishes excellent salt, which is found here in various pits, sloughs, and stagnant lakes, of which the most notable are Mochavskoe, Kanikovo, and Gvozdovskoe, situated respectively 10, 15 and 30 versts from Astrakhan. In the lagoons or salt sloughs there are salt veins through which the salt rises. On the surface, the heat of the sun causes the formation of flakes of salt as clear as crystal and as thick as one's finger. It has a pleasant odor of violets. Anyone who wishes may carry it off, paying the Grand Prince a duty of only one kopek for two puds. The Russians do a thriving business with it, transporting it up the shores of the Volga, piling it up in great quantities, and shipping it all over Russia.[180]

Some hint of the scale of output in the region is given by an order to the military commander of Astrakhan' in 1672 'firmly and constantly, and at a low price, to send two hundred thousand puds of salt every year to Simbirsk or Nizhnii Novgorod'.[181] These supplies for state use were, of course, only part, probably a small part, of the region's total output. Merchants, as well as the crown, exploited these resources. In 1644, for example, Nadei Sveteshnikov took 50,000 puds of salt from Astrakhan', and expected to get more than 5,000 rubles for it.[182] Grants to individuals to work Lake Elton were made in 1655.[183] In 1727 'on the meadow side opposite Tsaritsyn there is a great salt lake called Elton, 30 verstas beyond the Volga, in which they quarry salt and bring it to the Volga; between Tsaritsyn and Cherny Yar the salt surpasses any Astrakhan' *buzun* and is very white and pure and has the scent of raspberries'.[184] The area, however, was only safely in Russian hands after Peter's campaigns, yet as late as the 1740s it had to be defended against the Kalmyks (see p. 183). Baskunchak, apparently, only started to be exploited as late as 1771.[185] The view that 'taking salt from the deposits of the Astrakhan' lakes, chiefly Baskunchak and

[179]Margeret, *Estat*, 1 verso.
[180]Olearius, *Travels*, 325–6.
[181]'Zapiski ORSA', *IAO* (1861), II, 379.
[182]Bakhrushin, *Nauchnye trudy*, vol. II, 230.
[183]Kolominskii, 'Torgovlya', 14.
[184]Kirilov, *Sostoyanie*, 232 (1727).
[185]Semenov, *Geografichesko-statisticheskii slovar'*, vol. I, 218.

8 In 1885 Henry Landsell visited the 'Salt mines of Iletsk', actually a salt quarry. Comparing it with the salt-mines near Salzburg and Cracow, he remarked that 'the underground part of the business at Iletsk struck me as on an exceedingly small scale, nor did I see or hear anything abnormal in their working of the mines'. Nevertheless, at that time the workings covered more than a square mile in area and had reached a depth of nearly 500 feet.

Elton, became of considerable importance in the second half of the 17th century', would, though true in general, seem to need confirmation as regards the specific locations.[186] The same applies to the statement that 'the main quantity of lower Volga salt was sent to Astrakhan' and Gur'ev for the lower Volga, Yaik and Caspian fisheries'.[187] Enormous quantities of salt were undoubtedly used by the fisheries, but we do not know what proportion of the unknown total output went there.

When, in the 1640s, Nadei Sveteshnikov was developing his frontier salines at the great bend of the Volga near Samara, other Russian venturers had reached the Pacific. The penetration of Siberia in the

[186]Ustyugov, *Solevarennaya promyshlennost'*, 5.
[187]*Ibid.*, 306–7.

seventeenth century gave the Russians access to another major source of salt at Lake Yamysh on the upper reaches of the Irtysh. An instruction of 1626 refers to salt taken from the lake earlier, but it seems probable that any such expeditions were fairly recent; the instruction ordered salt to be collected, a survey of the lake made and a plan sent to Moscow.[188] To carry this out, 604 men were sent with 23 vessels (16 *doshchanniki* and 7 *lod'i*); they brought back over 29,000 puds of salt, and traders brought another 10,000; in 1625 the total had been just over 12,200.[189] These quantities fit fairly well with assumed capacities of 1,000 and 2,000 puds for *doshchanniki* and *lod'i* respectively.[190] The members of the expedition were paid 5 puds of salt each.

The Serbian adventurer, Križanić, who was in Tobol'sk in the 1660s, considered that Lake Yamysh was an inexhaustible supply of salt. 'There', he wrote, 'we would cheaply get many cattle, salt beef and mutton, and dry a great quantity of it in the sun and in the smoke. Siberia would be supplied with this and it would be sold to the Germans.'[191] He optimistically thought that salt exported from this lake to the 'Germans', i.e. non-Slav westerners, would compete with that they had from Portugal. Lake Yamysh and the wells at Ust'-Kut saline, however, supplied the treasury with only 31,000 puds in 1698 and 34,000 in 1699.[192] At that date the route along the river Irtysh from Tobol'sk was still so liable to attacks from the native peoples that salt could be won only with annual armed expeditions protected by strongpoints built around the lake. An instruction in June 1699 (over eleven double-column pages in length in its printed form) specified that twenty-five boats (*doshchanniki*) were to go for salt to the lake.[193] The salt collected by the expedition was to be carted in 1,140 sacks by horse and camel obtained from the natives to the boats. The boats were to be stamped on both sides with the state emblem of the eagle, and the salt, emptied from the sacks, was to be secured under matting. Salt belonging to individuals was in no circumstances to be carried. The leader of the expedition, moreover, was to 'watch carefully that no Russian people or foreigners of any rank brought the prohibited tobacco plant to Tobol'sk or secretly bartered it with the Kalmyk people and Bukharans; and that no one anywhere at the wharves made intoxicating beers and ales for themselves and for sale'.[194] The risks and

[188]*RIB*, vol. VIII, 376–7.
[189]*Ibid.*, 378, 419–20.
[190]Shunkov, *Ocherki*, 316–17.
[191]Križanić, *Politika*, 29–30, 388.
[192]Kolominskii, 'Torgovlya', 15.
[193]*AI*, v, no. 288.
[194]*AI*, v, no. 288: 527.

difficulties involved in exploiting this distant resource clearly prevented Križanić's extravagant expectations from being fulfilled. Lake Yamysh never became a major centre of Russian salt output.

The emergence of a large-scale and widespread industry in early modern Russia was gradual; the industry evolved in different ways and at different periods at its various locations. The earliest evidence is of rock salt from the south-west. The evaporation of sea water or surface brines in the White Sea area and the north-west is known from the twelfth century, though it is certainly much older in origin. A major change took place with the development of drilling, perhaps in the mid-fourteenth century. This technique, although at first not reaching great depths, enabled the industry to spread to new areas. From the mid-fourteenth century, too, there was a remarkable increase in the numbers of monasteries, many of which contributed much to the colonisation of remoter areas. Monasteries often had resources of men and money; they could provide the capital needed for the new techniques; they could make loans – and foreclose when they were not paid on time. Such considerations to some extent account for the part played by monasteries and other corporations or companies (often hidden in the records under the name of a single man).

The extension of the salt industry appears to have been started by individuals or groups; but monasteries and princes took an increasing part in it by the fifteenth century. The Trinity monastery of St Sergius, for instance, acquired considerable holdings by purchase and exchange; the monastery was following a policy for the active development of this industry as early as the first half of the fifteenth century.[195] Princes, too, were active in developing some salines with three or four salt-works in this period, but their direct involvement declined in the first half of the sixteenth century.

The new technique thus contributed to a great extension of salt getting. In the fifteenth century brine obtained from underground sources was being evaporated across much of what was to be the core of Muscovy, from Staraya Rusa in the west, through a cluster of locations along the Upper Volga and the valleys of the Kostroma and the Sukhona. The latter river, together with the Vychegda and the Pinega, flow into the Northern Dvina; along all these rivers there were important salt-workings, as well as to the west of the White Sea. On the Kama, far to the east, salt production may have started early in the fifteenth century, but definite evidence for what was to be a very

---

[195]*ASEI*, I, nos. 72 (*c.* 1430?), 118 (–1440), 120 (*c.* 1435–40).

important location only dates from 1579.[196] By this time the Stroganov family were active there and the first steps had been taken towards the acquisition of the Urals and Siberia. Astrakhan' had been taken in 1556.

The developments involved in the growth of the brine-based salt industry included an increase in trade. Before 1400 the Northern Dvina was a trade route for salt by cart and by boat; at Ustyug and at Vologda, which became perhaps the greatest salt market in Russia, the prince's representative was to receive two measures of salt for each boatload.[197] This was the route used by such large salt traders as the Solovki monastery in the White Sea.

In 1518 the St Joseph monastery of Volokolamsk was trading in Novgorod, Demon, Rusa and Beloozero and sent its factor (*kupchina*) or elder 'in winter on a hundred and fifty carts, and in summer on five boats (*strugi*), to buy or to sell . . . And if their factor or elder comes once a year to Rusa to buy salt, they buy salt and put it in sacks (*rogoziny*), but baskets (*lub'ya*) are not paid for.'[198] A will of this time mentions a sack of salt priced at 15 altyns.[199] This suggests a weight of over 15 puds since salt then often cost somewhat less than 6 dengas per pud.[200] Other evidence, however, shows that the sack varied in weight from 10 to 35 puds (163 to 571 kg); most frequently it seems to have been about 30 puds (over 1,000 lb).[201] It therefore seems unlikely that this 'sack' was simply that; work people would not have been able to lift them when they were trans-shipped.

Such monastic trade was often duty-free, or at least partly so, from the mid-fifteenth century.[202] In the case just mentioned, the Grand Prince allowed the monastery to sell duty-free any salt left surplus to their own consumption. 'But if they begin to buy, not for monastic consumption, and begin to sell again what they have bought, our customs officials and collectors of customary dues shall take the stamping impost (*tamga*) and customary dues from their goods as from trading people.'[203]

In 1583 the Trinity monastery had its right to buy iron for its salt

---

[196]Ustyugov, *Solevarennaya promyshlennost'*, 41.

[197]*ASEI*, III, no. 7, article 14 (1397).

[198]*AFZ*, II, no. 82. According to Kamentseva and Ustyugov, *Russkaya metrologiya*, 111–12, the sack was not a measure, but here it indicates an appreciable quantity, one liable to duty.

[199]*ARG*, no. 179 (before 21 December 1519).

[200]Man'kov, *Tseny*, 67, 175.

[201]Kolominskii, 'Torgovlya', 21; according to Kolominskii, there were three baskets to a sack. Savich, *Solovetskaya votchina*, 140–1.

[202]*ASEI*, I, nos. 202 (1447–55), 237 (1450), 245 (1453), 248 (1453–5), 295 (1461–6), 318 (1462–6).

[203]*AFZ*, II, no. 102 (1527, with confirmations to 1541) is similar, but equates the five boat-loads with 300 carts.

pans, and other consumables, confirmed and was to be liable to customs duties.[204] The Metropolitan received a right in 1564, confirmed
in 1569 and 1598, to a hundred loads of grain and salt or other consumables in winter, or a hundred carts or their equivalent in river vessels
(*sudna*) in summer, all duty-free.[205] The quantities of salt involved
were evidently considerable. The one vessel a year the St Joseph monastery of Volokolamsk was allowed to send to Beloozero and to Kargopol' duty-free for salt for the monastery's use carried 20,000 puds
(327,000 kg).[206] According to the Ves'egonsk customs charter of 1563,
these vessels were charged at double the rate for the boats (*strugi*)
mentioned above.[207] This may indicate that at this time boats were
considered to be half the size of vessels.

On occasion the exemption of monastic salt consumption from duties
was abused; at least a charter of 1517 specified that the St Joseph
monastery tenement in Degunino was not to be used to store or sell
'others' supplies of salt or any other good as their own supplies';
violation of this results in a penalty of two rubles and the stamping
impost was to be exacted.[208]

In the sixteenth century, then, the northern monasteries played a
large part in the salt trade, some as producers and traders, others as
traders only. The main monasteries involved were Solovki, St Nicholas of Korel', Antonii of Siya, the Saviour of Priluka and Cyril of
Beloozero.[209]

Prices for salt rose during the century, but not as much as for a
number of other foodstuffs.[210] It seems that the extension of the salt
trade to new areas, the increase in the amounts produced, and a fall in
the cost of iron-pans in the second half of the sixteenth century, all
helped to damp down a rise in salt prices.[211] The import of salt
through the Baltic was an additional factor. Prices rose in the 1550s
when trade with Livonia declined, but fell in the 1560s when the Narva
navigation developed considerably.[212]

In general it seems that in the early period individuals and companies
of individuals paid a rent to the Grand Prince or treasury for brine
used, whereas most monastic and boyar salt-works were privileged,

[204]*AAE*, I, no. 320.
[205]*AFZ*, III, addend. no. 1; no. 2 is similar but more detailed.
[206]*AFZ*, II, no. 395 (1589).
[207]Sreznevskii, *Materialy*, vol. III, 558–9.
[208]*AFZ*, II, no. 80.
[209]Man'kov, *Tseny*, 62; Kostomarov, *Ocherki torgovli*, 153.
[210]Man'kov, *Tseny*, 67–9.
[211]Man'kov, *Tseny*, 71.
[212]Khoroshkevich, *Torgovlya*, 262.

freed from such payments and from transit dues in many cases.[213] Such exemptions were often restricted to salt for use by the monastery; salt for trade was liable to the usual exactions. This distinction between deals for own use and trade, presumably for profit, was common. There is some evidence of attempts to regularise transit and associated dues in the sixteenth century. The Dvina customs charter of 1560, for instance, specifies the charges to which boats carrying salt were liable: 2 rubles 40 dengas for each 1,000 puds; there were also payments to the weigh-men on any sales.[214] In the late sixteenth century the government tried to regularise the salt trade and the associated customs dues. In 1571 a customs charter was issued for the extensive Novgorod territories, which laid down the dues from merchants and those on sales.[215] Even at the end of the century, however, there was still considerable variation with a large number of small payments to be made. In all, these amounted to 10 dengas a pud.[216]

Salt, however, was an item of extractive industry, trade and taxation which had other aspects; it had something of an aura about it which may have been enhanced by its relative scarcity in the core areas of early Russia. It has been pointed out that the Russian term for 'hospitality', literally 'bread–salt' (*khleb-sol'*), enshrines the combination of farming and gathering; salt dominated Russian economics and society into comparatively recent times. More specifically, it had certain almost magical properties. One of the questions put to the church council of 1551 was about the fact that 'inexperienced priests on Easter Thursday put salt under the altar and so keep it till the seventh Thursday after Easter, and give that salt as medicine to people and livestock'.[217]

Yet, although it is clear that salt was a major item of internal trade in the late sixteenth century, old centres of production fell into disuse. This was partly owing to shortage of resources, fuel, and particularly the low salt content at some locations. New centres were developed largely on the basis of the deep drilling techniques, which seem to have been developed in the late sixteenth century. From this time new sources of capital and methods of organisation emerge. Changes in ownership and organisation of salt-works were often a sequel to the destruction of works during the wars and associated disasters of the early seventeenth century. According to a charter of 1618, the exten-

[213]Ostroumov, in *Ustoi* (1882), nos. 9–10, 139.
[214]Chaev, *LZAK*, xxxiv, 200–1.
[215]Chulkov, *Opisanie*, vol. i, i, 190.
[216]Kolominskii, 'Torgovlya', 23.
[217]*Stoglav*, ch. i, 41, question 24, 42.

Table 2.5. *Some technical indices, sixteenth–nineteenth centuries*

Date	Location	Salt (puds) per boiling per pan	per wks	Boilings p.a.	Output 1000 per pan (puds)	Firewood (fathoms) p.a. total	per pan	Salt (puds) per fathom
White Sea								
1 1563	Sukhoi Navolok, Obonega	28[a]		120–35 days	c. 4			
2 1564	Suma volost'			160 'nights'	6.3[b]	600		
3 16th–17th cents.	Nenoksa	48–50		120	5.76–6			
4 16th–17th cents.	Navolok			240–300	11.52–15			
5 1622	Balakhna		>350[c]					
6 17th cent.	Una							
7 1610	Kui saline			286	1.6			
8 1621/2, 1628/9	Una				3.3[d]			
9 1646/7, 1648–51, 1654/5	Una				7.1[e]			
10 1669	Chernoretsk	20						
11 1695/6					3.1[f]			
Centre[g]								
12 1622	Sol' Vychegda	~50[h]			4.1[i]			
13 1644–8	Sol' Vychegda				4.3[i]			
14 1651/2, 1654/5	Sol' Vychegda				4.2[i]			
15 1665/6, 1669/70	Sol' Vychegda				3.8[i]			
16 1674/5								
17 1708	nr. Ustyug Yarensk	60		120[j]	7.2			
18 1674								
19 1555	Tot'ma				5 (good) 4 (medium) 3 (poor)	24,000		11.1
20 1646	Sol' Bol'shaya, Kostroma	30–5						

S. H. H.

24	1700	Tyskorka monastery, Perm'			
25	1700	Novousol'e (Stroganovs)	120	300	10.5
26	1759	Chusova		36	

Nineteenth cent.

27	1800–25		250–300		20–24
28	1830–50				> 30
29	1850	Nenoksa			23.3
30	Late 19th cent.	Pomor'e			1
31		Ledenga, Tot'ma			10–14

Notes:

a 4 *korobya* per firing.

b Assuming 1 fathom gives 10½ puds.

c In 6 days.

d Assumes 2 works were operating.

e Assumes 3 works were operating (5.2, if 4 works).

f Assumes 4 works were operating.

g 1690s are omitted because of low outputs.

h In 3 days and 3 nights.

i These are the only years reported with boilings throughout the year.

j Each boiling took 2½ days.

k Per works; 6 per pan?

l See Table 2.3.

m No. of pans unknown.

Sources:

1 Zaozerskaya, *U istokov*, 106.

2 *AAE*, I, no. 268.

3 Zaozerskaya, *U istokov*, 117.

4 *Ibid.*

5 Vvedenskii, *Dom Stroganovykh*, 174.

6 Prokof'eva, *Votchinnoe khozyaistvo*, 56.

7 *Ibid.* 55–6.

8 *Ibid.*

9 *Ibid.*

10 Savich, *Solovetskaya votchina*, 102.

11 Prokof'eva, *Votchinnoe khozyaistvo*, 55–6.

12 Vvedenskii, *Dom Stroganovykh*, 174.

13 Prokof'eva, *Votchinnoe khozyaistvo*, 52–5.

14 *Ibid.*

15 *Ibid.*

16 *Ibid.*

17 de Bruyns, *Puteshestvie*, 274.

18 Geiman, *LZAK*, xxxv, 17, 21.

19 Ostroumov, *Ustoi* (1882), nos. 9–10: 135.

20 Bakhrushin, *Nauchnye trudy*, II: 231.

21 Vvedenskii, *Dom Stroganovykh*, 173–4; Zaozerskaya, *U istokov*, 148.

22 Ustyugov, *Solevarennaya promyshlennost'*, 288.

23 *Ibid.*, 248.

24 Kolominskii, 'Torgovlya', 12, 37.

25 Ustyugov, *Solevarennaya promyshlennost'*, 290–1.

26 Kolominskii, 'Torgovlya', 37.

27 Vvedenskii, *Dom Stroganovykh*, 173.

28 *Ibid.*

29 Savich, *Solovetskaya votchina*, 105.

30 Gomilevskii, *Sol'*, 76, 84.

31 *Ibid.* 77.

sive salines of the Trinity monastery of St Sergius had fallen 'empty from grain failures and plague'.[218] But this was not the only factor contributing to the changes in the industry in the seventeenth century. New and, for the period, virtually inexhaustible sources of salt were directly available from the late sixteenth century, when the length of the Volga was open to the Russians as a result of the capture of Kazan' (1552) and Astrakhan' (1556). These surface deposits came to be greatly exploited by around 1700 even though they were distant from the core of Muscovy. Their advantage was that they were cheaper to exploit. Throughout the seventeenth century these supplies of salt increasingly competed with production from other locations.

The winning of salt, therefore, can broadly be seen as undergoing some technical development; but it also involved changing the raw materials used, between the twelfth and the seventeenth centuries. The sea water and brines of similar low salinity were the main sources in early times; from the late fourteenth century, drilling (and, later, deep drilling especially) gave the Russians access to brines of greater strength.

Major difficulties had to be overcome, however, in the growth of the industry. Lack of labour does not appear to have been a major obstacle, but the forms of labour varied considerably. While skilled workers, such as pipe-men, received good wages, and were able to become men of substance in some cases, the men engaged in the actual production process were sometimes wage labourers, sometimes partly paid in kind, and their level of remuneration seems to have been little above subsistence. Such work people were often dependants, sometimes slaves or serfs. 'Hire', in fact, differed little from debt enserfment at times. Auxiliary labour engaged in wood cutting and supply, the transport of the salt and so on, was also often paid; such activities provided side earnings for the peasants in the areas concerned. Sometimes, however, provision of firewood and transport were imposed on the local population as an obligation. Even when wages were paid, therefore, the actual situation of the work people varied considerably and they were by no means always wage labour as we now understand the term.

Remote locations meant that even serf labour did not always feed itself. In some cases the work people had to be supplied with grain and other provisions from a distance. Transport of supplies and of output did not prove an insuperable obstacle, but the relative prices of salt and grain had to be such as to make the industry economically viable. The

---

[218]*SGKE*, I, no. 530, 598.

spread of the industry to new areas meant that some important new locations were on the frontier. This resulted in considerable expenditures on defence. In its most extreme form, at Lake Yamysh, in Siberia, it reduced the industry virtually to an annual raid to gather salt.

Lack of a credit system caused many difficulties in the industry. Even corporations such as monasteries lacked access to credit. 'Salt was sold by the Solovki stewards for ready cash. There was no credit; salt might rise in price and the monks feared a loss. In addition, grain and all sorts of other "stocks" were bought "for their own use" on the spot with the money the monastery obtained.'[219] These cash deals were, for the most part, not effected locally, but at a considerable distance. Most of the Solovki transactions, for example, took place at Vologda. This involved a time lapse before any cash surplus was available for use at the point of production; it also involved risks in transporting cash over considerable distances, sometimes in exposed frontier areas.

One method of coping with this difficulty was to arrange for a transfer of money through a government office. A merchant or trader needing money for his saline usually paid a certain sum of money, for example, into the Novgorod Office in Moscow (which administered Sol' Kama); in exchange he received a charter addressed to the military commander or customs officer at Sol' Kama authorising the payment of the amount there. An alternative was for the local steward to offer to convey the taxes collected in the area to Moscow when a convoy was about to be sent there. The money was, in fact, not conveyed, but used to finance the salt-works; only a detailed statement of the sums involved was sent to Moscow. The merchant then paid this amount into the Moscow Office.[220] Such methods were open to powerful men with business in different parts of the country including Moscow. They were particularly used by those with connections in the government offices such as the Kirillovs, who, as has been seen, were both owners of salt-works at Sol' Kama and clerks in the Novgorod Office.[221]

Smaller men had to operate from hand to mouth and take money in advance from their purchasers. In 1695, for instance, the men of Sol' Kama artisan quarter, appealing for concessions as regards their tax payments, pointed out that 'of old we, your orphans of Sol' Kama, before the fires and after them, provisioned our salt industry, prepared firewood and boiled salt, taking money in advance for the salt from the

[219]Savich, *Solovetskaya votchina*, 151.
[220]Ustyugov, *Solevarennaya promyshlennost'*, 287, gives examples of both procedures in the late seventeenth century.
[221]See pp. 53–4 above. Ustyugov, *Solevarennaya promyshlennost'*, 256, 287.

trading people of other towns'.[222] The only defence against such misfortunes as fires and other risks for such smaller men was for them to
co-operate in the face of the far greater resources and access to power
(sometimes even the holding of state offices) by the great merchants;
such defences, however, were limited since the men concerned were in
competition with one another. Perhaps it is for this reason that we find
dynasties of small and medium, as well as some large, salt-works owners. The family was, to some extent, an alternative form of protection
to the corporation. It sometimes acted as a substitute, at least in part,
for a credit system.

Indeed, even state support for the richer merchants was by no means
always to be relied on. Trading capital was weak and developing in
unfavourable conditions, even though it was applied boldly and on a
broad front.

This was reflected in the fact that it evolved no organised system of credit, a
circumstance which placed the entrepreneur in bondage to the treasury, the
main financial power in the land with available resources of money and
goods. Sveteshnikov died when being flogged to exact unpaid debts to the
treasury which he had incurred by taking furs at an artificial price intending to
trade in them.[223]

We have seen that in the late sixteenth century salt was liable to
various imposts amounting to 10 kopeks a pud. This level of exaction
seems in the main to have lasted till the middle of the seventeenth
century. In Sol' Kama, however, the seller paid 8 dengas and the
purchaser 12 according to a decree of 1634/5.[224]

In 1646 a new tax on all salt, except that from Astrakhan' and Yaik
used to salt fish and 'our caviare', was introduced.[225] The stated intention was to avoid arguments about the excessive burden of taxation by
substituting this tax for a number of other small imposts and trading
dues, as well as the monies collected to maintain the musketeers and the
post-horse system.[226]

We have ordered other small imposts from all the land and all former customary dues on salt and transit trading dues to be set aside everywhere; henceforth
there shall be no harm to anyone anywhere in the sale of salt. And when that
customary due on salt is collected in full into our treasury we have ordered
throughout the land to remit from all people the income from the musketeers
and post-horse monies and to pay the musketeers and post-horse income with

[222]Cited in Ustyugov, *Solevarennaya promyshlennost'*, 287.
[223]Bakhrushin, *Nauchnye trudy*, vol. II, 255. On Nadei Sveteshnikov see p. 56 above.
[224]Ustyugov, *Solevarennaya promyshlennost'*, 295.
[225]*AAE*, IV, no. 5 (23 February 1646).
[226]*SGGD*, III, no. 124 (18 March 1646).

the money of these customary dues on salt, because this customary due on salt will be equal for all; no one will be exempt or will pay in excess and everyone will pay without exactions. The musketeer and post-horse monies are collected unequally; for some it is heavy, for some light; and they pay for the exaction with great losses, and some do not pay because their names are not on the lists in the Military Office (*razryad*), nor in the registers of inquisition, and they all live in the uezd exempt; also foreigners who receive our grants and maintenance money and the foreign trading people, all will be paying along with the people liable to tax. And trading people are to cart this salt into all towns and uezds without the trading due (*myt*) and without any customary due; and they are to sell everywhere, where each one wishes, in accordance with the former price, but much price increase is not to be put on salt and no one anywhere is to engage in conspiracies about selling salt, so that there shall be no oppression and excessive losses to people of any rank.[227]

The new imposition, however, was fixed at 40 dengas a pud, four times what it had previously been. The salt excepted from the new tax was liable to an amount of 20 dengas a pud. The taxes were to be collected where the salt was produced and there were to be no exemptions. B.I. Morozov, I.P. Matyushkin and Nazarii Chistoi were exclusively to deal with the new tax in the Novgorod Office.

The reasons for the introduction of this measure are complex. The background, of course, was the financial difficulties facing the new dynasty of the Romanovs after the Time of Troubles. The Smolensk campaign in the 1630s had, in particular, shown the need to modernise the army and put it on a new footing. Costs escalated, growing perhaps two-and-a-half times between 1630 and 1680.[228] Attempts at economies had little impact. The former merchant from Yaroslavl', Nazarii Chistoi, proposed replacing direct by indirect taxation and the salt tax was the result.[229] Yet curiously, the surveys carried out at the time do not seem to have had financial aims and no general financial reform was envisaged in them.[230]

The new tax, in any event, was a gross miscalculation.

A year later . . . it was necessary to calculate how many thousands had been lost on salted fish – used in Russia more than meat – that spoiled because it was not properly preserved, owing to the high price of salt. Besides, much less salt was sold than before, and remaining in the packing houses, it turned into brine and dribbled away.[231]

[227] *Ibid.*
[228] Klyuchevskii, *Sochineniya*, vol. III, 216.
[229] Bakhrushin, *Nauchnye trudy*, vol. II, 49.
[230] Veselovskii, *Soshnoe pis'mo*, vol. II, 230.
[231] Olearius, *Travels*, 206.

The measure was repealed in December 1647 and Chistoi himself was killed by the people in the Moscow rising of 1648.[232] As he was killed the mob cried 'This is your lot for the salt, traitor.'[233] The rich merchant V.G. Shorin was also threatened and accused of raising the price of salt.[234] A strong element in the mob were evidently frustrated traders and dealers in salt.

The customs charter of 1653 replaced a number of petty imposts by a single tax of 10 dengas per ruble on all goods sold except salt; this was liable to 20 dengas a ruble.[235] Only the seller paid. This increased tax on salt does not appear to have met with opposition or to have had adverse effects on the salt trade. In part this was because if a trader declared his money to the customs officials he then paid 5 dengas a ruble on the value of his purchases (10 for salt) and received a quittance note stating the purchase was made with declared money. When he resold in another town the note was shown and he then paid only a further 5 dengas (10 for salt). Salt sent for sale elsewhere was taxed only when sold. The tax was, apparently, sometimes paid in kind.[236] In Astrakhan', which was under the administration of the treasury, there was a different arrangement. The dealers in salt themselves collected the lake salt and paid 6 dengas per 100 puds.[237] In addition, a weighing and pud tax of a denga a pud was retained there.

The new trading statute of 1667 made only a few changes. The tax on all purchases (including salt) from declared money was now 5 dengas and the amount to be paid on resales of salt, therefore, increased to 15 dengas; the total tax thus remained the same.[238] Finally, in 1705 a treasury monopoly in salt was decreed.[239] Salt now had to be supplied to the treasury at fixed prices. This measure was particularly disadvantageous to the smaller owners of salt-works and led to a further concentration of the industry in the hands of some monasteries and the larger individuals and groups of entrepreneurs.

In pre-Petrine Russia a major extractive industry developed based on native resources. It was a form of gathering which underwent considerable development in the half a millennium before the reforms of Peter the Great; by the late seventeenth century it required considerable investment and involved some wage labour; it also involved prob-

---

[232]Smirnov, *Posadskie lyudi*, vol. II, 33.
[233]Klyuchevskii, *Sochineniya*, vol. III, 222.
[234]Solov'ev, *Istoriya*, vol. V, 482.
[235]*SGGD*, III, no. 158; *AAE*, IV, no. 64.
[236]Kolominskii, 'Torgovlya', 24.
[237]*Ibid.*; *AI*, IV, no. 243.
[238]*SGGD*, IV, no. 55.
[239]*PSZ*, IV, no. 2009 (1 January 1705).

9 A portable salt container, nineteenth century. Such objects, woven from straw, bast or pine roots, were used as small containers for various consumables. This one originates from the Upper Volga region.

lems of storage, of transport, mainly by river vessels, and of distribution on a scale large for the time. Thus, it was an extractive industry with some limited specialised labour and wages; it also grew largely on the periphery of areas with some agricultural surplus. It was the shortage of agricultural produce both in the White Sea and in the frontier areas which involved the salt trade so intimately with the wider economy. Salt was a major item both in trade and also in taxation, even in the early period. 'Salt was a very important seasoning for food. The scale of the ancient Russian salt industry which became a most important trade convinces us of this. The development of this trade was one of the main causes of the colonisation of our North-East . . . This business evoked particular interest and demanded particular controls by the government.'[240] Under Peter the Great the controls had become a state monopoly.

[240]Artsikhovskii, in *ORK XIII–XVvv*, part 1, 300.

3

✻✻

Drink: ale and alchemy

When Vladimir, prince of Kiev, considered abandoning paganism, he rejected Islam as an alternative because, he said, 'Rus' loves to drink, we cannot be without it.'[1] At this period, before the Mongol invasions of the thirteenth century, mead was probably a common alcoholic drink in Russia. The term *med* means both 'mead' and 'honey'; usually in the sources of this period it refers to drink, but sometimes there are unequivocal references to honey used as sugar would be nowadays.[2] Mead was drunk by the nobility in the tenth century, to judge by the chronicle's account of Ol'ga's revenge for her dead husband in 945.[3] From the thirteenth century, the Novgorod princes had their mead-makers.[4] The Slavs in what is now European Russia were essentially forest people exploiting the resources of their environment by a combination of gathering and cultivation; the gathering of honey from wild bees in the forest was the source of the raw material for mead. Thus it seems probable that mead was made throughout the whole area occupied by the Rus' and at all levels of society, even though there is no direct evidence for this.

The other common drink of Kievan times was kvas, a very lightly fermented, almost non-alcoholic, beer.[5] Home-made kvas is nowadays fermented from malted rye, barley or wheat and rye, wheat or buckwheat flour or from pastry, bread or rusks; sugar, honey and various fruits, berries and herbs are used to flavour it.[6] A twelfth-

---

[1]*PVL*, I, 60 (986).
[2]The *Kievo-Pecherskii paterikon* mentions that boiled wheat was mixed with honey and served at table.
[3]*PVL*, I, 41–2.
[4]*GVNiP*, no. 1 (1264). These officers are mentioned in the later contracts between town and prince.
[5]Sreznevskii, *Materialy*, vol. I, 1203.
[6]Korolev, *Russkii kvas*, 20. *Novyi i polnyi rossiiskoi khozyaistvennoi vinokur*, vol. II, 144–5, gives recipes for apple and pear kvas; Korolev, *Russkii kvas*, 4 writes that at the present time 'wild apples, pears, cranberries, red whortleberries, cloudberries, strawberries, blackcurrants and raspberries' are chiefly used.

century manuscript mentions 'much drink and kvas'.[7] It is this which seems to be referred to by Tedaldi, even though the drink he mentioned in 1581 was made with oats: 'Water mashed with oatmeal, then cooked, is the general drink; the oats relieves the badness of the water, and makes the men fat.'[8]

Beer is mentioned from the eleventh century onwards. The terms then used were *ol, oll* or *olovina* (cp. English 'ale'), a hopped beer; *siker* (from Gk. σίκερα) was evidently a virtual synonym. Malt for the tax-collector, or justice (*virnik*), at the rate of seven buckets a week was specified in part of *Russkaya Pravda*, the old Russian law, dated to the 1030s.[9]

Mead, kvas and beer were evidently adequate to meet the demands of Rus' for alcoholic drink, in Kievan times, but there were also some imported wines. Beer, locally produced, was sometimes a substitute for costly, imported, communion wine. A prince's cellar, sacked in 1146, held wines and meads, as well as much else.[10] In the early thirteenth century a prince was assumed to drink imported wine, but also ale.[11] 'Woe to your strong men drinking wine and your noblemen supping ale', exclaims an eleventh-century source.[12] A cleric gave some good advice to his brethren: 'do not drink without limit, but enough and not to drunkenness'.[13] It is noteworthy that churchmen drank; perhaps this was not owing to laxity, but to an amalgam of pagan and Christian elements. They also evidently attended feasts of lay people at which there was drinking.

What of those who go to lay people and drink? The holy fathers order clerics to accept piously and with a blessing what lies before them; when they enter [where there is] playing, dancing and howling, all are to ensure that their feelings should not be defiled by seeing and hearing, as is commanded by the fathers, or they should entirely avoid those feasts, or leave them when it is suspected and considered that there is great temptation and unbridled enmity.[14]

An allegedly late thirteenth-century text mentions

. . . those who still keep the devilish customs of the thrice-cursed Hellenes and

[7]Sreznevskii, *Materialy*, II, 122
[8]Shmurlo, *Izvestiya*, 19.
[9]*PRP*, I, 80, section 42; 75.
[10]*PSRL*, 2, 333.
[11]*PSRL*, 2, 747 (1226).
[12]In Sreznevskii, *Materialy*, vol. II, 660.
[13]'Pouchenie Arkhiepiskopa Luki k bratii', *Ruskiya dostopamyatnosti*, part 1, 10.
[14]'Poslanie Ionna Mitropolita Ruskago', *Ruskiya dostopamyatnosti*, part 1, 1815, 95 (eleventh or twelfth cent.).

create certain devilish spectacles on God's festivals, with whistling and calling, with howls summoning some shameless drunkards, and fighting with staves even to the death and taking the trousers off those killed. This is a reproach to God's festivals and an offence to God's churches.[15]

This combination of spectacles, games, dancing, wind–music and fighting persists well into the seventeenth century. The reasons for this will be dealt with later.

An inscription scratched into the plaster of St Sophia, Novgorod, and palaeographically dated to the late eleventh century, refers to a particular type of ceremonial binge. 'Radko, Khotko, Snovid and Vitomir drank a flagon here at Ugrin's bidding; may god bless what he gave us. And give him salvation. Amen.'[16] Perhaps Ugrin fell off the scaffold. Or maybe this was a topping–out ceremony imported by the Hungarian (Ugrin)? The Novgorod ceremony for building a house involved burying a horse's head or skull beneath the floor; several of these have been found, dating from eleventh to fourteenth centuries. One was buried in association with a scoop, suggesting that drinking was involved.[17]

In the period following the Mongol invasions mead and beer remained the commonest intoxicating drinks, but there may gradually have been a change in their relative importance; at least there seems no adequately clear basis for the blunt statement that, 'as formerly, the basic drink was mead'.[18] It is true that the Nomocanon of the thirteenth century permitted three cups of mead a week to be drunk during days of abstinence, and during fasts allowed only one cup to be drunk when fish was eaten.[19]

In addition, there is chronicle evidence for mead being drunk and for the plundering of mead from lords' cellars.[20] The Moscow prince had extensive bee forests at least from the fourteenth century and an administrative department was developed to deal with them. The butler, the man responsible for drinks in a great lord's household, was called *sytnik*, from the term for honey water (*syta*).[21] It thus seems that in the centuries immediately after the thirteenth-century Mongol invasion, mead became increasingly a lord's drink.[22] Colonisation and

[15]'Pravilo Kirilla Mitropolita Ruskago' (1274?), *Ruskiya dostopamyatnosti*, ch. 1, 114.
[16]No. 145 in Medyntseva, *Drevnerusskie nadpisi*, 97–100.
[17]Sedov, *KS*, 68, 20–8.
[18]Artsikhovskii in *ORK XIII–XV*, 1, 302.
[19]*RIB*, vi, 1, 122.
[20]*PSRL*, 4, 85 (1328).
[21]Galton, *Survey*, 12.
[22]Khoroshkevich, *Torgovlya*, 328, notes that costly imported honey sold mostly to lords.

cultivation disturbed or destroyed the wild bee population and made honey a luxury consumption item.[23]

Most charters in the post-Kievan period which use the term *med* refer to honey, often as an item of produce rents and measured by weight. In 1378, however, troops beyond the river P'yana (i.e. 'Drunk') found 'mead and beer, they drank themselves very drunk, of a truth they were drunk beyond the Drunk'.[24] In fact, the relatively little evidence we have suggests that beer was a common, if not the commonest, intoxicating drink from the fourteenth century; it was at this period that *pivo*, originally meaning 'drink' in general, came to indicate 'beer' in particular.[25] A charter of 1391 noted that monastic peasants had to grind malt and brew beer.[26] Probably beer grew in importance for the mass of peasants as mead was increasingly restricted to consumption by lords. From the late fifteenth century there are many references to the consumption of beer by peasants, often accompanied by a ban on uninvited attendance by officers of the prince. The Grand Prince in 1455–62, for instance, laid down that his servants, boyar people 'and anyone else uninvited, shall not go for beer to their monastery people [i.e. dependants], whoever may live under them in that village and the hamlets'.[27] A similar prohibition was issued against the Grand Prince's dependants who 'go uninvited for festivals, feasts and fraternities (*bratshiny*) and do them [the Metropolitan's peasants] violence, take mead, beer and ale (*braga*) from them by force'.[28] Ale was sometimes liable to tax in the sixteenth century.[29] That beer was commonly brewed in the late sixteenth century seems implied by the vagueness of the rule on a monastic estate that 'if anyone has an ale, the steward is to have a gift'.[30]

Kvas does not appear to be mentioned in the documents of this time; it undoubtedly continued to be made, but perhaps because of its very low alcoholic content it is unlikely to have produced the problems connected with intoxication which would feature in the documents. This scarcely alcoholic drink was probably the day-to-day drink of most peasants.

[23]Križanić, *Politika*, vol. I, 3, noted how potash production interfered with the gathering of honey.

[24]*PSRL*, 4, 73.

[25]Sreznevskii, *Materialy*, vol. II, 930–1.

[26]*Cambridge Economic History*, vol. I, 540. The charter is translated in full in Smith, *Enserfment of the Russian Peasantry*, 39–40.

[27]*ASEI*, I, no. 264. Cp. nos. 356 (1467–74), 462 (1478–82); II, nos. 127 (1448–70), 386 (1470) and many others.

[28]*AFZ*, I, no. 146 (1425–62). Cp. nos. 147 and 148 (1464–73).

[29]*AFZ*, II, no. 129 (1534). Also *ARG*, nos. 18, 23, 29, 32, 34, 249.

[30]*AFZ*, II, no. 391 (1591).

All the drinks so far mentioned might be hopped. In parts of north European Russia wild hops were found.[31] They were also found on special hopfields, perhaps cultivated.[32] Hopfields sometimes evidently belonged to the settlement rather than to individual tenements.[33] The law book of 1589 laid down that hopfields and orchards were not available for redistribution in certain circumstances.[34] In some areas hops were a regular item of produce rents at least from the fifteenth century.[35] Sometimes such payments might be commuted.[36] In Novgorod and Pskov hops were a regular item of trade from the thirteenth century; prices fluctuated considerably, and this suggests that demand at times outstripped supply.[37] Monasteries consumed considerable quantities of hops; one in Vladimir was allowed to purchase annually, duty-free, 40 puds of honey and 50 puds of hops.[38] Hopped drinks were especially intoxicating; in the mid-fifteenth century the Venetian Iosaphat Barbaro commented that Russian mead and ale were hopped and that 'a drink results as stupefying and intoxicating as wine'.[39] Such hopped drinks, as they could be kept longer in cask, might have a higher alcohol content resulting from imperceptible evaporation of some of the water. Paolo Giovio, basing himself on information supplied by a Russian interpreter in 1525, noted that the people 'drink mead which they make from honey and hops. It will keep for a long time in caulked barrels and acquires value with age.'[40] He added that 'apart from that, they use beer and ale [*cervisia*], as we see among the Germans and Poles; these drinks are made from wheat and rye or barley and are offered at every feast'.[41] It is, thus, understandable why the term for hops (*khmel'*) also meant 'drunkenness' and the related adjective meant 'drunken'.

 Brewing mostly took place for special occasions. A late fifteenth-century document refers to the preparation of mead, the brewing of beer and ale 'for St. Boris's day, or for some lord's festival, or for a

[31]*ASEI*, I, nos. 196 (1447–55), 373 (1467–74); *AFZ*, I, nos. 12, 32, 33; 100 (9 December 1525) 101 (15 November 1525); *SGKE*, no. 51 (1519–20); *GVNiP*, no. 122 (fifteenth century), 120; *Pam Ryaz*, no. 83 (1576–7).

[32]*ASEI*, III, no. 56 (*c.* 1462–9); *Pam Ryaz*, no. 27 (1556–7).

[33]*SGKE*, I, no. 61 (24 April 1528).

[34]*PRP*, IV, 434.

[35]*NPK*, III, 738; cp. 682–3; V, 579–80; *ASEI*, I, no. 221 (second half of sixteenth century).

[36]*NPK*, I, 439–41.

[37]*GVNiP*, nos. 1 (1264), 2, 3, 6, 7, 9, 10, 14, 15, 19, 22, 26 (11 July 1471); *P2L*, 163–4 (1476).

[38]*ASEI*, III, no. 92 (22 October 1623). The pud is 16.38 kg, 36 lb.

[39]'Viaggio alla Tana', in *Barbaro i Contarini o Rossii*, 133, 158.

[40]Gerbershtein, *Zapiski o Moskovitskikh delakh*, Iovii Novokomskii, 'Kniga o moskovitskom posol'stve', 272.

[41]The Russian translation mistakenly renders *cervisia* as 'vodka'.

wedding or birth, or for Easter week'.[42] The Grand Prince's officers were to be informed and the man could then hold a drinking party 'for three days. But between those festivals he is not to keep drink by him. Nor is he to keep mead, beer and ale for sale.'

The nature of the occasions mentioned in this document vary. There is the major festival of the Orthodox year, Easter; a saint's day or a lord's festival (probably his name-day), and, lastly, the celebration by a kin-group or neighbours of a wedding or a birth. Other commonly mentioned festivals include Christmas and the feast of St Nicholas.[43] The earliest mention of such celebrations may be a fraternity (*brat'-shchina*) held on St Peter's day, 1159.[44] A monastic statute of 1391 specified that 'if the abbot arrives at any village for a fraternity, the contributors (*syptsi*) each give the abbot's horse a *zobnya* of oats'.[45] From about the mid-fifteenth century onwards there are more than fifty charters which refer to peasants and other dependants holding such communal feasts and fraternities (*piry i bratchiny*). The earliest of these, dated about 1445–6, forbad uninvited guests and prince's officials to go to a monastery's people 'for ales and for fraternities'.[46] The latest seems to be one dated 1623, but with confirmations to 1686.[47] The majority occur before 1550; eight are dated 1504.

It seems possible, despite the overlaps between them, to make some distinctions between the festivals, feasts and fraternities. 'Festivals' sometimes signified both the others; in the main, however, the term was used to refer to church festivals, celebrations of a formal religious nature. Festivals, of course, might include a feast as part of the celebration and, indeed, the central rite of the church was a ritual meal. In the majority of charters, however, 'feast' meant a ritual meal, sometimes on a saint's day, but probably of calendrical or local significance not necessarily of a formal religious nature; family occasions such as births, christenings, marriages, deaths were also celebrated by feasts. Sometimes feasts were more than a private family celebration; the fraternities of contributors associated with them had rights, including judicial rights, and duties, but it is unclear whether fraternities were responsible only for public celebrations on saints' days or also dealt with private family occasions.

There is at least a hint that family occasions preceded the feasts and

---

[42]*AFZ*, II, no. 124 (1462–1505). St Boris' day was 2 May or 24 July, Old Style.

[43]Tereshchenko, *Byt*, vol. V, 150, noted the two chief 'fraternities' as the Archangel Michael (6 September) and the winter St Nicholas (6 December).

[44]*PSRL*, 2, 495.

[45]*AFZ*, I, no. 201.

[46]*ASEI*, II, no. 448.

[47]*ASEI*, III, no. 92, 127, 128.

10 Commemoration of parents, 1630s. Food is being placed on the graves of parents. The food appears to be some sort of small pasties or cakes and fish.

fraternities institutionalised by the emergent state and that they were not liable to exactions, while fraternities were, at least on monastic estates. As early as the mid-fifteenth century the Grand Prince had granted the Metropolitan certain immunities in some of his villages (including one called P'yanitsino (*p'yanitsa* means 'drunkard')); his boyars' people were 'not to ride to them uninvited to an ale'.[48] Such occasions gave opportunities for exactions. 'If any peasant happens to have a small private ale (*osobnoe pivtso*) at a birth or to commemorate parents, our [monastery] steward is to have nothing from that; but from a fraternity he is to have two dengas'.[49] Elsewhere the steward has a 'gift' from any ale held.[50] Another monastery decreed that 'if any peasants begin to brew beer, they are to make a declaration to the steward, but are not liable to any payment'; if they brewed without a

[48] *AFZ*, I, no. 145 (1445–61).
[49] *AAE*, I, no. 348 (1590).
[50] *AFZ*, III, no. 391 (9 September 1591).

declaration, they were fined.[51] The same statute distinguished simple hospitality from a celebration:

If anyone invites someone to eat bread or to drink, that is allowed, but if the steward or the court investigator is informed that they ate or drank very much (*silno*) at a certain peasant's, the fine for that is two rubles to the monastery, and the peasant at whose home they ate or drank very much [is to pay] whatever is exacted, and those exactions are to be paid to the steward and the court investigator without going to court.

A statute for peasants on a court estate, however, specified that 'if any man in a village or hamlet happens to have a feast or fraternity, they are not to go uninvited to drink at his feast and fraternity; but if anyone is invited to a feast or fraternity, when he has drunk he is not to spend the night there'.[52] There is evidence, then, of concern not to impose excessive or unspecified demands on some local populations.

The feast was 'the knot bringing together all the threads of the emergent sociality of ancient times'.[53] It was the most obvious expression of contemporary communal life. Zabelin was dealing, however, with the formal feasts of the tsar' and upper classes and, although he noted that the system of precedence observed at feasts might have originated around the domestic hearth, he did not expand on this.[54] For the common people the significance of feasts lay elsewhere than in their mechanical function of providing a forum – especially important in a predominantly oral culture – where men of all conditions could meet. In fact, uninvited officials and others were frequently forbidden at feasts and fraternities which were apparently restricted to the relatively homogeneous social group of neighbouring peasants or, in towns, corporations of trades people.

The Pskov law has a laconic statement that 'the fraternity judges like judges'.[55] The Dvina statute of 1397 laid down that 'if a fight occurs at a feast and they accept forgiveness without leaving the feast, the prince's representative (*namestnik*) and his official (*dvoryan*) are to take nothing; but if they accept forgiveness after leaving the feast, then they give the prince's representative a wool *kunitsa* each'.[56] Other statutes indicate some of the judicial aspects of feasts and fraternities. The two institutions do not appear to be sharply differentiated in this connec-

[51]*AAE*, I, no. 357 (31 March 1593).
[52]*AAE*, I, no. 201 (20 April 1544).
[53]Zabelin, *Domashnii byt*, vol. II, 348.
[54]*Ibid.*, 355.
[55]*PSG*, para. 115; this section has been variously dated between 1241 and the early fourteenth century: *PRP*, II, 283.
[56]*ASEI*, III, no. 7, para. 3. Cp. a similar clause in a statute of 1509, *ASEI*, III, no. 27, para. 20.

tion, though there may have been conflicts between them over the right to judge.[57] Indeed, a charter issued by the Grand Prince in 1453 appears to grant damages to festivals as well as feasts and fraternities for manslaughter, theft or any other losses caused by uninvited participants.[58] A similar but later charter mentioned the same three institutions.

If anyone comes uninvited to those people of theirs to drink at a feast or fraternity or on a festival and there causes any loss, I order an exaction to be had without going to court and without investigation from those who go uninvited, on horse or on foot, to those people of theirs to drink at a feast or fraternity or on a festival.[59]

This phraseology allows a distinction to be made; there might be a feast or fraternity on a festival, so probably only these two institutions are referred to here.[60] The Beloozero statute of 1488 forbad uninvited officials at feasts and fraternities and added that 'if anyone comes uninvited to their feast and fraternity, they send him off and are not themselves liable; but if anyone takes drink by force (*silno*) while with them and causes some loss, he is to pay for that without going to court and is to be penalised by me, the Grand Prince'.[61] A statute granted the Pereyaslavl' fishermen in 1506 had a similar clause, but the penalty for any damage caused was to be twofold.[62] If 'an uninvited man does not go off from the feast or fraternity, but takes drink by force' he was liable to a twofold exaction.[63]

Fraternities and feasts also had certain duties as well as rights. They were sometimes evidently liable to a payment in kind from the beer brewed.[64] This was called *nabor* or *nasadka*; both terms occur with this meaning only from the early sixteenth century.[65] The amount was, apparently, one 'bucket' (*vedro*), almost three gallons (as a measure the

[57]Popov, 'Piry i bratchiny', 32.

[58]*AFZ*, I, no. 187.

[59]*ASEI*, I, no. 327 (1462–78).

[60]Cp. *AFZ*, I, nos. 147 (1461–2), 148 (1464–73), 188 (13 December 1464) where the phrasing is more doubtful; but no. 190 (15 October 1490) is clear.

[61]*ASEI*, III, no. 22. Cp. a statute of 1509 with a similar regulation: *ASEI*, III, no. 27, para. 23. *Silno*, unfortunately, means both 'powerfully' and hence 'a lot', and also 'by force'; in some contexts, as here, it is ambiguous.

[62]*ASEI*, III, no. 25. Cp. *AFZ*, nos. 70 (1504), 87 (1523).

[63]*AFZ*, I, no. 97 (1473).

[64]*ASEI*, III, no. 27, para. 24, (20 July 1509); *AAE*, I, no. 201 (20 April 1544).

[65]*ASEI*, III, no. 27, para. 24; Yakovlev, *Namestnich'i, gubnyya i zemskiya nastavnyya gramoty*, no. 16 (1547–56), 47; *AAE*, III, no. 37 (5 June 1614); Popov, 'Piry i bratchiny', 23.

nasadka amounted to two-and-a-half 'buckets', about 7 gallons).[66]

The persons excluded from uninvited attendance at feasts and fraternities were officials and others. In the Grand Prince's charter to the Metropolitan in 1504 they were specified as: 'the officials and court investigators of our Moscow representatives and our volost heads, and any other people of our representatives and the people of volost heads, and my, the Grand Prince's people of manorial settlements, and boyars' people [i.e. slaves] and peasants [i.e. serfs] and those of monasteries, and anyone else'.[67] Other documents include the royal kennel-men and grooms.[68] There are many similar lists.

Such persons had been alleged to offer violence to those celebrating; 'they take mead, beer and ale (*braga*) from them by force and beat and rob them'.[69] Probably such impositions gave rise to the aphorism that 'an uninvited guest is worse than a Tatar'. It seems unlikely, however, that the numerous charters which include regulations about feasts and fraternities are all to be accounted for solely as part of the regularising of exactions associated with the limitation and, in the 1550s, the final abolition of the system of livings (*kormleniya*) allowing officials to live off local populations. Undoubtedly, the period from the mid-fifteenth to the mid-sixteenth century saw the dominance of Moscow become the tsardom we know as Muscovy, with all the attempts at regularisation that that subsumes; but why does the concern with feasts and fraternities take the form it does?

At the start of the period boyar people were not to go uninvited to an ale at certain estates of the Metropolitan see in Yur'ev uezd.[70] The charter granted the Metropolitan in 1504 for the same area forbad officials and court investigators of the Grand Prince's representative, their other people, the people of the Prince's manorial settlements, boyar people and peasants, those of monasteries and anyone else 'to go uninvited to drink at feasts and fraternities'.[71] In general, the immunities granted the see over this period were reduced.[72] Why, in such circumstances, were feasts and fraternities somewhat more explicitly protected? We do not know whether these celebrations were used as

[66] Yakovlev, *Namestnich'i*, 47. Kamentseva, Ustyugov, *Russkaya metrologiya*, 50–1, calculated the value of the *nasadka* as a measure (assuming the Novgorod and Moscow measures were commensurate).

[67] *AFZ*, I, no. 70 (March 1504).

[68] *AFZ* III, no. 11 (20 June 1564).

[69] *AFZ*, I, nos. 147 (1461–2), 148 (1464–73).

[70] *AFZ*, I, no. 145 (1448–61). See note 48 above.

[71] *AFZ*, I, no. 150 (March 1504). See note 67 above.

[72] Cherepnin, *Russkie feodal'nye arkhivy*, vol. II, 200. See also Kashtanov, *Sotsial'no-politicheskaya istoriya*, 218f.

recruitment opportunities by officials and local lords on the look-out for labour, but one charter hints at this.[73] If it were so, then the greater attention paid to feasts and fraternities in the early sixteenth-century charters is in part a royal policy protecting peasants against excessive exactions and labour recruitment. This was taking place within the context of attempts to limit immunities to the church, so such protection was essentially a weapon directed against the church hierarchy in order to strengthen the power of the Grand Prince.

Formal church festivals were distinguished from the informal, and sometimes irreverent, festivities which encompassed both local and domestic celebrations. Not only this, the church was troubled throughout Russia's history by various aspects of such celebrations. Vladimir may have accepted Christianity because Christianity, unlike Islam, did not forbid drink, but from Kievan times the church was concerned about excessive drinking and also about other aspects of popular rituals which included the feasts and fraternities.

Why the church was concerned, and the particular aspects of popular rituals about which it was concerned, are matters of dispute: was it concerned because it saw the popular celebrations as essentially pagan; or was its opposition based on the fact that the jollifications reduced church attendance (and, perhaps, therefore church income) and that drunkenness was abhorrent in itself? In any event, festivals, feasts and fraternities were not always sharply distinguished from one another and the popular celebrations contained a mixture of elements: there were features to be explained by the mundane attraction of alcohol, but there were also pagan features.

A major change took place with the growth of the power of Moscow; this itself probably increased social tensions, and feasts and fraternities might increase in response; there were increased attempts to control social life and these took many forms. According to the testimony of foreigners, in Russia in the late fifteenth century the brewing of beer, the making of mead and the use of hops were forbidden. 'Seeing that the people there, owing to drunkenness, abandon work and much else that would be useful to them, the Grand Prince issued a prohibition on the making of ale and mead and the use of hop flowers in anything at all.'[74]

They are great drunkards and are exceedingly boastful of it, disdaining those who do not drink. They have no wines, but use a drink from honey which they make with hop leaves. This drink is not at all bad, particularly if it is old.

[73]*ASEI*, I, no. 264 (1455–62). Translated in Smith, *Enserfment*, 63.
[74]Barbaro, 'Viaggio alla Tana', in *Barbaro i Contarini o Rossii*, 133, 158. See note 39 above.

However, their sovereign does not allow everyone to prepare it freely, because, if they were free to do so, they would be drunk every day and would kill one another like beasts.[75]

Albertus (Pighius) Campensis stated that 'the prince forbad them, under the severest penalties, mead, ale and all intoxicating drink save on certain particular solemn occasions in the year'.[76] Herberstein, who was in Moscow in the early sixteenth century, noted that 'drinking mead and beer is forbidden to the common folk save at certain times of the year, at Christmas, Shrovetide, Easter, Whitsun and a few other fixed seasons. They celebrate on these occasions more on account of the drink than from reverence.'[77] As we will see, this last statement may not be entirely true; it is virtually impossible to distinguish love of alcohol from ritual drunkenness involving some reverence, not necessarily Christian, of course.

In the central areas of the Moscow state, then, drinking took place, evidently within the home, either by the family or by a larger group who formed a fraternity for the purpose of sharing both costs and enjoyment. There is little evidence before about the mid-sixteenth century of special drinking houses; the lack of such places no doubt contributed to problems of control. At any rate, there is little if any attempt to control drinking closely, at least in the core of the emergent Russian state; in fact, we have much evidence of concern to avoid interference, especially interference by officials with drinking in people's own homes. There were regulations aimed only at limiting the right to brew intoxicating liquor to certain specific times of the year, or to particular occasions, and to obtain income from the declarations made.

In areas more subject to influences from the Baltic region we find a somewhat different pattern. A section of a Pskov law book which is believed to date from the early fourteenth century laid down that: 'The prince's people are not to hold strong drink (*korchma*) in their tenements, either in Pskov, or in the subject towns; nor are they to sell mead by the bucket or scoop, nor by the barrel.'[78] This may hint at drink being used by the prince's slave officials to gain a hold over the population. Here, too, it appears that at this stage sales of drink took place from dwellings. In 1473/4 the Master of the Teutonic Order agreed on oath not to let strong drink, beer and mead from his area

---

[75]Contarini, 'Viaggio in Persia', *ibid.*, 204–5, 328–9. Contarini was in Moscow in 1476–7.
[76]*De Moscovia*, 8 recto.
[77]Sigmund von Herberstein, *Description of Moscow and Muscovy, 1557*, 93.
[78]*Pskovskaya sudnaya gramota*, in PRP, II, 301. The three items listed are presumably measures.

11 In the tavern, mid-eighteenth century. Farnos, the Russian equivalent of Punchinello, and his wife, Pigasiya, are here depicted visiting the tavern run by a man trusted on oath to deal with the duty on alcohol sales. The fantastic garb of Farnos, his cod-piece and cap, as well as his prominent red nose, underline the sexual implications of the doggerel inscription:

> In your red felt cap
> Is it you, Ermak, you man on oath, we've found?
> I'd bow to you to the ground,
> But I'm loaded with a tufted cap.
> Would you know Farnos?
> Do you want to view, never fear,
> My fine nose, my wife Pigasiya?
> Have you seen such news?
> Have you heard of us?
> Though we're not rich,
> We have our humpbacked noses,
> Though we're uncomely, we don't wear sacking,
> But a liking for drink we're not lacking.
> Yesterday, lashing out cash,
> From you we didn't budge;
> Tipsy, we didn't begrudge
> Our spending spree.
> Sighing and suffering now we be.
> We come to you for a drop of gin,
> You can't ignore this plight we're in.
> Call for a can and set up the beer,
> We'll even pay our debts, no doubt,
> Or we'll knock your stuffing out.

into Pskov.[79] The term *korchma* also meant a 'tavern', a place where drink and food were to be had (but not one operating a state monopoly of alcoholic drinks). In the late fifteenth century, however, the term seems to have retained its meaning of 'strong drink'. 'The German merchant is not to trade in Pskov in strong drink or beer, but apart from strong drink and beer any good may be freely taken into Pskov.'[80] Later, when control of drink became more important to the administration, the term *korchma* came to mean 'illicit drink'; this meaning here seems possible, but unlikely.[81] Spirits in the late fifteenth century were evidently imported from Riga and Derpt (Yurevets).

The tavern, then, was at first a dwelling place where food and drink were available for sale; sometimes it became something more specialised. It was found mostly in the Baltic (Pskov), west Russian (Smolensk) and southern areas, but was unimportant in the central areas of Russia.[82] The defeat and incorporation of Novgorod into the Moscow State in 1477 and the similar fate of Pskov in 1510 led to new problems. The Baltic trade bringing in, legally or illegally, strong drink (as well as providing other foreign contacts) resulted in measures to protect the Russian population from contamination.

Herberstein claimed that the tsar', Vasilii Ivanovich (1505–33), built an establishment where his servitors could drink beer and mead 'because other Russians are prohibited from drinking mead and beer, save for a few days in the year'.[83] It is noteworthy that there is no mention, either here or elsewhere in Herberstein's account, that spirits were then available in Russia.[84] Michalo Lituanus, who was probably never in Moscow (and, almost alone among foreigners writing about Russia at the time, considered Russians a sober people), stated that Vasilii founded 'Nalevvki', as he called it, after the capture of Smolensk in 1514. He did this, 'for the leisure of our [i.e. the Lithuanian] mercenary soldiers and called it by the name "Drunken" as an insult to our people, for Nalei means "pour"'.[85] Michalo was writing about 1550. He also noted, perhaps with greater reliability, that 'in the Lithuanian towns there is no trade more frequent than the production of ale and spirits from rye'.[86] His date for the origin of Nalivki may not be invented

[79]*P3L, PL*, II, 196.
[80]*GVNiP*, no. 78 (13 January 1474), 134. Cp. *PL*, II, 196; *PSRL*, 4, 248–9.
[81]See Sreznevskii, *Materialy*, I, 1413.
[82]Pryzhov, *Istoriya kabakov*, 34.
[83]Herberstein, *Zapiski*, 99.
[84]An English edition of Herberstein, *Description of Moscow and Muscovy*, 59, mentions 'brandy', but this is a mistake.
[85]*De moribus* in *Arkhiv istoriko-yuridicheskikh svedenii*, book 2, section 5, 32–3.
[86]*Ibid.*, 30.

even if spirits were consumed there; in 1515 the Joseph of Volok monastery was instructed not to keep 'burnt wine' (*goryachoe vino*), i.e. brandy, and hopped drinks.[87] 'If anyone brings to the cell mead or brandy, or beer or mead kvas, or ale, no one of you is to have or drink it and you are to tell me who brings it.'

There is another version of the origin of this quarter for mercenaries in the south of Moscow: Catholics lived there, though without a church;

> They came to this quarter with the right to sell wine, beer and so on which the Muscovites themselves were not allowed since they, being too inclined to drunkenness, to which the sovereign himself is very hostile, are not permitted by him to make and sell beer, apart from eight days before and after Christmas when they are allowed to drink because of the festival.[88]

Tedaldi had been in Moscow in 1551–4, as well as frequently after that till 1565. The information from Michalo and Tedaldi suggests that Catholic Lithuanian mercenaries, not unexpectedly, also engaged in trade and were granted certain rights with regard to drink (perhaps including spirits, though they are not mentioned) in the first half of the sixteenth century; they were, however, restricted to a particular quarter of Moscow. It is not till 1578, however, that there is an unambiguous reference to foreigners selling spirits. According to Boch 'the Livonians and Germans are allowed by the prince to sell beer, hydromel or mead and that drink called aqua vita'.[89]

It is believed by some that spirits or vodka, i.e. distilled alcoholic drinks, reached Russia in the late fourteenth century.[90] Spirits (*vino*), unlike vodka, were distilled only once; confusingly, however, *vino* also indicates wine. It seems unlikely that alcoholic products would reach Moscow from Genoese colonies on the Black Sea coast after the Tatars were converted to Islam in 1389. Indeed, even the rare and costly imported wines consumed at feasts by princes and boyars ceased to come by this route.[91] Wine is not listed among the goods carried by the Surozh merchants trading with the Crimea.[92] A more likely route might be the Baltic; there were close relations between the Teutonic Order and Pskov, the Hanseatic League had a yard in Novgorod and

[87]*DAI*, I, no. 212.

[88]Shmurlo, *Izvestiya*, 19.

[89]Schmidt, 'Iohannes Boch in Moskau', *Russische Revue* (1887).

[90]Pryzhov, *Ocherki*: 196; Billington, *The Icon and the axe*, 86, 660–1. *BSE*, 3rd edn, 24, 1, 327, goes further: 'The production of spirits underwent considerable development in Western Europe and Russia in the 14th century.' See also *BSE*, 3rd edn, 5, 175.

[91]*ORK XIII–XVvv.*, 1, 304.

[92]Syroechkovskii, *Gosti-surozhane*.

there were other links. The import of red and white wine by this important trade route was evident at least from 1436.[93] In 1476 the Archbishop of Novgorod presented the Grand Prince with a barrel of red and another of white wine as a parting gift; this was clearly a great luxury.[94] There is no mention of spirits, however, only of wine as a Novgorod import.

In fact, there seems a 'complete absence of information on drinks like present-day vodka', according to one Soviet authority, and such drinks spread to Russia only in the sixteenth century 'as written sources demonstrate'.[95] Recently, a western historian has asserted that the Russians 'learned from the Tatars the art of distillation' in the sixteenth century.[96] Unfortunately, neither author gave any sources for these statements. In fact, it appears that spirits, known in Russia in the first half of the sixteenth century, came in from the West, but were at first restricted to consumption by foreign mercenaries.

In 1544 Ivan IV sent an official to establish eight strong drink houses (*korchemnykh dvorov*) in Novgorod.[97] These presumably were houses intended to operate a monopoly by the tsar' of drink sales. They led to such drunkenness that Feodosii, Archbishop of Novgorod, protested against taverns and, on 27 December – the time of year is probably significant – 1547, the tsar' set aside the strong drink (*korchma*) and the drink-shop drink (*pitie kobattskoe*).[98] The 'strong drink' (if *korchma*, as it seems, is to be taken in that sense here, and not as 'tavern') and the 'drink-shop drink' almost certainly indicate spirits, as tends to be confirmed by the statement that follows this. 'The reeves of the town quarters and streets, 30 men, were given two barrels of beer and six buckets of mead and one and a half buckets of burnt wine [i.e. brandy] as an allocation.'[99] This appears to indicate that spirits, generally available through the tsar's monopoly, were replaced by a limited allocation to celebrate Christmas distributed by local officials.

Administrative control of drink was also attempted by an institution, new towards the middle of the sixteenth century; this was the drink-shop (*kabak*) which sold state-produced or state-licensed drink, especially spirits; it was run either directly by men on oath or other officials or was farmed out in return for a money payment. In an attack

---

[93] Nikitskii, *Istoriya ekonomicheskogo byta*, 163, n. 3; Khoroshkevich, *Torgovlya*, 323–32.
[94] *PSRL*, 30, 180.
[95] Artsikhovskii, *ORK XIII–XVvv.*; part 1, 304–5.
[96] Pipes, *Russia under the Old Regime*, 157.
[97] *PSRL*, 30, 205.
[98] *DAI*, 1, no. 41; *PSRL*, 30, 151.
[99] *PSRL*, 30, 151; the text reads *gor'koe vino* ('bitter wine'), but this is presumably an error for *goryachoe vino*.

on Kazan' in 1545 the outskirts of the town and the Khan's *kabaki* had been burnt.[100] Despite their Islamic faith the Khans had such drinking places, but, as usual in Islamic countries, they stood outside the town. On his return from Kazan', Ivan IV 'forbad the sale of vodka in Moscow, allowing only the members of his Oprichnina to drink it and for their drinking bouts he built a special establishment at Balchuga [in central Moscow] called in Tatar *kabak*'.[101] This institution then spread to other parts of Muscovy, according to Pryzhov, and he lamented the change. In the Tatar *kabak*, as in the inn, one could eat and drink; in the Moscow drink-shop (*kabak*) the order was drinking only, and drinking only by the common people, i.e. the peasants and the men of the artisan quarters, 'for they alone were prohibited from making drink at home; all other people drank in their own homes and, in addition, had the right to hold drink-shops'.[102] The monstrous appearance of such drinking establishments influenced the entire subsequent history of the Russian people.

The triumph of the drink-shop, however, was not immediate, if we are to believe Anthony Jenkinson, an English merchant in Russia in 1557. 'In every good town there is a drunken tavern called a *korchma*, which the emperor sometime letteth out to farm and sometimes bestoweth for a year or two on some duke or gentleman in recompense of his service; and for that time he is lord of all the town, robbing and spoiling and doing what pleaseth him.'[103] Jenkinson's remarks call attention both to the financial aspects of drinking and to the presence of institutions for drink in towns only.

The tsar's drink policy had both moral and financial aspects. He himself made this clear when he raised issues

... about the taverns granted in towns and in dependent towns and in volosts; they have been granted from of old, but now any royal representatives and those holding livings should set aside the ale-due from those lands, and there should be no tavern at all, since great harm is done to the peasants by the tavern and destruction to their souls.[104]

Concern for administrative control of social and even private drinking is demonstrated by such documents as a charter to a number of

---

[100]Karamzin, *Istoriya*, vol. VIII, 93.

[101]Pryzhov, *Istoriya kabakov*, 49; his *Ocherki*, 221. Dit'yatin, in *Russkaya Mysl'* (1883), IV, 9, 40, mistakenly stated this was after the conquest of Kazan'.

[102]Pryzhov, *Istoriya kabakov*, 50.

[103]Hakluyt, *Principall Navigations*, 337.

[104]Number 4 of Ivan IV's 'questions' for Metropolitan Makarii, February 1550, in *PRP*, IV, 577–8.

volosts in the Northern Dvina area.[105] 'If any people on the Penezhka and the Vyya and on the Sura begin to keep a tavern, the elected heads [three names] and their fellows, ten persons, shall hold the tavern securely, so that . . . the volost peasants keep no drink for sale.' There was to be no competition with government sales; the tsar' was to have his income assured. Any peasant found with drink for sale was liable to heavy penalties: 2 rubles to be paid to the Grand Prince and 2 to the volost people; those caught drinking were to pay ¼ ruble. 'If any people happen to brew an offering (*kanun*) for a festival, to commemorate their parents, or for a christening or a birth . . . those people are free to brew drink and to drink for about five days or a week if they have made a declaration.' The profits to be made one way or another are hinted at by the statement that 'the elected officials themselves are not to hold drink for sale'.[106] There was a similar formula in the oath taken by the officials: 'illicit drink is to be seized in accordance with the sovereign's charter; and judges themselves are not to hold illicit drink'.[107] These regulations are similar to those in the Vaga statute of 21 March 1552.[108] The statutes of the time for royal representatives, however, continued to be concerned with their intrusions and exactions.[109]

If anyone at the pogost or in a volost' has a feast or fraternity, he takes the official a bucket of drink, a *nasadka*, whatever drink he happens to have, and bread and a chicken. But if he does not want the *nasadka* of drink, the bread and the chicken, they give a denga for the drink, one for the bread and one for the chicken. The official and other people of the royal representative, apart from the court investigator, are not to ride uninvited to them to a feast or fraternities.

In 1571 on Friday of Easter week – again a noteworthy time of year – the privy clerks, Semen, son of Fedor Mishin, and Aleksei Mikhalov Staroi, rode into Novgorod and forbad the boatmen to ferry people over the Volkhov; they ordered them to cross by the Great Bridge. They also forbad the dealers in spirits – another noteworthy fact – to trade, and they set up a checkpoint on the Great Bridge. If they caught a dealer with spirits on him, or a man who was drunk, they ordered him to be beaten with the knout and cast into the water from the Great Bridge.[110]

[105]Published by Kopanev in *Istoricheskii arkhiv*, vol. VIII, 9–20 (25 February 1552).
[106]*Ibid.*, 17–18.
[107]*PRP*, IV, 198 (1556–82).
[108]Yakovlev, *Namestnich'i, gubnyya i zemskiya ustavnyya gramoty*, 103–13, esp. 109–10.
[109]Yakovlev, *Namestnich'i, gubnyya i zemskiya ustavnyya gramoty*, nos. 16 (1547–56), 45–9.
[110]*PSRL*, 30, 158.

The church, of course, mostly stressed the moral and social problems arising from excessive drinking wherever it took place. According to the Metropolitan's Justice, a document of about 1390–1430, if a wife went to a feast 'with other people', this was adequate grounds for a divorce.[111] The church, or at least some of its best publicists, made a sustained effort against drink in the mid-sixteenth century.

The church council of 1551 was much concerned with the evils of drunkenness, especially in monasteries. A chapter of the results of the council's deliberations is devoted to intoxicating liquor.[112] It was not proper for there to be drink in monasteries for 'it is from this that there is drunkenness and drunkenness is the beginning and end of all evil deeds'. Drink was permitted, however, as authorised by the Holy Fathers, but it was not to be drunk 'to drunkenness'. The drinks prohibited in monasteries were hopped alcoholic drinks and spirits; kvas made from grain and with honey was allowed, while Frankish wines might be drunk as allowed 'to the glory of God; but not to drunkenness'.

There were also complaints by churchmen about lay drinking and its associated activities.

But here we see that in the town called Pskov and in all Russian towns there are taverns and whores. For drunkards never frequent taverns without whores. But if the taverns are not removed – this is known, that there is both drunkenness and whoring for the unmarried and fornication for the married – there shall be retribution for this on those who grow rich thereby. Lord, show mercy and lead our tsar' into the ways of righteousness, let him remove them, and not only this, but any intoxicating drink. For if there be no drunkenness in our land, there will be no whoring for married women and there will also be no killing, apart from brigandage: for if any evildoer intends brigandage, sometimes he will achieve it. An attack overcomes the thoughtless who fails to remain vigilant. For if, in the world's custom, men and women indulge in intoxicating drink, then certain sacrilegious persons will come, playing psalteries, viols, drones and drums and other devilish games and playing pranks before married women, leaping and singing ribald songs. Seeing this, the wife, who is already seated as if overcome by drunkenness, has lost the strength of sobriety and is a prey to the desire for satan's game; her husband has also weakened and his mind is inclined to other women and he glances here and there with his eyes and caresses them; and each man gives a drink and kisses another's wife and then embraces will be accepted and insidious speeches woven and devilish mating.[113]

---

[111] *ASEI*, III, no. 8.
[112] Kozhanchikov, *Stoglav*, ch. 12, 174ff; Honcharenko, *Stoglav*, ch. 52.
[113] Ermolai Erazm, *LZAK*, XXXIII, 198 (1540s or early 1550s).

Complaints such as these contain a mixture of very different elements and their nature is not always immediately obvious. Certainly, their vigour and the fact that they continue at least into the late seventeenth century stress their importance, but the reasons for that importance call for comment. Apart from the objection to drink increasing sexual desire, and sometimes resulting in performance, Ermolai-Erazm raises other matters: 'sacrilegious persons', musicians, players, singers and 'devilish games'. He omits some items to be found in other ecclesiastical objections to popular celebrations: masking (perhaps subsumed by his 'devilish games'), bears, fisticuffs. These are not a chance collection, but at the least a complex implying a live low culture, irreverent in nature and containing elements of non-Christian ceremonial, something quite sufficient to call forth the wrath of the Christian clerics having a struggle both to ensure the supremacy of their religion in a widely scattered population and to cope with heresy and princely pretensions. Moreover, we have seen that the feasts and fraternities that institutionalised popular celebrations of different kinds existed throughout the sixteenth century. The church was not dealing merely with recalcitrant individuals, but with social bodies that had both princely support and popular participation in their customs.

Objections to such traditions, which seem only partly to have been entertainments in the usual sense, were, as has been seen, of long standing. The fighting was often fisticuffs (*kulachnyi boi*), as described by Herberstein.

The sturdy young lads commonly have some ground within the town where they gather on holidays. As the custom is, one of them gives a whistle, upon which they rush upon each other, striking and punching each other with fists, knees and feet in the face, throat, belly or genitals so that some are always carried off half-dead. This takes place for the honour of holding the fort longest and also to harden them to blows with which, when given in earnest, they will be familiar.[114]

Fisticuffs were particularly frequent at Shrove-tide and have been associated with ancient feasts for the dead which included contests on the grave of the dead.[115] Such fistfights were condemned by the church council of 1551, along with many other popular rituals.[116] Many burials took place in the spring because the severe and continuous frosts prevented the digging of graves. As Turberville put it:

[114]*Description of Moscow and Muscovy*, 42.
[115]Zelenin, *Volkskunde*, p. 352. See also Kotlyarevskii, 'O pogrebal'nykh obychayakh'.
[116]Honcharenko, *Stoglav*, chs. 52–4, 216–23, also 234.

> The bodies eke that die unburied lie till then
> Laid up in coffins made of fir, as well the poorest men
> As those of greater state; the cause is lightly found,
> For that in wintertime they cannot come to break the
> ground.[117]

Giles Fletcher made a similar observation.[118]

Whistling, howling and calling are also likely to be more than simply that. Even today in Russia whistling in public is frowned on and this perhaps hints at something sacral about it. The 'whistle-dance' (*svistoplyaska*) was held annually on the fourth Saturday after Easter in Vyatka, allegedly to commemorate the men of Ustyug mistakenly killed by their allies of Vyatka in a night battle in 1480. It seems at least a possibility, however, that the whistle-dance had more general links with the commemoration of the dead. In the mid-sixteenth century similar ceremonies occurred elsewhere. The commemoration for the dead in nineteenth-century Vyatka included a contest of dolls hurled across a ditch to the continuous accompaniment of clay pipes and whistles in the form of ducks.[119] *Svistoplyaska* in modern times also had the meaning of a wild ne'er-do-well.[120] Calling had not only the sense of shouting, but also of luring birds and animals, perhaps with overtones of charming them. In the sixteenth century 'early on Easter Thursday they burn straw and call the dead'.[121] Calling was also associated with wizards (*volkhvy*) and with feeding and keeping bears.[122]

The churchmen objected most to the wind instruments. Psalteries and viols were mentioned, but horns and pipes and especially bagpipes seem to have aroused particular hostility. The horn and pipe have sexual connotations in many languages. In addition, in Russian the term *duda* and its cognates are associated with drink, often only mildly alcoholic, and also with drunkenness.[123] This suggests an origin in the period before distilled spirits were generally available. There appears to have been at least some general opposition to music as early as the twelfth century: 'moreover, do not listen to music, neither the pan-pipes, nor the trumpet'.[124] The entertainer or jester (*skomorokh*) was

---

[117]To Spencer.
[118]*Of the Russe Commonwealth*, ch. 26.
[119]Zabylin, *Russkii narod*, 65. Was the duck shape a deliberate reminder of the ancient Russian duck shaped scoop (*kovsh*) from which people drank in common?
[120]Dal', *Tolkovyi slovar'*, vol. IV, 65.
[121]Kozhanchikov, *Stoglav*, ch. 41, question 26, 142.
[122]Kozhanchikov, *Stoglav*, ch. 93, 264; Honcharenko, *Stoglav*, ch. 53, 219.
[123]Dal', *Tolkovyi slovar'*, vol. I, 1243–4.
[124]Sreznevskii, *Materialy*, III, 274.

sometimes a piper or played the panpipes.[125] The most characteristic instrument used, however, was the psaltery. Along with trumpets and drones, drums, psalteries, devilish songs, dancing, hopping and various other things were regarded as impious.[126] It has been suggested that whirling, dancing, rhythmic singing and drumming were means of achieving states of exaltation or trance and were used in fortune-telling.[127] The drum was indicated by a term (*kudes, kuddes*) which was used of a shaman's drum, but which in Russian was also reminiscent of a word for a sorcerer or soothsayer (*kudesnik*). It is, therefore, probably significant that 'the land of Perm' . . . is full of idolatry . . . wizardry, divination, enchantment and sorcery'; such a remote, basically Finnish area might well have been one of the sources for features of shamanism to penetrate Russian culture.[128] Much popular music and its performers, therefore, had associations which could not be tolerated by the church even if, as no doubt was sometimes true, those involved did not intend any hostility to Christianity, but merely sought entertainment and support from custom.

Similar considerations apply to some of the other entertainments to which the church objected. Masking was 'an archaic part of the Russian Christmas-tide ritual; it retained a series of masks the prototypes of which go back to the early forms of religion. First here we should name the group of zoomorphic masks.'[129] These included the horse, bull and bear, as well as the hen which is the one most clearly associated with comedy. The horse provided a crude measure of peasant wealth: peasants were divided into those with and those without horses.[130] The Novgorod finds of horse skulls in the foundations of houses also points to the symbolic importance of the animal in popular Russian culture at the time.[131] The bull and the games played in this mask are erotic and go back to a fertility cult. There was also a bear cult known in early Russia from the eleventh century which probably gave rise to the mask of that animal and perhaps to other games involving wild or trained bears.[132] The bear and the goat were also symbols of abundance and fertility.

---

[125]*Ibid.*

[126]*Domostroi*, ch. 23.

[127]V. Smirnov, *Narodnye gadaniya v Kostromskpom krae* (1927), 39, cited in Chicherov, *Zimnii period*, 195. See also I.M. Lewis, *Ecstatic religion*, 39.

[128]Sreznevskii, *Materialy*, vol. II, 1357 (fifteenth century).

[129]Chicherov, *Zimnii period*, 195.

[130]*Ibid.*, 200.

[131]See n. 17 above.

[132]Voronin, 'Medvezhii kul't', esp. 66, 86. Kozhanchikov, *Stoglav*, ch. 93, 264; Honcharenko, *Stoglav*, ch. 93, 219.

12 A musical bear and goat, nineteenth century. The bear and the goat as
trained animals long continued the tradition of masking and entertainment. In
this nineteenth-century woodcut they 'play, dance and drink a tot together'.
The couple at table have been drinking spirits and tea supplied with hot water
from a samovar.

Laments and howling at the burial of the dead were usual. The
overbreathing in the laments may be a relict trace of another means of
achieving a state of trance. Giles Fletcher commented on the 'ordinary
women mourners that come to lament for the dead party and stand
howling over the body after a profane and heathenish manner'.[133] The
songs at the funeral feast and other occasions, however, often had
humorous and sexual implications associated with ancestor worship. In
the mid-sixteenth century in cemeteries 'men and women come together in villages and churchyards on Trinity Saturday and weep at the
graves with great lamentations. And when the jesters and pipers begin
to play, they stop weeping and begin to hop and dance, to clap their
hands and sing satanic songs; at those cemeteries are deceivers and
cheats.'[134]

'Players and organists and psaltery-players and comedians play at lay
weddings and sing devilish songs; when they ride to the marriage
ceremony in the church, the priest is there with the cross, they run

[133]*Of the Russe Commonwealth*, ch. 26. See also Tatishchev, *Leksikon*, 326–7, on howlers (*klikushi*)
    'possessed by devils' as late as the 1720s.
[134]Kozhanchikov, *Stoglav*, ch. 41, question 23, 140. Cp. Olearius, *Travels*, 40–1 for a seventeenth-
    century description.

before him with all those devilish games.'[135] This was condemned; so were the entertainers or jesters who 'eat and drink forcefully with peasants in the hamlets, steal goods from halls and beat people on the roads'.[136] Drunkards and dice-players were condemned.[137]

And false prophets go on foot through the country districts and villages, men and women, maids and old women, naked and bare-footed with their hair uncut and loose, they tremble and beat themselves and say that saints Pyatnitsa and Nastasiya appear to them and command them to order Christians to dispense (*zavecheti*) offerings; and they order no hard work to be done on Wednesday or Friday, and the women not to spin, nor wash clothes nor light fires, but they order other blasphemous things, not in the Holy Scriptures, to be done.

Among games 'leading many to laughter and debauch' there was transvestism.[138] Moreover, 'they summon kvas, and charm the taste and celebrate drunkenness'.[139] At Rusala, about St John's day, and on the eve of Christmas and Epiphany, 'men, women and maidens gather for night games (*pleshchevanie*) and unseemly talk, for devilish songs and dances, and for impious deeds; there is defilement for the young men and seduction for the maidens; when the night passes, then the strong go off to the river with great cries, like devils they wash with water and when matins begin they depart to their homes and fall as if dead from much groaning.'[140]

The main popular celebrations, then, seem not only to be connected with a calendar of festivals closely linked with the agricultural year, but to have included a number of elements linking the agricultural year with a cult of the ancestors, presumably in order to assure fertility to humans, plants and animals. Feasting and drinking played a central part in the winter and spring ritual celebrations. At Christmas-tide the ceremonies included feasting in cemeteries and lighting bonfires at which the dead were invited to warm themselves.[141] At Shrove-tide the jollifications included feasting and drinking, as did the week after Easter known as *Radonitsa* or *Radunitsa* (supposedly from *rod*, meaning 'kin-group'). Trinity or Whitsun was also marked by similar commemorative feasts.[142]

---

[135] Kozhanchikov, *Stoglav*, ch. 41, question 16, 135–6.
[136] *Ibid.*, question 19, 137.
[137] *Ibid.*, ch. 92, question 20, 137; Honcharenko, *Stoglav*, ch. 93, 219–20.
[138] Kozhanchikov, *Stoglav*, ch. 93, 265; Honcharenko, *Stoglav*, ch. 93, 220.
[139] Honcharenko, *Stoglav*, ch., 220; Kozhanchikov, *Stoglav*, ch., 265 has a slightly different version.
[140] Kozhanchikov, *Stoglav*, ch. 41, question 24, 141.
[141] Propp, *Russkie agrarnye prazdniki*, 17–18.
[142] On *Radunitsa*, see Tereshchenko, *Byt*, 5, 27–31, also 6, 173–98.

There was, thus, a duality of beliefs. 'The fierce struggle for Christianity developed in the Moscow State did not result in victory for the ruling class. The people, in performing a ritual linked with the productive life of the agriculturalist, perhaps unconsciously opposed the Orthodoxy which remained foreign to them.'[143] In the sense that the rituals survived into the twentieth century, this is no doubt true; but it is extremely difficult to assess the meaning of such celebrations for the participants at different times.

The drinks consumed on such occasions were kvas, beer and mead. Spirits are unlikely to have been generally available.[144] We know less about the food. Probably pottages of some sort were the commonest form of dish, but all the items mentioned were derived from grain. Some such dishes had ritual aspects.

The Vaga Statute of 1552 specified that

> If any people happen to brew [or 'boil'] an offering (*kanun*) for a festival or to commemorate their parents, or for a christening or a birth, and those people report about that to the elected officials (*izlyublennye golova*) . . . and those officials allowed those people to brew drink freely and to drink for about three, or four or five days; and when that term of days is past, the elected officials take the drink from those people and impose a fine on them in accordance with our decree.[145]

Kanun had the meaning, among others, of 'offering' in a general sense, but also specifically of boiled food or drink which was sometimes placed on the altar, despite the objections of some churchmen.[146] This custom was evidently sufficiently established in the mid-sixteenth century for an altar to be regularly used for it.

> A second altar is called the frumenty one (*kuteinik*); both the boiled wheat (*kolivo*) and the offering and other food (*brashno*) are taken to it for good health. On Easter Sunday itself cheese and eggs and other food (*yad'*) which Christians are permitted, and the frumenty and the offering and other food (*brashno*) for the use of the churchmen is brought and, in addition, a short service is sung for the departed souls.[147]

In the nineteenth century *kanun* was defined as a fool with honeywater, or pancakes with honey, or frumenty for the dead.[148] These

---

[143]Chicherov, *Zimnii period*, 172.

[144]For a contrary opinion, see Leont'ev in *ORK XVIv.*, 2, 54.

[145]*AAE*, I, no. 234 (21 March 1552); a similar statute (25 February 1552) for three Dvina volosts is in *Istoricheskii arkhiv*, VIII, 9–20.

[146]Sreznevskii, *Materialy*, vol. I, 1191. Popov, 'Piry i bratchiny', 37, regarded *kanun* as drink for a festival.

[147]Honcharenko, *Stoglav*, ch. 40.

[148]Dal', *Tolkovyi slovar'*, 210, 2.

items, too, hint at non-Christian rites and probably account for clerical opposition to their being set on the altar.

Kut'ya, here translated as frumenty, a pottage of whole grains, seems, at least in early times, to have been an offering; in 1103 'the Russian princes and warriors all prayed to God and made their vows to God and his Mother, some with frumenty, some with charity to the poor, some with contributions to monasteries.'[149] It was eaten in recent times at feasts in commemoration of the dead and on Christmas Eve. A century ago an observer noted in Pinega that, 'apart from the church commemoration, they remember the dead with pancakes, another sort (called *oladyshi*), thin porridge (*salamata*) and frumenty. They eat the frumenty when it is blessed by the priest.'[150] *Kut'ya,* like English frumenty, was made with the whole grain of wheat, but also with barley or imported rice with honey-water and raisins.[151] The whole grain, i.e. the seed, indicates its symbolic importance, implying the possibility of growth; it is linked with a cult of dead ancestors.[152] By Christians, no doubt, it might have been taken to symbolise the Resurrection, though no evidence has been found for this.

Certain prohibitions were associated with frumenty. It was forbidden to set water by it or to place eggs on it.[153] Like the host and candles, it was not to be accepted from those who opposed church regulations. The doubts about the acceptability of frumenty, and other items, are reflected in the complaint, in 1499, that 'certain unsanctified persons bless gifts brought to the church, that is to say, rolled grain or frumenty for the dead; we henceforth forbid this; frumenty and beer should not be brought to the altar, but only the host, candles and incense and wine'. Within a generation, however, another document laid down that 'frumenty may be blessed honourably in praise of the saints and frumenty blessed to give rest to the dead, but it is ruled that no lunch and dinner for the dead be blessed, nor sprinkled with water, and no eggs are to be put on the frumenty'.[154] In the mid-sixteenth century, apart from incense, church wine, candles and the host, offerings (*kanon*) for health and repose of the soul and, at Easter, cheese, eggs and meat, and 'on other days' wheat-rolls, pastries, loaves and pancakes, as well as all sorts of fruit, were set on the altar.[155] These, as

[149]*PVL*, 184.
[150]Efimenko, *Materialy*, ch. 1, 137.
[151]Herberstein, *Notes upon Russia*, vol. 1, 70–1, noted the constituents.
[152]Propp, *Russkie agrarnye prazdniki*, 16.
[153]Sreznevskii, *Materialy*, vol. 1, 1381.
[154]*Ibid.*
[155]Kozhanchikov, *Stoglav*, question 26, 56.

well as 'beer, mead, kvas and ale', were prohibited.[156] Such food was 'not only a means of satisfaction, but also an act linking oneself and one's household to the forces and potency which were ascribed to the dish eaten. Such phenomena include frumenty and also eggs for the Resurrection of Christ and of the whole of nature.'[157]

There was, then, a certain area of ritual food associated with feasts, and perhaps fraternities, which was at times suspect from the point of view of the Christian church, and this area is associated with the commemoration of the dead ancestors of the kin-group. There were probably circumstances in which it was difficult to make a sharp distinction between the church's attitude and that of a group of kin or neighbours. Kin-groups or fraternities might well venerate an ancestor, or alleged ancestor, and not clearly distinguish this from the veneration of a local saint. There are certainly saints who appear to have been exceptionally popular among the peasants; for instance, St Nicholas and Pyatnitsa or Paraskeva ('Friday'). The doubts about frumenty should not necessarily be taken to indicate outright conflict between Christian and pagan; they seem, rather, to indicate that grey area where the church was trying to assimilate some non-Christian elements which were alive even in the sixteenth-century Russian countryside. A unique document perhaps illustrates this situation; a loan contract with a monastery includes the phrase that 'the abbot and monks are to make as much beer as they can in memory of Stepan' (evidently the debtor's father).[158] The monastery was thus called on to commemorate Stepan in the customary non-Christian way.

Spirits appear to have reached central Russia from the West around 1515, but were not then widespread. By the middle of the century, however, a number of problems about the social and economic aspects of drinking had come to the fore. The tsar' was concerned about the moral problems of drunkenness, but at least as much about the income to be derived from control of drink. The attempt to introduce the drink-shop demonstrated this, as did the increasing concern with control of the officials or tax-farmers involved. At the lower social levels and in the country-side the tsar' appeared as a defender, in some sense, of the feasts and fraternities; this is linked with the growth of the central power as against that of the royal representatives, their officials and, later, the entertainers or jesters they supported or protected.

Even before spirits became common (and afforded increased oppor-

[156]*Ibid.*, ch. 12, 73. Cp. chap. 13, 74. Honcharenko, *Stoglav*, chap. 12, 48, adds frumenty and bread to the list.
[157]Propp, *Russkie agrarnye prazdniki*, 30.
[158]*GVNiP*, no. 152 (1448–9).

tunities for control), drink, though still mostly produced and consumed in the home, had become a commodity, often sold from the home. The tavern and drink-shop were restricted to towns, and to a relatively few towns at first; spirits were available perhaps only in Moscow and Novgorod. The feasts and fraternities reinforced custom and kin-group by their ritual celebrations, whether Christian, pagan or simply as entertainment. The less intermittent, less personal sales of food and drink in the tavern, however, provided a meeting place for a wider spectrum of society; for that very reason it seems to have come under suspicion from the authorities.

The church, too, was greatly concerned both about drinking and about the feasting and associated activities which were either disapproved of as too frivolous, or condemned as conflicting with Orthodox belief. This disapproval contributed to increased measures undertaken by the tsar', but at times put a brake on his concern to increase taxation income by increasing drink sales.

Despite the changes of the mid-sixteenth century domestic brewing long continued. Hops continued to be mentioned on a par with grain in customs charters, for example.[159] Foreigners continued to mention kvas, beer or mead, but not spirits. Even those who dined in the presence of the tsar' in the late sixteenth century comment more on mead than any other drink. In the late 1560s Turberville expressed in humorous fashion a common view of Russian drinking habits.[160]

> I left my native soil, full like a retchless man,
> And unacquainted of the coast, among the Russes ran:
> A people passing rude, to vices vile inclinde,
> Folk fit to be of Bacchus traine, so quaffing is their kinde.
> Drinke is their whole desire, the pot is all their pride,
> The sobrest head doth once a day stand needfull of a guide.
> If he to banket bid his friends, he will not shrinke
> On them at dinner to bestow a douzen kindes of drinke:
> Such licour as they have, and as the countrey gives,
> But chiefly two, one called Kvas, whereby the Mousik lives.
> Small ware and waterlike, but somewhat tart in taste,
> The rest is Meade of honie made, wherewith their lips they baste
> And if he goes unto his neighbour as a guest,
> He cares for little meate, if so his drinke be of the best.

During his mission to Moscow in 1583–4 Sir Jerome Bowes was granted generous provisions of food, drink, as well as other necessities and provender. The drink consisted of a quarter of a bucket of cherry

[159]*LZAK*, xxxiv, 201–2 (1560).   [160]To Edward Dancie.

mead, a quarter of raspberry mead, half a bucket of 'burnt wine', one bucket of 'sodden meade called obarni', i.e. from scalded honey; three buckets of sweet, ten of white and fifteen of ordinary mead; four buckets of sweet beer and fifteen of 'beer'.[161] He thus had almost sixty times more mead and thirty-eight times more beer than spirits.

An ambassador in 1604 mentioned no spirits in describing a formal dinner with the tsar'.[162] Mead continued to be a noble drink, competing at such banquets with imported wines.

The 'Mousik' continued to have kvas and some mead, as well as beer, as everyday drinks. A verse of 1609 in praise of a London beer gives a curious list of Russian drinks.

> Nor all those Drinkes of Northren Climes,
> Whose Brewings shall fill up our Rimes,
> Brant, Rensque, and the cleere Romayne,
> The Belo, Crasno, and Patisane,
> Peeva (to them as is our Beere)
> As Meade Obarne, and Meade Cherunck,
> And the base Quasse by Pesants drunck
> With all the rest that whet the sprites
> Of Russes and cold Muscovytes.
> Not all these Drinkes nor thowsand mor,
> Can reach the fame of Pimlyco.[163]

The beers described, white (Belo), red (Crasno) and from clear honey (Patisane), would seem, in fact, to be meads.[164] Meade Obarne (i.e. *obarnyi*) was made from scalded or heated honey, the Cherunck (presumably *cheremkhovyi*) was flavoured with bird cherries.

The 'Peter' plan of Moscow, dated between 1596 and 1598, regarded as the first realistic plan of Moscow, mentions 'Ale prisons, prison for drunkards' on what is now Nogin Square.[165] Overall, therefore, there seems little doubt that even in Moscow spirits had not become a standard everyday drink for the mass of the population in the late sixteenth century.

It is in the late sixteenth century that there is the first evidence for spirits produced in Russia. In 1588 a fine of 4 rubles was exacted in the St Joseph monastery, Volokolamsk, from those who had distilled its

[161] Hakluyt, *Principall Navigations*, 493–4.
[162] *Sir Thomas Smithes Voiage and Entertainment in Rushia*, F.v. Quoted on p. 114 below.
[163] *Pimlyco, or, Runne Red-Cap* (London, 1609). I am grateful to W. Ryan for calling my attention to this item. Robert Nares, *A Glossary*, col. II, 707, commented on 'Quasse': 'I suspect that this is merely a misprint for *quaffe*, or drink.'
[164] Ustryalov, *Skazaniya*, vol. III, 213; Margeret, *Estat*, mentions '*Patisini mieud*, qui veut dire, Medon de miel vierge', f. 32.
[165] Sytin, *Istoriya planirovki*, vol. I, 64, 71.

13 Feeding the poor, sixteenth century. A twelfth-century Russian prince, Andrei Bogolyubskii, is shown giving support and food to poor commoners who are distinguished by their short-skirted garments and, in most cases, bare feet. The food on the table includes a triangular item, probably a pasty, frequently depicted in such scenes of upper class meals.

grain.[166] In 1597, significantly in Easter week, a survey official rode into a hamlet on an estate of the Patriarch and 'tormented the peasants, and Mikhailo demanded from them beer and spirits and food for himself and for his horse'.[167]

In 1600 a monastery complained that some junior boyars were continually making beer and spirits and their slaves, peasants and labourers were selling it. An instruction was issued that

[166]*Slovar' russkogo yazyka XI–XVII*, vol. II, 183. Curiously, this is the monastery which was prohibited from holding spirits in 1515 (see p. 88 above).
[167]*AFZ*, III, section 2, no. 109, 163.

You are to observe closely that the junior boyars, Osip Ostrenov and his brothers, and other junior boyars in the Kurmysh uezd, are to distill spirits and brew beer for themselves in their tenements. But the slaves in their tenements, and the peasants in their hamlets, are not to make beer and spirits for themselves, nor to keep illicit drink nor to sell spirits to be taken away. If any junior boyar begins to keep illicit drink or to sell spirits to be taken away, you are ordered to take the drink and the stills from them and to impose a penalty on them. If drink for sale is taken for the first time, you are ordered to have a penalty of five rubles from each man and are ordered to imprison him for one month. If anyone sells a second time, you are ordered to have a penalty of ten rubles, and the offenders are to be beaten in the market place with the knout, and cast into prison for half a year.[168]

These penalties are the same as those later specified in the Code of Laws of 1649, with certain additions.

The class implications of drink were clear to foreigners in Russia at the end of the sixteenth century. 1500s

Large tubs of sweet mead and beer were set for the people in different places in the Kremlin and each was able to drink. Drinking beer and mead is the greatest pleasure (for Muscovites), especially when they are able to drink as much as they wish, and in this they are masters; most of all [they love] vodka which is forbidden all of them except the gentry and merchants' stock.[169]

In 1611 a prince was accused of various abuses against some monastic peasants. Among other offences the prince's men had ordered the peasants 'to distill spirits and brew beer and prepare all sorts of provisions from their peasant grain'.[170] This material does not disagree in date with the earliest known Russian manuscript on distillation which is later than 1542 and may be early seventeenth-century.[171] In the 1620s the stills in Verkhotur'e had to be more closely controlled.[172] By the late seventeenth century internal customs books record triple and quadruple stills.[173]

Towards the end of the sixteenth century, therefore, distillation was more widely known, and perhaps practised, in Russia, but mainly along the routes from the Baltic and White Sea. A German work on the subject, printed in Strasbourg in 1537, was the basis for up to ten manuscripts on distillation produced in Russia in the late sixteenth or

[168] *AFZ*, III, section 1, nos. 43, 76 (27 October 1600).
[169] Isaak Massa, *Skazaniya*, 65, referring to 1599.
[170] *AFZ*, II, nos. 428, 484.
[171] Bogoyavlenskii, *Drevnerusskoe vrachevanie*, 74.
[172] *AI*, II, no. 153.
[173] Sakovich, *Iz istorii torgovli*, 40, 83.

14 Distillation, seventeenth-century. The western dress is significant.

early seventeenth centuries.[174] These were specialist works, not intended for or achieving popular levels. Alchemical concepts, however, had become outmoded in the West before this exemplar was produced. So it did not, for example, focus on the 'quintessence' or *aurum potabile*. As a result Russia never passed from ale to alchemy, but directly to an early form of pharmaceutical chemistry, although alchemists were employed in the early seventeenth century. Christopher Pukhner, an alchemist, was replaced by another, Tomas Vins, whose pay and conditions working in the apothecary department were: 50 rubles a year, 5 rubles a month for food, and 3 cups of spirits, 2 pots of mead, 2 pots of beer a day, 12 chets of oats and 18 bales (*ostramki*) of hay a year.[175]

[174]Hieronymus Brunschwig, *Das Neüwe Distilier Buoch*; this is a posthumous work based on that of Brunschwig who died c. 1512. Bogoyavlenskii, *Drevnerusskoe vrachevanie*, 72, 74.
[175]*AI*, III, no. 239 (15 February 1645).

PART II

****

State appetite, peasant diet

4

****

Controls and code:
the seventeenth century

The seventeenth century opened in Russia with a series of disasters commonly known in the West as the Time of Troubles. There were a series of famines, a number of internal risings and invasions by Swedes and Poles. The tsarevich Dmitrii died in mysterious circumstances in 1591 and the last of the Rurikids in 1598; thereafter various pretenders claimed the throne. It was not until 1613 that Mikhail was chosen tsar' and became the first Romanov to rule Russia.

The famine in the opening years of the century was very severe and impressed both Russians and foreigners. Conrad Bussow from Lüneburg, for instance, who was in Russia from 1601 to 1611, gave the following account:[1]

This dearth started in 1601 and continued till 1604 when a ton of rye cost 10 or 12 florins (whereas formerly a ton usually cost no more than 12 or 15 Moscow coins) and the famine throughout the country was greater even than that during the siege of Jerusalem . . . But, I vow to God, it is the absolute truth that I saw with my own eyes people lying on the street; in the summer they ate grass and in winter hay, like cattle. Some were already dead; straw and dung protruded from their mouths, and some (*bona venia*) ate human dung and hay. Not to be counted is the number of children who were killed, cut up and boiled by their parents and parents by their children, guests by their hosts and, on the other hand, hosts by their guests. Human flesh, finely minced and baked in pies, i.e. pasties, was sold in the market as animal flesh and eaten up, so that the traveller in those times had to beware with whom he put up for the night.

Bussov went on to describe tsar' Boris's charity which 'caused the poor peasants in the countryside to abandon everything and quit their homes, and, with wives and children, rush to Moscow to receive this money'; he claimed that up to 500,000 persons received a denga a day. The poor who died were provided with burial clothes and buried at the tsar's expense. According to, evidently unreliable, information

[1]Bussov, *Moskovskaya khronika*, 222–4.

given to Bussov 'by reliable clerks in the offices and by trading people, in Moscow alone more than 500,000 people died of hunger during this dearth'. Bussov added some other information scarcely to be believed. He stated that several ships laden with grain arrived at Ivangorod (Narva) from the German ports, but 'Boris did not want the shame that grain from other lands be bought and sold in his country which was rich in grain ... No one was allowed to buy a single barrel on pain of death.' He added that Boris sent to find any stocks of grain in the country. They 'then discovered many untold ricks of grain 100 and more fathoms long which had stood 50 and more years unthreshed in the fields such that trees had grown through them'.

More convincingly he noted that 'the devil of greed, allowed by God as a punishment for the whole land, so seized the rich Moscow profiteers that they started to buy up the tsar's grain, and that of the princes, boyars and monasteries, on the quiet through the poor and at a low price and then to resell it to the poor much dearer'. This account is not dissimilar from several others, though with some variations.[2] In the summer of 1601 there had been 'ceaseless rain, and the rye and the spring-sown grain was soaked and remained in the field over the winter'.[3] The following year

... frost killed the rye in flower and in both these years rye was bought in Kazan' for one and a half rubles and for 60 altyns; in Moscow and in Nizhnii [Novgorod] it was bought at 3 rubles a chet' and there was a great famine and great loss to people. In Moscow the sovereign ordered the dead to be interred; they buried about 100 and 90 and 300 a day; in 7 months 50,000 people died.[4]

This implies an average daily death rate of about 200 ('100 and 90') during these seven months. Bussow's figure of 500,000 dead is excessive; it is probably several times the population of Moscow at that time, and therefore improbable, even allowing for the influx of those seeking charity. According to another foreigner more than 120,000 people died and were buried in three graveyards.[5] This statement probably derives from a Russian source and is perhaps closer to the truth.[6] On the basis of a count ordered by the tsar' there were 127,000 dead in Moscow alone.

Whatever the actual death toll, the causes were only partly natural; problems of distribution and speculative hoarding played a great part

[2] Cp. Massa, *Skazaniya*, 77–81.
[3] Tikhomirov, in *IZ*, 10, 94, citing a contemporary document.
[4] *Ibid.* See also *PSRL*, 14, 1, 55. Palitsyn, 'Skazanie', 523, apparently refers to 1603, but was taken by Karamzin, *Istoriya*, vol. XI, 120, as referring to 1601.
[5] Margeret, *Estat*, 33v.
[6] Palitsyn, 'Skazanie', 524.

in the calamity. By late 1601 the tsar' had already taken action against such speculation, to judge from a document sent to Sol' Vychegda.[7] The church, the Stroganov family, the men of the artisan quarter, peasants, traders and others, including 'all the local rich people', were alleged to have 'much grain of all sorts, threshed and in stack'. 'The price of grain at Sol' Vychegda rises from hour to hour and is dearer from day to day, more than before; great need is imposed on the men of the artisan quarter and the volost people that they are unable to buy bread from the factors, bakers and roll-makers at such a great price.' The tsar' ordered that in Moscow 'and in all towns of our, the tsar's, dominions, the grain factors and all those people who have increased the price of grain and advanced money for grain, purchased grain and shut it away and concealed it are to be sought out'. No one anywhere was to increase the price of grain, though how this was to be effected was not disclosed. However, any hoarded grain found was to be sold at a decreed price: rye 1/2 ruble a chet, oats 1/4 ruble, barley 4 grivnas. There were to be no wholesale transactions in grain and distillation was forbidden, as was the brewing of beer, though with certain exceptions.

A few weeks after this decree, on 28 November 1601, the tsar' sent a memorandum on the release of peasants to a chamberlain, V.P. Morozov.[8] The tsar' and his son 'ordered the peasants in all their state to be given the right to move because of taxation and fines'. In fact, the right was for the junior servitors to make arrangements about peasant transfers between themselves. Movement was limited to the autumn St George's Day (26 November, i.e. two days before this memorandum!) and the following two weeks; not more than two peasants were allowed to be moved and the rights granted did not extend to the Moscow uezd or apply to the crown estates, the black volosts, the church or higher social ranks. Almost exactly a year later, on 24 November 1602 (two days before St George's Day), a similar decree was sent to Novgorod.[9] It disclosed that, despite the earlier regulation, peasants had been mistreated and held against their will. These efforts to regulate transfers of serfs between the minor servitors were probably evoked by the famine which had a particularly adverse effect on such servitors who lacked the resources of their superiors and the church. The exclusion of the Moscow region from the decree of 1601, however, is a puzzle; perhaps the tsar' believed that the measures against speculation and his own charity in Moscow would be enough to control the danger of social unrest in and around the capital.

[7] *LZAK*, IX, section 3. Cited in *Vosstanie I. Bolotnikova*, 68–73 (3 November 1601).
[8] *AAE*, II, no. 20. Translated in Smith, *Enserfment*, 101.
[9] *AAE*, II, no. 23.

Although the precise nature of the link between the famine and the measures about enserfed peasants at this time is not entirely clear, in August 1603 the link between the famine and the situation of slaves, often household servants, was explicitly recognised.

If any boyars and gentlemen, men of the Departments, junior boyars, merchants and any serving people, traders and others have sent their slaves from their tenements and have not given them manumission charters or handed them their bondage deeds and order them to feed themselves and those slaves of theirs are dying of famine, and many others are fed by the charity of the Sovereign Tsar' and Grand Prince of All Russia, Boris Fedorovich, and no one will accept them because they have no manumission charters . . .

then such slaves were to be given manumission documents in the Department of Slave Cases (*Prikaz kholop'ya suda*).[10] A contemporary noted that during the great famine 'everyone saw how it was impossible to feed a numerous household of slaves (*chelyad'*) and they began to set their slaves free, some truly, others dissembling . . . but many . . . had the means to feed their domestics for a long time, but wished to accumulate much wealth and so released their household'.[11] In September 1603 the slave rising led by Khlopko broke out.[12]

The famine, then, had a direct impact on the social disturbances in Russia in the early years of the seventeenth century. The results of the bad weather were crop failures; but these might not have led to outbreaks of violence had there been less speculation and better distribution. The social structure ensured that, where patriarchal and paternalistic attitudes failed to withstand the adverse circumstances, slaves starved while the wealthier lords survived, sometimes in considerable luxury.

About half a century earlier, in 1553, the first Englishmen had arrived in the White Sea, an accidental by-product of an expedition to discover a north-east passage to the riches of Cathay. Richard Chancellor was conveyed to Moscow and, finally, had audience of Ivan IV, the Dread. He was much impressed by the luxury of the court and by its ritual; both the wealth and the court arrangements he noted help towards understanding the early seventeenth-century situation as regards provisioning of this highest level in the land.

The Englishmen attended a dinner in the presence of the tsar':

In the middes of the roome, stoode a mightie Cupboorde upon a square foote, whereuppon stoode also a rounde boord, in manner of a Diamond, broade beneath, and towardes the toppe narrowe, and every steppe rose uppe more

10 *AI*, II, no. 44.
11 Palitsyn, 'Skazanie', 107.
12 Kusheva in *IZ*, 15, 91.

narrowe then another. Uppon this Cupboorde was placed the Emperours plate, which was so much, that the very Cupboord it selfe was scant able to sustayne the waight of it . . . There were also upon this Cupborde, certaine silver caskes, not much differing from the quantity of our Fyrkins, wherein was reserved the Emperours drinke . . . The Emperour, when he takes any bread or knife into his hand, doth first of all crosse himselfe upon his forehead: they that are in speciall favour with the Emperour, sitte upon the same bench with him, but somewhat farre from him: and before the comming in of the meate, the Emperour himselfe, according to an ancient custome of the kings of Muscovy, doth first bestow a peece of bread upon every one of his ghests with a loud pronunciation of his title, and honour, in this manner: The great Duke of Muscovie, and chiefe Emperour of Russia, Iohn Basiliwich, (& then the officer nameth the ghest) doth give thee bread. Whereupon all the ghests rise up, and by and by sit downe again. This done, the Gentleman Usher of the Hall comes in, with a notable companie of servants, carying the dishes, and having done his reverence to the Emperour, puts a young Swanne in a golden platter upon the table, and immediately takes it thence againe, delivering it to the Carver, and seven other of his fellowes to be cut up: which being per-fourmed, the meate is then distributed to the ghests, with the like pompe and ceremonies. In the meanetime, the Gentleman Usher recieves his bread, and tasteth to the Emperour, and afterward, having done his reverence, he depar-teth. Touching the rest of the dishes, because they were brought in out of order, our men can now report no certaintie.[13]

The 'mightie Cupboorde' for the display of the tsar's plate was called 'the Sovereign's'; three other sideboards accommodated the drinks, the food and the biscuits, bread and rolls.[14] These sideboards were the apex of a complex system of provisioning that will be described later.

There are many other accounts of formal dinners for embassies in the late sixteenth and early seventeenth centuries. The ostentatious display of precious plate, the numerous dishes and, especially from the turn of the century, the many varieties of drink were all intended to stress the wealth and power of the ruler. Most accounts by foreigners show that the intention was fulfilled, even though many commented on a lack of beauty and elegance in the setting; some were less than enthusiastic about the dishes served and others noted that the ceremonies sharply reduced the time available for eating. Not all were as impressed as the writer who recorded Sir Thomas Smith's mission in 1604:

Then the *Emperor* sent from his table by his noble servitors, to my lord and the kings Gent. 30. dishes of meate, and to each a loafe of extraordinary fine bread. Then followed a great number of straunge and rare dishes, some in

---

[13]Hakluyt, *Principall Navigations*, 286–7. Herberstein had given a similar account in 1549; see *Notes upon Russia*, vol. II, 126f.
[14]Zabelin, *Domashnii byt*, vol. II, 367–8.

15 The tsar' at table, sixteenth century. The tsar' dines at a separate table. This does not appear to be noticeably raised above the level of the tables at which other dignitaries are eating. In the centre of the room is a 'cupboard' of shelves which diminish in size as they ascend. This displays pots and other vessels. The object in the left foreground seems to be a heating stove decorated with tiles.

Silver, but most of massie gold: with boiled, baked and rosted, being piled up on one another by halfe dozens. To make you aperticular relation, I should do the entertainment wrong, consisting almost of innumerable dishes: Also, I should overcharge my memory, as then I did mine eyes and stomache . . .

For our drinkes, they consisted of many excellent kindes of *Meandes*, besides all sortes of Wine, and Beere. I assure you I had rather drinke to you a daily health in them, then make you long after their pleasantnesse, considering the colde and sower voyage you must undertake, before you tast of their vigor and sweetnesse.[15]

Jan Buczinski, secretary to False Dmitri I, invited Peyerle, a native of Augsburg, to Russia. The latter has left a description of a formal feast in 1606:

There were neither spoons nor plates on the tables; they first served vodka and exceedingly tasty white bread, then they served various dishes of food, mostly hashes, but badly cooked; among them was a huge pie filled with small fish;

[15] *Sir Thomas Smithes Voiage*, F. (ob.).

16 The tsar' at table, seventeenth century. The tsar' is placed at a table raised well above the other diners. Icons are on the wall above him; church dignitaries are on his left, laymen on his right. The 'cupboard' of shelves diminishing in size as they rise is now built round the central column.

the dishes were not served all at once, but one at a time: there were very many of them, but all tasteless, partly from an excessive amount of oil, partly from the honey which the Muscovites use instead of sugar. They also served numerous drinks, particularly various kinds of mead, a drink prepared from cherries, plums, grape juice and so on.[16]

Lev Sapieha, too, dined in the presence of the Emperor, but then, again, 'as for plates and napkins, they have never heard of them, the Emperor himself uses none; they eat very good fish, but badly served because it was in Lent when they eat no eggs, butter, nor any milk products'.[17] This report then elaborates on the sumptuousness of the tsar's table and the rituals associated with it. It stresses some of the deficiencies as regards condiments and other niceties: 'on these tables there is only bread, salt, vinegar and pepper, but no plates or napkins'.[18] Lack of individual plates meant that servings were small portions intended to be shared between neighbours close enough at table to manage with fingers. Plates, spoons and knives were, in fact, only

[16]Peyerle, in Ustryalov, *Skazaniya*, vol. II, 58–9.
[17]Margeret, *Estat*, 31.
[18]*Ibid.*, 31v.

provided for particularly honoured guests, mainly some western ambassadors.[19] Drinks, however, were abundant; Margeret mentions Spanish wine, vodka and various sorts of mead including mead 'made of pure honey, not strong, but as clear as spring water and very delicate'.[20]

Foreign visitors noted not only certain deficiencies they saw in the tsar's feasts, but also the tendency to rely on the number of dishes and of drinks to create an air of luxury. Samuil Maskiewicz, a Lithuanian gentleman who served with the Poles under Żółkiowski, was at a dinner given for the Hetman in September 1610. He commented:

The dishes were Russian; I did not like one of them, apart from the farinaceous dishes, which were similar to the French. There were other pasties, too. They served various meads, each time they served a new kind, to show how many there were in the Moscow State. Our people wanted to drink and asked them for as much as they liked to offer, but of one kind, not mixing one with another; the Muscovites did not agree and went on in their own way.[21]

Many accounts comment on the excellent qualities and several varieties of bread. According to an inventory evidently drawn up for the information of the Poles in 1610–13, for Easter Day the tsar' was served with four varieties of bread, thirty-six different fish dishes and a few others. On a meat day the tsar' was served five varieties of bread, followed by sixty-three dishes, the first of which was: '2 swans, and the swans were on top of 2 biscuits in which were 6 spoons of fine flour (*muki krupichatye*), 40 eggs, and in the sauce 2 spoons of brown sugar, the giblets of the two swans and on the swans, in the sauce and the swans giblets 30 zolotniks of saffron, and in the giblets 12 parts of beef'. The dishes included several loaves or cakes (*korovai*) which were made with sixty or forty eggs, sometimes with some filling such as cheese, eggs or fungi; at least ten pies, savoury and sweet; duck and hare; eleven dishes of mutton and sheep's liver and kidneys; three pork dishes; four beef dishes; as well as sausages, tripe and stomach from unspecified animals. Fish was poorly represented, presumably because fish days were so numerous that it was avoided when possible; only 'carp with meat' was mentioned. On the other hand, there were a dozen chicken dishes, three of which were soups; there was but one dish of the humble cabbage soup (now regarded as *the* national dish). The total of eggs used in preparing this one meal was 757.[22] Lest this should seem somewhat sumptuous, the list for Christmas ran to 130 items, apart from the initial varieties of bread,

[19]Zabelin, *Domashnii byt*, vol. II, 369.

[20]Margeret, *Estat*, 32.

[21]Maskiewicz, *Pamiętniki*, 52. Cp. the diary of the Polish ambassadors Olesnicki and Gasiewski in Ustryalov, *Skazaniya*, vol. II, 162.

[22]*AI*, II, 356, 429–31.

which were nibbled with vodka.[23] On St Philip's fast, after six varieties of bread, there were still fifty-one dishes, but all were fish or flour.[24] The number of portions might reach 500, though each was small. The reason for this was the custom of presentation (*podachi*) of food being sent after the feast not only to all who had been present, but to others whom the tsar' wished to honour with his grace and favour.[25] Such provisions were likely to be of superior quality to those available elsewhere.[26] Nevertheless, the ritual, as well as the social and economic, aspects of such gifts should not be overlooked.

The Emperor sends to each noble at home, and to all whom he favours, a dish of meat called Podatdh [i.e. *podacha*, a 'presentation'] and this is done not only at festivals, but once each day and is observed very strictly whatever happens. If the emperor is not inclined to feast an Ambassador, according to the custom of the country, after an audience the Emperor sends him to dine at his residence with the following ceremony. First, he sends him some chief gentleman in cloth of gold, his mantle and hat decorated with pearls; he rides on horseback before the dinner to announce the Emperor's graciousness to the Ambassador and also to keep him company at dinner. He has fifteen or twenty servants around his horse; two men walk behind him, each carrying a cloth rolled like a bale; two more follow carrying salt-cellars; then two with containers full of vinegar; then two others, one carrying two knives and the other two spoons, all richly decorated; the bread follows this, carried by six men, two by two; then follows the spirits and after this a dozen men each carrying a silver pot of about three *chopines* each [i.e. about 1¼ litres], full of various kinds of wine, mostly strong wine of Spain, the Canaries and other places; after these as many large cups of German work are carried; then follow the meats, that is, first, those that are eaten cold, then the boiled and the roast and, last, the pies; all these meats are carried on great silver plates, but if the Emperor favours the Ambassador, all the plate put on his table is of gold. After come eighteen or twenty large vessels, each carried by two men, full of various kinds of mead; then follow a dozen men carrying five or six large drinking cups; and, after everything else, two or three carts follow full of mead and beer for the commons; everything is carried by the musket-men who have been entrusted with this and who are very well-dressed. I have seen up to three or four hundred carry meats and drinks for a single dinner in the manner described and have seen three dinners sent to different Ambassadors in one day, some being sent more, some less, nevertheless, with the ceremony described above.[27]

---

[23] *Ibid.*, 434–8.
[24] *Ibid.*, 433–4.
[25] Zabelin, *Domashnii byt*, vol. II, 373.
[26] *Ibid.*, 738.
[27] Margeret, *Estat*, 32–3.

In 1601, at a time of famine, the daily allowance of food for an ambassador was generous.[28]

Daily: 2 rolls (*kalash*)
      2 1–denga loaves   The ambassador's gentlemen received 1 roll
                                 and 1 loaf each

Every two days:
      a heifer costing 60 kopeks
      4 sheep   each $7\frac{1}{2}$ kopeks
      9 chickens $2\frac{1}{2}$
      a side of ham   12
      200 eggs   10
      5 pounds of butter $1\frac{1}{2}$ each
      a bucket of sour cream   5
      $\frac{1}{4}$ pud (9 lb) of salt $2\frac{1}{2}$
      $\frac{1}{8}$ quarter of groats   4
      onions, garlic and cabbage   6 kopeks

The drink allowance was 5 cups (*charki*, i.e. one sixtieth of a bucket, about a third of a pint) of spirits a day, as well as quantities of wine and various meads.

It was not only western emissaries who had such allowances.[29] In 1644 an ambassador from the Khan of Bukhara arrived in Moscow with his brother, four servants of the Khan and five of the ambassador (there was also a messenger (*gonets*) who seems not to have been on a daily allowance). The daily allowances per person (apart from exceptional grants on arrival and departure in 1645) (a) before and (b) after having audience of the tsar' are shown in Table 4.1.[30] It is interesting that Muslims were granted an allowance including alcohol; perhaps it was intended for the Russian servants of the embassy or for resale.

Apart from such provisioning of embassies, which might be regarded as normal, sometimes extraordinary supplies of luxury foodstuffs were granted, at least in the later seventeenth century. When the Polish emissaries departed after the feast for them on 25 November 1667 they received an abundance of sugar and spices 'for the road' from the Fruit Store (*Ovoshchnaya palata*).[31] The items were conveyed to the emissaries' residence by an official of the Drinks Office. During their

[28] Zabelin, *Domashnii byt*, vol. II, 727.
[29] See Olearius, *Travels*, 96, for another example.
[30] Bukharskie dela, 1619–1743, list 5, cited in M. Yu. Yuldashev, *K istorii torgovykh i posad'skikh svyazei Srednei Azii s Rossiei v XVI–XVII vv.* (Taskent, 1964), 97–8. I am grateful to J.M. Rogers for this reference.
[31] See Table 4.2.

Table 4.1. *Allowances for Bukharan embassy*

	Ambassador (a)	Ambassador (b)	His brother (a)	His brother (b)	Servants of Khan (a)	Khan (b)	Ambassador (a)	Ambassador (b)
Money (kopeks)	$7\frac{1}{2}$	12	3	6	3	5	$2\frac{1}{2}$	3
Drink:								
spirits (cups)	4	5	2	3	2	3	1	2
mead (pots)	6	6		1		1		
beer (pots)	6	6	$3\frac{2}{5}$	2	$3\frac{2}{5}$	1	1	1

stay in Moscow they had received quite considerable additional quantities of spices. (See Table 4.2.)[32]

The 'loafe of extraordinary fine bread' served Sir Thomas Smithe, like the fine bread commented on by so many other visitors, was a roll (*kalach*) made of wheat flour. In the late seventeenth century this bread was evidently baked for the court in the form of rolls, about 4 to 7 feet (1.2 to 2.1 m) in length (the length of a Russian stove) and 6 or 7 inches (152 or 177 mm) across. They were probably cut into pieces the size of the usual individual roll.[33] Salt (as well as pepper and vinegar) was provided for every four persons at a feast.[34] Three set phrases were used by the tsar' to invite guests to dine with him; one of them gave the Russian word for hospitality its literal meaning: 'you will now eat bread and salt with me'.[35] Herberstein had noted in the early sixteenth century that 'bread is used by the prince to express his favour towards anybody, but when he sends salt, it is intended to express his affection – indeed it is not possible for him to show greater honour to anyone at an entertainment given by himself, than by sending him salt from his own table'.[36] The custom of sending salt to express affection, however, seems to be absent in the accounts of seventeenth century visitors; could this be owing to lack of observation on their part, or lack of affection on the part of the tsar', or perhaps to an increased stress on specifically Christian elements in the ceremonial?

The church calendar sharply differentiated between fast days and others; this was the main constraint on the food available at the tsar's

[32]Zabelin, *Domashnii byt*, vol. II, 405–6.
[33]Kotošixin, *O Rossii*, fol. 26v.; Zabelin, *Domashnii byt*, vol. II, 32. The size of rolls was supposed to vary with the price of grain; see pp. 129f below.
[34]Zabelin, *Domashnii byt*, vol. II, 369.
[35]Zabelin, *Domashnii byt*, vol. II, 365.
[36]Herberstein, *Notes upon Russia*, vol. II, 128.

Table 4.2. Allocations to Polish embassy (1667)

	amounts (pounds) distributed: (a) after a feast					(b) during their stay	(c) Total
	Benevskii	refendarius	crown undergroom	gentlemen	(5 persons)		
Loaf sugar	20	20	12	1		83¾	136
Cinnamon						15 }	20
Chinese	1	1	½				
German	1	1	½				
Saffron	1	1	1			15	18
Muscat nuts	1	1	1			10	13
Cloves	1	1	1			15	18
Muscat colour	1	1	1			15	18
Cardamon	1	1	1	½	2½	10	16
Dry ginger	1	1	1	½	2½	15	21
Pepper	3	3	3	1	5	80	95
Anis	5	5	4	2	10		26
Rice	5	5	4	2	10	40	66
Raisins	3	3	2	1	5	2	16
Figs	3	3	2	1	5	40	54
Currants	3	3	2	1	5	40	54
Prunes	3	3	2	1	5	40	54
Almonds						20	20
Dried pears						20	20
Caraway, German						10	10

Source: Zabelin, Domashnii byt, vol. II: 405–6.

table. It determined the nature of the foods to be served, but probably had less effect on the quantities, except in the case of those fasts which were more strictly observed. In the late seventeenth century the ritual was evidently quite severe.

Meat dishes are prepared for the tsar's table and for distribution on Sunday, Tuesday, Thursday and Saturday. On the fast days, Monday, Wednesday and Friday, and during fasts, fish dishes and pies are made for the tsar's table with olive, nut, linseed or hemp oil; in Lent and the Assumption Fast the dishes prepared are raw and cooked cabbage, gilled fungi (*gruzdi*), raw and cooked milk-caps in brine and berry dishes, without oil, except for the Day of the Annunciation. The tsar eats once a day on those fasts, on Sunday, Tuesday, Thursday and Saturday, and drinks kvas; but on Monday, Wednesday and Friday during all fasts he eats and drinks nothing, save for his, the tsaritsa's and his children's name-day. When the hierarchs and boyars are at the tsar's table on a festival, on those fast days they are served the same dishes as the tsar. Similarly, when the tsar has ambassadors, emissaries and messengers of other states arriving or departing on the fast days or during fasts, they are sent fast dishes, fish and pies with oil, with the tsar's table [i.e. dishes from his table]; but the daily ration is given them during fasts and on the fast days, not in accordance with the fasts, but meat and fish as is ordered . . . And during those two fasts, apart from Sundays and Saturdays, when the tsar and the tsaritsa do not eat, presentations of food are not sent to any of the boyars and those close to the tsar.[37]

The ceremonial of the tsar's feasts and the presentations of food to embassies was of such importance that they took place even during the famine of 1601–3.[38] Apart from the regular supply of food allowances for ambassadors already mentioned, there are presentations of food, such as that sent to Boris Godunov's intended son-in-law, a Danish nobleman, in September 1602: 'a hundred heavy gold dishes with foodstuffs, numerous goblets and cups with wines and meads'.[39] Yet, when the young man was to be met by the tsar's military commander at Ivangorod on the journey to Moscow, the latter had written that the post-horse men had grown thin from the dearth and their horses had been lost.[40]

The ostentatious display of abundance even in time of famine, however, should not deflect us from considering some of the wider implications of provisioning the court. The organisation of its supplies, their treatment and distribution were complex and affected not only the court, those with whom it had diplomatic relations and its servants;

---

[37]Kotošixin, *O Rossii*, fol. 117–18.

[38]*Razryadnaya kniga 1559–1605*, 338 (6 July 1602), 348 (10 October 1602), 350 (1 September 1603), 352 (2 February 1604).

[39]Karamzin, *Istoriya*, vol. XI, 50; *Razryadnaya kniga 1559–1605*, 346–7.

[40]Solov'ev, *Istoriya*, vol. IV, 400.

such matters had a wider impact on some parts of the country and certain aspects of the economy.

The four sideboards or cupboards at the tsar's feasts were physical representations of the organisational structure involved in provisioning the court with food and drink. The sovereign's sideboard with its display of precious plate represented the palace administration, formally dealt with by the Department of the Great Palace (*Prikaz Bol'-shogo Dvortsa*). The other three had more immediately functional purposes, as has been mentioned above, but they also represented the three establishments subordinate to the Department of the Great Palace and responsible for drinks, for foodstuffs and for bread. These were simply known as establishments or offices (*dvory*). A detailed description of the organisation and its responsibilities was given by Kotoshikhin in the 1660s, but the main structure had existed for long before that. It is perhaps noteworthy that Kotoshikhin's chapter on the tsar's offices lists six; of these, only the treasury and the stables were not directly concerned with food or drink.

The Department of the Great Palace was headed by a boyar, a butler, a chamberlain and a member of the council, with two or three clerks; the boyar was second in rank only to the tsar's groom, the greatest officer after the tsar'.

The men of the artisan quarter of more than 40 towns are administered as regards tax liability and dues in that Department and the farms and imposts on oath each year from drink-shops and customs, from waters, mills and fisheries; the crown's dues in grain and money and all kinds of dues and hay from those villages and volosts, and the farm of fishing and other appurtenances, and the farm of ferries and bridge tolls, in money; the trading and handicraft people of Moscow free settlements, eight settlements: cauldron-makers, pewter-smiths, blacksmiths, carpenters, fishermen, tent-makers, potters and stove-builders and brick-men, and they are liable to the same dues as other men of the artisan quarter and are to work on anything to be done at the tsar's court without money payment.[41]

Apart from other dues, the money income from this group was given as 120,000 rubles a year. Also, the Department had 2,000 rubles from duties on sealing documents and 3,000 from certain dues on the rivers Moskva and Yauza. A total of 125,000 rubles was thus reckoned to be available; it was used for church-building, for charity and 'for all sorts of palace expenditures and for the purchase of palace provisions', as well as for the maintenance of certain retainers (musicians, messengers

[41]Kotošixin, *O Rossii*, fol. 128–9.

etc.).[42] Unfortunately, we do not know what proportion was spent on provisions; it seems likely that most of it was.

The Drinks Office (*Sytyannoi dvor*) had a staff of five officials who were in charge of more than thirty cellars, 'apart from the cellar with overseas drinks'.[43] All drinks in the cellars stood on ice which was only changed in March each year. Under these officers were twelve cupbearers (*charoshniki*), about forty scriveners (who were responsible for the distribution of drink and had to account for the silver, copper, pewter and wood vessels used), and fifty drink-men (*sytniki*) (who carted the vessels with drink and also acted as candle-bearers). There were also 200 other men: distillers, brewers, watchmen and coopers who 'distil spirits, brew beer make mead and the vessels and go through the cellars decanting and pouring off the drink'.[44]

Each day the expenditure of drink, apart from that taken for the tsar and tsaritsa, their sons and daughters, is close to 300 buckets [about 825 gallons] of simple spirits, spirits with poppy and double- and triple-distilled; 400 and 500 buckets [about 1,100 and 1,375 gallons] of beer and mead; if at any time there is insufficient mead, spirits [wine?] is given in accordance with the account.[45]

On feasts, name-days or birthdays, the amount might reach four or five hundred buckets of spirits and two or three thousand buckets of beer and mead. Flavoured, raspberry and other beers and honey-water, fine berry and apple meads, and 'Romanee, Rhine, French and other overseas wines go to whomever is indicated, daily and weekly. But it is not possible to record what goes on the tsar's expenditure.'[46] A generation later, in 1697–8 the main state expenditures were on the court and the royal family; 6,000 rubles were spent at Archangel on imported wines and spices.[47] In 1700, the Drinks Office supplied Peter I with 2,113 buckets, 11 pots, 10 cups.[48] The drinks were distributed to

. . . ambassadors, emissaries, messengers and embassy people on a daily basis, as ordered; to the Greeks and Greek hierarchs and the Kizilbash [i.e. Persian] merchants; to the high officers of the tsar, the tsaritsa and their children living at the court; daily to the tsar's handicraft people of all ranks; and daily to the Don and Cherkas Zaporozh'e cossacks; also when there are festivals and the tsar has meals for rulers and boyars and whoever eats at his table; also on

[42] *Ibid.*, fol. 129v.
[43] *Ibid.*, fol. 108–11.
[44] *Ibid.*, fol. 111, 109v.
[45] *Ibid.*, fol. 110–110v.
[46] *Ibid.*, fol. 110v.
[47] P.N. Petrov, *ZORSA*, IV (1887), 335, 338.
[48] Zabelin, *Domashnii byt*, vol. II, 715.

festivals for the priests and deacons of the tsar's churches, cathedral and ordinary, and for the musket-men, as ordered.[49]

All these expenditures had to be diligently recorded and the authorising memoranda checked against the record books 'so that there is no cheating'.

The raw materials required to produce the range of domestic drinks consumed came from a variety of sources.[50] Malt was supplied from the tsar's granaries administered by the Grain Office (*Zhitennoi dvor*), but hops, perhaps because they were wild, were bought from market stalls. Raspberries, black currants, stone-brambles, strawberries and bird-cherries were obtained from peasants on crown estates near Moscow. Apples, cherries, pears and plums came from the tsar's orchards in Moscow and in villages. Spirits to the value of 30,000 rubles a year were distilled by contractors – trading people and drink-shop farmers – who were given advances against sureties. Since the fixed price was 8 altyns a bucket, this implies a total of 125,000 buckets (more than 340,000 gallons). Failure to supply resulted in confiscation of the contractor's home and property and beating with the knout. Other spirits were distilled in the Pharmacy Department (which also produced oils, soap and preparations from spices); Romanee wine was sometimes used as the raw material.[51]

Imported wines were bought, from the customs and drink-shop incomes, in Archangel. An instruction of 1649, for example, ordered the purchase of 5, 6 and 9 barrels of different qualities of Romanee; 3 barrels of white and 3 of red Baster (a Canary wine); 2 barrels of Alicante; 2 of Rhenish; 10 of French 'best'; a barrel of Malmsey; a barrel of white and a barrel of red Muscat; 2 of Canary (*kinarei*) 'best' and 10 of 'good church wine'.[52] The concern for such imports was shown a few years after Kotoshikhin wrote his account of Russia when the tsar' ordered 'the immediate despatch of sheepskins, felt and matting and ropes, so as to bring safe to Moscow before the big frosts' his Frankish wines and spices.[53] A report from Archangel the following year mentions Romanee, Rhine and Alicante wines.[54]

The Food Office (*Kormovoi Dvorets*) had three officials as well as about 20 scriveners and 15 junior cellarers. The provisions of meat and

[49]Kotošixin, *O Rossii*, fol. 109v.–10.
[50]*Ibid.*, fol. 111–12.
[51]*AI*, III, 291 (vi) (1645).
[52]*DAI*, III, no. 55 (June 1649).
[53]*DAI*, v; no. 98 (3 October 1669).
[54]*DAI*, vi, 18 (I) (21 September 1670); items (II)–(v) mention the same wines. See also p. 123 above.

fish, both fresh and salt, were stored in 15 ice-cellars or in dry stores.[55] There were more than 150 master cooks, under-masters and apprentices, dishwashers, water-carriers and watchmen. They were equipped with silver, pewter, copper, wood and iron vessels. The general responsibilities were similar to those already described for the Drinks Office. The dishes for each day for the tsar's table, for the members of his family, for those living in the palace, for those spending the day or the night there, for guests (including embassies), the presentations of food for boyars, members of the council and others around the tsar', for the court servants, priests, deacons, musket-men and handicraft workers, all had to be recorded and distributed 'according to the registers and the annual lists'.[56] The presentations of food evidently did not always reach the intended recipient and disputes resulted from such offences to honour which sometimes led to physical punishment or imprisonment.

'Each day more than 3,000 items are distributed for the tsar and the tsaritsa, their children and as presentations to boyars, apart from the other expenditures mentioned above and birthdays and festivals.'[57]

Contractors undertake to supply at the Palace, like the spirits contractors, all sorts of foodstuffs for the tsar's table and for distribution, meat on the hoof and all sorts of slaughtered animals, all sorts of live and dead birds, cheese, eggs and butter, linseed, hemp and olive oil, buckwheat and millet groats and other suitable supplies to the value of 30 or 40 thousand rubles or more, apart from what comes from the crown volosts and peasants.[58]

Close to Moscow, and in some nearby villages, there were also dairy farms supplying soured cream, milk, cheese and butter. That near Moscow had 200 cows. If there were any deficiencies, supplies were bought by the treasury in the market stalls. Other supplies were purchased in Archangel and from Germans in Moscow.

Stocks of fish are brought, summer and winter, from the towns down the Volga, from Nizhnii Novgorod, Kazan', Astrakhan' and from Terek, from the tsar's fisheries; they sell what remains after the tsar's expenditure of any fish supplies. The fish supplies brought from down the Volga are: large, medium and small salt beluga and sturgeon; beluga and sturgeon steaks brined in barrels; dry and cured beluga and sturgeon back and belly; barrels of brined sterlet; ling roes, livers of beluga and sturgeon (*ksenimaksy*); beluga and sturgeon caviare, granular and pressed in cheeses; sturgeon gristle, cured russnase in wands. About 400 barrels a year of fish supplies come from Great Novgo-

[55]Kotošixin, *O Rossii*, fol. 112–16v.
[56]*Ibid.*, fol. 112v.
[57]*Ibid.*, fol. 114v.–15.
[58]*Ibid.*, fol. 115.

rod and from Ladoga, of whitefish, Ladoga whitefish (*lodoga*) and white fish
roe. About 200,000 puds a year of sea trout and salmon from Vologda,
Archangel and the Kola strong-point. It is reckoned that of those fish supplies
the yearly expenditure for the tsar's table amounts to more than a hundred
thousand rubles at the selling prices in trade. Live fish for the tsar's table is kept
in nurseries at Moscow in rivers and ponds; the live fish are sturgeon, russnase,
sterlet, salmon, pike, bream, pike-perch, perch and every other sort of good
ones fit to set before the tsar. The crown fishermen and tax-liable people catch
the best fish in the Volga and others in rivers and lakes.[59]

Fish, however, was also bought from tradesmen. In 1624, for example, a trader from Kazan' brought 1,805 beluga and sturgeon and 140
small ones (counted as 70 full-sized ones), 150 stellate sturgeon, and 300
sides and bellies.[60] From Nizhnii Novgorod 40 barrels of large mesh
caviare (*okhan*), 20 puds of soft roes and 1½ puds of isinglass were
bought.[61] The expenditure there on fish in fifteen of the years between
1648 and 1670 was more than 62,000 rubles; in 1653 alone the amount
was more than 6,000.[62] Fish was also bought in Pskov, a region famous
for its delicious smelts.[63] Arrangements had to be made for the transport
of fish. In 1680, for example, the results of the spring fishing with bait in
Astrakhan' required seventy-one teams with sacks and ropes and each
team was to have its own teamster.[64] Live fish, of course, were a greater
problem and required special equipment. They were brought from
Beloozero in perforated boats (*strugi*) to stock the tsar's ponds in Dmitrov; fresh fish went to Moscow, but any torpid ones were salted and the
small ones were given to the fishermen.[65] An acknowledgement for a
similar consignment from the Sheksna noted 564 sterlet (and 6 pike)
caught, gave the number of each size, but noted only 558 sterlet received
alive at the Dmitrov ponds. Six sterlet and six pike were received
salted.[66] At about this time the stores at the Beloozero fishery included
112 puds of salt, 104 vats, 19 perforated boats, 9 sets of hempen gear, 4
reams of paper, 3 puds of candles, 200 mats, 117 bast ropes, a steelyard
and iron weights.[67] In 1677 8 salmon 'scattered with ice' were despatched to the tsar'; the pass given the carrier ordered him 'to travel the
road in haste, day and night and to dally nowhere, not for an hour'.[68]

[59]*Ibid.*, fol. 115v.–16v.
[60]*DAI*, II, 53 (12 March 1624).
[61]*DAI*, VI, 60 (I) (31 August 1672). Cp. (II) and *Ibid.*, X, 38 (I) (6 September 1682).
[62]*DAI*, VI, 60 (III).
[63]*DAI*, X, 38 (II) (1 December 1682).
[64]*DAI*, IX, 75.
[65]*DAI*, VI, 108 (28 May 1674).
[66]*DAI*, X, 38 (II) (29 May 1688).
[67]*DAI*, XI, 23 (after March 1684).
[68]*DAI*, VII, no. 59.

Other delicate and perishable foodstuffs were also given special attention as regards transport. A report from Astrakhan' detailed 2 barrels of black grapes, 120 bunches in 2 tubs, and 1 of white with 70 bunches; these were in syrop. In addition, 150 bunches of black grapes were sent 'not in syrop' and 300 water melons. To protect the fruit from frosts – the journey upstream must have taken them well into the autumn – there were felts and sheepskins. The men had been instructed 'to go in haste, day and night, so as to reach Moscow before the frosts'.[69]

The Bread Office (*Khlebennoi dvor*) was smaller than the other sub-departments of the palace organisation. It had a cellarer, two scriveners and about twenty junior cellarers and fifty master bakers, of loaves, rolls and pies, and watchmen. It evidently had some functions other than the baking and distribution of its products in the late seventeenth century: 'a Department has been instituted with that cellarer to note the receipt and expenditure of bread supplies and for investigation and decision'.[70] The supplies of rye and wheat came from the Grain Office. The flour was made at the tsar's mills in Moscow and in villages. Apparently, the bakery items produced, loaves and rolls, were made without salt, 'not because they grudge the salt, but because that is the form'.[71] This means that salt was placed on top of these items in the traditional ceremony of hospitality.

The Grain Office, too, was subordinate to the Department of the Great Palace. It had about 300 granaries in which to store the grain it received from three sources: the tsar's crown villages; the towns down the Volga, and the fields which were sown for the tsar'.[72] Kotoshikhin gives little other information about this office. There was, however, also a Bread Grains Department (*Khlebnoi Prikaz*); this had an officer and a clerk and an income from the towns, volosts and villages allocated to it of 20,000 rubles a year. This office was responsible for the lands tilled for the tsar' in its areas (i.e. the third source of the grain received by the Grain Office).[73]

Overall, then, the organisation within the palace concerned with food and drink for the tsar's table had a staff of a dozen or so officers, some of very high rank, and 600 or more men dealing with the receipt, storing, preparation and distribution of the provisions. These figures do not include hundreds of other servants, guards and other attendants

[69] *AI*, IV, 133 (15 August 1658). See also *DAI*, IV, 60 (1659–60) and *AI*, V, 131 (1658).
[70] Kotošixin, *O Rossii*, fol. 116v.
[71] *Ibid.*, fol. 117.
[72] *Ibid.*, fol. 118v.–19.
[73] *Ibid.*, fol. 161v.

who were used as extras on ceremonial occasions. Supplies were obtained from all parts of Russia, from Archangel in the north to Astrakhan' in the south, from Pskov in the west to Kazan' in the east; they came from crown estates, as the result of labour rents, as rents in kind and by purchase. They involved provision of special transport facilities. Purchases were made from market stalls outside the Kremlin walls and from international traders in Moscow and Archangel. Imports came from as far away as the Canary Islands (circumnavigating Scandinavia to reach Moscow), Central Asia and India. Large quantities of grain were regularly allocated as pay to the palace servants, and given to the tsar's attendants and the military in Moscow; embassies received many costly imported spices. Thus, in modern terms, the palace was not only a consumer of victuals; it was also a distributor and even, to some extent, a producer. It generated a demand which had an impact, the scale of which is unknown, both at home and abroad.

The presentations of food and drink had both economic and honorific aspects and these were of differing importance at different social levels. The economic aspect was not the same as our present-day use of the term based on a developed market with commodities and established prices readily available for virtually every item of our daily existence. The provisions supplied, at least those to the boyars and others close to the tsar', were not all readily available on the market; yet, even if they could have been ascribed a price, the recipients regarded them not as part, or in lieu, of a salary, but as an honouring gift. The honorific aspect was felt to be of crucial importance, as can be seen from the nature of the disputes that arose. The gift helped to define status and reinforce allegiances between ruler and noble. Those attendant on the court were not being paid in kind; they were servitors by birth (*sluzhilye po otechestvu*), distinct even from the servitors by choice (*po priboru*), let alone the mass of the dependent, tax-liable (*tyaglye*) population who were bound to perform whatever tasks were imposed on them. For the boyars and others in the first category the ritual importance of eating and drinking together, physically or symbolically, or from the same dish was a bond strengthened by the meanings attached to bread and salt. The grain given 'to all ranks of palace people and junior clerks', to 'distillers and watchmen, cooks, bakers and other ranks' was not a presentation, but a grant (*zhalovanie*).[74] In this case comparable grain was available on the market and the economic aspect of the transaction was more to the fore; the grain was pay in kind. Moreover, at the rate of 15 or 20 chets each a year, the total for

[74] *Ibid.*, fol. 117.

this allowance alone would have amounted to about 850 or 1,150 tons, large enough to have made an appreciable impact on the market.[75]

On certain exceptional occasions food and drink were distributed by the crown on a wider scale in Moscow to the population in general. At the coronation of Boris Godunov in 1599, as we have already seen, mead and beer were provided for the people as part of the general celebrations.[76] Probably such donations to the general populace of Moscow were normally to be expected whenever such joyful occasions presented themselves, perhaps especially when it was advisable to gain as much popular support as possible. Of course there might be quite different circumstances inducing the distribution of charity.

On a less happy occasion, two years later Boris distributed money and grain during the famine. Famine conditions probably stimulated, but did not initiate, legislation on the weight and price of bread.

Formerly in this country they paid no heed to weight when bread was baked; only [during the famine] was a decree issued on weight and the price of bread determined. Then the bakers, to increase its weight, baked it so that it was half water, so the situation became worse than before. Although some were severely punished, this did not help. The famine and people's wants and bitterness were too great.[77]

This view, however, is not entirely accurate. There had evidently been some control of bread during the reign of Fedor Ivanovich (1584–98) when weight schedules (*izvest'ki*) had been issued, allegedly, annually.[78] This pre-famine attempt to control bread prices in Moscow was referred to by the Land Office (*Zemskoi prikaz*) when the bakers made a complaint in 1631. The tradition had evidently survived both the famine and the Time of Troubles, but it is not confirmed by other evidence; however, Fedor Ivanovich was responsible for much building in Moscow, including 'merchants' chambers for the satisfaction and supply of traders', so there may have been some basis for it.[79] The earliest schedule of an Assize of Bread, however, seems to be that for 1619, when the Romanovs were ruling and engaged in supervising the recovery and reorganisation of the country. On 25 May 1619 Foma Durov and the clerk Vasilii Martem'yanov, in accordance with a decree of the tsar' issued with the boyars' assent, submitted to the Land Office a schedule of their weighing of bread and rolls, 'how many grivenkas weight in loaves of bolted and coarse flour and in rolls, and how much maintenance go on

---

[75] *Ibid.*
[76] Massa, *Skazaniya*, 65.
[77] Massa, *Skazaniya*, 81.
[78] *Ukaz o khlebnom i kolachnom vesu*, 54, 55.
[79] *PSRL*, 14, 1, 7.

loaves and on rolls'.[80] The amounts for maintenance were the same as those later given in a memorandum of 30 November 1623, but also included details for loaves from coarse flour; the latter amounts were less because there was no allowance for salt, bolting or 'candles and broom'.[81] The two officials had five representatives altogether to assist them and verify their findings, two from the merchant guilds and three from the localities, the 'black' hundreds. The decree, however, specified that four men on oath a year were to be chosen from the local hundreds and supplied by the Land Office, the department which dealt with the running of Moscow.

In 1623 two town stewards (*gorodovye prikashchiki*), their fellows and an unspecified number of men on oath were instructed to ensure that loaves and rolls conformed to a schedule with which they were supplied; this was presumably the schedule drawn up by Foma Durov in 1619. In fact, it seems probable that the 1619 schedule continued in use until the crisis of 1626.

In a document dated 11 March 1626 the tsar' ordered Nemir Fedorovich Kireevskii and the junior clerk Isak Levont'ev 'to deal with bread matters at Moscow'; this was the standard phrase used for the following years. The department people of the Land Office (*Zemskoi dvor*) and the Great Income (*Bol'shoi prikhod*) were to ensure that loaves and rolls were sold at the correct price throughout Moscow.[82] The reason given was that, through the oversights and blunders of these administrators, 'the Moscow bakers make loaves and rolls for sale which are small for their price and sell them dishonestly, thereby imposing burdens and losses on junior and all sorts of people'.[83] The bread officials were to be supplied by the Land Office with men on oath and with lists of the bakers and traders in bread; they were to buy a quarter each of wheat flour and of bolted and of coarse flour, weigh them (the *chetvert'* was a measure of capacity) and get the bakers to make rolls and loaves of various sizes from them; then they had to estimate the maintenance costs and compare their results from the former schedule supplied with the memorandum of instruction. The results, which were expected to increase the size of rolls and loaves, were to be communicated to the bakers and traders who were to be summoned to the officials' house. Offenders were to be fined and the records and money were to be taken to the clerk at the Military Office (*Razryad*) who was also to be

[80]*Ukaz o khlebnom i kolachnom vesu*, 30.
[81]The 1623 memorandum is translated in Smith, *Peasant Farming*, 256f. *Ukaz*, 35, 44; the 1619 additions are correct, unlike one given in 1623.
[82]*Ukaz o khlebnom i kolachnom vesu*, 8.
[83]*Ibid.*

given a copy of the new schedule.[84] The memorandum to the Land Office authorising the necessary measures was issued two days later and evoked the swift response that the office had no such lists of bakers and roll-makers, nor $2\frac{1}{2}$ pud, pud and $\frac{1}{2}$ pud weights; the weights smaller than half a pud and the men on oath were supplied. Two months later, in May, these ten representatives complained in a petition that they had been kept for more than two months instead of seven to ten days as with former representatives concerned with weighing bread and rolls.[85] This raised the question of why there were ten, not four, representatives; there were also four additional men to carry the scales and small weights. Five representatives and two men carrying scales worked alternative days.[86] This petition was dated only ten days after a fire in Kitaigorod, an area which included the main market, and in the Kremlin, when 'the palace, all the departments and churches were burnt'.[87] This no doubt exacerbated the existing problems of administration and the bakers may have counted on the old schedules being destroyed in the burning of the Departments.

The matter dragged on throughout the summer of 1626; the tsar' called for a report and the Land Office searched its records and produced the documents from Foma Durov's period in office.[88] The bakers complained that it was no longer possible to work to the weights established by Nemir and Isak; the costs allowed had been too small: 'how we, your orphans, are to be fed and to fulfil our tax liabilities to you, the sovereign, that has not been disclosed . . . The weights were established by the altyn [i.e. 6 dengas], but now they weigh your orphans to a denga or a kopek [2 dengas]; formerly, lord, they did not weigh us to five dengas . . . [lacuna]'.[89] Nemir was accused of weighing the flour with chaff and everything else included; whereas the loaves and rolls were supposed to be taken to the weigh-house and a report then made to the tsar', he had failed to do this; the bakers claimed to have been waiting ten weeks for some action on their complaint and asked for another gentleman to replace Nemir. In October the tsar' was still calling for a report on the matter.[90]

At some stage a confrontation was arranged between Nemir and the bakers. Nemir declared he was being slandered. It seems possible that this may have been so. The bakers asserted that formerly men of the

[84] *Ibid.*, 8–11.
[85] *Ibid.*, 12–13.
[86] See also *ibid.*, 36, 49, 50, 53, on staff numbers and problems.
[87] Tatishchev, *Istoriya*, vol. VII, 167 (3 May 1626).
[88] *Ukaz*, 33, 29–30, 44–5.
[89] *Ibid.*, 31.
[90] *Ibid.*, 32.

'merchant and cloth guilds and trading people of other hundreds' had been involved in the weighing, but Nemir had only had men on oath from the 'black' hundreds; it would be reasonable to expect that the former would favour high prices, the latter, as consumers, low ones.[91] Evidently in the summer of 1627 the bakers complained, possibly a second time, but this is not clear.[92] They pointed out that Foma Durov's schedule (in 1619) had been established with the help of trading people, but that Nemir had weighed the loaves and rolls in winter with the help of men on oath from the 'black' hundreds; costs had been cut as a result. They were obliged to bake without profit and at a loss 'fearing your, the sovereign's, anger; and because of this many of our brethren have stopped baking loaves and rolls'. The reference to weighing in winter was explained in a subsequent document:

Formerly Nemir Kireevskii weighed rolls and loaves in winter, and winter weighing is more advantageous in weight than summer because the flour in the bin is chilled (*vyzebaet*) and settles in the measure; but now they bring hot flour from the mills and the flour stands in a heap in the measure and it is a loss in rolls and bread compared with the winter one.[93]

Nemir himself, on several occasions during 1627, pleaded to be allowed to retire and indeed claimed that this retirement had been authorised on 13 July 1627.[94] His final appeal pointed out that he had served since 1626 till the time of writing, evidently the summer of 1627. It went on:

Lord, formerly many of my brethren dealt with your, the sovereign's, affair for two or three weeks; but, lord, in the present year since Easter week 1628 [*sc* 1627] till now I, your slave, lie sick on my death bed and old age has seized me, your slave, and my eyes see little; I am near to death, ending my life in sickness . . . Tsar', please have mercy!

On 13 August 1627 the tsar' ordered Nemir's release from his duties; we do not know whether he was, in fact, released other than by death.

The names of thirty-four gentlemen, including both Foma Durov and also Timofei Iskanskoi (who was appointed to deal with bread on 25 April 1628), were noted as being 'in place of Nemir'.[95] Yet Timofei Iskanskoi was 'to take from Nemir Kireevskii the tsar's instruction . . . and from Nemir Kireevskii the itemised schedule of weights of bread and rolls.'[96] Moreover, like the gentleman listed, he was 'in place of

---

[91] *Ibid.*, 33.
[92] *Ibid.*, 41–2.
[93] *Ibid.*, 58 (14 July 1631).
[94] *Ibid.*, 38–40.
[95] *Ibid.*, 46, 40–1.
[96] *Ibid.*, 46.

Nemir'; the chronology, then, is obscure. What appears to have happened is that Timofei Iskanskoi served from 1628 to 1631; in February 1631 Gavrilo Fedorovich L'vov replaced him.[97] Shortly after that the bakers made another complaint, claiming that they were unable to keep to the weights established in 1626 for the curious reason that 'the price of grain is not the same from year to year' and because Gavrilo had not made any test weighings.[98] Gavrilo, for his part, said he had not been allocated a clerk or any trusted men. When he was given the men required, and weighed 'in the second week of St Peter's fast' and made cost estimates, he allegedly failed to allow the bakers anything for labour and taxes in their costs; he dragged the matter out and did not take the loaves and rolls baked for the test to the Military Office and the Great Customs House. Furthermore, the clerk made an error in writing up his report, which Gavrilo overlooked.[99] Probably for this reason, on 15 August 1631 he was replaced by Grigorii Ivanovich Svin'in and the junior clerk Ivan Protasov.[100]

It therefore appears that towards the end of the sixteenth century an attempt was made to establish bread prices in Moscow. The famine created a situation very favourable to speculation and had to be met by donations from the tsar's stores.[101] From 1619 the evidence is more precise and makes clear that regulation of bread prices became a regular feature of Moscow life, even though there were conflicts of interest between bakers and consumers, and the administrative system was flawed. The fact that, apart from the tsar', a number of central institutions were involved, the Land Office, the Military Office, the Great Income and the Customs, is important; it shows the extent of concern with conditions in Moscow. There appears to be no evidence at all that similar control of weight and price was even attempted elsewhere. It almost looks as if the Moscow market was treated as an extension of the tsar's table: the Land Office signals the presence of Moscow itself, but the Military Office, which played an important part in organising the court servitors and servants, appears to have been the department mainly responsible for this attempt at regulating a primary foodstuff in the capital.

The seventeenth century saw much effort devoted to regulating drink. This was not limited to Moscow, though Moscow practice

---

[97] *Ibid.*, 51.
[98] *Ibid.*, 54–5.
[99] *Ibid.*, 56–7.
[100] *Ibid.*, 58–9. We have already seen that in 1638 grain-based trades formed a considerable part of those then recorded (Ch. 1).
[101] See p. 129 above.

played a special part; it was state-wide largely because alcohol was a major source of state income, but also because the advent of spirits on a fairly wide scale and as a commodity led to problems of anti-social behaviour, partly real and partly imagined. Throughout the seventeenth century there was concern over drinking, the disturbances that were associated with it and all sorts of 'criminal activity' ranging from dicing and cards to suspected plots against the crown. There was concern, too, about non-Christian traditions and rituals which involved drinking and the eating of ritual foods. Laws were made and the church proposed reforms, but the Romanov state concern for income and against any centres of potential opposition was the dominant factor in the situation.

As early as at the time of the famine in 1601, Boris Godunov had tried to prohibit the production of alcoholic drinks from grain; this was, of course, an extraordinary measure in exceptional circumstances. The charter on this sent to Sol' Vychegda specifically refers to the distillation of spirits.

Moreover, we formerly wrote you that at the artisan quarter of Sol' Vychegda and throughout Usol'e uezd, both the archiepiscopal and monastic servants, peasants and all sorts of people should not distill any spirits on their own (*odnolichno*) by any means and not hold vessels for spirits by them; and you were ordered to send round men on oath from the artisan quarter, from Sol' Vychegda, throughout Usol'e uezd to the stans and volosts and they were to be ordered to search out diligently in accordance with our decree on illicit drink and henceforth institute a firm prohibition so that at the artisan quarter at Sol' Vychegda and in the whole Usol'e uezd drink for sale was held nowhere; and you on your own, in accordance with the former and with this our charter, at the artisan quarter at Sol' Vychegda, and peasants and all sorts of people in the whole Usol'e uezd, in the stans and volosts, should not make beers and spirits. But if anyone has to brew not too much beer for great need, for great festivals, for the memory of their parents, for a birth or a wedding, [let them], but with great care, so that there is no excessive expenditure of much grain on their intoxicating drink.[102]

This not only stresses the continuing importance attached to ritual feasts, which the tsar' was forced to recognise, even, or perhaps especially, in famine conditions, but also hints at the association between salt production and vodka consumption we have already noted. Furthermore, it shows that the state had not yet established effective control over the production of alcohol, or even of spirits which were evidently quite widespread in some areas before the Poles had captured Moscow.

[102]*LZAK*, IX, section 3, II, 55–60 (3 November 1601).

17 A market, sixteenth century. The miniature shows a market with open-air stalls, stores, barrels, animals and carts.

In general, the mass of the people continued whenever possible to brew and drink their domestic mead or beer, as they had done for many centuries. A monastery regulation of 1602 still laid down that

If any peasant has an ale, a declaration is to be made and the payment is a denga a quarter of beer. But if any peasant has an ale and makes no declaration, he is liable to a fine of two rubles to be paid to the monastery. And they are to be ordered to drink quietly, so there shall be no fighting and violence and no criminal activity whatsoever.[103]

Quiet drinking, in fact, does not seem always to have taken place, even at such private celebrations. A complicated family affair in 1648 led to uncle and nephew being brought face-to-face, the uncle claiming that 'that nephew, Semen, was a criminal who had beaten many people and robbed them and boozed in drink-shops'.[104] Semen was condemned

[103] *AFZ*, III, I, no. 44 (1602).
[104] Zertsalov, *Novyya dannyya*, vol. XXII, 52.

'for his criminal activity and excessive drunkenness'. He was sent to a monastery under close arrest and was not to be allowed to escape or to have ink, paper or visitors; he was to be given the diet of an ordinary monk and he was to be watched carefully, it was added, to see that 'he did himself no harm'.[105]

A complaint to the tsar' in 1649 claimed that 'that Grigori Pertsov, lord, came to the premises at two o'clock in the morning, drunk, and started to beat me, your slave, and to rob, together with his friends and advisers'.[106]

Sometimes, however, private behaviour had public or state implications. Two brothers wrote a complaint to the tsar' about the disgraceful (and economically damaging) behaviour of their cousin. He had written his wife a threatening letter, ordering her to enter a nunnery; she was so scared, she did so. But, they went on,

Lord, the scoundrel and boozer has dispersed his household slaves and now, lord, that scoundrel has taken peasant boys and girls into his house; and, lord, in this year 1647 that scoundrel has squandered your, the Tsar's, grant and his estate held by service in Vladimir uezd, 17 peasant tenements; and that scoundrel Vasilii, lord, drinks continually; lord, that scoundrel has fled from God's mercy with his swipes and on the Lord's feast days he does not visit God's church because of his swipes; and that same scoundrel and boozer, lord, rides round his peasant tenements in Kashira uezd with spirits, drinking continually, and he makes the peasant girls drink a lot and orders them to sing songs before him and orders them to dance, and creates all sorts of disorders.[107]

Poor Vasili was arrested and sent to the Great Palace.

At times disturbances evoked protest from churchmen in terms not of general moral principles, but of the inconvenience caused. At three festivals in the year, the Assumption (28 August), the Presentation of the Holy Mother of God in the Temple (4 December) and in memory of Cyril the Wonder Worker (22 June), trading people came from towns and volosts with goods and traded by the St Cyril of Beloozero monastery for three or four days. On such occasions

The Beloozero customs men and drink shop men on oath ride to the monastery for our customs dues and bring drink from the drink shop, spirits and beer, and set themselves up at the monastery's hostel and sell that drink by the cup and by the bucket; there are insults to the brethren and all sorts of confusion from that, and there are quarrels and many fights among the drinkers themselves and criminals even kill some people.[108]

[105] *Ibid.*, 53.
[106] *Ibid.*, vol. XIX, 45.
[107] *Ibid.*, vol. XXI, 48.
[108] *DAI*, I, 229 (13 July 1602).

The festival market was therefore prohibited near the monastery, it was to be moved away, and no drink was to be taken there. The deaths mentioned do not appear to be the main motivation for concern here, despite the fact that one might expect manslaughter to be of great importance to Christians.

The concern to avoid the violence which sometimes followed from immoderate consumption is readily understandable from both state and church viewpoints. Some aspects of what may be called the moral concern about drinking and activities associated with it, however, may be of less ready access to us. These were of particular concern to the upper levels of the church hierarchy and are partly to be explained in terms of the feasts and fraternities and the non-Christian traditions discussed earlier (chapter 3). In the first half of the seventeenth century such traditions aroused strong opposition from the head of the church. Filaret, the father of tsar' Mikhail Romanov, had been joint ruler from his return from Polish captivity and his election as Patriarch in 1619 until his death in 1634; so there was an additional reason for such church views to be taken seriously by the state authority. The tsar' was opposed to such apparently innocent activities as games of cards and dice; these were regarded as divination and might, therefore, involve sorcery aimed against the Orthodox sovereign and the established system. Perhaps this attitude reflects a fundamental uncertainty, since it seems to imply a belief in at least the potential efficacy of non-Christian, or, in more general terms, magical rather than religious, practices. Whether there are traces of dual belief here or not, tsar' and Patriarch, state and church, united in their formal opposition (whatever their private practice) to a cluster of rituals, traditions and activities which were associated with communal drinking. This was so despite the state concern to encourage drinking for the sake of revenue.

A crier was sent round Moscow in May 1627, 'round the market-places and the main streets, the crossroads and alleys, and the small markets, on more than one day, so that henceforth no persons shall gather for any disorder beyond Old Vagankovo'; offenders were to be arrested and beaten with the knout in the market-place.[109] The final sentence of this brief item supplementing the law book makes the meaning clearer: 'And a memorandum has been sent to the New Department about it, that they should not go beyond Vagankovo for disorder with drink shop drink.'

Another supplement, issued by Patriarch Filaret in the same year, ordered a crier to cry

[109] *AI*, III, VIII, 92.

... along the rows and streets, the free settlements and the hundreds, that they are not to go with hobby-horses (*s kabylkami*) and the lay people are not to gather for games, so there shall be no confusion for Orthodox Christians (*krest'yanom*) and they are not to cry the kalends [*koleda*, a sort of pagan carolling], spring [*ovsen'*, celebrated on Christmas Eve] and ploughs.[110]

The non-Christian element in such activities was evidently clear to Patriarch Filaret and the survival of such rituals in Moscow itself at this date is noteworthy; they were not restricted to the countryside. The dates in the year of these two documents are significant. In May 1627 both Ascension and Whitsun would have been celebrated (since Easter Sunday fell on 25 March). In December every year the winter cycle of festivities was celebrated. Why, like other orders of the period, they were only issued at the very moment concerned is strange.

A vividly detailed complaint from a group of priests in Nizhnii Novgorod to the Patriarch Iosaf in 1636 specifies such 'disorders' or popular festivals.[111]

Instead of spiritual joys, they cultivate devilish joys; they spend these days [Christmas and Epiphany], lord, in many Hellenic and devilish games. From Christmas to Epiphany, lord, they perform games from house to house; and very many men and women gather together for that evil sight and perform games of every sort of devilish fantasy with many evil images; they curse God's mercy and His Immaculate Festival. And, lord, they make bast hobby-horses and bisons and decorate them with linen and silk fringes and they hang bells on the hobby-horse and put shaggy animal masks on their own faces and similar clothing and behind they fix tails, like visible devils, bearing shameful members on their faces and devilishly revelling in every way and displaying the shameful members; others beat drums, weaving and dancing and doing other unsuitable things, and in this manner, lord, they go not only from house to house, but also along town streets and through villages and hamlets, like furious whores, and are not ashamed before God's image and the honoured Christian name, but create great hindrance, lord, for Christianity.[112]

On the sixth Thursday after Easter, on the Feast of Christ's Ascension they also oppose the Feast of Christ's Ascension. They go to the Monastery of the Cave, since the church of the Ascension is there, two verstas from the town; men and women walk from the town, lord, and ride in from the villages and hamlets, and tavern-keepers, lord, with drink shops and with all sorts of intoxicating drinks, and players, bear-men and jesters with devilish implements, all gather, lord, at the Monastery of the Cave and think to celebrate in this fashion; bear-men with bears and dancing dogs, jesters and players with

[110]*AI*, III, x, 92 (24 December 1627).
[111]N.V. Rozhdestvenskii, *ChtOIDR*, 201 (1902), book 2, miscellany, 1–31; text is on 18–31.
[112]*Ibid.*, 24–6.

masks and shameful instruments of debauchery, with drums and pipes (*surny*) and all sorts of satanic attractions to debauchery and, lord, creating evil devilish attractions, getting drunk, dancing and beating drums, sounding the pipes and going in masks and carrying shameful things in their hands and doing other improper things such as Satan taught them to oppose to the Festival of Christ's Ascension.[113]

The priests claimed that, apart from Christmas, there were four annual shameful gatherings of all the people: the Ascension, just described; the seventh Thursday after Easter 'at cemeteries'; the Descent of the Holy Ghost (i.e. Whit Sunday); the birth of John the Baptist (24 June) when 'they gather for similar shameful play and drunkenness'.[114] 'They ride in from villages and hamlets and there are very many people involved in abuses, and they are full of killings as was pointed out for the monastery of the Cave.'[115] It was claimed that 'every sort of illegal thing has multiplied'.[116] The Patriarch issued a memorandum on disorders in the Moscow churches clearly based on the complaint from Nizhnii Novgorod.[117]

There appears to be little difference between what worried the church authorities and the tsar' at the *Stoglav* Council in the mid-sixteenth century and their worries in the first half of the seventeenth century.[118] The administrative and economic setting, however, was changed. The financial demands on the state during and in the immediate aftermath of the Time of Trouble had led to emergency loans and taxation in the period 1614–19.[119] The military commanders, who were the tsar's representatives in charge of areas of the country, had patronised and protected the jesters; but by the 1630s the regularising activities of state and church were reinforced by the start of a reform movement.

This was the period, immediately following the election of Mikhail Romanov as tsar', when the new ruler was attempting to assert control over the devastated country and to regularise taxation. The following account shows some of the problems which existed.

A kvas and beer (?*suslo*) drink-shop was opened in Beloozero, on the tsar's orders, evidently in 1614. The first month's profits, 13 rubles 2 altyns 1 denga, were sent to Moscow, but marauding cossacks seized two cartloads of malt on the way. Moreover, while Lithuanians were still in the vicinity of Beloozero the local people moved a hut (*izba*) of

[113]*Ibid.*, 26–7.
[114]*Ibid.*, 27–8.
[115]*Ibid.*, 28.
[116]*Ibid.*, 30.
[117]*AAE*, III, no. 264 (14 August 1636).
[118]See Chapter 3 above.
[119]Veselovskii, *Sem'sborov*.

the drink-shop into the town on rollers, another building was taken for firewood by cossacks and foreigners, and a third structure (*klet'*) was taken into the fort by a man who claimed he had bought it from someone killed by the cossacks. The men on oath were hurriedly making kvas and beer in the town until the drink-shop was restored. Those who had carted off the drink-shop were ordered to re-establish it – clearly a nonsensical order, made to avoid any state expenditure – malt was to be sent to the drink-shop 'when there are no criminals, but if there are any criminals [i.e. invaders], we forbid malt to be sent to the mill for grinding and order malt to be ground in hand-querns'.[120]

A major concern about drink, from the administrative point of view, was that there should be no challenge from any quarter to the monopoly of the state drink-shop (and the considerable income it generated for the state). The head official of a drink-shop in Beloozero was instructed 'to watch carefully that in the artisan quarter the gentry and junior boyars and foreigners, the musketeers and gunners and anyone of the men of the artisan quarter in the town hold no drink at all for sale apart from the drink shop'.[121] A newly arrived commander of the musketeers, however, 'gave the musketeers freedom to hold drink for sale in the town and those musketeers act violently towards him [the head official] and do not allow him to take from them the drink for sale'. Such illegal drink was to be seized by force with the help of as many musketeers as needed, supplied by the local military commander, and the offenders punished. There were no doubt many such conflicts of interest in the confused early years of the Romanov dynasty.

An instruction of 1618 stated that 'the prohibited drink is ordered to be removed and given to the drink-shop official to be sold to the drink-shop; those dealing in prohibited drink and those consuming it are to be liable to exactions in accordance with the Sovereign's former order'.[122]

At Sol' Vychegda the Stroganovs had a cathedral church and, beside it, two drink-shops with the market-place around. Here, church and drink were closely connected; the cellars of the church were used to store drink so that 'from those spirits there is a great smell in the church.'[123] 'From under that church the men on oath sell spirits by the bucket and by halves, quarters and eighths; and they measure out spirits for the drink shops, for the bars; the spirits which they accept for the drink shop they put under that church.' This, of course, did not

[120]*DAI*, II, no. 36 (13 March 1615).
[121]*AI*, III, no. 44 (7 November 1614).
[122]*AAE*, III, no. 129.
[123]Cited in Vvedenskii, *Dom Stroganovykh*, 215.

contribute to decorum in the church. 'If anyone buys spirits under the church, an eighth or a quarter, they are to drink those spirits on the spot. When they sing matins or vespers in the church, the revellers sing songs and engage in every sort of disrespect.'[124] Ivan Stroganov himself was one of the drink-shop officials, so it is perhaps scarcely surprising that it was not found possible to remove the drink from the church. 'It is not possible to move the spirits from under the church until they are sold because the barrels are great, old ones of pine and fir, the hoops are also pine; under many barrels there are drains and as soon as those barrels are moved from their places, the hoops will not take it and there will be a loss of the spirits.' The treasury was no doubt well content; in 1619 the returns over eighteen months were increased by more than 1,000 rubles over the previous period.[125]

Sales in outlying areas, both Russian and native, were evidently profitable, as we have seen from drink being taken to fairs and festivals. Yet occasionally, restrictions were imposed on sales to native people. In 1606 a grant had prohibited the sales of Novgorod spirits and meads in seven Lop districts when the area had been ascribed to Novgorod. Subsequent confirmations included ones dated 1648 and 1650 which 'ordered the Lopari and peasants of the Lop pogosts to be protected', and no impositions to be made on them so that they may live in peace'. This order was to be given each year to the newly elected head officials 'without being kept back'.

As the result of a petition from 'the lay people of all seven Lop pogosts', the Olonets and other pot-house sworn men were 'prohibited from going to the Lop pogosts with spirits and with beer or mead and so cause loss and ruin to the peasants of the Lop pogosts'.[126] We do not know why there was such concern to protect these people against the abuses of those selling drink, and perhaps even against the introduction of spirits. Usually every opportunity was taken throughout the seventeenth century to encourage the controlled sale of drink in order to ensure and, if possible, increase state income.

From 1620, the exceptional taxes of 1614-19 were stopped and arrears were not exacted; direct taxes in money and in grain were reduced.[127] The old basis for taxation, the land tax, had been eroded by changes in the late sixteenth and early seventeenth centuries and there was evident concern about the burden on the tax-payers. At the same time, financial needs remained high; it was in these circumstances that

---

[124]*Ibid.*
[125]*Ibid.*, 216.
[126]*AI*, v, 140 (10 May 1686).
[127]Veselovskii, *Soshnoe pis'mo*, vol. II, 197–8.

there was some shift to indirect taxation. Customary tolls (*tamozhennye poshliny*) and drink-shop income became an important part of revenue. At that time, however, these were not treated entirely as indirect taxes. The amount collected in one year was evidently taken as the sum, plus some small increment if possible, to be expected in subsequent years. It was regarded, thus, almost as an allocated tax. Officials responsible for collecting this revenue were personally liable to make good any shortfall. The system, as in the late sixteenth century, was either to farm out these taxes or to use elected or appointed officials (the drink-shop head and men trusted on oath). Whether such indirect taxes became more important than direct taxes in the seventeenth century is unclear. In 1679/80 they amounted to 53% as against 44% of direct taxes.[128] This may not have been the situation every year, however.[129] Certainly, the indirect tax revenue was important in the towns, especially major trading centres, but it is not yet clear that it was 'the largest single item of income in the Russian budget from the 1580s to the end of the seventeenth century'.[130]

Certainly the decade from 1619 saw an increase in the number of drink-shops and the income derived from them, whether by state officials or through tax-farmers, grew considerably.[131] By 1626 there were evidently twenty-five drink-shops in Moscow alone.[132] There was also an increase in drunkenness. By the middle of the seventeenth century 'in Moscow and in free settlements around Moscow many people making a living by trade and farmers of drink-shops reside'.[133]

Other aspects of the process of restoration and of control over drink were important enough to be recorded in the Pskov chronicle.

Prince Vasilei Turenin and the clerk Tret'yak Kopnin established a brewery (*varnitsa*) for the Sovereign, to brew for the drink-shops; and they took the church wine from the trading people for the Sovereign, for the trusted men on oath to sell at a high price; and the empty church and monastic heritable estates were confiscated for the Sovereign, the monastic donors were driven off; no monasteries or churches were built and even on the feast days of those churches there were no due vespers; deliberately they were given on farm to kvas-makers, carters, caulkers and bath-men for payment, with yearly additions and higher increments, and public clerks too.[134]

[128]P.N. Milyukov, *Gosudarstvennoe khozyaistvo*, 74.
[129]Veselovskii, *Soshnoe pis'mo*, vol. I, 36–8.
[130]Bushkovitch, *The Merchants of Moscow*, 159.
[131]Veselovskii, *Soshnoe pis'mo*, vol. II, 538.
[132]Veselovskii, 'K voprosu o sostave i istochnikakh xxv glavy Ulozheniya', *RIZh*, 1–2 (1917), 29.
[133]*AAE*, IV, 45 (1648). See also the 1649 Code of Laws, Ch. 18, paras. 21, 23.
[134]*PL*, II, 281 (1626–8).

Here direct control of supplies could be exercised as the drink-shops were not producing their own drink. In 1628–9 the Moscow men, Khmelevskoi, a guarantor of Ivan Nikitich Romanov, and his fellows, bought the drink-shops at Moscow and sold spirits at 4 altyns a measure (*stopa*), and they reduced the measure. After that, Vaska Boldin bought the farm in the garrisons and the volosts, in Pechki and in Talavsk and in Eliny and in Usitvy, to establish new drink-shops.[135]

Evidently strong drink continued to be imported in the seventeenth century even though internal production was firmly established and widespread. A charter of 1636 mentions that 'they bring brandy (*vino goryachoe*) and all sorts of fine German drink from the sea coast to Solovki monastery'.[136] Imports, in fact, were probably restricted to fine wines and brandies not produced in Russia, items for consumption only by the privileged. Foreigners were particularly suspect when it came to drink. In 1639 a search of villages belonging to a monastery in Suzdal', remote from the coast and not directly on major trade routes, disclosed that 'Russian people and Germans [i.e. non-Slav westerners] and all sorts of foreigners keep by them prohibited drink for sale, spirits, beer and mead, also tobacco, raw and ground, and they trade and make a living by that prohibited drink.'[137] It would be interesting to know who were 'all sorts of foreigners'. In 1643 a number of priests and deacons from nine parish churches in Moscow had complained about 'Germans', including women, buying tenements in their parishes and causing 'all sorts of defilement for Russian people', including holding in their houses 'all sorts of illicit drink'.[138] This was evidently especially evil because some Russians lived with them. The foreigners were, incidentally, paying high prices for houses (twice or more what Russians paid) and the parishioners, according to the complaint, were moving out. Whether the foreigners themselves produced this drink, imported it or acquired it locally is not stated; in any event, official concern is evident.

The situation in Moscow provided the basis for the legislation which was intended to apply to the whole country in the Code of Laws of 1649.[139] The New Department (*Novyi prikaz* or *Novaya chet'*) was established in 1619 and administered the drink-shops in Moscow and those formerly dealt with by the Vladimir, Galich and Kostroma de-

[135] *Ibid.*
[136] *AAE*, III, 390.
[137] *AYu*, no. 101.
[138] *AI*, III, 92 (XXXVI). On hostility to foreigners at this period, see S. Baron, 'The origins of seventeenth century Moscow's Nemeckaja Sloboda', *California Slavic Studies*, V, 1–17.
[139] *Sobornoe ulozhenie 1649 g.*, especially chapter 25.

partments.[140] By the mid-20s a great merchant (*gost'*) was chosen each year by the Merchant Hundred and the Cloth Hundred to head it; the 'black' hundreds and free settlements chose the men on oath. In addition, a gentleman or junior boyar was appointed as a virtual police officer to each of the thirty or so Moscow districts for the seizure of illicit drink (and tobacco); the 'black' hundreds chose men on oath and ten-men from every ten tenements who were responsible for drink and tobacco in their areas. Drunks on the streets were arrested and taken to the New Department to be dealt with. The Musketeer Office supplied men to assist with searches, to guard the takings and drink sold outside the shops and to deal with scuffles. The system of elected officials and the involvement of more than one Department is similar to the arrangements for control of bread, but much more elaborate, presumably because of both revenue and fear of social disorders.

Provincial towns had a simpler system. There were no police, except in a few towns (Great Novgorod, Pskov, Kazan', Astrakhan'); in some towns there were only military commanders and heads of the drink-shop (Beloozero); in others only head officials (Ustyug Department towns).[141]

Torture was common in Moscow practice; it is mentioned in eleven of the twenty-one articles of Chapter 25 (dealing with drink) of the 1649 Code. It is rarely mentioned in provincial experience. Fines and punishments, too, were lighter in the provinces before the Code.[142]

One of the changes involved in the increase in indirect taxation in 1620 was that head officials, whether elected by those liable to tax or appointed by government without election, were now used on a considerable scale in towns other than their own. Even ordinary members of the town artisan quarters began to be sent as men on oath to collect tolls and excise elsewhere. This evoked many complaints from the Merchant and Cloth Hundreds since such service was particularly onerous. The men concerned had to leave their livelihood and live among strangers; if they acted in the government's interest, they incurred local hostility; if they sided with the locals, they were liable for any shortfall in revenue collected and could not rely on the locals, or their own townsmen, for help.[143] Such men, too, had to be the most experienced since they had to operate on their own; this meant a loss of good men from their community. Complaints from those liable to tax came to a head in the summer of 1648 when there were disturbances, partly

[140]Veselovskii, 'K voprosu', in *RIZh*, 1–2 (1917), 28.
[141]*Ibid.*, 27–9.
[142]*Ibid.*, 32–4.
[143]*Ibid.*, 41–2.

caused by other dissatisfactions as well, in many towns.[144] The wealth-ier men in Merchant and Cloth Hundreds did not then dare to call for additional new members for service in other towns and only did so early in 1649.[145] Meanwhile, concessions had been made and service in other towns had been all but abolished.

The drink-shop officials had functions not only of police, at least in Moscow and a few other towns, but also had privileges as regards justice until the 1649 Code attempted, but failed, to abolish these for the men on oath.[146] Tax farmers were not liable to be brought to court until after the expiry of their farm and the revenue and accounts had been dealt with.[147] This was sometimes a lengthy process, since it could take over a year to collect drinking debts and settle the finances.[148] The farmers were usually then tried by the Department concerned in Moscow, not the military commander in the locality. This caused many disagreements between consumers and the officials; also between the local military commanders (whose administrative responsibilities were restricted here) and the officials. The drink-shop officials were agents of the treasury in the locality, virtually indepen-dent of the local administration from about 1630 and freed from local claims for redress. Sometimes, however, there was an important dis-tinction between tax-farmers and their servants, who came from other towns, and the men trusted on oath, who were locals and therefore subject to local pressure. Members of the family of the latter group not living independently were not subject to local justice by the military commander in Tot'ma in 1629.[149] These considerable concessions fol-lowed from the priority given to achieving revenue and were neces-sary to ensure that officials could be found to operate drink-shops.

The drink-shop itself was not only a retail outlet, often it also pro-duced the drink it had on sale. The trusted head official of a drink-shop in Velikie Luki, Ivashko Vodop'yanov ('Water-drunk'), took over a somewhat dilapidated drink-shop in 1646.

There is a brew-house with . . . and the brew-house has rotted, its roof and wall have collapsed into the river. There is a caulked hut (*oshmanik*) and . . . unsound, the roof, the laths and trusses have rotted and the ceiling has per-ished, all the staging has rotted and the corners have fallen in and it now rests on its underpinnings; there is an old cellar (*pogrebishche*) under a lean-to, and

---

[144]*DAI*, III, no. 47; *AAE*, IV, no. 28.
[145]Veselovskii, 'K voprosu', *RIZh*, 1–2 (1917), 42.
[146]*Sobornoe ulozhenie 1649 g.*, ch. 10, section 153.
[147]Veselovskii, *Trudy po istochnikovedeniyu*, 122, 132.
[148]*Ibid.*, 142.
[149]*Ibid.*, 141.

the cellar has collapsed, undercut by the water, and the lean-to and roof have rotted and fallen in. In the brew-house the old decanting (*spusknye*) vessels and the kvas ones are all unsound, they have rotted and it is impossible to brew beer any more in any of the vessels and in . . . or the spirits ones. There is an old copper brewing boiler; the boiler is unsound, it leaks and its weight is unknown because it is encircled beneath its brim with a wide iron and has iron lugs.

The survey then went on to account for this sorry state of affairs.

At Velikie Luki, lord, your, the Sovereign's, drink shop was entirely flooded by the river Lovat' on 17 December. The basement doors were not to be seen from either side in the water, and the water was halfway up the doors in the caulked hut, and in the hut, your, the Sovereign's, drink for sale now stands on crates (*perevodiny*) under the ceiling; and the stove was carried away from the hut by all the water; as the doors had disappeared your, the Sovereign's drink could be seen and the old building, the new heated building and the ice-house under the drying room, where the men on oath formerly sat, and now sit at the counters, with your, the Sovereign's, drink, and all the counters were flooded and the water poured over the ice-house and froze, and the old heated building with the room is frozen . . . and now, lord, by day we sell your, the Sovereign's, drink on the river ice, and at night we sit with your, the Sovereign's, drink in the reception room; and to safeguard your, the Sovereign's drink shop monies (*kazna*), we have taken away the hall partition by the reception room and made a stairway from the river ice, the former stairway from the tenement was carried off by the water, because . . . and the brew-house, lord, was all flooded and the doors are not to be seen; and now, lord, we brew beer . . . and we hire vessels; the vessels have been carried off from the brew-house and all the [market] rows have been flooded and there is now nowhere to put your, the Sovereign's, drink, spirits, beer and mead in your, the Sovereign's, drink shop in store for the summer; the water poured over the ice-house when the drink shop and the rows were flooded and the staging in the ice-house was taken off by the water, it froze and it is impossible to clear it.[150]

In addition, the drink-shop had also had to be closed for five days for a fast and prayers for the tsar' during which 'they eat no flesh, neither meat nor fish, nor butter and drank no intoxicating drink'. No wonder the income declined.

Other natural calamities could also affect the takings. A poor harvest could have disastrous effects. In 1634

There is great poverty in Sol' Kama artisan quarter and in the uezd; there are few drinkers at the drink-shop and no markets at Sol' Kama or in the volosts in the uezd since there was a harvest failure in 1633 to 1634, and the remaining grain and hops have frozen; and the men of the artisan quarter and the volost peasants are suffering exactions for payment of their taxes, the soldiers'

---

[150]*DAI*, III, 22 (before 22 March 1647).

money, the post-horse maintenance and all the communal payments; and others are wandering here and there.[151]

The risks involved in being a drink-shop official were great, and were by no means restricted to natural disasters as may be seen from an appeal from two head officials in the White Sea area in November 1647 and the administrative response to it.[152]

And, lord, in past years under former head customs officers there were many traders and venturers of all sorts who would come in autumn to Kholmogory and to Dvina uezd from Ustyug and from the Vaga and from all other towns and uezds with stocks of grain and with goods; and from the Murmansk Sea and other places with fish and blubber; and from the Maritime volosts with goods and money; and from Novaya Zemlya with walrus hides and blubber, and with ivory. The Kholmogory artisan quarter and uezd people traded in all sorts of goods with those who came and all those local traders and venturers and those who had come, all sorts of people, drank much, buying the drink shop drink in your, the Sovereign's, Dvina drink shops; the musketeers of Archangel town and the Kholmogory strongpoint also drank much, buying the drink shop drink in the drink shops; and, thus, no small sum was collected as your, the Sovereign's, customs duties and profits from the drink shop.

In 1646, however, the trade had fallen off.

For that reason there is a great shortfall in your, the Sovereign's, customs impost, and there are now many fewer drinkers compared with previous years in autumn in your, the Sovereign's, Dvina drink shops. And the musketeers of Archangel town and the Kholmogory strongpoint do not drink at all and now in autumn buy no drink shop drink in your, the Sovereign's, Dvina drink shops, because the musketeer officers at the town and in Kholmogory have forbidden the musketeers to drink and to buy drink shop drink; if any musketeers drink in drink shops on credit or against an article deposited, they forbid those musketeers to pay the money for the drink shop drink to the men on oath at the drink shop, and order the musketeers to have the articles deposited, without payment, from the men on oath; but if any musketeer officers in charge of 50 men, or those in charge of ten, or ordinary rankers come for spirits for feast days or to commemorate relatives, or for christenings, or for wakes, we, your slaves, do not dare to give them spirits without your, the Sovereign's, decree; this, too, causes a great shortfall in your, the Sovereign's, drink shop impost.

They appealed to the tsar' not to be held liable for this shortfall which was owing to changed circumstances.

On the reverse the document bears a note indicating that their appeal was rejected; they were not only to be liable for twice the

---

[151]Cited in Vvedenskii, *Dom Stroganovykh*, 216.
[152]*DAI*, III, 34.

amount of the shortfall, but, it was added, 'they are to be punished for their carelessness'. The punishment was not specified. In March, 1648, nevertheless, the same two men were still in office; this suggests that there were ways of bending many of these paper rules. If this had not been so, it seems unlikely that even the profits to be made would have justified the risks involved. The two officials wrote querying the small number of men on oath assigned them, insufficient, they considered, to deal with the salt tax, for which they were also responsible.[153] They were allowed eighteen men on oath additional to the sixteen already selected but were warned 'to collect the tax with great zeal, without blunders, so as, compared with the previous year, to make a great profit for the Sovereign's treasury'.[154]

Drink was supposed to be sold only against immediate cash payment, but even in court villages, under the control of the tsar's own administration, debts occurred as a result of drinks being 'chalked up' ('notched up' on wooden tallies would probably be more accurate). In 1650 the tsar' had to order a steward of one of his villages in Suzdal' uezd to recover 'eighty one rubles twenty four altyns and a denga drink money owed by debtors and drinkers'.[155] The money was not immediately forthcoming.

The problem of shortfalls was raised, probably in 1648, by men of the artisan quarter in Pskov who complained that shortfalls were exacted from them without any investigation. The response was that any shortfalls investigated 'without deceit' and found genuine were not to be exacted from Pskov. The Novgorod Chet' was then uncertain whether this decision, not in the 1649 Code, was generally applicable.[156] Shortfalls occurred for a variety of reasons:

. . . at Arkhangel on the [Northern] Dvina if there are few trading vessels appearing from overseas; in Nizhnii Novgorod shortfalls occur if fewer vessels appear with fish and salt from Great Perm' and Astrakhan'; in Vologda, Kargopol' and other maritime province towns, Vyatka and Perm' Usol'e shortfalls occur from grain failure and frost; in other towns shortfalls are caused by lack of trades and by large state taxes, though the head officials and men on oath have done their duty.

The tsar' with the assent of the boyars ordered shortfalls to be dealt with by enquiry in this way.[157]

The last chapter of the 1649 Code of Laws attempted to regulate

---

[153]*DAI*, III, 39 (I).
[154]*Ibid.*, (II).
[155]*DAI*, III, 77 (1650–1).
[156]Veselovskii, 'K voprosu', *RIZh*, 1–2 (1917), 43–4.
[157]*Ibid.*, 45.

matters relating to drink in detail. It was done by extending Moscow practice to the rest of the country with little or no modification. Severe penalties were now applied to the provinces as well as Moscow; both heavy fines and physical punishment and imprisonment were to be imposed on those keeping illicit drink, and similar penalties, but without imprisonment, applied to those drinking. Torture was to be used to establish the facts. There was a continuing class differentiation in the legislation. 'If anyone's people [i.e. slaves] or peasants [i.e. serfs] or yard-slaves are brought in and, when questioned, those people brought in tell them to whom they sold the spirits they had stolen from their boyars, those people brought in are to be tortured about selling the spirits, [in order to determine] whether their boyars knew about that'.[158] The production of spirits, because of the equipment and capital required, thus seems to have been largely in the hands of lords, presumably not always on a legal basis. This is evident from another section of this law which lays down that

The ten-men are to look and watch carefully in their tens [i.e. their districts] that, if any gentlemen and junior boyars whom anyone shall set up in tenements have spirits in accordance with declarations, those gentlemen and junior boyars shall have no extra spirits above what is in the declaration and shall not let anyone into their tenements without a declaration.[159]

This control of strong drink was one means by which in the course of subsequent centuries lordly and state exploitation of the enserfed peasantry was realised. An item of domestic production and consumption had been converted into an instrument of exploitation. In the mid-seventeenth century, when serfdom was finally legally imposed on the Russian people, they were also virtually deprived of the right in law to produce any domestic alcoholic drink. The increased availability of spirits was more easily controllable and the central authorities used this to attempt to impose a monopoly and to extract considerable income in the process. The disturbances of 1648, however, created a climate which did not encourage the elaboration of legislation adequate to deal with the many problems involved even in regard to state revenue from alcohol. We have just seen how, within a year of the Code, a supplementary decree on shortfalls in revenue had to be issued.

Fundamental changes were introduced in 1652, but the origin and concerns of this reform were different from those of the Code of Laws. Broadly, the concerns about drink in the first half of the century focussed on the state need for revenue. The 1649 Code attempted to

[158]*Sobornoe ulozhenie 1649 g.*, ch. 25, para. 6.
[159]*Ibid.*, ch. 25, para. 20.

ensure a state monopoly over spirits (from which the privileged classes were exempt) and control over the consumption of other drink; it showed no concern over aspects of social behaviour associated with drinking which had so disturbed some church leaders even before the Code was issued. In 1652 the latter concern became more prominent, even affecting the revenue aspect; the reform 'was imbued with a resolution, unusual for the Moscow government, to sacrifice fiscal aims for abstract ideas'.[160] Over the following years, the results shook the economy and led to changes in the pattern of social behaviour before there was a reversion to something similar to the previous system.

In response to clerical complaints about irreligious activities in which drink played a part, on 5 December 1648 the tsar' issued a decree:

We have been informed that in Belgorod and in other towns and uezds lay people of all ranks, their wives and children, do not go to God's churches during the holy singing on Sundays and the Lord's days and the major festivals and drunkenness has multiplied among people of all sorts, and every sort of disorderly devilish activity, frivolity and jesters with all sorts of devilish games.[161]

To prevent the deceit and damage caused by 'much augury and wizardry', people were ordered to attend church and a whole series of activities were proscribed. The first of these was immoderate consumption of intoxicating drink; then, all those items known from clerical complaints for several hundred years; jesters, music, masks and so on. Fortune-telling by pouring molten tin or wax and by cards, as well as games of chess and knucklebones, were prohibited, as were dancing dogs and bears, curses, bawdy songs, dancing, hand-clapping, devilish performances, fisticuffs, swings etc.[162]

Swings appear to be an innovation; at least they were not mentioned amongst such devilish activities in the sixteenth-century *Stoglav*, yet it is difficult to understand why they should have appeared in Russia as late as this. Perhaps it was rather that the clerics had only just realised some of their implications. There were various types of swing: some were suspended seats; rotating around a horizontally mounted axle, others were simple ropes hanging from a pole.[163] The ritual of swinging started at Shrove-tide, the earliest the weather allowed swings to be set up, and took place at all festivals.[164] In the mid-seventeenth century

---

[160]Veselevskii, in *ChtOIDR* (1907), book 1, miscellany, 38.
[161]Cited in A.A. Belkin, *Russkie skomorokhi* (1975), 175.
[162]*Ibid.*, 177.
[163]One of the latter type was depicted at a wake in a nineteenth-century Hucul community in Paradzhanov's film *Shadows of Our Forgotten Ancestors*.
[164]Propp, *Russkie agrarnye prazdniki*, 127.

Olearius noted that it was mainly an activity of young wives.[165] There were evidently deaths from this seemingly innocent occupation, however; in 1648 priests from Nizhnii Novgorod complained that 'many dash themselves to death' on swings.[166] No doubt swings could be dangerous and priests were concerned to reduce such risks. The association of swinging with other elements of the abhorred 'Hellenic games', however, suggests that there was more to it than that, or even than a puritanical distrust of simple pleasures. Possibly the rhythmic movement was used to induce a trance-like state; this might account for some of the involuntary falls. It may even be that this is a relict derived from an ecstatic cult of the ancestors. Young married women might perhaps be thought especially apt to engage in swinging and dancing since they were excluded from some other activities in the male-dominated society of that time, yet there seems no hint that swinging was associated with the female saint Paraskeva. Possibly too, the church reform movement itself contributed to the re-emergence or development of such entertainments by insisting on the closure of shops and workplaces on holy days.

On 19 December 1648 the tsar' was informed of similar devilish activities in Moscow and on 22 December issued a decree prohibiting them and attempting to suppress drunkenness among priests and monks. This decree was extended to cover the whole country and has survived in a copy sent to Shuya on 24 December.[167]

In November the tsar' had considered one complaint which incidentally stated that it had been ordained that on holy days 'Orthodox Christians should not trade after the hours decreed and refrain from drunkenness.'[168] This does not appear in the 1649 Code of Laws, although there is a paragraph about holding courts of justice on Sundays and other holy days, and laying down that 'three hours before evening, trade is to stop and the market-rows are to be closed'.[169] Here the tsar' appears to have followed the pattern established by the Patriarch who, in 1647, had laid down exactly the same regulation for early closing on Saturday in order to ensure Sunday church attendance.[170] The complaint about the matter omitted from the Code may therefore have been part of the churchmen's propaganda campaign.

The reform movement directed against excessive drinking and the associated abuses was largely mediated by a group of active churchmen

---

[165]Olearius, *Travels*, 169–70.
[166]Cited in Belkin, *Russkie skomorokhi*, 173.
[167]*Ibid.*, 178–80.
[168]*Ibid.*, 174.
[169]*Sobornoe ulozhenie 1649 g.*, ch. 10, para. 25.
[170]*AAE*, IV, no. 324 (14 July 1647).

known as the Zealots of Piety who were in contact with the tsar'
himself. The most important members were Ivan Neronov, Nikon
(the future Patriarch), Avvakum (who was to be the main opponent to
Nikon's ecclesiastical reforms) the Vonifat'ev, the tsar's confessor.[171]

There is considerable evidence of the hierarchs' and the tsar's concern about drinking and drunkenness, especially in convents and monasteries, both immediately before and after the Code of 1649.[172] Priests
and monks were to abstain completely from drinking and swearing
'not only in church, but also in the world'. In Novgorod in 1651 sales
of spirits were stopped for a fortnight at Easter, despite this being an
optimum period for sales; moreover, from 1 September 1651 there was
to be only one drink-shop in Novgorod. Nikon, then still Metropolitan of Novgorod, was not satisfied with this and pressed for a pot-
house 'like the Moscow pot-house' and the abandonment of any attempt to maintain the former level of revenue, pointing out that 'at a
single drink-shop, lord, it is impossible to collect as much as in
many'.[173] He also called for no attempt to exact any shortfall. The
Novgorod farm at this time was valued at 4,882 rubles. The closure at
Easter alone had caused a decline of 425 rubles, according to the tax-
farmer.[174] The conflict between morality and revenue, or church and
state interests, was sometimes ingeniously avoided: in October 1651 a
drink-shop was removed from the Patriarch's settlement opposite Kostroma to crown land.[175]

It was at this time that two Frenchmen, Jean and Charles de Gron,
arrived in Russia.[176] Little more is known of Charles, but Jean submitted a project on 17 November 1651 to show how the tsar' could
'annually increase his income more than two or three hundred barrels
of gold'.[177] De Gron envisaged the export of naval stores (timber,
hemp, iron, pitch 'and other such goods as are useful for seagoing'), the
building of a fleet, a massive development of overseas trade and the
import of luxuries.[178] This plan was read to the tsar'.

Another, evidently later, project was somewhat similar in stressing
the availability of timber, iron, hemp, flax for sailcloth and so on, but

[171]N.F. Kapterev, *Patriarkh Nikon*, 105–68.
[172]Pascal, *Avvakum*, 163.
[173]*ChtOIDR* (1907), book 1, miscellany, 38–9 (20 July 1651).
[174]*Ibid.*, 39–40. This rate would have given well over 10,000 rubles a year.
[175]Pascal, *Avvakum*, 165.
[176]30 September 1651: Baklanova, 'Yan de-Gron', *Uch. zap. In-ta. istorii RANION* (1929),
vol. IV, 111.
[177]Cited *ibid.*, 114. See also Kurts, *Sostoyanie Rossii*, 80, n. 1.
[178]Baklanova, 'Yan de-Gron', 115–17. De Rodes, in Kurts, *Sostoyanie Rossii*, 81.

18 The meal of the pious and the dishonourable, eighteenth century, but based on much earlier models.

Beneath the sun, in the top left-hand corner, the text reads:

This meal is of ungrateful people, idle talkers, blasphemers, shamefully laying bare the devil's words, eating without saying grace.

The angel of the Lord turned his face away from them, and standing he weeps seeing the devils with them.

Beneath Jesus Christ, on the right-hand, the text reads:

This meal is of pious people eating at table with the saying of grace.

The angel of the Lord attends, blesses those eating and drives away the devils, obscuring them by the power of Christ.

Christ is associated with the pious, so probably the sun is to be related in some way to the dishonourable. The humans depicted within the central arch both upstairs and downstairs are all males. There is a visual parallel between the figures on the viewer's left. In the upper scene, a young man listens attentively to a preacher. In the lower one, two women eye a servant equally attentively, encouraged by a female devil. At the right on the main table is what looks like a bottle of vodka. The erotic theme is reinforced by one of the musicians having bagpipes.

added 'people and the wherewithal to feed them'.[179] This seems to be the only reference to foodstuffs. The Swedish agent in Moscow, de Rodes, noted the arrival of de Gron as early as 20 October and commented on his specious project on 11 December.[180] He also mentioned the tsar's intention to export grain because of high prices in the Netherlands. At the end of January 1652 he noted that

> More than 10 thousand lasts of grain are expected to reach Archangel this year and they intend to continue this each year. In order afterwards to bring a much greater quantity, all (the Russians) rest on the idea of destroying the vodka for which, up till now, they have gathered and destroyed an enormous amount of grain, since in a year they distill many thousands of barrels in the whole country.[181]

The losses in excise revenue would be made up four times over, he stated.

On the basis of such evidence it has been argued that the abolition of the drink-shop, its replacement by the pot-house and the limitations on sales, introduced by the 'drink-shop reform' of 1652, aimed to increase grain available for export by reducing internal consumption.[182] This may have been an element in some calculations of policy, though consideration of grain as an export commodity seems less likely to have arisen from de Gron's projects, than from the indemnity paid to the Swedes, through de Rodes, in 1650.[183] This was partly in cash, but partly in rye. The collection of this grain in Pskov contributed to the disturbances there in 1650 and was part of the background to Nikon's limitation of alcohol sales in Novgorod the following year, before de Gron's arrival in Russia and his project of November.

Before mid-February 1652 the tsar' ordered the head officials and tax-farmers in the towns not to keep great stock of drink since from the next year (i.e. 1 September 1652) there were to be no drink-shops, but one pot-house in each.[184] A number of other restrictions were imposed.[185] In August an assembly considered the problem of regulating the consumption of drink.

> The 11th day of August, having taken counsel with our father and priest, the most holy Nikon, Patriarch of Moscow and All Russia, and with the Metropolitans and Archbishops and with all the Holy Chapter, and having

[179]Baklanova, 'Yan de-Gron', 119–20.
[180]*Ibid.*, 118–19. Kurts, *Sostoyanie Rossii*, 79–81.
[181]De Rodes, 31 January 1652, cited in Kurts, *Sostoyanie Rossii*, 95.
[182]Bazil'evich, 'Elementy merkantilizma', 14–15. Cp. Baron, in Olearius, *Travels*, 145.
[183]Olearius, *Travels*, 215.
[184]*DAI*, iii, no. 109 (1653) refers to a decree of 18 February 1652.
[185]Veselovskii, 'Kabatskaya reforma 1652 goda', *Ezhemesyachnyi zhurnal*, 4 (1914), 61.

spoken with the boyars and the chamberlains and with all our men of the council about drink-shops, we have decreed: there is to be but one pot house (*kruzhechnyi dvor*) in all towns, large and small, where hitherto there were drink-shops; and spirits are to be sold for consumption off the premises by the bucket and the pot, and to be sold by cups (*charki*), they are to make a cup of three [old] cups and to sell one [new] cup per man, but I forbid them to sell more than the one cup decreed to [any] one man; and drinkers are forbidden to sit or to be allowed to drink at or near the pot house; and no drunkards and boozers and dicers are allowed at the pot house. Spirits are not to be sold during Lent and at Assumption and on Sundays throughout the year; nor are spirits to be sold at the fasts of Christmas and St. Peter, on Wednesdays and on Fridays. Clerics and monks are not allowed into pot houses nor are they to be sold drink; no spirits are to be sold from the pot houses to any persons on credit or against a deposit or to make anyone become bound [as a dependant]. In summertime sales are to be after lunch, from the third hour of the day and to cease an hour before evening; in wintertime, after lunch, too, from the third hour, and to cease at dusk. There are to be pot houses in our large court villages; but in the small ones with few inhabitants there are to be no pot houses; and in all large villages there is to be one pot house each. All pot houses shall be held by men on trust and the best men shall be selected in towns and villages for the pot houses on oath; the spirits to be distilled for the pot houses by the men on oath and the contractors shall be agreed in the Departments; but if any beer or mead remains in the taverns till St. Semen's day in the year 161 [i.e. the year from 1 September 1652], that beer and mead is to be sold in the first month, September, and in October there should be no beer and mead for sale at all.[186]

Sales were thus limited to not much more than two hundred days a year. The concern to avoid drink, particularly on credit, being used to bind debtors is expanded in a later section: 'so that henceforth drinkers liable to exaction because of debts for drink and held by the officers of the court (*pristavy*) and in prison shall not needlessly die and there shall be no harm to the soul of the drink shop head as regards the drinkers'. This statute also strictly prohibited private sales of drink or holding undeclared drink or distilling it. All this is similar to the provisions of the Code of 1649; the change from drink-shop (*kabak*) to pot-house (*kruzhechnyi dvor*) appears to be a novel, but clear-cut, administrative decision.

When we look further at the statute, however, we see that it is not quite so clear-cut. First, despite the apparent abolition of the drink-shop, that term continued to be used in many contexts; there are references in the statute itself to the drink-shop registers, money, head officer, provisions, expenditures, till etc. Secondly, the statute was concerned with at least two aspects of drink: as a source of revenue, and as

[186]*AAE*, IV, no. 59 (1).

a factor in social disturbances, the former was predominantly a state concern, but the latter was a matter for both state and church.

State concern for revenue is shown in general and in detail. 'I have ordered the drink-shop monies to be kept carefully, to be expended less than in previous years, only for the most necessary expenditures which are not to be avoided, so that it may be more profitable for our treasury.' The officials were to collect 'from that drink shop and the tolls a profit greater than formerly'. This was the general concern. If expenses were higher than before owing to the officials' lack of zeal, they were liable to twice the amount involved and were to be punished. Detailed concern specified even that the officials were

. . . to put monies collected in the boxes, the men on oath are not to put the monies anywhere other than in the boxes, not in purses, in pockets, under dishes or plates; the head official is himself to seal the boxes with his seal, and the head official and the men on oath are jointly to take the money from the box weekly or monthly, and to write in the books separately how much any man on oath collects on spirits and in tolls; I have forbidden much money to be owing to the men on oath and the head official is to make a list of income and expenditure month by month in the drink shop collection books.[187]

Prices were fixed at a considerably raised level, probably at least 50% more than before, presumably intended to make good any losses resulting from the restricted opening times. Unfortunately, there remain gaps and obscurities about prices. Since beer and mead prices were not raised, there was presumably an increase in consumption of those drinks.

State concern also extended to the problem of social disturbances.

I have ordered the head official and the men on oath that drinkers should drink at their pot house quietly; that there should be no evil, brawls, killings or any other criminal activity, nor welcome for thieves and brigands, walking or riding, at the drink shop; they are not to accept any unknown people as tipplers at the pot house.[188]

A regulation a year later expanded this by inserting 'that they are not to have from anyone, as deposit for drink, any crosses or icon mounts, books or any church utensils, or the goods of thieves or brigands'.[189] Here state and church concerns intermingle.

Church concerns seem to dominate in a section dealing with jesters.

At the pot-house jesters with drums and pipes, with bears and with little dogs should not come, and no devilish games at all should be played by any means, and I order a strict regulation to be made about that; if at the pot-house any

[187]*AAE*, IV, no. 59. [188]*AAE*, IV, nos. 59 (16 August 1652), 70.
[189]*AAE*, IV, nos. 63 (16 August 1653), 96.

Table 4.3. *Sale price of spirits (dengas)*

	bucket	½ bucket	¼ bucket	pot (1/10 bucket)	cup (1/100 bucket)
1 *1652*[a]					
Perm', Cherdyn', Sol' Kama	180	150 (300)	120 (480)		3 (300)
2 *1653*	[b]			30 (300)	3 (300)
3 *1652*					
Cherdyn', Sol' Kama	480	240 (480)	120 (480)		4 (400)
4 *15 March 1660*					
Perm', Cherdyn', Sol' Kama	300			50 (500)	5 (500)
5 *12 Oct. 1660*					
Moscow	600	300 (600)	150 (600)	75 (750)	8 (800)
All towns except below Kazan'	600	300 (600)	150 (600)	75 (750)	6 (600 sc. 800?)
6 *26 Sept. 1661*					
All towns					10 (1000)

Notes:

[a] Beer and mead was to be sold 'as before'.

[b] To be sold by the bucket in three items: 30, 25 and 20 altyns a bucket i.e. 180, 150 and 120 dengas. These amounts are the same as those for a bucket, ½ and ¼ buckets in 1.

1 Rate per bucket is shown in brackets.

2 In 1625 a bucket of spirits in Moscow had, allegedly, cost 2 rubles (400 dengas), but in other locations in the first quarter of the century it had cost between 10 and 30 altyns (60 and 180 dengas). Probably the Moscow item was vodka, not spirits, implying a price of 200 dengas for the latter. M. Smirnov, *Nizhegorodskie kazennye kabaki* (Nizhnii Novgorod, 1913), 13.

3 In the second quarter of the century at Nizhnii Novgorod spirits sold at 50 to 200 dengas a bucket, according to the measure used; the wholesale price in 1650 varied from 50 dengas to 160 dengas a bucket; retail sale prices were higher. *Ibid.*

4 In 1669 129 dengas a bucket was considered a high *cost* price. *DAI*, v, 93 (1).

Sources: 1, 2, 4, 5, 6 *DAI*, iv, no. 73 (i–iii).

3   *AAE*, iv, no. 63.

jesters with drums and pipes, with bears and with little dogs, start to come and to play any devilish games, I order you to take those jesters and bring them before yourself; and those people who are brought for the first time I order to be beaten with rods; if any jesters are discovered with that devilish game and are brought in a second time, I order those jesters to be beaten with the knout, and I order a fine of five rubles a man to be exacted from them; and I order the drums, pipes, lutes and horns to be smashed to pieces; and I order the masks to be burnt; and you are to write about the fines money, how much has been exacted from whom, and to send to us, to Moscow; I order you to send your note and to hand over the fines money to the Department of the Great Palace.[190]

There is some evidence suggesting that attacks on jesters in this period even resulted in changes in music: helm-shaped psalteries became less widespread, as did horn-players.[191]

The jesters had been to some extent patronised and protected by the military commanders who acted as the tsar's regional representatives. Probably the income derived from drink-shops and the entertainments associated with them encouraged such protection; jesters provided professional entertainment and not all the income from sales of drink would necessarily reach Moscow as revenue. In the seventeenth century, however, the officials and tax farmers responsible for excise were exempted from the military commanders' justice. This limited the incentives to the commanders to concern themselves with protecting jesters who, by the mid-century were under attack by some influential church leaders.[192] Other less risky means for deriving income from drink became available at this period.

The reform of 1652 'completely failed to take account of the habits of the population and of the means at the government's disposal to carry it through'.[193] Concessions were soon made. As early as April 1653 the sick and weak 'who do not drink spirits' were to have beer and mead 'as before'. The price was to be determined locally; since such drinks were easily made at home it would have been quite unrealistic to fix prices, especially at an increased level. In 1653–4 the officials at Archangel were making spirits, beer and mead; they were, incidentally, instructed to mix any bad stocks with good drink in order to sell it.[194] Also in April 1653 'from the pot-houses in all towns the head officials and men on oath are to sell spirits in kopek [i.e. two-denga] cups, as it was sold at drink-shops in the towns before this'.[195] Prices were reduced because 'in many towns and at villages and hamlets in the uezds, apart from the pot-houses, many illicit drinking places have been created where they secretly sell spirits cheap'.[196]

In 1652 private distilleries were ordered to be destroyed 'apart from

[190]*AAE*, IV, no. 63 (16 August 1653). *AAE*, IV, no. 59 (I) (16 August 1652), has only minor differences.
[191]I.V. Tynurist, 'Gde vo gusli zvonili?', *Etnograficheskie issledovaniya severo-zapada SSSR*, 27–8.
[192]See pp. 139 and 145 above.
[193]Veselovskii, 'Kabatskaya reforma', 62.
[194]*DAI*, III, nos. 116 (I), 488.
[195]Veselovskii, 'Kabatskaya reforma', 62.
[196]*Ibid.*, 63.

those brew houses in which, in accordance with the sovereign's decree, there are contractors for spirits for the sovereign's Distribution Warehouse, for Moscow, and for the pot-houses for the towns'.[197] Moscow, through the Departments, was to organise the supplies of spirits. The state monopoly was crucial; yet insuperable difficulties faced the state and there were immense advantages for the suppliers. Where the excise had previously been farmed out the Departments had no information about the quantities supplied, nor had they any means of estimating what was required at the new prices. Any losses now fell on the state; moreover, the contractors often demanded, and sometimes achieved, payment in full in advance. Here was a great opening for enterprise and it was not neglected by some of the highest in the land.

A decree of 1657 lists about 125 persons who, having failed to fulfil contracts, were not to be given further contracts or any advances.[198] The list includes not only several boyars and relatives of the tsar', but also even peasants of the Patriarch Nikon himself. It seems unlikely that such peasants were acting for the Patriarch (despite the evidence of an informer that Nikon, after his condemnation, used to get women drunk in his quarters).[199] It is also unlikely that they were without any support from officials of the patriarchal estate. By the time of the 1662 riots in Moscow traders were complaining that the clergy, the military and the justices, avoiding and disdaining every government rule, were then holding all the largest and best crafts, trades and markets.[200]

The 1652 reform also encountered external difficulties. Had hopes of deflecting grain from alcohol production to export motivated the reform, any such expectations must have been dashed by the outbreak of the Anglo-Dutch war early in 1652. This devastated the trade through Archangel. At the same time the demand for state revenue sharply increased in order to sustain the war against Poland, which started in October 1653 and lasted until 1667. In March 1654 an extraordinary 10% tax was exacted and this was repeated in the autumn; plague was then raging in the centre of the country, part of the north-west and the Upper Volga region and made the situation even worse.[201] In such circumstances it was only to be expected that greater weight would be given to concern for revenue, rather than morality. However concerned the tsar', who appears to have formally initiated the reform, and

[197]Cited in Veselovskii, 'Kabatskaya reforma', 61–2.
[198]*Ibid.*, 64.
[199]Solov'ev, *Istoriya*, vol. VII, 358.
[200]Bazil'evich, 'Elementy merkantilizma', 6, 14, citing A. Zertsalov, 'O myatezhakh v gorode Moskve i sele Kolomenskom'.
[201]Bazil'evich, 'Elementy merkantilizma', 16.

the leaders of the church may have been about public morality and Christian decorum, the demand for state revenue thus asserted its predominance almost at once.

There was continual concern over competition with the state monopoly of spirits. The head official of a pot-house in Kolomna complained in 1653 that, when the pot-house was shut because of fast days, soldiers came and openly sold spirits by the cup from flasks. 'And on any days when the pot-house is open the soldiers go round the pot-house, to the market-place and along the market-rows and in the artisan quarter in the free settlements in tenements and streets and continually sell spirits.'[202] They produced drink where they were stationed and their commander protected them. The official could not collect tax from them because they had threatened to kill him. They played cards and dice. There had been a riot involving over two hundred soldiers which resulted in the death of one of the men on oath and a workman and attempts on the life of another man on oath. An armed guard of twenty or so men had been organised to prevent intending drinkers from reaching the pot-house so that the soldiers themselves could sell to them. The major himself was alleged to be a known seller of spirits and to be selling spirits he had bought at the pot-house to his own soldiers. By 1659 the men on oath on the Northern Dvina were not only urged to brew beer and make mead, but to sell them 'measuring up to the sales of former years and the purchase of stocks so that it shall be more profitable for our treasury; and drinkers are not to be driven away from our pot houses'.[203]

The decline in revenue resulting from the reform and the confusion it caused was a contributing factor in the depreciation, first, of the silver coinage, exacerbated by the wars with Poland, and later Sweden; it then drove the government to issue copper coins. In 1658 silver and copper coins circulated on a par, but silver steadily increased in value till late 1661 when, in three months, they doubled in value; by mid-1663 they had increased again almost four times, then being thirteen times their 1658 value.[204] The impact of this depreciation of the coinage was delayed, probably because it took place in a weakly monetised economy. Gradually, however, inflation made itself felt, especially when the war against Sweden went badly at the end of the 1650s and the government exacted the musketeers' money tax in kind at 700 chets each of rye and oats per sokha unit in 1661-2.[205] Inflation evoked

[202] *AI*, IV, 74 (I) (25 December 1653).
[203] *AAE*, IV, no. 111 (15 May 1659).
[204] *AAE*, IV, no. 144 (II) (9 November 1663).
[205] Bazil'evich, 'Elementy merkantilizma', 18-20.

widespread disorders in many towns, including Moscow in June 1662.[206] The copper coinage was abandoned in June the following year. The old system of drink-shops was restored the following month; only a few restrictions remained.[207] No drink was to be sold near monasteries or churches on feast days, nor was drink to be sold in the first week of Lent or Easter Week, on Sundays, or on Wednesdays and Fridays in Lent or the Assumption fast (in August). The fines for illicit drink were doubled. The reform of 1652, thus, failed to outlast either the war with Poland (1653–67) or the ascendancy of Nikon (condemned by the Synod in 1666).

[handwritten: 1663 July]

There were, of course, continuities throughout the second half of the seventeenth century; some documents, in fact, read as if the reform had never taken place. One of 1678 specifies (incorrectly) the deficit in the sums collected at the pot-house in the Beloozero artisan quarter in the previous year compared with the amount in 1651, twenty-seven years previously, and before the 1652 reform.[208] According to the officials at Beloozero

Their deficit relative to 1651 was caused by the fact that in that year, they claim, drink was sold at the pot-house and at many bars; and they rode out to the uezd with drink and sold it at festivals and fairs, and in that year they gave drink on credit and against deposited goods, and grain was cheaper.

Now circumstances had changed. 'The people of the Beloozero artisan quarter are impoverished and there have been few drinkers at the pot-house.' The reply from the administration was to organise a detailed enquiry with a battery of questions, including:

. . . how much swipes and brewed beer the trusted head officials had at the distillery and the price per chet of any grain which went for swipes and the beer-mash and the price of a bucket of spirits from swipes, and also from the beer-mash, and the price at which spirits and beer were sold by bucket, by pot and by cup; and how many buckets of spirits and beer and provisions remained in the present year 1678 unsold, and where they put those spirits.

The maltsters were also to be closely questioned, as were 'the clerks, the distillers and brewers and the work people'. There was to be a great general investigation to check against any possible deception. Moreover, the military commander of Beloozero was instructed to watch the investigators.

---

[206]V.I. Buganov, *Moskovskoe vosstanie 1662 g.*, 33–5.
[207]Veselovskii, 'Kabatskaya reforma', 65.
[208]*DAI*, VII, no. 66, (II).

You are to watch carefully lest the people investigating, gathering in family groups (*skopyas' sem'yami*), give false results of their searches at the instigation of the head officials and men on oath; and during that investigation I forbid the head officials and the men on oath to be at Beloozero; they are to be sent for a time wherever is suitable, so that they do not bribe or persuade those investigating.

If the investigators failed to do their duty they were to be 'severely punished and for their fault they shall be taken with their wives and children to Moscow, to live there for ever on service'. As if this punishment were not terrible enough, their property was to be seized as a contribution to making good the deficit.

In 1664, twelve years after the reform, the small drink-shops in the Kholmogory artisan quarter had some time before been ordered to be done away with and replaced by a single pot-house; 'and our, the Great Sovereign's, drink, spirits, beer and mead, shall be sold in one place on the days decreed'.[209] This probably refers to the decrees of 1652 and 1653, which ordained prohibited days and forbad credit. In 1664, however, 'in the Kholmogory artisan quarter the head officials of the pot-houses . . . sell Russian and German spirits and vodkas by buckets, pots and cups from the spirits cellar, and at Kholmogory artisan quarter in six places and not on the days decreed'. They were also alleged to sell at various prices and on credit; they were fiddling the books by claiming to be distilling when they were not, and so on. The Dvina military commander queried whether there was to be one pot-house rather than several drink-shops, closed days etc. The reply referred to a decree for all Novgorod Department towns: 'In accordance with the decree of our Great Sovereign, the drink-shops were abolished in all places in towns where they were and there was ordered to be one pot-house for each; but henceforth pot-houses are forbidden, but drink-shops are ordered to be, as they were before, where they existed before this.' The trusted head officials were to be responsible for the excise revenue, not the military commanders. Obviously, all was not clear even in this important trade centre.

In July 1677 involvement of the military commanders in the work of customs officers and the head officials of drink-shops was forbidden in the Pskov region; the elders of the land and all the people of the artisan quarter were to elect the officials.[210] The administration was evidently in disarray; the Novgorod Department could not find relevant documents; it was not known for how long the farm of a drink-

[209]*DAI*, IV, no. 139 (March 1664).
[210]*DAI*, VII, no. 66 (1).

shop in Krasny, near Pskov, had been granted. Similarly, information was sought about the farming out of kvas sales at the market baths in Archangel. The farm year was rarely precisely stated; cases occur indicating a year starting on 1 February, March, June or November as well as September.[211] Most of the establishments on farm were granted for periods of three or five years. Usually they were held by men of the artisan quarter, but on the estates of the high nobles, drink places, and sometimes markets, were farmed 'to peasants'; these were probably their nominees.

Military commanders sometimes were called on, as an interim measure, to deal with the drink-shop dues 'according to the new trading statute and the statutory regulation and the memoranda', but were not to interfere with the tavern officials.[212] Detailed instructions followed on how these officials were to act. All the men of the artisan quarter were to watch the officials carefully to see they did not steal from the treasury, or have free drinks; that they kept their books accurately and did not trade their own stuff duty-free, gave no credit and took no money for themselves. The officials were to etablish whether it was more profitable to distill spirits or to buy them on contract. They were to engage in no abnormal expenditure without authorisation from the Treasury Department.

The Sol' Vychegda town and uezd chief tolls and pot-house official for 1669 responsible for 'spirits, and for buying rye malt, barley malt and hops for the beer mash for distilling spirits', complained that in Velikii Ustyug, without the tsar's authority, the military commander had forbidden the distillery contractors to buy grain in order to produce spirits. He had, therefore, been obliged to purchase 500 buckets of spirits on credit 'at no small price, of necessity, so that your, the Great Sovereign's, Usol'e pot-houses should not be without spirits'.[213] He paid what was considered the high price of 20 altyns (120 dengas) a bucket. This official claimed to be a tilling peasant, illiterate and not engaged in crafts, trades or commerce 'I, your orphan [i.e. dependant], am not rich, am in debt, and hitherto, lord, have never been on such service of yours, the Great Sovereign, and do not know about your, the Great Sovereign's, tolls and pot-houses.' The two men on oath were young, twenty and eighteen, and poor (*nedostatochnye*), had never before performed state service and did not know about tolls and pot-house matters. The result was that these officials, lacking resources in money and grain, could get no credit because

[211]*DAI*, vii, no. 66 (v).
[212]*DAI*, vii, no. 66 (iv) (28 January 1681), Beloozero.
[213]*DAI*, v, 93 (i).

Knowing our scant and poor existence, no one trusts us. And, lord, many men of the artisan quarter and volost peasants engaged in trade, for want of trade, and tilling peasants and holders of hamlets have been impoverished and fallen into great debt from grain failures and the payments imposed on the hamlets; and the spirits contractors will not make agreements without money; they ask no small sum to supply us.

The grant to these officials was, apparently, 50 rubles, whereas the previous year the amount granted the former head official had been 200 rubles. Sales of spirits and beer had not fallen and soon there would be nothing to pay with. The maltsters were asking high prices

. . . because, lord, in the present year 1669 half or less of the rye in the fields has grown, and the barley, oats and wheat, the peas and hops have perished from frost and hops are to be bought at a high price, twice or more that of previous years.

And in the present year, lord, 1669, the head tolls and pot-house official, Aggei Svin'in and his fellows newly erected at Shilyuga, at Lal *pogost*, at your, the Great Sovereign's brewery and distillery, stills, a boiler, seven settling tanks, two stills, eighteen pipes.

But he refused to hand the newly equipped works over to the new official without payment. Subsequently a payment of 200 rubles was authorised.

There were, too, difficulties in accounting in the late seventeenth century; these may be illustrated by a memorandum dated 18 October 1677.[214]

And as soon as this memorandum reaches you, in accordance with the former and this decree of the Great Sovereign, you land reeves and all the people of the [tax] commune are to receive, from the head official and the men on oath of the past year 1676–7 at the drink-shop, their draft (*chernye*) drink-shop registers before all the men of the artisan quarter and over the hand of the head official and the men on oath; you elect three or four persons from the group among yourselves, from the artisan quarter best and middle and junior people; and you order those people to take account in truth of the registers of the head official and the men on oath, and order them to write fair copies (*belye knigi*) and, checking the fair copies with the draft registers in the Land Office, order the fair copies to be read aloud, more than once, to people of all ranks. This is to check that: the head official of the drink-shop and the men on oath have recorded the drink monies in full compared with what was collected; that all items of expenditure have been given in accordance with the decree; that they have not left anything for themselves from what was collected; and, after taking account of the registers of the head official and the men on oath and all putting their hand to it, send them with the registers to be accounted for to

[214]*DAI*, VII, 56.

the Great Sovereign, to Moscow by the first winter road, without waiting for any other decree from the Great Sovereign about it; and they shall suffer no delays or losses from the report in Moscow.[215]

The last phrase must have raised a hollow laugh; Moscow red-tape (*moskovskaya volokita*) had long been established and was a by-word.[216]

With so much concern for excise duties as a source of revenue and the organisational and administrative problems encountered, it is not surprising to find attention given to suspected smuggling. Pronka, an apple-seller, was walking home in Moscow at half past twelve on the night of 24–5 September 1684. By All Saints Gate he saw a couple of Ukrainian carts and 'simply said "I bet that chap's carrying undeclared stuff"'.[217] No doubt he wished later he had kept quiet. The watch seized him and took him with one of the carts to the Malo-Rossiya Department. They found three (later two!) three-bucket barrels of double distilled spirits and a flask, about half a bucket of ordinary spirits. These had been sent from his mother in Kiev to Osip Vasil'ev Klimashevskii.

Both state concern over revenue and the individual's concern to avoid the state's monopoly, if at all possible, were related to the price of spirits. Crull, in 1698, claimed that: 'Bath-stoves being so common in *Muscovy*, that there is not a village so small, but has one or more of them . . . But as the Taverns and other Houses where strong Liquors are sold, infinitely out-number the Bath-stoves, so the Revenue arising from them to the Czar is incredible.'[218] He also claimed that some were farmed out at 2,000, 6,000, 10,000 or 12,000 rubles a year. This is almost certainly an overstatement in some respects, even though the revenue achieved was very considerable. Korb, too, regarded the drink-shop income as second in importance to tribute and annual tax; he estimated the income as 200,000 imperials at this time.[219]

In the late 1670s there were evidently more than a hundred official outlets for trade in spirits, but we do not know how many more.[220] Altogether, there may have been a few hundred of some size and importance and at least as many others. Olearius, who had been in Muscovy in the 1630s, claimed in 1656 that three drink-shops in Novgorod had given an annual income of 6,000 rubles, and that 'under

---

[215]Similar, but not quite such detailed, instructions are found in *DAI*, vii, 66 (iv) (1681).
[216]*DAI*, vi, 52 (ii) (1672) for instance, stipulated that allowances were to be paid at the times decreed, in all years, 'without Moscow red-tape'.
[217]*DAI*, xi, 80.
[218]J. Crull, *The Antient and Present State of Muscovy*, vol. i, 184.
[219]Korb, *Diary*, vol. ii, 145–6.
[220]*DAI*, vii, no. 66 lists almost a hundred, mostly drink-shops.

the new order, the sum is greater yet. There are around a thousand such taverns in the country, though not all are as profitable.'[221] Van Klenck, later in the century, recorded that a new drink-shop in the Polish settlement took 136,000 ducats from November to mid-January but this, of course, included the cycle of Christmas festivities.[222]

Supplies for the pot-houses were sometimes considerable and might come from a remote distillery. There is an order of 20 November 1677 for the Shuya distillery to produce 1,000 buckets of very good spirits, 'sparkling and without any burning taste'; this was to be done 'with great haste' so that it could reach the Novomeshchanskii pot-house in Moscow 'by the winter road of the present year 186', i.e. the winter of 1677–8. Moreover, the cost, including cooperage (it was envisaged that the Shuya house would need to acquire additional barrels) and transport, was to result in retail sales at less than 10 altyns [60 dengas] a pot, that is 600 a bucket; if costs were to be higher, an estimate was to be sent 'immediately, with deliberation, before anything was started or spirits distilled'.[223] The reasons for this apparently exceptional urgency were not stated.

Pot-houses were sometimes supplied with spirits from a central Despatch Warehouse (*Otdatochnyi dvor*) in Moscow. We have details, obviously estimated, of one such operation in 1683, for which the allowances to the men on oath amounted to 4,204 rubles (Table 4.4).[224] Deliveries to the Warehouse or to local pot-houses had to include a supplement of five pots above every ten buckets to allow for seepage and ullage, an allowance of 6.25%.[225]

Some sketchy impression of possible profits from sales of spirits may be formed from the meagre information in Table 4.5. Profits were very high. Even if we dismiss all the figures showing more than a hundred percent profit in one year and take the exceptionally high-cost, evidently extortionate item in 1667 (4), profit still amounts to 25%. The sale of 1,000 buckets of spirits here gave a profit of 600 rubles. Nevertheless, state thirst for money was such that at Dedilovo in 1683 an investigation was set up in order to determine how shortfalls of $29\frac{1}{2}$ rubles and almost 19 rubles had occurred.[226]

Available information is not enough even to hazard a guess as to the total revenue from alcohol. It appears, though, that quite apart from

[221]Olearius, *Travels*, 199.
[222]*Voyagie*, 104.
[223]*DAI*, VII, no. 60.
[224]*AI*, v, no. 106 (5 May 1683).
[225]*DAI*, v, no. 93 (III) (1663).
[226]*DAI*, x, no. 88.

Table 4.4. *Supplies of spirits and costs (1683)*

Destination	1 Price		2 Transport		3 Quantity (buckets)	Totals for:		
						4 Spirits (1 × 3)	5 Transport (2 × 3)	6 Total (4 + 5)
	alt.	d.	alt.	d.		rubles		
Sol' Kama	7	4			1,800	414	180	594
	8	2			6,200	1,550	620	2,170
	8	4	3	2	2,000	520	200	720
Cherdyn'	8	2			2,000	530	200	730
Kaigorodok	9	0			1,000	270	100	370
					13,000	3,284	1,300	4,584
Allowance for men on oath								126
Total								4,710

Source: *AI*, v, no. 106.

any state encouragement of drink consumption in the interest of revenue, Russians did not lack a tendency to drink in the seventeenth
century. 'On holidays they are allowed, even given the pre-eminent
right, to make themselves drunk without punishment; one may then
see them lying on the streets, frozen by the cold, or carried to their
homes, piled one on top of another on carts and sledges.'[227] Reitenfels
observed that women, clergy and the monks were also addicted and
added: 'Although the Russians try to excuse their constant drunkenness, for they preferably drink vodka day and night, by the fact that,
apart from ancient custom (the whole north has of old drunk much), it
is essential for them as a defence against the cold; nevertheless, they do
not fully succeed in removing the shameful stain of drunkenness.'[228]
Other foreigners in Russia at the time had practical objections: drunkenness interfered with work. Christian Marselis and Andrew Butenant
complained about drink being brought for sale to the workers at their
copper works near Olonets by the head officials of the pot-house or
drink-shops. Drunkenness led to many quarrels, crimes and manslaughter among both skilled men and ordinary workers.[229] The officials were forbidden to take drink to the area.

   Not only foreigners in Russia were concerned about the extent of
drunkenness. Satirical writings were quite frequent in the seventeenth
century, some reproducing material even from the sixteenth cen-

[227]Reitenfels, 'Skazaniya', 145. Originally published in Padua in 1680.
[228]*Ibid.*, 146; see also 155. Cp. Olearius, *Travels*, 142–6; and many other foreigners.
[229]*DAI*, ix, 33 (1678).

Table 4.5. *Percentage profit from spirits sales*

Date	Amount involved (buckets)	Cost (dengas/bucket)	Selling price[a] (dengas/bucket)	Gross profit (%)
1 1663		108[b]	600	455
2 1669	500	120	600	400
3 1664	500	220	600	173
4 1667	1,000	480[c]	600	25
5 1667–8	5,312	111	600	440
6 1683	13,000	72[d]	600	733

Notes:
[a] See Table 4.4, p. 167 above.
[b] Fixed as maximum to be paid.
[c] 10 altyns (60 dengas) a pot, i.e. 480 dengas/bucket. This is stated to be dear.
[d] Estimate, clearly optimistic; see Table 4.4 above.
Sources: 1, 2, 5 *DAI*, v, no. 93;   4 *DAI*, vii, no. 60;
         3   *DAI*, iv, no. 139; 6 *AI*, v, no. 106.

tury.[230] From the second half of the century we have a sharp lampoon in the form of a parody of vespers; this not merely condemned the moral evils of drunkenness, as had frequently been done before, but pictured the economic evils resulting from the drink-shop.[231]

Church concern about drinking by clergy and monks continued throughout the second half of the century. In 1660, for example, the monk in charge of a monastic salt-works at Staraya Rusa was warned that the stewards 'should not visit drink-shops, drink and tipple (*brazhnichali*) and should not impose taxes and drive away peasants, but should defend the peasants and give no offence to anyone'.[232] If they did not, the Patriarch Nikon would hold them in disgrace and they would be severely punished 'without mercy'. The same year the Metropolitan of Novgorod sent a memorandum to the Tikhvin monastery calling attention to a decree forbidding lords to import spirits for sale by barrels or by buckets, that is for large-scale or wholesale trade.[233] The penalties were severe: forfeiture of the lord's estate, and 'if any of their people and peasants begin to distill spirits and sell them without

[230]V.N. Peretts, 'Iz starinnoi satiricheskoi literatury o p'yanstve i p'yanitsakh', 432–3.
[231]V.P. Adrianova-Peretts, *Prazdnik kabatskikh yaryzhek*, 5, 8; the reconstructed text is on 50–84.
[232]*AAE*, iv no. 114 (February 1660).
[233]*DAI*, iv, no. 88 (31 October 1660).

their knowledge, the hands of the people and peasants are to be cut off and they are to be exiled to Siberia'.

Tikhvin, with its busy settlement of artisans and traders, was warned three years later by Archimandrite Iosif.[234] 'Offence is caused by scoundrels; those living in the artisan quarter make undeclared illicit alcoholic kvas for sale in many places and secretly sell it.' He prohibited them from dealing 'in illicit drink, tobacco, spirits, beer and fermented kvas; nor are you to have any dice, cards, illicit drink and whores or any refuge at all in the artisan quarter for prohibited criminals'. Drink might be permitted, however, to commemorate relatives, for weddings and so on. Drinking places were often found where trade took place; this was frequently close to a monastery, so the church became involved. At Makar'evo, near Nizhnii Novgorod, the fair held in June or July was attended by officers seeking runaway serfs and other offenders; this caused such disarray and consequential losses from tolls, and extra demands for maintenance, that the officers were prohibited. The monastery was to judge any cases arising during the fair.[235]

Sometimes, however, the church was more directly involved with the conduct of its own clergy. The Metropolitan of Novgorod and Velikie Luki ordered clerics, deacons, hieromonks, monks and elders found in pot-houses in Novgorod to be brought to his establishment, 'as well as any of those ranks who are drunk in the [market] rows and on the streets'.[236] The Metropolitan's officials dealing with such offenders were warned not to take bribes.

The joint tsars, Ivan and Peter, authorised the Zvenigorod pot-house to be removed in 1682

... and for there to be henceforth no pot-house in that town; and instead the pot-house is to be in the crown village of Mikhailovskoe, in Moscow uezd, because the Zvenigorod pot-house stood close to the cloister of the Venerable Father Sava Storozhevskii, and from that monastery inexperienced monks go to the pot-house to drink and dishonour the holy cloister.[237]

When the two young tsars were to visit this monastery in 1684 (Peter was then twelve) beer, small beer, kvas, sour cabbage soup and mead were to be prepared for them as in former instructions.[238] Firewood, workers, all sorts of vessels and anything else needed for these modest, non-spiritous drinks, not characteristic of Peter's subsequent consump-

---

[234] *AAE*, IV, no. 143 (July 1663). See also *AYu*, no. 349 (1).
[235] *DAI*, X, no. 41 (1673, confirmed in 1682).
[236] *AI*, V, no. 203 (10 December 1690).
[237] *DAI*, X, no. 21 (13 July 1682).
[238] *DAI*, XI, no. 63.

tion, were to be provided by the monastery or the people of the artisan quarter.

Indeed, a more characteristic description of the drink situation a few years before the start of Peter's reforms is that given by a visitor in 1689.

They prepare for their fast by an equal number of carnival days during which the disorder is then so great that the foreigners who stay in the suburbs do not dare to leave and come into the town; for they beat one another like wild beasts and become drunk on brandy and other drinks so strong and fierce that they are the only people in the world able to drink them; and, again, there is nothing surprising if they lose what little reason they naturally have and stab one another with large knives like bayonets.[239]

Within a year or two, in the early 1690s when he was about twenty, Peter had institutionalised his bouts of drinking. These usually took place with his close companions, after his 'mock' battles on land and sea or to celebrate the launching of a ship for the navy, as well as at established annual festivals. 'Just as, in the mock battles on land and sea, Romodanovskii was generalissimo and admiral, while Peter was a captain, bombardier or skipper, so, at the feasts, Nikita Zotov was head of the company, "The Most Jokey Father Ioanikit, Patriarch of Presburg, Kokui and All-Yauza".'[240] Peter was merely a deacon. The 'Patriarch' later became the 'Prince-Pope' with a conclave of twelve cardinals and a suite of bishops, archimandrites and other officers 'bearing nicknames which under any censorship regulation, will never appear in the press'.[241]

What was the significance of this College of Drunkenness? Was it simply a coarse form of relaxation after heavy work or a carelessness about behaviour?[242] Did the change from 'Patriarch' to 'Pope' involve a change from Orthodoxy to Catholicism as the object of parody?

Foreign observers were prepared to see in these outrages a political and even an educational tendency directed, as it were, against the Russian church hierarchy and even the church itself, but also against the vice of drunkenness; the tsar', they alleged, was trying to mock that to which he wished to weaken addiction and esteem; allowing the people a chance to be amused, the drunken

[239]Foy de la Neuville, *Rélation curieuse*, 190–1.

[240]Solov'ev, *Istoriya*, vol. VII, 474. The title (*Vseshuteiishii otets Ioanikit, presburgskii, kokuiskii i vseyauzskii patriarkh*) mimics that of the true Patriarch Ioakim; but is an amalgam of Western and Russian elements; Kokui was the location of the foreign settlement at Moscow; the Yauza was one of the tributaries of the Moskva which ran through the town. Cp. Schuyler, *Peter the Great*, vol. II, 451.

[241]Klyuchevskii, *Sochineniya*, vol. IV, 40. See also Korb, *Diary*, vol. I, 255–8.

[242]*Ibid.*, 39.

ПОСТАРИНЕ, КОГДА НАСТОЛЪ ПОСТАВЯТЬ ВСІПЬ. ХОЗЯЮШКА
САМА ФОЛЖНАПОДНЕСТЬ. ДЛЯ ПРОЧИЩЕНІЯ ГЛОТКИ, ГОСТЯМ
ПОЧАРКЕ ВОДКИ. ДЛЯ ЛУПЧЕЙ КУШАТЬ ИМЪ ОХОТКИ. АДАКЪ
ПОДНОСЬ ИМЪ СТАНЕТЬ ПОДАВАТЬ. ДОЛЖНА ОНА ПОТОМЪ
ГОСТЕИ ПОЦАЛОВАТЬ; Я МОДА ПОХВАЛЮ ТАККЮ. ИЛИШЪ
ОДНО ПОКРЫТИКХЮ. НАПИЩЪ ТО ОХОТЫ ПРИДАЕТЬ
ХОЗЯИКИНЪ ПОЦСЛУИ ПОСКРОМОСТИТЬ ГУБЫ. СІВОДКИ ЗУБЫ
ДОЕ СТЛИ ТЫ ДУРНОІ ХОЗЯЮШКА. МОИ СВЕТЬ. ТОКИ
ВОДКУ ПОДНОСИ. КОКЪ КОНЧИТСЯ ОБЕДЪ.

19 Old-time hospitality, mid–eighteenth century.
An eighteenth-century meal with the wife in attendance. The doggerel
inscription is roughly as follows:

> The wife herself in days of yore,
> Serving, to the table bore
> A glass, to cleanse the taste,
> Of vodka each one's lips to baste
> To raise their ardour for the feast.
> And as she held the tray for each,
> She offered every guest a kiss.
> Such a custom's worth our praise,
> I'd only one objection raise.
> I say what raises up their ardour –
> The good wife's kiss will scent their lips,
> Their teeth will smell of vodka sips.
> But if you've no good looks, my friend,
> Then serve the vodka at the end.

company taught it to combine disdain for prejudice with revulsion from filthy debauch. It is hard to weigh the element of the truth in this view; but all the same it is a justification, rather than an explanation.[243]

What is undoubted, though it has hitherto not perhaps been adequately stressed, is the element of continuity in the form of these drunken revels. Even after the creation of Petersburg, up to about 200 people joined in drunken celebrations with public processions at Christmas-tide; Easter was marked in similar fashion.[244] When the fool (*shut*) Yakov Turgenev was married in January 1694 (Christmas-tide was a traditional time for marriages), boyars, chamberlains, members of the Council and palace people of all ranks followed in the procession; 'they rode on oxen, goats, pigs, dogs, and wore ridiculous dress: fibre sacks, bast hats, dyed kaftans trimmed with cats' paws, grey variegated kaftans trimmed with white tails, straw boots, gloves of mouse-skin, bark caps'.[245] Bears were also used on occasion.[246] Aspects of traditional celebrations, especially at Christmas-tide and Easter, involving drink and animals which had formerly had cult associations, were part of these rituals. These old traditions perhaps included some parody of church rituals; such was the lampoon of vespers mentioned above. An attitude of mockery sprang from the great stress on ritual; 'strictly demanding external fulfilment of church procedure, the pastors were unable to induce a proper respect for it, because they themselves attached insufficient importance to it'.[247] 'Here is no subtle or cunning anti-church calculation of politicians, but simply the coarse feeling of powerful revellers disclosing a common fact, the deep decline of church authority.'[248] The conflict with the church in such celebrations was, as we have seen, of long standing. Whatever the specific motivation for Peter's College of Drunkenness, whatever its intended impact on the Russian church and society, its actual impact was assured by its forms making use of popular elements with a long history. In this respect, as in so many others, Peter marks, Janus-like, both the continuing influence of old Russia and the start of the new. Peter introduced elements of West European carnival into some public celebrations, but non-Christian elements in the revels, derived from a cult of the ancestors, also marked the birth of the Russian Empire.[249]

[243]*Ibid.*, 41.
[244]*Ibid.*, 40–1.
[245]Solov'ev, *Istoriya*, vol. VII, 474.
[246]Klyuchevskii, *Sochineniya*, vol. IV, 40.
[247]*Ibid.*, 42.
[248]*Ibid.*
[249]V. Miller, *Russkaya maslenitsa*, 29. Cp. Bakhtine, *L'oeuvre de François Rabelais*, 270. Sakharov, *Skazaniya*, II, VII, 72, noted that Peter opened the Shrove-tide celebrations by swinging with his officers.

5

****

Steppes and counter-measures: the eighteenth century

In the eighteenth century some major changes took place in Russian diet: upper class diet had long differed from that of the mass of the people in terms of quality and quantity, now it also came to differ in style. Imports increased and were in the main restricted to upper class gentry tables; West European cooking had an increasingly strong impact at this social level from the reign of Peter the Great (1689–1725). The creation of the Russian Empire (Peter was declared Emperor in 1721), which resulted from Russia becoming a Baltic power, had important consequences for the diet.

St Petersburg was built in the early years of the eighteenth century and it was used by Peter as the centre for the court and the capital of Russia. He made considerable efforts to ensure that it was a capital city in the western style. This activity created a vast market for supplies of all sorts: building materials, naval stores, food for tens of thousands of workers and for court, military and naval officers, as well as for the foreigners who gathered there, and provisions for the naval and military forces. Despite Peter's success in creating a Russian navy, the merchant marine trading to Russia remained foreign. All this meant that the port of St Petersburg not only was the entry for a range of luxury foodstuffs and equipment but also had a sizeable community of West Europeans, some of whom maintained good tables and kitchens. Both imports and example contributed to the changes which took place.

The imports included cooks.

From Peter's time the Russian nobility and the rest of the gentry borrowed the West European tradition of cookery and introduced it among themselves. Rich grandees visiting Western Europe brought back foreign cooks. At first these were mainly Dutch and German, in particular, Saxon and Austrian, later they were Swedish and predominantly French.[1]

---

[1]Pokhlebkin, *Natsional'nye kukhni*, 10.

Peter himself contributed greatly to this process in two ways. First, he sent many Russians abroad to learn various skills; some acquired a taste for western food during their sometimes lengthy stay abroad. Second, he himself visited Western Europe and recruited many foreigners to serve in Russia from the time of the Grand Embassy (1697–8). Most of these, of course, were concerned with military, naval and industrial affairs, but this influx of about a thousand foreigners with diets different from the Russian probably prepared the way for the changes which followed on the subsequent development of St Petersburg. Moreover, many of Peter's associates were foreigners and he himself developed a taste for some western food and drink. He had a partiality for Limburger cheese and favoured Hungarian wine, but also had a sailor's hearty appetite.[2] Peter, too, after 1704, acquired Johann Velten, the Saxon cook to the Danish ambassador to Russia.[3] This was crucial in that it set the fashion for Russians in Peter's circle. This fashion then filtered down to at least part of the nobility and gentry, not many in number perhaps, but important in terms of influence. In the second half of the eighteenth century cooks were so regularly recruited from abroad that foreign ones almost completely replaced Russians in the households of the higher gentry.[4] Indeed, when what was probably the first Russian cookery book appeared in 1816 its author claimed that it was no longer possible to give a full description of Russian cooking, but that one had to be satisfied with what people still remembered.[5]

As a result of West European influences upper class meals were modified in two main ways. First, the formal meal no longer started with bread and vodka as in the sixteenth and early seventeenth century, or cold soups as later, but with open sandwiches of meat, fish or cheese. Ham, smoked tongue, salt beef, sausage, herring, pickles in brine, all cold, were served; 'all this was very salt, with a lot of pepper and garlic'.[6] Caviare, cured salmon and sturgeon were used, as well as items in aspic.[7] Such food sometimes constituted a meal. This development was a stage in the emergence of the Russian *hors-d'oeuvre*, called *zakuski*, of which the great range known today only arose in the nineteenth century. The development of *zakuski* did not involve any major change in the diet; it used foodstuffs which, apart from cheeses, were already common place. As late as 1786 we have it on the author-

[2]Klyuchevskii, *Sochineniya*, 4:33.
[3]von Staehlin Storcksburg, *Original Anecdotes*, 275.
[4]Pokhlebkin, *Natsional'nye kukhni*, 10.
[5]Levshin, *Russkaya povarnya*, cited by Pokhlebkin, 11.
[6]Just Juel, the Danish envoy in 1709, cited in Mel'gunova, *Russkii byt'*, 83.
[7]Pokhlebkin, *Natsional'nye kukhni*, 10.

20 Tiled stove, eighteenth century.

ity of Catherine II herself that 'scarcely any cheese is made in the whole of Russia'.[8] No doubt she had in mind hard and other matured cheeses; cottage or cream cheese was probably generally available. This seems

[8]Cited in Bartlett, *Human Capital*, 132.

to be implied by the views of two merchants in the 1790s that imported cheeses were an unnecessary delicacy, since anyone could make
them for themselves.[9]

A modification introduced at such eighteenth-century upper class
tables was that, as imported wines became commoner in the course of
the century, they were sometimes served with these preliminaries,
together with the well-established vodka. Hungarian wine continued
to be popular at court after Peter's day.[10] One of the earliest English
Governesses in St Petersburg wrote in the mid-1730s that there was 'no
Want of good Diet, no more than there is of good Liquor, Claret,
Burgundy, *Tockay*, Arrack, Brandy, with several other fine Liquors,
they have very reasonable'.[11] She only noted the absence of port;
otherwise, she believed 'there is no Part of the World where the *English*
live better than they do at Petersburgh'.[12] Towards the end of Peter's
reign the enterprising Pososhkov praised the vodkas, beers and meads
that God had given the Russians. It was all right for foreigners to keep
their own foreign drinks in their houses and to entertain freely whomever they wished with Rhine, Alicante or Hungarian wines, but if
they sold any, they should be fined a hundredfold its value and their
stocks confiscated. 'In my opinion,' he added, 'it were better to cast
money into the water than pass it overseas for drink.'[13] The relatively
low import of wines towards the end of the century (see Table 5.1)
suggests that their use was not widespread and perhaps, even for the
westernised gentry in general, wine was still a drink intended to indicate status, but not necessarily a matter of preferred taste. Comments
by the same governess upon the choice and quality of fish, game, meat,
fruit and vegetables would seem to justify her view that the 'Diet of
Russia is excellently good, and, in my Opinion, this Place is very fit for
an Epicure'.[14] She immediately went on to write: 'for, in short, Eating
and Drinking take up a third Part of their Time'. Whether epicures are
to be identified by the time spent at table may be open to doubt
(especially by those who have had to eat in Soviet restaurants), but it is
clear that these accounts relate to the English community in St Petersburg and the upper class westernised Russians, perhaps 1% of the total
population.

The second way in which West European influences modified upper

[9]Kahan, 'Costs of "Westernization"', *Slavic Review*, xxv, 1, n. 5.

[10]von Manstein, *Contemporary Memoirs*, 257.

[11]Justice, *A Voyage to Russia*, 21.

[12]*Ibid.*, 57, 20–21.

[13]*Kniga o skudosti i bogatstve*, 135–6.

[14]Justice, *A Voyage to Russia*, 19, 20 (fish); 21 (game); 20 (meat); 39, 40 (fruit and vegetables);
    59–60.

class meals was that sugar gradually came to replace honey. This seemingly small change resulted in quite large consequences in the course of the century. Tarts, pastries and sweetmeats were modified and developed and, as tea became a commoner upper class drink from the 1770s, a new meal, afternoon tea, emerged.[15]

The first sugar refinery in Russia was established in Petersburg by a merchant of foreign ancestry, called Vestov or Westhoff, and his associates, in 1723.[16] This relied on the import of cane sugar coming into the new port. Sugar, loaf and crystals, as well as products such as sugared biscuits and confectionery had been imported into Russia through Archangel in the 1670s.[17] At first in the eighteenth century imports of refined sugar were prohibited, presumably to protect the native industry, but later they were allowed on payment of a 15% tariff.[18] Around the middle of the century Canary and 'semi-Canary' (*polukenarskii*), loaf sugar, 'simple', white and 'red' crystallised sugar and raw powder (the cheapest) was imported.[19] These varieties were mentioned in the 1757 tariff. They were all cane sugars and were imported by way of Lubeck, Hamburg, London, Amsterdam, Copenhagen and Danzig.[20] In 1755–62 about 500 puds (8,100 kg) a year of crystallised sugar was imported from China; during the reign of Catherine II this figure had risen to 1,500 to 2,500 puds (24,000–40,000 kg) a year.[21] This type of sugar was used in black tea predominantly.

Sugar works, processing imported sugar, are documented from the 1770s, in the interval between the two closures of Kyakhta and just before the first mention of samovars.[22] In Kaluga in 1772 Peter Korobov had a works which had the following output.[23]

Canary, called refined	5,600r
Ordinary, called molasses	3,600
Crystallised sugar	624
Black syrop	200

---

[15]Tea as a beverage is dealt with in chapter 6 .

[16]Solov'ev, *Istoriya*, vol. IX, 481; Lyubomirov, *Ocherki*, 192–3, 253, 532, 536, 549.

[17]Kurts, *Sochinenie Kil'burgera*, part 2, ch. 1, *passim*.

[18]Brokgauz–Efron, *Entsiklopedicheskii slovar'*, vol. XXIX (57), 16.

[19]Chulkov, *Opisanie*, vol. IV, iv, 311. I have been unable to establish the precise meaning of the term *polukenarskii*; there is no mention in *Slovar' Akademii Rossiiskoi* (1789–94).

[20]*Ibid.*, vol. VII, ii, 190–3.

[21]Samoilov, *Sbornik statisticheskikh svedenii*, vol. II, 7. Korsak, *Obozrenie*, 68, 88.

[22]Chulkov, *Opisanie*, vol. VII, ii, 190–3.

[23]*Ibid.*, vol. VI, iii, 591.

The 1782 tariff laid down the following rates of duty:[24]

Canary and semi-Canary, also refined	per pud	1r.	40k.
Molasses in small and large loaves		1	20
Simple sugar, called lump		1	00
White and red crystallised		1	60
West Indies granulated sugar imported through Europe (this had to be certified as such by Russian consuls or local magistrates)			20
Granulated sugar processed in Europe,	per ruble estimated value		20
Light treacle	per pud	1	80
Black treacle			60

By this time a wide range of sugars were being imported into Russia from the West and this development is associated both with the growth of tea as a meal and the more general introduction of sweetmeats taken after a meal (*zaedki*) and other sweetstuffs formerly made with honey.

In 1793–5 sugar was a major item in imports from the West (in value terms), averaging almost 6 million rubles a year; total imports were then running at almost 28 million rubles a year.[25] This luxury was costing over four times as much as the next foodstuff, coffee, and about five times as much as the imported wines declared.[26]

The simple diet of the mass of the Russian people was not greatly changed for much of the eighteenth century. The English governess already quoted 'observ'd, they need not lay by much to provide for Food; for they can make an hearty Meal on a Piece of black sour Bread, some Salt, an Onion, or Garlick'.[27] 'As to Drink', she added,

They love the strongest liquor they can get; and if they cannot obtain it honestly, they will steal it; for they will not be debarr'd from this sort of Intemperance. But the Liquor commonly sold for the Use of poor People, is Quash [i.e. kvas]; compounded of Water that is thrown upon the Malt after the Goodness is drawn off; and runs upon several Sorts of Herbs, as Thyme, Mint, Sweet Marjorum, and Balm.[28]

It is not surprising, therefore, that Pososhkov, justified his argument

[24]*Ibid.*, vol. IV, iv, 798–9.

[25]Kahan, 'Costs of "Westernization"', *Slavic Review*, XXV, 1.

[26]Storch, *Supplementband*, 53–4, cited in Kahan, 'Costs of "Westernization"', *Slavic Review*, XXV, 1, 44. A. Semenov, *Izuchenie istoricheskikh svedenii o rossiiskikh vneshnei torgovle i promyshlennosti s poloviny XVII-go stoletiya po 1858 god*, part 3 (St Petersburg, 1879), 23–5, 29–30; cited by Volkov, *IZ*, 71, 156.

[27]Justice, *A Voyage to Russia*, 18.

[28]*Ibid.*, 18–19.

Table 5.1. *Luxury imports of foodstuffs into Russia through Europe ('ooo rubles p.a.)*

	St Petersburg and Archangel 1726	St Petersburg 1751–3	1758–60		Declared value	Duty 1793–5	Total
				puds			
Sugar	11.3	310.7	499.9	49,037	5,595.2	332.4	5,927.6
Coffee	*a*	35.8	55.5		1,315.3	141.5	1,456.8
Wines	141.2*b*	454.1	570.8		1,137.3	204.7	1,342.0
Fruit		75.4	90.3		903.6		903.6
Beer and porter					386.9	131.5	518.4
Spices					284.5	26.3	310.8
Cheese					121.3	9.8	131.1
Total imports					27,886.0		

Notes:
a 494 puds
b 'Drinks' (*napitki*)
Source: Storch, *Supplementband*, 53–4. A. Semenov, *Izuchenie istoricheskikh svedenii o rossiiskikh vneshnei torgovle i promyshlennosti s poloviny XVII–go stoletiya po 1858 god*, part 3, 23–5, 29–30.

for exporting manufactured goods, rather than raw materials, because 'bread and food with us is much cheaper than over there'.[29]

The items constituting the diet had changed little, perhaps, but there were considerable changes in the organisation, production, storage and distribution of food supplies. The state grew in the course of the eighteenth century, in the sense both of internal development and of expansion to new areas. This involved new or increased demands for supplies and finance; some of these demands were realised through a growth of trade and the market. New attempts at state intervention in production, and especially in storage and distribution were also made. These changes affected major items of the common diet such as salt, grain and alcohol, and we will now look at these items in turn.

The state monopoly in salt established in 1705 did not long outlive Peter's reign. It was unpopular, since townsmen were obliged to sell the salt on behalf of the state (this obligation lasted till 1785); state costs were high and profits low. A shortage of cash also hindered trade. Free trade would allow barter to take place.[30] In 1727 a decree was issued

[29]Pososhkov, *Kniga o skudosti i bogatstve*, 147.
[30]*Ibid.*, 213.

21 A gingerbread board, probably eighteenth-century.
The peacock was a popular design for such boards.

restoring free trade in salt from the following year.[31] But, in its turn, this was shortlived. The tax of 5 kopeks a pud failed to produce the returns expected by the state and in 1731 the monopoly was restored; at this time a Salt Office was organised alongside the other Departments of state.[32] Again, there were problems, in part arising from the changing internal and external situation of the country.

In 1733–5 Russia was involved in the war of the Polish succession and in 1735–9 in war with Turkey; during the same period internal expenditure by the court, largely on luxuries, rose considerably and continued to do so during the reign of Peter's daughter, Elizabeth (1741–61). By the late 1750s court expenditure was running at the rate of at least 1.7 million rubles a year.[33] Demand for cash, much of it having to be in forms acceptable to foreigners, therefore increased and prices rose. The constraints imposed by the existence of serfdom put a particularly high value on labour and this, in its turn, meant that

[31]*PSZ*, VII, no. 5219 (31 December 1727/5 January 1728); Solov'ev, *Istoriya*, vol. x, 147.
[32]Troitskii, *Finansovaya politika*, 160–1.
[33]*Ibid.*, 239. In 1725 such expenditures had been less than 0.5: *ibid.*, 224, 243.

transport costs rose sharply. State taxation, however, was collected with considerable delays and there were enormous arrears. Between 1720 and 1732 arrears on tolls and drink-shop income amounted to 13.5 million rubles; for Novgorod alone the arrears for 1737–43 on tolls and drink-shop income was almost half a million rubles.[34] The Senate repeatedly called for information, but with little success.

By the mid-1740s the financial difficulties were so great that in Malorossiya supplies of provisions and fodder to magazines for the army were to be paid for, not in money, but in canvas from the state mills.[35] In 1749 the army was in difficulties because of lack of money; the Main Provision Office was to be paid as soon as possible, it was decreed, 'for there is an extreme situation as regards the most necessary affairs: the grain suppliers are complaining that they have not been paid on time and will in future refuse to supply provisions'.[36] The troops were said to be short of over a million rubles, including 300,000 for provisions.

It was against this general background that proposals were made which would increase state income from indirect taxes, including the revenue from salt. There were, however, real difficulties. In 1744 the Senate had to turn its attention to a great problem for the people, a lack of salt resulting from interrupted supplies from the Stroganov works in Perm'.[37] Salt production in general reached a peak of 6.5 million puds in 1741 and then declined over the following years; sales peaked in 1741 and 1743.[38] The shortage was made worse by soldiers pushing aside the peasants and buying up the supplies; other dealers also had preference. The Procurator-General of the Senate himself 'rode to the shops at 11 o'clock on 9 February but found salt sales had stopped; he found a great number of peasants and other base persons [*podlost'*] who declared they had not managed to buy salt for several days'.[39] The Senate ordered salt to be sold only to peasants! Even so, salt had to be brought in from St Petersburg, probably imported salt. This incident was treated as if it were a problem of distribution and profiteering; but the claims of the Stroganovs, and others, in this period point to a number of deeper economic and social difficulties.

The Stroganovs, the largest salt producers in Russia, claimed that transport charges alone exceeded their allowed expenses. They asked

[34]Troitskii, *Finansovaya politika*, 250; Solov'ev, *Istoriya*, vol. XI, 250. See also Troitskii, *Finansovaya politika*, 247–9.
[35]Solov'ev, *Istoriya*, vol. XI, 399, 459.
[36]*Ibid.*, vol. XII, 12–13.
[37]*Ibid.*, vol. XI, 250.
[38]Troitskii, *Finansovaya politika*, 161, 169.
[39]Solov'ev, *Istoriya*, vol. XI, 251.

for their works to be taken back by the Treasury, since they could not operate them profitably; they also urged that a commission should examine their accounts. The key factors seem to have been two. First, labour had greatly increased in cost and was difficult to find. At Perm' there were no workers available with stamped passports, officially allowing them to be hired, 'and they are ordered not to accept written ones', presumably because they were likely to be spurious.[40] Transport contractors were asking 'an unbearable price' for carrying the salt to Nizhnii Novgorod. The situation of other suppliers at Astrakhan' was similar; here, too, there was a shortage of labour; the men on the boats were paid an advance and then ran away, the contractors were asking 19 kopeks a pud 'which has never been known'.[41] A contributing factor to the high cost of transport was the risk of losing labour when boats were searched for runaway serfs at various points on the long river route. The Salt Office confirmed that contractors and workers suffered insults and delays, and had to pay bribes and, as a result, 'there was a great deal of muddle in the hire of workers on the boats'.[42]

The second factor was a technical one: shortage of fuel. The Stroganovs claimed that nearby forest had been cut down and they had to get wood from a distance; there were losses as a result of shallow rivers and storms; they were getting wood from hundreds of verstas up the Kama and were unable to pursue the contractors who had been given considerable advances but had failed to deliver. Demidov, another major salt producer, was in a similar situation. The Senate response to these difficulties was to send a few thousand men under a major-general and to insist on the delivery of the 3 million puds of salt expected from the Stroganovs, 'otherwise a terrible danger will threaten', the Salt Office claimed. The smaller Perm' producers were not able to supply such quantities; Demidov, who produced over a quarter of a million puds, had stopped work; the transport of the lake salt (*buzun*) from Astrakhan' was hindered by lack of workers.[43] The Stroganovs, for their part, claimed that they could not produce 3 million puds because they would only have 139,187 fathoms of wood; this would produce 2,780,000 puds.[44] This is an interesting statement; it implies an output of 20 puds a fathom, considerably higher than the 10–15 puds they had been producing in the previous century and equivalent to nineteenth-century output levels (see Table 2.5, p. 66).

[40] *Ibid.*, 251, 341.
[41] *Ibid.*, 342.
[42] *Ibid.*
[43] *Ibid.*, 343.
[44] *Ibid.*

Such was the situation in 1744 and 1745. In 1746 there were similar problems; the Stroganov salt production was down to less than 2½ million puds; Demidov's to less than 100,000. The Bakhmut state works was also in difficulties for want of labour and the Senate ordered workers to be sent from Voronezh and Belgorod.[45] Other sources of supply were considered. The salt and brine (*tuzluk*) from Lake Elton, about ninety miles east of the Volga in the Saratov administration, was found suitable for human consumption. A colonel was sent with an expedition to erect a wooden fort to protect the site from Kalmyk attack and from smugglers. Salt was to be collected and then carted to Dmitriev and Saratov, a distance of nearly 150 miles (240 km). Boats were to be built in Kazan' and Vyatka uezds – there was a lack of timber in the steppes – and the salt transported upstream. The intended development of this rich deposit of salt was a result of the shortage of fuel available for the Stroganov works in Perm' and the fact that Astrakhan' *buzun* had become so costly because of high transport costs.[46] At Nizhnii Novgorod Perm' salt cost the state 9 kopeks (excluding transport charges to Nizhnii), but that from Astrakhan', of inferior quality, cost 18 kopeks a pud. So, the Stroganovs were still ordered to produce 3 million puds in order to avoid an 'ultimate shortage' in salt.[47] Astrakhan' was envisaged as supplying local needs only; but, of course, the fisheries there used large quantities of salt for preservation which thus found its way into the central areas of Russia. When, in 1745, P.I. Shuvalov had proposed a uniform price for salt throughout Russia of 35 kopeks (prices then varied from 3 to 50 kopeks a pud), Astrakhan' and Krasnyi Yar were to have salt at half that price 'so that the fish dealers should not add much to the salt–fish without which the people cannot manage'.[48]

Finally, the Senate recognised in mid-1748 that the Stroganovs could not continue to produce salt in the old way as a result of the rise in costs.[49] In 1750 Shuvalov's proposal was implemented; the price rise, however, failed to produce the expected profit; though part of this state income was used to reduce the poll-tax, the new price encouraged smuggling of lake salt and measures had to be taken against this.[50]

By 1751, however, there were evident results from the exploitation of the south, especially Lake Elton: more than 4 million puds reached

[45] *Ibid.*, 401–2.
[46] *Ibid.*, 457.
[47] *Ibid.*, 458.
[48] *Ibid.*, 461.
[49] *Ibid.*, 502.
[50] *Ibid.*, vol. XII, 115.

the stores at Nizhnii Novgorod from Lake Elton and more than 700,000 puds of Astrakhan' *buzun* as well.[51] For the following year the Stroganovs were to produce not more than 2 million puds. The increased exploitation of such southern sources, despite the continual difficulties encountered, was no doubt a factor in the closing of some other salt-works which were technically uneconomical. The Staraya Russa area, for instance, apparently produced less than 2 puds per fathom of timber (a tenth of that produced by the Stroganovs); it was closed in 1753 and the north-west was to be supplied from Perm'.[52] By 1754 the Perm' salt producers were no longer asking for labour supplied by the Treasury and it looked as if the Lake Elton supplies might be still further developed when P.I. Shuvalov daringly proposed the construction of a pipe-line to take the brine from the lake to Dmitriev on the Volga.[53]

The outbreak of war with Prussia in 1756 put an end to any such plans. The allocations from income from salt to reduce the poll-tax ceased and the price of salt was raised to 50 kopeks a pud. At first the half-price for Astrakhan' was retained, but it was abolished later the same year.[54] By 1761, in an attempt to get its priorities right, the Salt Office asked for a reduction in the sum it had been told to supply for war needs; the Office had to supply funds to the Empress' chamber.[55]

Almost at the start of her reign in 1762 Catherine II reduced the price of salt to 30 kopeks in general, and 10 kopeks to the fish dealers in Astrakhan' and Krasnyi Yar and 15 to those in Archangel; the expected loss of income was to be made up by increases in the liquor excise.[56] At the same time the salt from Lake Elton was to be replaced by that of better quality from Ilek. This was a salt dome, worked from 1754, by quarrying, not mining. Three hundred convicts were sent to work this rock salt in 1773; presumably it was this which gave rise to our jocular references to Russian 'salt-mines'. State sales were to continue, but salt was also to be allowed to be sold outside the monopoly at 30 kopeks a pud; there was nothing to fear if salt began to be sold at a high cost, if they gave false weight, or mixed sand and dirt with it, because the buyer would then purchase from the Treasury, it was thought. A year later, however, the price was raised to 40 kopeks because money was

[51]*Ibid.*
[52]*Ibid.*, 175.
[53]*Ibid.*, 206–7.
[54]*Ibid.*, 381.
[55]*Ibid.*, 642. Court expenditure had risen from 4.4% of state expenditures in 1725 to 10.9% in 1767: Troitskii, *Finansovaya politika*, 243.
[56]Solov'ev, *Istoriya.*, vol. XIII, 118.

needed for the salaries of officials.[57] Problems continued; Perm' salt remained both more attractive to consumers and cheaper to the Treasury. At Nizhnii Novgorod it cost little more than 8 kopeks a pud to the state, 14 or 15 kopeks including transport, but Lake Elton and Ilek salt cost 17 kopeks for transport and then had to be stored, and any consequent losses borne, by the state.[58] From 1764 to 1768 a commission enquired into the salt trade; it seems to have achieved virtually nothing, but in 1781 a new Salt Code was issued.[59] This was associated with the reorganisation of local government after the defeat of the greatest peasant rising of the eighteenth century, that led by Pugachev. The continuing concern with the maintenance of essential supplies for the population had been demonstrated three years before the rising by a requirement to have a constant two-year reserve of salt.[60]

Salt requirements were estimated on the basis of 12 to 18 lb (5.4 to 8.2 kg) for each registered male and female and stores were to be set up in each area to hold two years' supply. The Code envisaged that these reserves would be completed in 1786, an intention not, of course, realised.[61] Inter-regional stores were also to be established in order to help with distribution from particular sources. Following the Code there was an attempt at a more rational distribution system, which was evidently intended to reduce the high transport costs involved (46–94% of retail price), largely as a result of high labour charges and the general inflation during this period (see Table 5.2).[62] The intention was to provide each region with supplies from a nearby or relatively accessible source of salt. The state stores distributed salt in ways which differed according to the quantity involved. Sales of over 50 puds were made after advance written application and a guarantee that the buyer was not trying to buy up the market; obviously, however, such purchases must often have been for the purpose of trading locally in salt. Amounts between 10 and 50 puds were supplied immediately on written request; sales of less than 10 puds were met straight away; amounts smaller than 1 pud were supplied not from the stores, but from nearby stalls run by townsmen hired by the local authorities (until 1785, however, townsmen had been obliged to sell salt on behalf of the state).[63]

The cost of salt to the consumer, assuming an average 15 pounds a

[57] *Ibid.*, 233.
[58] *Ibid.*, 234. Le Donne, 'The Salt Code of 1781', *Jahrbücher*, 22 (1975), 166.
[59] *PSZ*, XVI, nos. 12, 105 (23 March 1764); XVIII, 13, 137 (20 (30) June 1768); XXI, 15, 174 (16 June 1781). Le Donne 'Salt Code', 161–90.
[60] *PSZ*, XIX, nos. 13, 784 (7 April 1732). Cp. XX, nos. 14, 980 (1 February 1780).
[61] Le Donne, 'Salt Code', 173f.
[62] Based on Le Donne, 'Salt Code', 171, 178, 179, 184, 186.
[63] Le Donne, 'Salt Code', 189.

Table 5.2. *Salt consumption, costs (1788) and intended production (1789)*

	Consumption (puds)	Total (mln puds)	Cost (kopeks per pud) Production	Transport	Total	1789 Production required (mln puds)
Perm' salt			8–9			5.295
Moscow	711,845			$11\frac{1}{3}$	$26\frac{5}{8}$	
Smolensk	650,000			17	$32\frac{1}{2}$	
Vyatka	460,000			$15\frac{1}{2}$	25	
Tver'	450,000			$9\frac{4}{5}$	$25\frac{3}{10}$	
Vladimir	443,471			$9\frac{9}{10}$	$25\frac{2}{5}$	
Pskov	435,571			$26\frac{4}{5}$	$42\frac{3}{10}$	
Novgorod	431,974			$12\frac{3}{5}$	$28\frac{1}{6}$	
Kaluga	371,427			$12\frac{1}{3}$	$27\frac{2}{5}$	
Perm' region	199,738			$7\frac{3}{5}$	$16\frac{9}{10}$	
Olonets	50,000			$27\frac{1}{2}$	43	
Polotsk	95,988			$17\frac{4}{5}$	$33\frac{3}{10}$	
		4.3				
Ilek salt			$\frac{3}{4}$			0.275
Nizhnii Novgorod	440,000			$30\frac{1}{2}$	$30\frac{1}{2}$	
Ufa	219,274			$11-16\frac{1}{2}$	$13\frac{4}{5}$	
Kazan'	89,112			25	25	
		0.748				
Elton salt			$9\frac{3}{4}, 6\frac{3}{4}$			4.178
Orel	600,000			$24\frac{9}{10}$	$34\frac{7}{10}$	
Kostroma	505,600			$19\frac{9}{10}$	$29\frac{7}{10}$	
Tambov	422,000			$19\frac{4}{5}$	$29\frac{3}{5}$	
Penza	391,436			$7\frac{9}{10}$	$17\frac{7}{10}$	
Yaroslavl'	374,028			$20\frac{9}{10}$	$30\frac{7}{10}$	
Tula	370,000			22	$31\frac{3}{4}$	
Kazan'	318,954			$17\frac{3}{5}$	$27\frac{1}{5}$	
Saratov	246,316			$7\frac{9}{10}$	$16\frac{3}{5}$	
		3.228				
Astrakhan' salt			$5\frac{9}{10}$			0.966
Astrakhan' region	895,687			$2\frac{8}{10}$	$6\frac{4}{5}$	
Kursk	517,398			$19\frac{3}{5}$	$25\frac{1}{2}$	
Simbirsk	333,811			$23\frac{7}{10}$	$23\frac{3}{4}$	
Voronezh	315,000			$17\frac{9}{10}$	$23\frac{9}{10}$	
Caucasus	70,648			2	22	
Saratov	12,081			$\frac{4}{5}$	$\frac{4}{5}$	
		2.145				
Crimean salt			45			0.5
Khar'kov	299,490					
Mogilev	200,000					
Malorossiya		0.5				

Table 5.2. *(contd.)*

	Consumption (puds)	Total (mln puds)	Cost (kopeks per pud)			1789 Production required (mln puds)
			Production	Transport	Total	
Vologda and White Sea salt			$12\frac{1}{4}$			0.562
Vologda	252,059					
Olonets	98,828			$10\frac{3}{10}$	$22\frac{3}{5}$	
Archangel	85,000					
		0.436				
Balakhna			$13\frac{1}{2}$, $19\frac{1}{4}$			0.44
Ryazan'	420,000			$14\frac{3}{4}$	$34\frac{1}{4}$	
St Petersburg	308,329			$19\frac{1}{2}$	39	
Tambov	44,000			$10\frac{1}{2}$	30	
		0.772				
Staraya Russa			20			0.117
Pskov	85,422			$5\frac{3}{5}$, $6\frac{1}{2}$	$25\frac{3}{5}$, $26\frac{1}{2}$	
St Petersburg	31,973			$7\frac{2}{5}$	$27\frac{2}{5}$	
		0.117				

Source: Based on LeDonne, 'Salt Code', 171, 178, 179, 184, 186.

year, was 13 kopeks when salt cost 35 kopeks a pud, or $18\frac{1}{2}$ kopeks when 50 kopeks a pud. As a proportion of the total burden of tax and rent payments expressed in money terms, the expenditure by serfs of the gentry declined through the eighteenth century, according to one estimate, from about 10% in the middle to less than 3% at the end.[64]

However, it should be borne in mind that serfs continued to suffer from a shortage of cash and there was little possibility of salt being acquired other than through the market. In terms of serf expenditures on consumables, therefore, salt remained a major item for which there were no alternatives. In this sense the price remained a heavy burden. The great achievement in the second half of the century was that no major shortages were reported after 1760; but this seems likely to be the result of the effective incorporation of the southern steppe areas into the Russian administration at least as much as of direct government measures.

From the point of view of the state, moreover, the Salt Code of 1781 was a failure in that it did not increase revenue; indeed, by the end of the century the operation of the salt monopoly showed a deficit. No full account can be given of the financial aspects, but what is known

[64]Kahan, 'Costs of "Westernization"', Table 6.

implies that in 1762 the salt revenue amounted to 2.2 million rubles, declined to 1.1 by 1783 and showed a deficit of 1.2 in 1795. Despite the rise in price to 1 ruble a pud in 1810, the state continued to lose revenue and abandoned its monopoly in 1818. Economically, however, this trade was important for Russian eighteenth-century development. The scale of production reached 14 million puds in 1797; this had almost all to be transported to distant centres of consumption. It thus generated a labour demand and the development of transport and related services. This had two consequences, 'The very location of the deposits on the outer rim of European Russia from the desolate shores of *Pomor'e* to the inhospitable slopes of the western Urals and the barren lands of Astrachan' and the Crimea contributed to the integration of these borderlands into the Russian economy.'[65] On the other hand, the need for the resources of these areas drove the state and some entrepreneurs to make considerable expenditures and as far as the state was concerned such operations were not financially profitable. There were, however, no alternative sources of supply and concern for social stability, though not priced, clearly justified the state in making the efforts it did in the eighteenth century to ensure a more regular supply of salt in the enormous quantities demanded by the population.

Grain was the main provision for the army. The fifty-three levies (twenty-one of which covered all tax-liable population) for the new regular forces during Peter's reign are estimated to have recruited over 284,000 men.[66] These men had to be accommodated and provisioned during their training and then formed part of the armies, sometimes of great size, which were moved from one end of Russia to the other, from the shores of the Black Sea to the Baltic. The provisioning of these men in camp and in the field was a major problem.[67] In 1703, for instance, Sheremetev asked Peter about provisions: 'how much should be laid down and how is it to be carted: this winter or in spring, and if in the spring, then what are the stores in which these provisions are to be laid down, and the people who are to cart them, and the draught teams because all that should be prepared beforehand'.[68] The navy posed similar problems and also raised the special question of preservation of foodstuffs for use on long voyages.

Peter instituted a series of measures intended to cope with the prob-

[65]Le Donne, 'Salt Code', 187–8.
[66]*Ocherki istorii SSSR, XVIIIv., pervaya chetvert'*, 347.
[67]See van Creveld, *Supplying War*, on the nature of such problems for eighteenth-century armies.
[68]*PiB*, 2, 449.

lems of provisioning; these illuminate some of the issues and were important in that they affected the diet of a section of the common people and set some precedents for subsequent measures. Grain stores were set up, both for the military and as reserves for the population in case of shortages. The magazines (the term *magaz(e)in* was then introduced into Russian) were mainly supplied from the localities where they were situated until about 1705.[69] The famine of 1704–5 probably stimulated concern for supplies at this dangerous time. A Provisions Department (*provianskii prikaz*) was created and a provisions officer (*proviantmeister*) made responsible for food stocks and for forage for the army.[70] Much grain was requisitioned on the spot for the forces in Poland and Lithuania and this caused friction with the local population; armed soldiers had to be used in 1707.[71] At that time supplies for the Admiralty, flour, rusks and groats, were to be taken from the 'general magazine', not purchased locally.[72] Commanders of forts were to build grain stores to hold supplies, varying with the size of the garrison, for the current and two additional years.[73] Poor harvests and arrears in requisitions were a continual problem.[74] It was not until after the campaign on the Pruth in 1711 that the problem of supplies from the magazines seems to have been regularised; after that, supplies from magazines, not from local requisitions, became the main source of supply for the army. These stores were established to cover the whole country towards the end of Peter's reign, the main ones being in St Petersburg, Riga and on the rivers Don, Dnepr, Desna and at Astrakhan'.[75] Even then there were problems: in 1714 1,000 men on campaign fell sick as a result of the soldiers being issued with food appropriate for the five week fast of the Apostles; Peter demanded they be given oil and meat instead of dried smelts and water.[76] The Military Regulation issued in 1716 (a year of widespread famine) laid down the following norms for rations during military operations: 2 pounds of grain, 1 pound of meat, 2 cups (less than ½ pint) of spirits, 1 garnets (about a quart) of beer, 1½ garnets of groats a month and 2 pounds of

[69]Beskrovnii in *Ocherki*, 353.
[70]M.G. Romodanovskii was in charge of this department 1705–7; in 1708–10 it was reorganised and A.P. Saltykov took charge in 1711.
[71]*PiB*, 5, no. 1493, 8; nos. 1583, 82, 481.
[72]*PiB*, 6, no. 2062, 153.
[73]*Ibid.*, 449.
[74]E.g. *ibid.*, 10, 733 (1710).
[75]Beskrovnii, *Ocherki*, 354.
[76]Pokrovskii, *Russkaya istoriya s drevneishikh vremen*, 2, 241.

salt a month.[77] The famines which started in 1721, and lasted to 1726, were only brought to Peter's attention in 1723.[78] Peasants were reported to have made bread with flax seeds, acorns and chaff. The famines caused Peter to establish more stores and take other measures in the decree of 27 February 1723.[79] Apparently, warehouses for provisions for troops after Peter's reign were numerous only till 1732.[80] In 1735, however, magazines, to be stocked at low prices and to sell at moderate cost during famines, were again being urged.[81] Yet in the second quarter of the eighteenth century the Military Commissariat bought the main bulk of grain on the market and a considerable part of the resources allocated to maintain the forces was spent on provisions.[82]

Peter the Great devoted little attention to agriculture; but government measures, sometimes as a result of famines, combined with cultivation on some fertile areas more to the south of central European Russia to bring about some development. Probably the most important change was that the growth of demand resulted in a small rise in yields in the 1720s. 'The growth of the market demand for grain continually stimulated the idea of increasing its marketable output. Private and government initiatives coincided.'[83] In the early 1720s, too, a special office was organised in the Revenue College (*Kamer-kollegiya*) to deal with grain farming.[84] There were also a number of instructions to estate officials which show an increased attention to possible income from agriculture. There is limited evidence to show that some landowning gentry had then switched to market-oriented farming.

Partial data on grain supplies brought to Moscow are shown in Table 5.3.[85] Although, obviously, these figures are very incomplete, they suggest that by the 1730s gentry were playing a greater part than formerly in supplying the Moscow market with grain. The 1723 data

[77]*PSZ*, v, no. 3006 (30 March 1716). Ch. 20 is on the General Quartermaster and chs. 21–3 are on other quartermasters. The Naval Regulation, *PSZ*, no. 3485 (13 January 1720), book 4, ch. 3, specified the monthly (28–day) ration per man as: 5 pounds of beef, 5 of pork, 45 of rusks, 10 of peas, 5 of buckwheat and 10 of oat-meal, 4 of fish, 6 of fat, 7 buckets of beer, 16 cups of spirits ½ a pot of vinegar and 1½ pounds of salt.

[78]Leontovich, in *Severnyi vestnik* (1892), 3, 48. Bogoslovskii, *Oblastnaya reforma*, 463–5, Slovtsov, *Istoricheskoe i Statisticheskoe obozrenie*, 465ff.

[79]*PSZ*, vii, no. 4175.

[80]Shchepkin, 'Goloda v Rossii', 502–3.

[81]Solov'ev, *Istoriya*, vol. x, 481.

[82]*Ocherki istorii SSSR, XVIIIv. vtoraya chetvert'*, 46.

[83]Indova, in *EzhAI 1965 g.*, 154.

[84]*PSZ*, vii, no. 4175 (27 February 1723).

[85]Kafengauz, in *MIZ*, i, 462–3, 465, 470, 481–3, 485. A shortened version of this article is given in his *Ocherki vnutrennego rynka Rossii*, ch. 5, 232–61.

Table 5.3. *Grain supplies to Moscow (chets)*

	Oct.–Dec. 1723	Sep.–Dec. 1728	Sep.–Dec. 1731	Jan. 1735–1737
1 *By water*	26,982	15,230		147,308
2 *By land*	17,649	12,221	54,638	20,709
of which,				
by peasants	10,606	6,076	24,428	
by gentry	1,965	4,333	19,146	

Source: Kafengauz, in *MIZ*, I, 462–3, 465, 470, 481–3, 485.

are probably exceptional, since that was a famine year. The figures for water-borne grain are, in real terms, limited to 1737, since the bulk of the water-borne traffic reached Moscow in April; this trade was in the hands of merchants, mainly large-scale ones, not land-owning gentry.[86] The majority of these merchants were from Orel (thirty-four out of seventy-nine), but there were two small traders from Tula. In the 1720s and 1730s peasants supplied perhaps half the physical amount of grain coming on to the market. They sold small quantities and predominantly in autumn and early winter when money was needed for tax and rent. The landowning gentry tended to market later and in larger individual amounts.[87]

Rye overwhelmingly predominated in physical terms in the grain brought to Moscow, both by land and by water, but wheat was important and, since it was costlier, especially so in value terms. Overall, in the late 1720s, Moscow is said to have accounted for almost a third of Russia's internal trade.[88] Prices in the 1730s rose rapidly as a result of the famine of 1733–4; in Moscow rye increased two-and-a-half times, and most other grains about twice, but the costlier wheat about one-and-a-half times.[89] While some of the grain was re-exported from Moscow, sometimes even to St Petersburg, there was evidently considerable consumption within the city itself. In the 1720s there were an estimated 1,440 traders in grain; 614 of these were men of the artisan quarter (605 from Moscow) and 825 were peasants or others, mostly from nearby uezds.[90] In 1723, 510 (out of 757) regis-

[86] Kafengauz, *ibid.*, 501–6.
[87] *Ibid.*, 483f.
[88] *Istoriya Moskvy*, vol. II, 293.
[89] *Ibid.*, vol. II, 273.
[90] Kafengauz, *MIZ*, I, 474–5.

tered trading peasants were engaged in trade in foodstuffs. It is probable that the men of the artisan quarter, unlike the peasants, did not
hawk their wares round the streets and markets, but were more substantial dealers, at least with stalls.[91]

Just as the traders were predominantly local men, so the grain itself
came from no very great distance at that time. In the 1720s most of it
came from areas to the south and south-east of Moscow across the
Oka, then from more easterly regions such as Vladimir. 'In general the
radius for grain carted overland to Moscow scarcely exceeded 200
verstas [about 213 km] with the southern Black Earth districts closest to
Moscow predominating.'[92] We have already noted that, in 1737, the
majority of the merchants involved were from Orel, yet local but
widespread trade predominated.[93] The development of the Moscow
market therefore, was beginning to influence a more considerable area
of the country. In Moscow itself many, from small trading peasants to
great merchants, were involved; a category of intermediaries between
peasants and Moscow traders emerged (known as kulaks) and some
gentry used their houses in the city as warehouses from which grain
was marketed at suitable, or necessary, times. This was the background
to an increase in central Russia of the cultivation of buckwheat and
millet, as well as spelt and spring rye; these were predominantly southern crops, but wheat, too, spread and by the 1740s was well-established
quite far to the north.[94]

During Peter's reign the more southerly regions were not yet the
granary of Russia, as they subsequently became. In 1720, of the
111,200 rubles worth of commodities despatched to central Russia
(two thirds of the total amount passing through Kursk market), cattle
accounted for half; the next most important items were hides, wool
and sheepskins.[95] More than 13,000 cattle and 10,000 sheep were sent
to Moscow itself, but the total amount of grain, flour and groats
reaching Kursk market was only 1,148 chets.[96] Of this grain, 330 chets
of wheat is known to have reached Moscow.[97] Trade with the
Ukraine through Bryansk is believed to have been similar in nature at
this time, though oil seeds were an important item.[98] By the end of

[91] *Ibid.*, 474–6. See also p. 24 above for the seventeenth-century traders in Moscow.
[92] *Ibid.*, 464.
[93] *Istoriya Moskvy*, vol. II, 274.
[94] Indova, in *EzhAI 1965 g.*, 143.
[95] Kafengauz, *Ocherki*, 303.
[96] *Ibid.*, 303, 294, 296.
[97] *Ibid.*, 306.
[98] *Ibid.*, 315.

Table 5.4. *Annual internal trade in foodstuffs 1724–6*

		Moscow	Novgorod	Archangel	Exported from following guberniyas: Voronezh	Smolensk	N. Novgorod	Siberia	Total
Rye	(chets)	28,772	2,382	21,240	32,366	4,318	14,539	14,734	118,351
Rye flour	(chets)	26,076	5,804	2,291	23,196	354	25,631	17,957	101,309
Wheat	(chets)	4,337	52	96	3,584	119	5,561	209	13,958
Wheat flour	(chets)	8,997	1,280	163	152	33	25,961	1,085	37,671
Oats and products	(chets)	25,900	5,564	1,450	2,820	1,875	7,140	1,200	45,949
Millet	(chets)	1,152	63	—	1,178	—	816	—	3,209
Buckwheat and flour	(chets)	8,600	780	21	879	126	3,417	—	13,823
Wheat-rolls (*baranki*)	(number)	—	16,667	—	—	2,312,667	—	—	2,325,334
Cabbages	(number)	—	4,750	—	—	—	16,967	—	21,717
Honey	(puds)	7,991	788	104	13,199	1,461	2,067	6.5	25,616.5
Fungi	(puds)	619	80	159	—	—	113.5	—	971.5

Source: Ocherki istorii SSSR, Vtoraya Chetvert' XVIIIv, 150.

Peter's reign, therefore, links had been established with the Left Bank
Ukraine and with Sloboda Ukraine.

From here the produce of Ukrainian livestock raising went to the centre of the
country. Russian merchants bought up Ukrainian cattle, wool, hides, sheepskins, fat, honey, wax and tobacco. In this period purchases of Ukrainian grain
were still rare, but grain was very often bought to distill spirits from it on the
spot and this would then be transported north.[99]

After Russia had incorporated the fertile steppes down to the Black Sea
in the late eighteenth century, Kursk and other towns of Belgorod
guberniya continued to supply, not grain, but mainly cattle and livestock products to the central regions of Russia.[100]

   In the reign of Peter the Great, relaxation or removal of imposts had
applied to supplies of provisions for St Petersburg; in 1724 supplies had
been freed from exactions and two years later this was extended to
provisions for those engaged in building the Ladoga canal. Such remis-
sions continued later; for example, in 1752.[101] By this date, however,
major changes were about to be introduced.

   The exactions and abuses encountered by peasants, merchants and
others trading in grain and other produce was put forward as grounds
for a proposal to abolish internal customs tolls and to make good the
state's loss of income by raising the import duties from 5% to 13%.[102]
'By this means', wrote P.I. Shuvalov, the author of the project, 'the
indescribable evil and calamity which befalls the peasants and merchants as well as many others shall have its end.'[103] Such a measure was
doubtless also expected to help hold back rising prices which impinged
on the cost of labour. He argued that peasants were sometimes deprived of half the value of goods marketed by tolls, other payments
and swindling officials; yet, 'the main strength of the state consists in
the people', those who pay the poll-tax. But the abolition of the
internal tolls from 1754, though it undoubtedly benefited the many
peasants who were marketing grain and other produce, was of such
importance to the merchants that they presented the Empress Elizabeth
with a 54 carat diamond, as well as a gold plate, some silver ones and
50,000 rubles in cash, in January, before the reform had been imple-

[99] *Ibid.*, 322.
[100] Kafengauz, *Ocherki*, 294–8.
[101] *PSZ*, VII, nos. 4598 (13 November 1724), 4712 (3 May 1725), 4852 (11 March 1726); XIII,
    no. 10022 (17 August 1752).
[102] On this reform see M.Ya. Volkov, *IZ*, 71, 134–57. The decree is in part translated in
    Vernadsky, *Source Book*, vol. II, 386–7.
[103] Cited in Solov'ev, *Istoriya*, vol. XII, 179.

mented.[104] Tolls in Little Russia (Malorossiya) were abolished in the same year.[105]

Concern for the people was common among eighteenth-century administrators who recognised where taxes came from. Such views were expressed by P.I. Shuvalov, as well as others, on many occasions and especially in a wide-ranging proposal he made in the autumn of 1754.[106] The six points he criticised in the state of Russia at that time may be subsumed under three heads; population loss by emigration; food supplies; and incompetent administration. The first was to be dealt with by a mobile frontier force to be located in areas where grain was cheaper and there was enough timber. The third was to be answered by a career structure with adequate pay and training.

The second group of problems is of greatest interest here. This involved the taking of provisions and forage on credit, quartering of troops and the related abuses; but it also included the problems of fluctuating grain prices – famine when there was a harvest failure, and low priced grain when the harvest was good. In order to cope with this, Shuvalov proposed that three types of magazine should be established: first, to supply the military; second, 'capital' ones (presumably in St Petersburg and Moscow) to balance the price of grain within the state; third,

. . . at ports so that in the event of need at any time, particularly if there is a harvest failure in certain places, we may have a reliable reserve in the magazine stores and maintain the price of grain in equilibrium; for it is well known in what abundance grain grows in many parts of the Russian state and at what a low price the poor agriculturalists have to sell it to pay their state taxes, so that they themselves scarcely have the sustenance they need; and when even a single year happens to have a harvest failure, having no stock of grain, they suffer unbearable need.[107]

The magazines now were envisaged as having some part to play in areas other than military provisions. The magazines were to be built and provisioned from the profits resulting from the sale of spirits and were to be maintained from indirect taxes under the administration of an Office of State Economy attached to the Senate. The only apparent result, apart from a great deal of office correspondence, was that a decree was issued in 1760 to collect information on grain harvests and the price of produce. In 1761 landlords were made responsible for

---

[104]*Ibid.*, 183. V. Nashchokin, cited in Mel'gunova, *Russkii byt*, 227.
[105]Solov'ev, *Istoriya*, vol. XII, 200.
[106]*Ibid.*, 207–11; S.O. Shmidt, 'Proekt P.I. Shuvalova 1754 goda', *Istoricheskii arkhiv*, 6 (1962), 100–18.
[107]Solov'ev, *Istoriya*, vol. XII, 209.

establishing grain stores to provide for their peasants when harvests failed.[108] At the time of Catherine II's Commission on a new Code of Laws this inevitably led to widespread gentry submissions calling for state stores.[109] Catherine herself had ordered magazines to be established towards the end of 1762 in an attempt to counteract a rise in the price of grain in St Petersburg; she also sought a reduction in transport costs which, it was alleged, reduced merchant profit and so diminished supplies to the capital.[110] In 1765 she ordered magazines to be created in settlements of the 'economic' peasants, but only in the south, in Malorossiya and Sloboda Ukraine, are any stores known from the 1760s.[111] There was also a conflict of interest over grain exports at this period. Measures undertaken in 1762 halved the export duty on grain sent by the Black Sea or Caspian; in real terms this was not of great importance, but it demonstrates that state demand for income had precedence over the people's need for food.[112]

Poor harvests in 1785 and 1786 created a dearth; people were eating leaves, hay and moss.[113] By the following year there was widespread famine in many central areas of Russia. Lack of stocks of grain, exports, and too little attention paid to agriculture were among the many causes of the famine. The main cause, according to one contemporary observer, was that 'Voluptuousness usually involves laziness, and laziness weakens people for agricultural work; a tendency to luxury, the need created by it, compelled many peasants, despite their wishes, to go into the market, into trades or other crafts; they satisfy their luxury, eat and drink better, but the land they work remains deserted.'[114] We do not have to accept Shcherbatov's patriarchal conservatism, or even his accusation of voluptuousness, to recognise that the growth of the market and the social changes it involved had far-reaching consequences. Foodstuffs increasingly became commodities; it became easier to price food against income from a variety of sources and some found they could eat better by modifying, or even abandoning, their farming. Increased dependance on the market magnified the importance of stores to ensure that regular supplies were to be available to consumers; and state concern with magazines both demonstrates this fact and calls attention to the deficiencies of the market.

[108]*PSZ*, xv, no. 11203 (14 February 1761); confirmed in 1767 by *PSZ*, xviii, no. 13017 (26 November 1767).
[109]Dukes, *Catherine the Great and the Russian Nobility*, 128.
[110]Solov'ev, *Istoriya*, vol. xiii, 137.
[111]Murzanov, *Arkhiv IT v R*, 3 (1922), 130–1.
[112]Solov'ev, *Istoriya*, vol. xiii, 23, 117.
[113]Shcherbatov, 'Razsuzhdenie', *ChtOIDR*, book 1 (1860), 91.
[114]*Ibid.*, 82.

Table 5.5. *Magazines and grain (1799)*

Totals by region	Population (male)	Magazines	Rye planned in store (puds)
Central Industrial	1,947,775	8,402	21,630,241
NW crafts and trades	1,670,227	8,564	5,010,681
Central Black Earth	2,784,068	9,026	8,352,214
SW agricultural	1,545,047	4,743	4,635,141
Novorossiya, Slobod			
Ukraine	949,115	2,893	2,847,345
Mid-Volga	1,487,660	5,822	4,462,980
Urals	1,054,005	3,812	3,162,015
N.Totals	11,369,459	43,375	988,377

Source: Based on Murzanov, *Archiv IT v R*, 3 (1922), 31–3.

Private magazines began to appear in some peripheral areas (Olo-nets, Archangel, Lifland etc.) under Catherine, but the problem of provisions was not solved. Paul I in 1799 ordered magazines with a year's supplies to be set up in all state and private settlements.[115] Governors' reports were called for and the data supplied give a fairly detailed but erratic picture for forty guberniyas. The material on gen-try stores is so deficient that no conclusions can be drawn from it. The most complete series are data for state and crown magazines; regional summaries are given in Table 5.6. Even this material is incomplete and no very firm conclusions should be drawn from it. It suggests, how-ever, that state magazines tended to have in store a higher proportion of the intended amount of rye (3 chets per male of the population) than did crown magazines; the proportion varied between 5% and 16%. There appears to be a less clear-cut tendency for spring-sown crops; for them the proportion of the intended amount (3/8 chet per male) mainly varied between 16% and 58%. The proportion in store was highest in the Central Black Earth and the Mid-Volga. The south-west was, it seems, not yet fully exploited.

Thus, even in 1800 the policy of magazine stores initiated almost a century before by Peter the Great was still no great success. This is true even of the state magazines, those for which we have fullest data and which might be assumed to be under the most effective control. There seems no evidence to show that the fertile southern steppes were more

[115]Murzanov, *Arkhiv IT v R*, 3 (1922), 130.

Table 5.6. Magazines. Data for (a) State and (b) Crown estates

		Population	Magazines	Rye (puds)			Spring-sown (puds)		
				Plan	Actual	%	Plan	Actual	%
NW crafts & trades	(a)	495,274	1,755	1,485,722	151,226[a]	10	185,728	49,848[bc]	3
	(b)	105,611	149	316,702	1,734[d]		39,598	25,449[e]	64
Central industrial	(a)	431,893	2,042	1,319,679	190,838	14	161,961	97,940[f]	6
	(b)	939,918	319[g]	281,754	17,472	6	35,220	7,220	20
Central Black Earth	(a)	987,923	2,512[h]	2,963,769	467,916	16	370,472	116,948	32
	(b)	59,707	198	179,121	9,730[i]	5	22,391	3,911[i]	17
SW agricultural	(a)	660,485	1,186	1,981,455	115,117		247,682	92,923	
	(b)[j]	2,704	14	81,112	838[k]		1,014	348[k]	
Mid-Volga	(a)	721,899	3,009	2,165,697	278,578	13	270,712	156,983	58
	(b)	95,250	265	2,857,750	18,332[l]	6	35,719	10,006[l]	28
Urals	(a)	194,085	817	582,255	29,000	5	72,782	27,048	37
	(b)	42,795	75	128,385	4,396	3	16,048	5,963	37

Notes:
[a] Incl. spring sown. No figures for Vyborg
[b] Excl. St Petersburg; see[a]
[c] No figures for Vyborg, Novgorod
[d] No figures for Smolensk, Novgorod, Vyborg
[e] Smolensk had a surplus
[f] No figures for Yaroslavl'
[g] No figures for Moscow
[h] Ryazan excl.
[i] Excl. Tula
[j] Excl. Kiev
[k] Excl. Novorossiya
[l] Excl. Simbirsk, Saratov

successful than other areas. In fact, the impression given is that the old-established agricultural areas, the Central Black Earth and the Mid-Volga, remained the dominant supply base for grain.

A new crop, which was envisaged as a substitute for grain in deficit areas and, therefore, a potential addition to the diet of the common people, was the potato. While on the Grand Embassy in 1697–8 Peter the Great had sent a bag of potatoes to B.P. Sheremetov with orders to distribute them to different districts and encourage Russians to grow them.[116] Nothing further is known of this far-sighted initiative. In the 1730s, however, at Prince Biron's table 'the potato often appeared as a tasty, but not rare and delicate dish'.[117] This seems doubtful; even at court in the 1740s amounts served were very small and the potato was evidently still rare. There is some evidence of potatoes being grown on a limited scale in Russia before the Senate instruction of 1765 which aimed at their more widespread cultivation.[118] Some may have been introduced by men returning from Prussia at the end of the Seven Years War. The instruction itself noted this cultivation but added that 'until now there has been very little of it [i.e. the potato] among the people'.[119] The measures taken in 1765 were a response to an outbreak of disease in Vyborg and the report of the College of Medicine that the peasants there often suffered as a consequence of the failure of the grain harvest; this was a basis for fever and even plague. The College recommended growing 'earth apples which in England are called potatoes' as a measure to counter grain failures, especially in Finland and Siberia.[120]

There were great difficulties which hindered the spread of potato cultivation in eighteenth-century Russia and prevented it from being an effective substitute for grain at that time. The authorities themselves were not fully informed; a consignment of fifty-eight barrels (about 84 cwt) of potatoes were sent from St Petersburg to Moscow at the end of December 1765.[121] Apparently this had been done on the basis of information relating to the frost-resistance of Jerusalem artichokes. The result was that only a small amount survived the journey. Yields were low. Varieties used were often small in size and so bitter tasting that the common people baked, rather than boiled them; boiled they had to

---

[116]A review, probably by S.M. Usov, mentions this in *Trudy VEO*, ch. 1, section 4, (1852), 50, cited by Lekhnovich, *MIZ*, II, 265.

[117]*Ibid.*

[118]Lekhnovich, *MIZ*, II, 263, 266.

[119]*PSZ*, XVII, nos. 12, 406 (31 May 1765) refers to 'earth apples, called *potatoes* (kartofel')'. Part of the instruction is translated by Vernadsky, *Source Book*, vol. II, 452–3.

[120]Lekhnovich, *MIZ*, II, 280.

[121]*Ibid.*, 285–6.

have costly butter or some other addition to render them palatable.[122] The Old Believers were opposed to the potato; some believed it was 'that forbidden fruit which the first two human beings ate; therefore, whoever eats it disobeys God, violates the holy testament and will never inherit the Kingdom of Heaven'.[123] The turnip was, in any event, a traditional staple crop for much of northern Russia and the potato failed to displace it for much of the eighteenth century.[124]

As early as 1770 not only members of the gentry, but 'even many people of lower condition are trying to introduce' the potato.[125] Even by the end of the century, however, 'in the majority of regions in the country the turnip and other root crops with which, as Georgi noted, the potato had "to battle" firmly occupied its place in the Russian food ration'.[126] Despite efforts to encourage its spread, therefore, the potato had not become a regular item of mass consumption by 1800. In 1807 an author could still write in much the same way as Bolotov had done in 1770: 'in places where grain does not always ripen owing to severe climate, the Russian inhabitants have begun to grow it with considerable application, especially colonists'.[127] Nevertheless, the first steps had been taken; the potato had become a garden crop on a fairly limited scale in many parts of Russia and its potential uses were being explored. It was not until 1840 that it could truly be claimed that, in famine conditions, apart from the 'normal' additives such as pine or fir bark, dried and powdered straw etc., 'the main substitute used instead of grain is the potato'.[128]

In the earlier part of the eighteenth century the grain surplus which provided the basis for much distillation was to be found not to the south, but to the east of Moscow along the Middle Volga from Nizhnii Novgorod to Kazan', the so-called Lowlands (*Niz*). The *podzols* of the forest area first gave place there to the more fertile *chernozems* of the steppe, and development was aided by the fact that this was an area of old established cultivation not subject to disruptive raiding by nomads or interference from the Ottoman Porte.

Towards the end of the seventeenth century there had been a ten-

[122]Bolotov, *Tr.VEO*, XIV, 394.
[123]Tereshchenko, *Byt*, I, 310–11.
[124]Lekhnovich, *MIZ*, II, 274, noted a potato:turnip ratio of 1:12.5 for the 1770s in Ingermanland.
[125]Bolotov, *Tr.VEO*, XIV, 394.
[126]Lekhnovich, *MIZ*, II, 299. He estimated the sown area as 'scarcely exceeding a few tens of thousands of hectares'. *Ibid.*, 322.
[127]E.F. Zyablovskii, *Noveishee zemleopisanie Rossiiskoi imperii*, I, 175, cited in Lekhnovich, *MIZ*, II, 323.
[128]Keppen, *ZhMVD*, XXXVI (1840), nos. 4, 405.

dency for the distilleries, run by merchants contracting to supply spirits, to be located not, as formerly, at the pot-house or drink-shop (which often only produced beer or mead), but in the countryside where there were cheap and readily available raw material and fuel: grain and timber.[129] The result was that by the turn of the century the authorities were noting that liquor produced in state distilleries was more costly than that of the merchant works. They demanded that 'the spirits in the drink-shop distillery should be cheaper than the price at which the contractors supply spirits'; the latter, it was argued, had to hire land, bear the capital costs and provide for transport.[130] The varying price of grain at different locations does not seem to have entered into their calculations, and the overheads of state works seem to have been ignored.

In the light of considerations such as these, seven distilleries were re-organised or established in the period 1705–15 along the Middle Volga in the Lowland region.[131] They were state works intended to produce spirits at the low cost of the merchant works. A.D. Menshikov, Peter's favourite, however, was somehow able to grab five of these works and was only forced to give them up in 1715; this suggests that these distilleries were profitable, whether they were able to compete with the merchant ones or not. In fact, the works produced no more than 6–7% of state requirements at best (the years 1717–19 and 1745–54) and failed to compete with other producers.[132]

The numerous changes in the administrative arrangements for the increasing number of retail outlets for liquor suggests that Peter had found no way of overcoming the problem of effective state control in this aspect of Russian life. Sometimes, and in some areas, local officials were used to collect the excise revenue; at others, this revenue collection was farmed out. In 1699 local officials (*burmistry*) of the newly established town councils (*ratushi*) were responsible; in 1704 the inns (*postoyalye dvory*) in Moscow were taken over by the crown with a view to farming them out, but this intention was abandoned in 1705.[133] There were then attempts to increase state income and to channel supplies of liquor through the Treasury. The farm continued to exist, however, and was generally re-established in 1712. In 1716 landowners alone were to have the right to distill, but this measure was clearly ineffective: it had to be repeated in 1731, 1755 and 1765. When

[129]Volkov, *Ocherki istorii promyslov Rossii*, 53.
[130]*AAE*, IV, no. 320 (1699).
[131]Volkov, *Ocherki*, 60.
[132]*Ibid.*, 62.
[133]Pryzhov, *Istoriya kabakov*, 245–6.

the Revenue College (*Kamer-kollegiya*) was formed in 1717 it gradually took over responsibility for the liquor revenue: in St Petersburg in 1719 and in Moscow in 1722.[134] 'This college was founded by Peter the Great and was never effective; and this is not surprising, for the greater part of its presidents strove more to display to the Sovereign an increase in income in order to deserve well, and also themselves to receive a profit from the farmers, and showed little concern to bring it into good order.'[135]

The profits to be made from liquor were such as to encourage swindles of various kinds, whatever the system in operation. In 1705 Kurbatov had virtually been made responsible for state finance when he was appointed inspector of the town councils. That year he complained to Peter that the officials had not accounted for the liquor revenue for many years.[136] The following year he reported that Nikita Yamskoi and Mikhail Sarpunov and his son, men of Pskov, with other worthies were reported to have stolen customary dues and liquor profits of 90,000 rubles or more.[137] Kurbatov thus showed that both officials and tax-farmers were either inefficient or criminal. He also claimed to have saved, 'from newly built pharmacies and the extirpation of many illicit drink-shops', 100,000 rubles in Moscow alone in one year. Presumably the pharmacies sold the various medicinal cordials and liqueurs which gentry, too, would often produce domestically and sometimes sell. He seized illicit drink from a junior clerk who handled the registers relating to boyars. This man and his wife sold up to 400 buckets of spirits by the bucket and the glass and had much more seized. These supplies were bribes from members of the gentry who had given him up to 1,500 buckets in two years.[138] This example illustrates, again, the problems of controlling spirits, which could be produced on many gentry estates and which were readily disposed of. To some extent spirits acted as a substitute for cash in a society which was both weakly monetised and lacked adequate funds for salaries.

The problems facing Peter in this sector of financial administration were difficult, but were somewhat mitigated by the fact that, even towards the end of his reign, the liquor revenue accounted for 11.4% of budget income; by the middle of the century it amounted to about

---

[134] *Ibid.*, 248–50.
[135] Shcherbatov, *ChtOIDR* (1859), III, 2, 71.
[136] Solov'ev, *Istoriya*, vol. VIII, 324–5.
[137] *Ibid.*, 326.
[138] *Ibid.*

20%.[139] By mid-century alcohol production was taking place in somewhat different circumstances.

The major change in the social position of producers during the first half, especially the second quarter, of the eighteenth century was the growth in the number of gentry distilleries. By the end of Peter's reign there were at least forty-five distilleries held by landowners and officials. The majority of these, however, were not in areas where the majority of serfs were privately owned; the largest group (twenty-three or twenty-four works) were in the Kazan' region where there were still few privately held serfs.[140] The gentry works at this stage were mostly not of small size.[141] Like the merchants in whose footsteps they were following, the gentry were evidently using hired labour and even hired land in regions where grain was available, and cheap; it was only after Peter's reign that the industry came to be based in manorial works using serf labour.

The growth of serf-based spirits production in the quarter-century after Peter's death was assisted by the procurement system established in 1728; by this date gentry supplies of spirits were increasing, but, apparently, already encountering difficulties from a shortage of demand. Yet Moscow alone required 250,000 buckets of spirits for sale in 300 houses on every street in the town.[142] The authorities responsible for the excise in St Petersburg and Moscow negotiated with the contractors to establish two prices: a gross price and a lower, concessionary, one. The authorities then had to enter into contracts for the supply of spirits: first, with the very few contractors willing to supply at the concessionary price; second, at the gross price with any gentry wishing to supply the state from the production for their own domestic consumption; and only then were contracts permitted with the contractors who had held out for the full price agreed.[143] It was also made financially easier for landowners to send supplies to the towns. They were allowed to sell spirits to the state from their output for domestic consumption. This resulted in numerous small producers supplying spirits and probably a fall in the average size of gentry distilleries.[144] Supplies from the crown distilleries had overriding priority and were paid the full price.[145]

[139]Chechulin, *Ocherki*, 153–4.
[140]Volkov, *Ocherki*, 63–4, 333–5.
[141]*Ibid.*, 293–4.
[142]Pryzhov, *Istoriya kabakov*, 255.
[143]Volkov, *Ocherki*, 68.
[144]*Ibid.*, 294–4.
[145]*Ibid.*, 74.

Table 5.7. *Merchant (a) and gentry distilleries (b)*

	1720s (a)	1720s (b)	1730s (a)	1730s (b)	1740s (a)	1740s (b)	1750s (a)	1750s (b)
Number of:								
works	224	47	310[a]		335[b]		298	278
stills etc.			3,679	10,213[c]			4,052	15,000[d]
volume (buckets)			39,288	80,360[e]			62,046	134,000[f]

Notes:
[a] Incl. 8 not working
[b] Incl. 28 not working
[c] Of which 'Factory' distilleries 1,800
[d] 'Factory' distilleries were 2,775, i.e. increase of 50% over 1730s figure; applied to total, this gives 15,000.
[e] Of which 'Factory' distilleries 20,000
[f] 'Factory' distilleries were 87,618, i.e. about 85% increase over 1730s figure; applied to total this gives 148,000. The average volume of a still in 1730s was 8 buckets; applied to the number of stills in 1750, this gives 120,000. 134,000 is average of these two estimates.
Source: Volkov, *Ocherki*, 34–5, 55, 63, 65, 233–4.

The result of the measures of 1728 on gentry supplies of spirits to the state was considerable (see Table 5.7). In the 1730s there were an estimated 7,000 domestic distilleries in the hands of landowners and officials; such gentry production was basically for domestic consumption, but also delivered supplies to the state.[146] This type of production was particularly well-established in the south where the homesteaders (*odnodvortsy*) and Ukrainians retained the right to distill.[147] An incomplete report shows that in 1730 8.1 thousand buckets were supplied by gentry from domestic output and this rose to 98 thousand in 1738; Moscow alone was supplied with 107,000 in 1739 and 132,000 in 1740.[148] Although supplies on offer were then more than twice the amount required, and large stocks had accumulated, in 1740 the Senate decided to accept the total amount, but to stop the system started in 1728. Gentry were to enter into contracts competing equally with other contractors.[149] This decision was ineffective. Gentry 'domestic' production had developed into some large-scale factory production and this source of money income was not to be foregone easily. The

[146] *Ibid.*, 34–5.
[147] Pryzhov, *Istoriya kabakov*, 227–43.
[148] Volkov, *Ocherki*, 68.
[149] *Ibid.*, 70.

decision, therefore, resulted mainly in gentry complaints about competition from the merchants.[150] Proposals then put forward to prohibit merchants from distilling and undertaking contracts to supply spirits were finally realised in the 1750s.

In the early 1730s the state was procuring at least 1.563 mln buckets of spirits a year and in fact probably something like 2 mln.[151] We do not know at all precisely the contribution of different producers to this amount, but the gentry 'domestic' output was only a small part of the supplies provided by the gentry officially; it is probable that gentry sometimes also found a ready market for illicit sales to peasants on their estates. Early in the eighteenth century many new drink outlets, both drink-shops and bars, had been opened, some in private settlements.[152] As gentry authority grew after Peter's death it seems possible that such sales increased.

Most supplies came from a fairly limited number of larger distilleries held by high officials and gentry and from merchant works among which small works sharply declined in numbers. Available information is summarised in Table 5.7. It appears that potential output, calculated from the capacity of stills etc., was in excess of state requirements, perhaps greatly so. If this excess potential were realised, it would have been a source from which illicit drink could be obtained. However, the calculation is uncertain in itself. For the period 1740–early 1750s one official estimate was as follows:[153]

Work season (months)	12	8	6
Output of 12-bucket still	500	333	250
Implied output per bucket of capacity	42	28	21

Another contemporary estimate, however, was 40–50 buckets of spirits per bucket of capacity. There were also other possible sources of supply, at least on a smaller scale. It seems impossible, therefore, to be at all certain of the scale of illicit drink output, but it was considerable and probably increased towards mid-century. The total amount of spirits available exceeded the state procurement even without that produced for domestic consumption and this may mean that the figures are inaccurate, that there was already excess production capacity or that an amount, perhaps equal to as much as half the state procurement, was

[150] *Ibid.*, 86.
[151] *Ibid.*, 35–6.
[152] *Ibid.*, 35.
[153] Volkov, *Ocherki*, 76.

disposed of illicitly. These possibilities are not, of course, entirely mutually exclusive. Finally, the figures indicate a significant rise in production and in state procurement only in the second half of the century. They seem to imply a per capita consumption towards mid-century of roughly a fifth of a bucket of spirits a year, somewhat more than 4 pints.

The balance between supplies from merchants and gentry landowners in the quarter-century after Peter the Great's death may be illustrated from the figures from contracts to supply Moscow.[154] Gen-

	1726 buckets	%	1739 buckets	%	1750 buckets	%
Merchants	75,000	86	212,500	66.5	128,500	47.5
Landowners	12,000	14	107,000	33.5	142,000	52.5

try and merchant deliveries both increased greatly during the period of the contracting system established in 1728, with landowners taking an increasing share. By mid-century the landowners' share was over half and merchant deliveries were declining, even though the capacity available in their distilleries had increased. Serf labour and the legal advantages of the gentry had resulted in their dominance in this industry.

In the mid-1730s the system of advance payment to contractors was stopped because 'the supply of spirits on contract began to exceed the Treasury's demand for these spirits'.[155] This implies that the rise of gentry distilleries, apart from gentry domestic distilling, was very rapid. Certainly in the second quarter of the century there was a great increase in the number of distilleries run by gentry, an increase of perhaps four or five times; there were 45 gentry distilleries existing in 1719–25 and 278 such works in 1753.[156] This development was associated with the growth in the marketing of gentry grain and of gentry agriculture based on labour rents. Distilling was for some landlords the most convenient means of linking their estates with the market and of increasing their money income. This was done legally by sales to the state, but at least in some areas at some times gentry sold direct to their own dependents even though this was illegal.

Most important on the social scale, however, was the change from the use of hired labour to that of the serfs on the estates. The gentry distilleries on hired land early in the eighteenth century were undercut

[154]*Ibid.*, 77.
[155]*Ibid.*, 37. Volkov repeats this opinion *ibid.*, 75.
[156]*Ibid.*, 65.

by merchant production. They were replaced by a massive growth of manorial works which by the early 1750s 'were located on the land-lords' own lands, basically on the estates of large and medium sized lords'.[157] The majority fully satisfied their demand for grain from their own resources, but although some were obliged to purchase grain, all used grain grown by means of labour rents. It was labour rents, too, that provided the work force for the distilling. In this way, costs of production were sharply reduced. The crown estates to some extent also took part in this process. The relatively few crown distiller-ies in the first quarter of the century included only one which sent any output to market; this was located in Sevsk uezd. In the 1730s supplies from this works and from other estates in the Ukraine were sent to Moscow and St Petersburg; this production was extended so that by the 1750s eleven crown works were supplying the market and they, like the gentry works, were based on the use of enserfed peasants performing labour services.[158]

A survey of 1,295 gentry distilleries in 1753 demonstrated something of the scale and concentration of the industry. 264 gentry with con-tracts to supply spirits had stills with a total volume of 37,239 buckets, about 60% of total known gentry capacity.[159] In 1754 the average total capacity of stills per gentry works was just under 150 buckets, but 5 works had a total capacity of 7,583 buckets.[160] Gentry distilleries each producing more than 20,000 buckets of spirits a year also appeared in the 1750s. This group basically included dignitaries with high court, military and administrative posts who had works with stills of more than 500 bucket capacity. The largest supplier at this time was Count P.I. Shuvalov, a statesman who, as has been mentioned above, had much to do with determining government policy.[161] He held estates in the Kazan', Alatyr' and Penza areas and undertook to supply 20,000 buckets to St Petersburg from his Alatyr' distillery in 1750 and 45,000 buckets from two works in 1754.

Early in 1753 P.I. Shuvalov was granted 30,000 rubles to find means to increase the revenue from drink-shops and salt.[162] In fact, he proposed to abolish internal customs and to make good the loss of revenue by a uniform tax on imports and exports. This was not the only measure propounded by Shuvalov which was of benefit to the merchants. He also proposed the formation of a Bank for Merchants in

[157]*Ibid.*, 66.
[158]*Ibid.*, 71–3.
[159]*Istoriya metallurgiya*, 438–9.
[160]Volkov, *Ocherki*, 296.
[161]Volkov, *Ocherki*, 304–5. See pp. 183–4, 194–5.
[162]Solov'ev, *Istoriya*, vol. XII, 178.

St Petersburg.[163] The same year, 1753, the Gentry Bank was established with funds resulting from the liquor excise.[164] The Shuvalov family had considerable influence at this time; P.I. Shuvalov's brother, Aleksandr, was head of the Secret Chancery in 1746; his cousin, I.I. Shuvalov, became favourite to the Empress Elizabeth. P.I. Shuvalov, however, was neither a mere hanger-on of the court, nor a proponent of gentry entrepreneurship at the expense of the merchants. He considered his own interests, and those of the gentry in general, would be best served if trade and industry in Russia were developed as fully as possible.[165] To a certain extent the term 'merchant' is misleading, since in the Russian context it often signifies a legal category; P.I. Shuvalov, however, though a count and a high court dignitary, a representative of the highest and richest gentry, was also functionally one of the greatest merchants in the land. His son, A.P. Shuvalov, also became the largest supplier of spirits in his day; he delivered more than 258,000 buckets in 1765; at a delivery price of 60 kopeks this would have produced a gross income of more than 150,000 rubles.[166]

In 1754 landowning gentry were granted virtually the sole right to undertake contracts for the supply of spirits to the state monopoly.[167] This might be interpreted as the outcome of a conflict between two classes within the broad functional category of merchant; between serf-owners and those hiring labour. Even so, the result, like so many of the cluster of economic measures undertaken in the 1750s and 1760s, confirmed and reinforced the predominance of the entrepeneurial land-owning gentry. Distilleries owned by merchants were to be sold to the gentry or to be destroyed, except in certain peripheral areas in the north and east where there were as yet no gentry works.[168] Landlords were also allowed to produce alcohol for their own domestic consumption on a scale according to their position on the Table of Ranks: from 1,000 buckets a year for those of rank 1, to 30 for those of rank 14.[169] They were, moreover, allowed to deliver spirits to any town where they had a dwelling. In 1755 it was decided to abolish state alcohol production as well but this plan was not carried out.[170] A protectionist policy was realised in the tariff of 1757.

[163]Solov'ev, *Istoriya*, vol. XII, 199–200.
[164]*Ibid.*, 177.
[165]Rubinshtein, *IZ*, 38, 250; Volkov, *Istoriya SSSR* (1957), 2, 89–95; *IZ*, 71, 137.
[166]Pavlenko, *Istoriya metallurgiya*, 443–4, 445. Kahan estimated an income of 225 r. per household as the requirement for western goods in a gentry household in 1790s.
[167]*PSZ*, XIV, no. 10261 (19 July 1754).
[168]*Ibid.*, no. 10490 (12 December 1755).
[169]*PSZ*, XIV, no. 10466 (19 September 1755).
[170]*PSZ*, XIV, no. 10356 (13 February 1755).

The measures undertaken in the 1750s were reinforced by Peter III freeing the gentry from compulsory service in a Manifesto of 1762.[171] Under Catherine II the economic and social dominance of the gentry reached a peak. Landowners' involvement in the running of their estates and the trades and crafts which could be based on them grew. It was, in effect, the basis for a further upsurge in agricultural production and especially that intended for the market in the second half of the eighteenth century.

Supplies of spirits came from some new areas. The acquisition of the Black Earth steppes meant that for the first time in its history Russia had an area capable of producing a grain surplus. In just over half a century from the death of Peter the Great the southern part of the steppe zone, including the Crimea, was acquired and settlement encouraged in order to secure this vast area and develop its potentialities.[172] The fortified line about Tsaritsyn had been established about 1720. By the Peace of Küçük Kainarci in 1774 the Russian frontier ran along the lower half of the Bug, then up the Dnestr and east to a point south of Mariupol'. The Russian Empire had thus acquired an extensive area of fertile soil south of, but then incorporated into, New Russia (Novorossiya which had been formed in 1764), as well as toeholds on the Black Sea and the Sea of Azov. The peace foreshadowed the next stage in the southward expansion; the Crimea was annexed in 1783 and the frontier advanced to the Dnestr in 1793. Odessa was founded in 1794 and became, in the following century, a major port for the export of grain southwards.

The Black Earth areas that had been acquired remained sparsely settled throughout the eighteenth century, but gave a basis for somewhat higher yields (see Table 5.8), though with considerable fluctuations, and for the cultivation of crops, such as millet and spelt, which could only be grown with difficulty further north. The south-west remained at levels of yield roughly comparable with those of the Volga area. The result was that in the late eighteenth century the central Black Earth region had considerable surplus grain, while the central regions of the country continued to have deficits (Table 5.9).

Supplies of spirits in the late eighteenth century continued to come from the old-established regions, but there was a significant shift westwards from the Lowland of the Middle Volga. Penza remained outstandingly important; its landlords supplied over 600,000 buckets of spirits from 46 distilleries in 1795–6.[173] Tambov, immediately to the

[171]Dmytryshyn, *Imperial Russia*, 57–60, has a translation of the 1762 manifesto.
[172]See R.P. Bartlett, *Human Capital*.
[173]Pavlenko, *Istoriya metallurgiya*, 448–9.

Table 5.8. *Crop ratios (selected years, mainly 1790s)*

	Years[a]	Rye	Wheat	Oats	Barley
Central industrial					
Moscow	1795	2.6	2.6	0.3	2.3
Vladimir	1795	1.7	2.3	—	—
Kaluga	1793–6	*3.0–3.4*	*2.5–3.1*	*2.7–3.3*	*3.0–3.5*
Kostroma	1795	1.8	2.2	—	—
Yaroslavl'	1796	*1.4*	*2.1*	*2.2*	*2.0*
Volga				3.2	
Nizhnii Novgorod	1792, 1795–7	2.1–3.1	0.8–2.6	2.3–4.6	1.9–3.2
Kazan'		—	—	—	—
Simbirsk	1793–5	1.5–2.7	1.4–2.3	1.0–2.5	0.9–4.5
Saratov	1791–2, 1794	*1.6–4.1*	*1.5–4.2*	*5.2–6.3*	*3.5–4.8*
Central Black Earth					
Tula	1782	*5.3*	*3.75*	*5.2*	*5.5*
Ryazan'	1794, 1796	*1.9–3.5*	*1.7–2.0*	*2.5–3.5*	*2.1–5.4*
Orel	1793, 1795–6	*3.5–4.3*	*1.8–3.6*	*1.3–4.4*	*1.5–14.6*
		4.0	2.1		
Kursk	1795–6	*3.1–5.2*	*1.0–3.9*	*1.8–4.5*	*2.2–3.5*
Tambov	1794, 1796	*2.3–3.2*	*1.8–2.2*	*3.0–3.4*	*1.4–2.5*
Voronezh	1791–2, 1795	*2.5–5.7*	*1.7–3.6*	*2.7–6.0*	*1.8–3.9*
Penza	1795–7	*3.1–5.9*	*1.6–2.0*	*2.2–4.4*	*1.2–1.6*
South-west					
Khar'kov	1786	*3.6*	*2.0*	*3.5*	*3.0*
Chernigov	1791	*3.5*	*2.1*	*3.2*	*2.5*
Novgorod-Seversk	1793–6	*3.2–4.9*	*2.2–3.6*	*1.4–2.5*	*1.7–1.9*
Kiev[b]	1791, 1799	*2.4–5.0*	*0.8–3.9*	*1.3–5.1*	*1.2–4.6*

Notes:
[a] 1795, the year for which most data are available, in Roman. All other years in italic.
[b] The lower figure in each case is for 1799.
Source: Based on Rubinshtein, *Sel'skoe khozyaistvo*, 444–52.

west, was the next most important supplier (362,000 buckets). Figures are not available for Voronezh, but Kursk, further to the south-west, supplied 269,000 buckets. The forest–steppe interface was important because it had the advantages both of somewhat better soil and climate, and wood to fuel the works. Between the borders of the steppe and Moscow, both Ryazan' (359,000) and Tula (202,000) were sizeable production regions, with Kaluga (332,000) to the west of them. These three regions, and Smolensk (226,000), formed a semi-circle round the immense market of Moscow. Moscow region itself supplied 215,000 buckets; in 1795 sales of liquor in Moscow amounted to 762,000 buck-

Table 5.9. *Grain surplus or deficit (mln chets) (a) 1780s (b) 1790s (c) early 1800s*

Region	Commodity Surplus			Deficit		
	(a)	(b)	(c)	(a)	(b)	(c)
Central industrial	—	—	—	5–6.5	3–4	3–4
North-west			(0.5–1.5)	3.5	3.5	(1)
Central Black Earth	5	11	10–17			
Volga			4–5		1–2	1

Source: Based on Rubinshtein, *Sel'skoe khozyaistvo*, 374–80.

ets, almost 1.6 buckets (4 gallons) per head of population.[174]

Further to the south-west, and extending onto the open steppe, the regions of Chernigov and Kiev supplied 597,000 and 587,000 buckets respectively.[175]

This was the background to the development of the distilling industry in the late eighteenth century. The expansion southwards, however, was considerably constrained by lack of population and by transport difficulties, both physical and economic.

In 1765 the exclusive right of gentry landowners to distill was re-affirmed.[176] A year later the fee for stills, then 50 kopeks, per bucket of capacity, was abolished, though stills continued to be officially regis-tered until 1781.[177] The start of this period, which lasted until the Regulations on Distilling, issued in 1781, was when gentry freed from compulsory service in 1762 were returning to their estates. They were entitled to produce spirits for domestic consumption, as we have seen, on a scale depending on their position on the Table of Ranks, the lowest being allowed 30 buckets a year; surplus amounts should have gone as deliveries to the state, but it is doubtful that much did. Be-tween the 1760s and the 1780s the number of gentry contractors in-creased only from 157 to 211 (Table 5.11). While the range of amounts to be delivered increased greatly, the average declined from about 12,000 to about 9,000 buckets. There was, therefore, some small in-crease particularly in the number of those delivering less than 10,000 buckets. There were, indeed, some very small deliveries, as little as 10 or 20 buckets.[178] The average for deliveries up to 5,000 buckets, how-

[174]Le Donne, 'Liquor Monopoly', 206.
[175]Rubinshtein, *Sel'skoe khozyaistvo*, 450.
[176]*PSZ*, no. 12448 (9 August 1765).
[177]*PSZ*, no. 12708 (28 July 1766).
[178]Le Donne, 'Liquor Monopoly', 180.

Table 5.10. *Spirits output and procurement by source*
i Estimated actual output
ii Estimated potential output (mln buckets)

Output		1730s	1740s	1750s	1760s	1770s	1780s	1790s
1 State	i	0.2	0.2	0.3	0.4	0.8		1.5
	ii	0.5–0.6	0.35	0.5				
2 Gentry	i	1.0–1.5	1.0–1.6	–1.7	1.9–	2.1–		3.4–4.5[a]
	ii		2.2	1.7				9.2[b]
3 Merchants	i	1.1	1.1					
	ii	1.3	1.4	1.7–1.8				
4 Total	i	2.3–2.8	2.3–2.9			2.3–	2.9–	4.9–6
	ii	3.0	4.0	3.9–4.0				
5 *State* *procurement*		1.6–2.0		1.6–2.0		2.2	1.9[c]	5.5[b]

Notes:
[a] 4.5 including Chernigov and Kiev output
[b] Sales
[c] From gentry only
Sources: Korsak, *Obozrenie*, vol. III, 288–9; Le Donne, 'Liquor Monopoly'; 175, 207; Pavlenko, *Istoriya metallurgiya*, 441, 443, 449–50; Shcherbatov, *ChtOIDR*, I (1860), 100; Tolstoi, *Istoriya*, 173; Volkov, *Ocherki*, 35–6, 75, 85, 302, 356.

ever, was 1,666 buckets, so there was no apparent mass of landlords involved in spirits deliveries even late in the century. This, of course, does not imply that landlords did not, almost always, produce spirits allegedly for domestic consumption. The industry that supplied the state continued to be dominated by large-scale gentry entrepreneurs and the overwhelming majority of gentry landlords were not recorded as producing spirits for sale.

Supplies, delivered under contracts made for four-year periods, were channelled through state stores which accepted deliveries three times a year.[179] The stores also handled state supplies; these were increased in this period, partly as a response to the threatened decline in state revenue as a result of the famine of 1767. A notable feature of the second half of the century is that state production grew from less than half a million buckets to about 1.5 million and increased its share to about a quarter of total deliveries.

The merchants, no longer allowed to distill, were allowed, on the other hand, to be tax-farmers responsible for sales of liquor. Indeed, in this period production and distribution were supposed to be separate

[179]Le Donne, 'Liquor Monopoly', 179–80, 192.

Table 5.11. *Spirits contracted to be supplied, Gentry contractors and deliveries ('000 buckets) (1765 and 1779–83)*

Spirits contracted to be supplied	1765				1779–83			
	Suppliers no.	%	Deliveries	%	Suppliers no.	%	Deliveries	%
−5	} 112	71	355	19	114	54	190	9
5–10					45	21	283	13
10–20	27	17	356	19	24	11	309	14
20–30	3	2	82	4	12	6	27*	13*
30–40	6	4	206	11	4	2	130	6
40–50	1	1	43	2	3	1	129	6
50–60	8	5	822	45	1	1	57	3
60–70					2	1	132	6
70–80					1	1	70	3
80–90					0	0	0	0
90–100					1	1	100	5
100–					4	2	485	22
	Total 157		Average 12		Total 211		Average 9	

Source: Pavlenko, *Istoriya metallurgiya*, 443, 446.
*Sic. Probably deliveries should be 270; average delivery would then be 10.

activities entrusted to distinct social groups. The possibilities of making a profit from liquor sales were great, but the perseveration of Muscovite attitudes into the late eighteenth century interfered, and reduced merchant desire to engage in this business. The state regarded the tax-farmer 'as an agent in whom fiscal responsibilities were vested because his reliability was guaranteed by his property'.[180] It was a service to be exacted by the state, rather than a contract to be agreed between the two parties to the profit of both.

In 1756 a single tax-farm system was envisaged for the whole country and the gentry were to be allowed to take part in the farm.[181] In effect, however, the threefold system of state officials, or men trusted on oath or tax-farmers collecting the liquor revenue continued till 1766. The general farm began in 1767 on the basis of four-year contracts but other means also continued sometimes to be used.[182] The

[180]*Ibid.*, 185.
[181]Pryzhov, *Istoriya kabakov*, 261.
[182]Le Donne, 'Liquor Monopoly', 185; *PSZ*, XVII, nos. 12444 (1 August 1765), 12446 (1 August 1765).

principle of the farm being open only to merchants was not, in fact, long observed, if it was at all. Because insufficient merchants made bids, gentry and, in the 1770s, others, including serfs provided their lords guaranteed them, were allowed to participate.[183] There may have been some attempt to increase the number of contracts, but this was evidently not consistent policy. The farm for St Petersburg and Moscow, the two largest consumer areas in the country, was treated as a single unit.

State concern for the farm led to the farmers obtaining exemptions from many impositions borne by other townsmen.[184] They were also given considerable authority over those serving under them. These rights to judge and punish for disputes and fights are reminiscent of those granted the ancient feasts and fraternities, while cases relating to their handling of the farm, dealt with by the treasury, not the ordinary courts, recall the privileges of the seventeenth-century farmers. The farmers also acted as a sort of police in the search for illicit liquor. They inspected transport coming into town; peasants were no doubt accustomed to such treatment and its associated bullying and bribery, but the gentry resented it and 'their complaints found a persistent echo in their *nakazy* [instructions] to the Commission summoned in 1767 to draft a new code of laws'.[185] The farmers maintained a force of retired military men to assist in ensuring stills were registered and regulations were observed in the drink-shops; this private force was supplemented by dragoons detailed from the army to deal with smuggling into the two capitals. 'Pitched battles were sometimes fought in which the police did not always gain the upper hand.'[186]

The reform of local administration in 1775 meant that the gentry in effect had control of the countryside, including police functions.[187] Serfs were then allowed to participate in the farm, if guaranteed by their lord, and this was one means by which smaller gentry could legally be involved in liquor sales. The differential between the state's purchase price (85 kopeks) and costs was eroded by rising prices for grain, fuel and transport and this encouraged gentry to make other, illegal, arrangements.[188] It also led to a rapid expansion of liquor production in the 1790s and the spread of illicit trade in liquor which Catherine's government vainly attempted to stop. In fact, widespread

[183]Le Donne, 'Liquor Monopoly', 188–200.
[184]Le Donne, *ibid.*, 186.
[185]*Ibid.*, 187.
[186]*Ibid.*, 187–8.
[187]de Madariaga, *Russia*, 283–4.
[188]Le Donne, 'Liquor Monopoly', 182.

gentry economic concern coupled with gentry dominance of resources, labour and administration made any such attempt derisory.

The upturn in production towards the end of the century was channelled into legal consumption through government stores which, under the Regulations on Distilling of 1781, were to hold in stock half the annual consumption. Ten to fifteen stores were located in each guberniya, then supposed to have a population of 300,000. This suggests that stores, on average, had to handle 10,000–15,000 buckets a year.

Following the 1781 Regulations on Distilling the local treasury chambers were to be in general charge of the farm or other arrangements. Their approval had to be given to outlets for liquor sales being established on gentry land; temporary sales points had to be covered by the contract; all sales had to be at the authorised price.[189] This was part of the general process of developing local administration at this time, while meeting gentry interests as fully as possible. If the farmer bought liquor from the state above the amount specified in the contract, he had to pay the full 3 rubles of the selling price; this curious decision evidently reflected the view that tax-farmers were state officials, not businessmen. If the farmer bought such liquor elsewhere, he was supposed to deposit it in the government store and pay the difference between his purchase price and the authorised selling price. The tax-farmers, dissatisfied with the new arrangements, asked for new drinking places, the right to sell off the premises from temporary outlets in new locations and for supplies additional to the amounts contracted, but were rebuked by the Senate for such improper demands; the Senate found in this 'a desire for impermissible enrichment'.[190] Competition was evidently not to be tolerated.

Throughout the century drinking places remained a problem. At the start of the century some new terms appeared: the hostelry (*avsteriya*), the liquor shop (*fartina*) and inn (*postoyalyi dvor*).[191] The distinctions between these institutions are not clear; the terms may simply have been modish innovations for old Russian institutions, but using western, mainly Polish models. As travellers from the West increased in numbers accommodation had to be provided for them. In 1757 the first hotel (*gerberg*) opened in Moscow.[192] At about this period, too, great two-stable inns were becoming common on the main roads to St

[189]*PSZ*, xxi, no. 15231 (17 September 1781). Pryzhov, *Istoriya kabakov*, 264. Le Donne, 'Liquor Monopoly', 198.
[190]*PSZ*, xxi, no. 15325 (14 January 1782). Pryzhov, *Istoriya kabakov*.
[191]Pryzhov, *ibid.*, 245–6.
[192]Solov'ev, *Istoriya*, vol. XII, 440.

Petersburg from the Baltic.[193] In 1746, however, the alleged revulsion evoked by the term *kabak* (drink-shop) led to an order that their signs should bear the name 'drinking place' (*piteinyi dom*).[194] This significant decision seems to have been ineffective, though; in 1765 and again in 1779 new orders to the same effect were made.[195] In fact, the legislation itself continued to refer to drink-shops (*kabaki*), just as it had in the seventeenth century.[196] The 1765 law had tried to raise the status of farmers by such measures as allowing them to wear a sword, calling them 'trusted servitors of the crown' and permitting the Imperial emblem to be displayed on drink-shops and liquor stores.[197] Reality, however, proved resistant to this long-continuing Russian belief that it could be manipulated by the magic of the word or sign. The revulsion, of course, did not extend to all, nor was it complete. The Court, landowning gentry and farmers were all willing and anxious to receive their income, however much they might object to the indelicate means by which it was realised. The people continued to frequent the drink-shops. The Empress Elizabeth in 1746 had ordered there should be no drink-shops or eating places on the main streets of St Petersburg; 'drink-shops are only to be in side streets and eating places are to be removed to the market-place'.[198] The Revenue Office (*Kamer-kontora*) pointed out to the Senate that drink-shops on the main streets had made 24,500 rubles a year, 'but now that amount is not collected'.[199] For the tax-farmers the main difference from the previous century was that the investigation of and penalties for default no longer involved torture and physical punishments.

The location and number of drink-shops was controlled closely. Farmers had no right to open or close them, but had to get authority to do so.[200] The state was primarily concerned for its revenue, not the farmers' profits.

Information on the number of outlets for liquor is sparse. Crude estimates for Moscow towards mid-century suggest sales per outlet considerably higher than elsewhere later in the century.[201] By the late eighteenth century there seem to have been a few hundred drink-shops in each guberniya; sales appear to have varied widely. For 1795, how-

---

[193]See K. Aluve, *Maa-kõrtsid ja hobuposti-jaamad Eestis* (Rural taverns and post-horse stations in Estonia) (Tallinn, 1976), with numerous illustrations and summaries in Russian and German.
[194]Pryzhov, *Istoriya kabakov*, 260.
[195]*Ibid.*, 262–3.
[196]See p. 155.
[197]Le Donne, 'Liquor Monopoly', 186.
[198]Solov'ev, *Istoriya*, vol. XI, 399.
[199]*Ibid.*, 400.
[200]Le Donne, 'Liquor Monopoly', 193–4.
[201]Cf. Table 5.12, below.

Table 5.12. *Outlets and sales*

	Drink-shops	Sales (buckets)	
		total	average
1728			
Moscow	300[a]	250,000[b]	833
1730s			
280 towns, European Russia	880		
		2.5–2.8 mln.	700–800
country districts	2,399		
1746			
Moscow	173[c]	270,000[d]	1,560 *or*, incl. uezd,
Moscow uezd	32[c]		1,317
1783			
Tula	174	161,000	925
Vladimir	232[e]	109,500	472 *or* 156
Tambov	337	153,293	455
Kursk	735	130,837	178

Notes:
[a] 'Houses'
[b] Procurement
[c] Hostelries and liquor shops (*fartiny*)
[d] 1750; excludes state's own supplies
[e] Plus 463 temporary outlets (*vystavki*)
Sources: Pryzhov, *Istoriya kabakov*, 255. Le Donne, 'Liquor Monopoly', 196. Volkov, *Ocherki*, 35, 77. Solov'ev, *Istoriya Rossi*, XI, 400.

ever, sales figures and population estimates by region have been published, so per capita consumption can be calculated. These figures show St Petersburg (4.1 buckets), Moscow (1.6) and Archangel (0.9) as areas with the highest consumption per male head. Orel (0.8) was the only other area with consumption above 0.5 buckets. The average for Russia, without the Ukraine or Siberia, was 0.5 buckets and cost 2 rubles. This was equivalent in cost to only half a chet or so of rye, but it was about twice the soul tax or half the annual rent paid by a serf in the 1790s.[202] This was a considerable burden when money income was low. The producer regions showed the lowest consumption: Nizhnii Novgorod, Kazan' averaged 0.4 buckets; Simbirsk, Penza, Ryazan', Tambov, Saratov, Voronezh and Kursk 0.3.[203] The two capitals, and

[202] Kahan, 'Westernization', Table 6.
[203] Estimates based on figures given by Le Donne, 'Liquor Monopoly', 206–7.

Archangel as a port, were exceptional for Russia; but if the high consumption there is to be accounted for in this manner, it might imply that foreigners, travellers and Russian traders were thirstier than others, or that administrative control was more effective at these locations. The low consumption figures for the producer regions, on the other hand, might suggest that domestic production and illicit sales were common. Since rye then cost 3–4 rubles a chet on the market there was a strong economic incentive to engage in domestic production.

Very roughly, it looks as though consumption of spirits was around a fifth of a bucket per male head of population till the second half of the eighteenth century. The quantities of spirits produced virtually doubled during the reign of Catherine II and at the end of it consumption had more than doubled and reached an average of half a bucket, more than 10 pints, for each male in the country.

During Catherine's reign a considerable proportion of the population became addicted to alcohol, but the state, too, became increasingly dependant on it. Budget revenue derived from alcohol grew from about 20% at the start of the reign, to over 30% at the end (see Table 5.13). Different authorities give somewhat different figures and there may be some confusion between gross and net revenue for the 1780s and 1790s. The statement that the 'liquor revenue which totalled 9,4 million rubles in 1782 rose first to 10,2 million in 1784, then began to decline inexorably until it reached 8,7 million in 1793' might be misunderstood.[204] First, the same author gives net revenue for 1792 as 8.6 million; 1793, therefore, shows a small upturn. Second, in 1793 'the total liquor revenue amounted to 15,6 million rubles of which 6,9 million was spent for the purchase of liquor and administrative overheads and 8,7 million constituted the net profit of the state. Three years later total revenue jumped to 22 million of which 15 million constituted the net profit.'[205] This seems to imply that the fall in net revenue, partly brought about by the disincentives to the farmers in the 1781 Regulations, was rapidly reversed by two new measures. First, the selling price of spirits was raised from 3 to 4 rubles a bucket in 1794. Second, a new system was instituted from the start of 1795. Farmers were allowed to purchase directly from producers, to retain the proceeds of sales of drink above the total sum in their contract and of any food sold. Gentry of all ranks were allowed to produce 90 buckets (243 gallons) of spirits a year for their domestic consumption; they also

[204]Le Donne, 'Liquor Monopoly', 198.
[205]*Ibid.*, 202.

Table 5.13. *Liquor prices and revenue*

	Delivery price	Sale price by		Liquor revenue 'ooor.	% total budget revenue
		bucket	cup		
1716		50	60	850	
1724		60 (1723)			11.4
1726		1.40[a]			
1742		70			
1747–9		1.20		1,062–1,263	
1749		1.88½	1.98	1,264–1,787	
1750	1.12[b]			2,667	
1751	50–70			2,200	–20
1751–3				2,273–2,362	
1755				2,663	
1756		2.23½	2.33½	2,500–3,450	
1759				3,133	
1762		2.53		3,450	
1763		2.54		4,376	
1765		2.54	2.64	4,295	
1766	60–80			5,767	
1767				5,085	
1768	70–90 (140)				
1769	70–100 (1767–70)	3.00		4,400	21–
				6,641 (1771)	
1771–5	85–92			6,644	
1775–9	85–100 (1775–82)			6,887	
1777				6,000[c]	25
1779–83				9,258	
1782				9,400	
1783				9,419	
1784				10,200	
1786				9,564	
1792				8,600[c]	19
1793			15,600[d]	8,700[e]	
1794		4.00			32.3
1795			24,100[d]	17,500	30
1795–9	90–110 (1790s)			169,000[e]	
1796			22,000[d]	15,000[e]	

Notes:
[a] Malorossiya
[b] Moscow, vodka, i.e. equivalent to 56 k. for spirits
[c] 'Net revenue'
[d] 'Total revenue'
[e] Profit

Sources: Le Donne, 'Liquor Monopoly', 180, 195, 198, 202–3, 205; Pryzhov, *Istoriya Kabakov*, 229, 260–5; Troitskii, *Finansovaya politika*, 159; Volkov, *Ocherki*, 31; Yakovtsevskii, *Kupecheskii kapital*, 155.

became eligible to bid for the tax-farm.[206] The result was that while the 1793 figures show net revenue as 57% of gross, after the new measures it was 73% in 1795 and 70% the following year; overheads had risen from 6.6 million to 7.0 million, but gross revenue had declined, presumably as a result of the increase in prices (see Table 5.13). This system, with some modifications, continued through much of the nineteenth century.

In the eighteenth century, therefore, state control of drink, especially spirits consumption became an increasingly important and profitable part of state revenue. The lack of an adequate state administrative apparatus was largely made good by using tax-farmers. These, together with those landowning gentry who produced for the state, made considerable profits, in money and in other ways. Their net money income is not precisely quantifiable, but this is perhaps less important than might seem at first sight, because the Russian economy remained weakly monetised throughout the eighteenth century despite the great growth in the market. For the gentry money was important as a means of obtaining commodities and services not produced on their estates; the growth of a westernised life-style created a demand which could not at first be met from their own production. For the merchants and other tax-farmers money was a source of capital. But profits in such a society must not be understood only as money. For both gentry and, perhaps even more so, for tax-farmers, the spirits they dealt in was also itself a medium of exchange especially acceptable as a lubricant for the creaking machinery of administration. The need for, as well as the possibility of, such bribery increased as a result of Catherine II's policies. 'The very decentralization of government achieved by the great reforms of the 1780s exposed many lower officials living on meager salaries to the temptations of handsome bribes by the wine farmers who were probably the largest handlers of liquid money in the province.'[207] The bribing with liquor disclosed by Kurbatov at the start of the century was made an integral part of the system by the 1780s, especially by the Senate's attitude to sales above the amount specified in the farmers' contracts. It is as if seventeenth-century Moscow attitudes were given a new lease of life in Catherine's reforms and only as a result of the system introduced in 1795 was the market effectively recognised.

The system of stores might have acted as reservoirs collecting supplies from a large number of small producers, but large-scale produc-

---

[206]Pryzhov, *Istoriya kabakov*, 264; Le Donne, 'Liquor Monopoly', 201–2.
[207]Le Donne, 'Liquor Monopoly', 191; see also 200.

ers, in fact, dominated throughout the century. Moreover, the concessions granted the gentry amounted to a virtually anti-merchant policy in Russian terms; in the second half of the century the merchants were penalised in various ways and deprived of access to serf labour, while gentry entrepreneurship was supported and itself supported a growth of peasant trades and trading at the expense of the merchants. The only improvement in the situation of merchants was that, though they continued to be treated as the state's unpaid tax collectors, they no longer operated under the threat of torture, the use of which died out in the reign of Peter's daughter, Elizabeth. The legal production and sale of spirits, therefore, failed to become an autonomous business activity in the eighteenth century; it remained, or rather it developed, as a means of generating state revenue. In this sense Catherine II hindered the development of the Russian market.

The main sources of supply of spirits shifted southwards, but along the borders of the steppes. The Ukrainian areas, however, were not fully integrated into the Russian market for three reasons. Unlike the Ukraine, the lands bordering the steppes were able to keep up with the demand for spirits and had ready access along the river routes to the central areas of the state; then, transport costs from the periphery, as we have seen in relation to salt, were high; lastly, the south had had its own traditions. The former Polish-Lithuanian and then Cossack areas had rights to domestic distillation which continued through much of the century; they also had the inn (*korchma*) and drink-house (*shinok*). The Russian drink-shop selling state liquor and the Russian system of regulation was only gradually extended there.[208]

These developments provided revenue for the state, much of it directly allocated to items of conspicuous consumption by the court. Their impact on the mass of consumers, however, was considerable. Consumption grew from about 4 pints of spirits for each male in Russia under Peter the Great to more than 10 towards the end of the century. Warfare, the growth of towns and industrial activity probably stimulated, if that were needed, such an increase; these changes or interruptions in daily life perhaps also contributed to a change in taste so that more people were demanding spirits, rather than being satisfied with the homely kvas, beer or mead. It seems quite likely that some such 'westernisation' among the town population may have taken place during Peter's reign, but it is hard to demonstrate. It would not conflict with, but simply reinforce the greatly increased state require-

[208]Pryzhov, *Istoriya kabakov*, 222–43.

22 An eighteenth-century woodcut (before 1766) showing a woman cooking pancakes in a Russian stove. She ladles batter into an iron pan which is held over the fire with the help of a long, removable handle fitting into a metal socket. This male and female coupling provides suggestive imagery to the woman's speech in the first part of this doggerel verse. In the second part, the man speaks:

Begone, begone! Get away from me,
I've nothing at all to do with thee.
You come here and pinch my arse,
Make my pancakes just a farce;
You're not allowed to pinch my bum,
Scorch the pancakes to a crumb.
I'll find a reason straightaway,
With a poker you belay;
Though it's shameful,
You'll be too painful
To appear. I'll not torment you,
But you had better disappear
Or, never fear,
With my poker I'll disgrace you

Though you beat me as you will,
Let me grab you by the bum,
For your buttocks seem such fun.
I came to you at home
And am glad you're here alone;
Though you spatter
Me all over with your batter,
I'll not quarrel;
Your true love only show
And we'll to bed together go.

ment for revenue at this period. This requirement, of course, increased
rather than diminished after Peter's death.

The addiction to spirits meant a stimulus to acquire cash; this involved some movement into by-trades and sometimes altogether away
from a largely self-supplying agriculture, a feature noted by contemporaries from the 1740s on.[209] In addition, as distillation improved, the
alcohol content rose and the Russian custom of downing spirits at a go
resulted in impressive drunkenness. Spirits largely ousted beer and
mead in public taste with great profit for state and farmer, but none for
the consumer. Yet the Russian consumer was at least partly to blame.
In the Ukraine, apparently, drinking customs differed sharply. There
wine, as well as spirits, were drunk in taverns where those drinking
could sit and talk as they sipped their drink. In 1787 it was reported
that the Ukrainians 'drink slowly and in small amounts; they chat

[209]Pryzhov, *Istoriya kabakov*, 257. Shcherbatov, 'Razsuzhdenie', *Cht oidr*, book 1; (1860),82.

rather. And when they do get drunk, there are few rowdy and quarrelsome brawls among them and few then come to blows'.[210] Even if this is a somewhat partial picture, it would be hard to find a Russian parallel.

The Ukraine might possibly have modified Russian drinking habits had closer links existed, but it seems unlikely; the Russian drink-shop was too well established and the state demand for revenue too great. Instead, we see continuities from the seventeenth century and earlier, greatly diminished and modified, but reinforcing the new system of revenue extraction. In Tver', Kostroma, Vladimir, Nizhnii Novgorod, Ryazan', Tambov and Voronezh, guberniyas forming a semi-circle round Moscow and mostly massive producers of spirits, the old Slav god of fertility, Yarilo, re-emerged as the god of vodka.[211] In Voronezh in 1765 his cult was celebrated during St Peter's fast with swings and with great drunkenness. Bishop Tikhon so successfully reproached the people for this that they broke the barrels of vodka and abandoned further celebrations of Yarilo. The tax-farmers, however, then denounced him for disturbing the people, 'teaching them not to drink vodka and thus destroying the treasury's concern'.[212] Two years later Tikhon had to retire. This conflict between humane concern for the consumer and the treasury's concern for revenue continued into the following century.

The structural changes which took place in the eighteenth century in Russia thus affected the diet of a large proportion of the population. This came about not merely as a result of the continuing growth of non-agricultural employment and of gentry demand for luxury items as a consequence of 'westernisation', both of which involved increased monetisation.[213] Gentry demand both for money rents and for labour and commodities other than land work and its produce also stimulated a change in peasant activities. Directly, gentry continued to develop a variety of manufacturing activities in manorial works using the labour of their serfs; distilling was an important example. Indirectly, gentry economic concerns were recognised by the government and resulted in legal changes. The result was that fewer people were directly feeding themselves and their families from their plots. The market for mass foodstuffs grew, while a minority developed new tastes.

[210]Shafanskii, *Opisanie Khar'kovskago namestnichestva* (1787), 93, cited in Pryzhov, *Istoriya kabakov*, 238.

[211]Pryzhov, *Istoriya kabakov*, 265.

[212]*Ibid.* See also Fedotov, *A Treasury of Russian Spirituality*, 235, 495.

[213]Kahan, 'The Costs of "Westernization" in Russia', *Slavic Review*, xxv, 1 (1966), 40–66.

Table 5.14. Tax per male soul (kopeks)

	1724	%	1749	%	1751	%	1758	%	1769	%
1 Total	149.2		141.1		164.08		225.66		270.32	
2 Direct	84.93		80.6		80.6		81.32		124.3	
3 Indirect	50.0	100	48.92	100	72.9	100	113.78	100	121.4	100
			46.66		10.59		06.83			
of which:										
(a) vodka	17.4	34.8	18.91	38.7	34.0	46.6	40.9	35.9	60.0	49.4
(b) salt	11.8	23.6	12.0	24.5	18.09	24.8	32.6	28.6	22.4	18.4
(a) + (b)		58.4		63.2		71.4		64.5		67.8
(c) toll duties	20.8	41.6	15.75	32.2	18.5	25.4	33.33	29.3	39.0	32.1
(d) other	0		2.26		2.3		6.95		0	

Notes: 1 does not equal 2 + 3
(d) has been calculated
Source: Based on Troitskii, *Finansovaya politika*, 219.

23 Kvas seller, *c.*–1780. The caption of the original reads: 'Espece de Ptisanne aigre qu'on vend communement aux Coins des Rues'.

Military activities on a previously unknown scale, the Northern War under Peter and the Seven Years War under Elizabeth, the Turkish campaigns under Catherine II, industrial development, the creation of St Petersburg, the growth of manorial works and of commercial farming, the growth of a transport system – all these meant an increased proportion of the population no longer supplying their food directly from their own holding. Increased supplies passed through the market. A contemporary noted the change in the 1780s. 'Bakers were extremely rare, but now bakers' signboards are seen on every street.'[214] In itself, of course, this is not an indication of any improvement in the diet; indeed, the reverse is likely to be the case, at least initially. The market offered an increased range of foodstuffs, some cooked, and almost all adulterated or stale. The state tried to regulate the new situation. In part, spirits and, for much of the century, salt were major sources of tax (see Table 5.14). They provided almost 20%

[214]Shcherbatov, 'Razsuzhdenie', 83.

of total tax in 1724, 36% in 1758 and just over 30% in 1769. In part, the state was obliged to interfere because the new circumstances involved considerable social risks: disease, famine, social disturbance and racketeering of all sorts and at many social levels; in part, the authorities were genuinely concerned for the welfare of the people who were recognised as the source of state wealth. At the end of Peter's reign Pososhkov had stressed that 'the tsardom is wealthy when all the people are wealthy according to their measure', not when the court was in cloth of gold.[215] Attempts to organise supplies, however, involved difficulties: merchants, other men, some with special skills such as accounting, materials and money were needed to develop and maintain a transport, storage and distribution system. Yet the state was desperately short of these resources. Even by 1800, these problems had not been solved There were also institutional restrictions hindering the full use of what was available. Above all, the state favoured the gentry and acted against other merchants. The passport system and serfdom, together with a severely restricted educational system, created a labour shortage; labour was, therefore, costly; the military and the court had first call on what money there was. Moreover, the state authorities tended to be more concerned with increasing taxation income from food than with ensuring adequate supplies for the population. Salt was an exception, for reasons not entirely of humanity.

[215]Pososhkov, *Kniga o skudosti i bogatstve*, 13–14.

6

✻✻

Tea and temperance

The Russians seem to have had no effective conception of China at least before late in the sixteenth century; the first report mentioning China relates to a venture by two atamans in 1567.[1] This report, however, is probably spurious; it coincides in some detail with one dated 1618.[2] The first Russian to drink tea may have been a cossack. Tyumenets, sent to the Mongol ruler in 1616. He reported that his mission 'drank warmed milk and butter, in it unknown leaves . . . and another fine (krasnoe), unknown leaf'.[3] He returned to Moscow with emissaries from the Khan and, allegedly, the first samples of China tea. In 1618 Ivan Petlin and Petrun'ka Kozylov set out from Tobol'sk and established direct contact with China, but the Emperor of China's letter remained in Tobol'sk untranslated into Russian for fifty-six years for lack of anyone able to translate it.[4] In 1638 the Mongol Khan is said to have sent 200 packets (bakhchas) of tea as a precious gift to tsar' Mikhail Fedorovich by the Russian emissary, Starkov, but the latter objected that tea was an unknown and superfluous article in Russia; the court of Moscow would prefer that the Khan should give the equivalent in sables.[5]

The first official mission to China was not till 1654. In that year the illiterate junior boyar, Fedor, son of Isak Baikov, was sent as an envoy to establish relations. He reached Pekin in 1656. His mission was not successful, however; he refused to kow-tow and he also, at first, refused

---

[1] Karamzin, Istoriya, vol. IX, n. 648.

[2] Kh. Trusevich, Posol'skie i torgovye snosheniya Rossii s Kitaem (M., 1882); F.I. Pokrovskii, 'Puteshestvie v Mongoliyu i Kitai Sibirskogo kazaka Ivana Petlina v 1618 goda', Izv. Otdel. Russkogo yazyka i slovesnosti imp. Akad. nauk, XVIII, book 4 (SPb., 1914), 258, 260; M.I. Sladkovskii, Ocherki ekonomicheskikh otnoshenii SSSR s Kitaem (M., 1957), 8.

[3] Cited in Sladkovskii, Ocherki, 15. Chinese hun cha (lit. 'red tea', i.e. black tea) might be meant here.

[4] Sladkovskii, Ocherki, 15–16.

[5] Baddeley, Russia, Mongolia, China, vol. II, 118, states that a bakhcha was a paper packet containing 3 Russian pounds of tea. Kovalevskii, Puteshestvie, vol. II, 125–6; Kozhin, MIZ, II, 706.

a ceremonial dish of tea. 'They then presented me with some *Thee*', as the English version of Baikov's account goes, 'made with Cow's milk and Butter, in the King's name, it being *Lent* I refused to drink it; they told me that I being sent from one great *Czar* to another mighty Prince, I ought at least to accept it, which I did and so returned back.'[6] Baikov, it is claimed, brought some tea with him when he finally returned to Moscow two years later.[7] There seems no hint of any difficulty in taking tea out of China, despite the story of an unnamed editor of the account of travels in China in 1665 by Dominic Fernandez Navarette. The editor asserted that he was often told in China 'that as well the Eastern as the Western Tartars put a great value upon the herb *Cha* or *Te*; whereof the most usual drink in that Kingdome is made', but, since export of tea was prohibited, they starved their horses for a few days, then fed them with tea and immediately set off for the frontier. Once past it, they killed these horses, took the tea from their stomachs, dried it and, he added, 'so carry it about to sell and make Drink of it'.[8] The second official Russian embassy to China, led by Perfil'ev in 1658, received, among a variety of presents from the Emperor to the tsar', ten puds (163 kg) of tea.[9] All this tea was sold in Pekin and jewels bought with the proceeds.[10]

Samuel Collins, physician to tsar' Alexei Mikhailovich, noted in 1671 that tea and anis was brought from Siberia.

The Chay is that which we call *Teah* or *Tey*, and *Bourdiam* is *Anisum Indicum Stellatum*, the Merchants say they use it (as we do in *England*) with Sugar, and esteem it a rare Remedy in diseases of the Lungs, *Flatus Hypochondriaci*, and distempers of the Stomach; 'tis bought over in papers about one pound weight, written on with *Chinese* Characters. They who travel into these parts are six years in their Journey, staying for winter way in some places, and summer in others.[11]

Unfortunately, he gave no indication of price.

In 1674 the Swede Kilburger, who had participated in an embassy to Moscow, claimed to have bought tea there at 30 kopeks a Russian pound.[12] He wrote that it was used mainly for medicinal purposes;

[6]In Churchill and Churchill, *A Collction of Voyages and Travels*, vol. II, 550. Baddeley, *Russia, Mongolia, China*, vol. II, 144.
[7]Prozorovskii, 'Chai'; Korsakov, *Obozrenie*, 58.
[8]Churchill and Churchill, *A Collection of Voyages and Travels*, vol. II, 367.
[9]Baddeley, *Russia, Mongolia, China*, vol. II, 168. Sladkovskii, *Ocherki*, 18, without citing any authority, says three puds.
[10]Bantysh-Kamensky, cited in Baddeley, *Russia, Mongolia, China*, vol. II, 168.
[11]*The Present State of Russia*, 75–6.
[12]Kurts, *Sochinenie Kil'burgera*, 113.

'they use it especially to avert drunkenness, if they take it before drinking; or to disperse the intoxication resulting from drink, if they use it after drinking'.[13] Kilburger himself refers to a work by Neuhoff as his source; in fact, Neuhoff stated that tea was very costly and it seems that Kilburger's price of 30 kopeks a pound was taken from Neuhoff's statement that 'a pound costs 5 Dutch shillings or 30 shtivers', i.e. 30 kopeks; but he immeditely adds: 'larger leaves 50 shillings, those still larger 5 Dutch guilders, 15 and, finally, 50 and 100 guilders'.[14] According to Neuhoff's prices, then, a pound of tea would have cost in Russian currency from 30 kopeks to 20 rubles. If Kilburger actually bought any tea in Moscow, it was the cheapest sort and he might have paid over 130 times as much for it, assuming prices there varied as much as those encountered by Neuhoff.[15]

It was in 1674, too, that the first Russian caravan went to China as the result of an initiative by a steward of a Moscow merchant.[16] After the treaty of Nerchinsk between Russia and China, agreed in 1689, state caravans, with private participation, took furs and other goods to Pekin and brought back to Moscow (two years after setting out) Chinese valuables, such as gold, silver, precious stones and also rhubarb fruits, silk and an insignificant amount of tea, the use of which in Russia was negligible.[17] The commodities requested as exports from China in 1693 by E. Ysbrants Ides (Elizar Elizarevich Izbrand), a Dutch merchant in Russian employ, were silver and medicinal plants, especially rhubarb. In 1694, at his death, the well-off agent of a merchant had one pound of tea, 'evidently for his own use'.[18] Prior to the establishment of a trading post at Kyakhta in 1727, there may have been about a dozen Russian caravans to China; they returned with gold, silver, pearls, precious stones, silks and other luxuries.[19] There seems to be little evidence to support the implications of the statement that 'from the end of the 17th century much tea was imported and sold in Moscow shops along with other everyday commodities'.[20] In 1698 a merchant who imported Chinese goods valued at over 32,000 rubles in Moscow prices brought in 5 puds 7 pounds of tea, valued (for tax purposes) at 20–5 rubles a pud in Moscow, about two thirds of a ruble

[13]*Ibid.*

[14]Neuhoff, *Die Gesandtschaft*, 324–6 deals with tea, and is quoted in Kurts, *Sochinenie Kil'burgera*, 25–6.

[15]Kilburger stated that a chet of rye cost 60–70 kopeks; *ibid.*, 177.

[16]Bakhrushin, *Nauchnye trudy*, vol. III, 1, 228.

[17]Samoilov in *Sbornik statisticheskikh svedenii*, vol. II (1854), 3; Sladkovskii, *Ocherki*, 26–35.

[18]Bakhrushin, *Nauchnye trudy*, vol. III, 1, 235.

[19]Sladkovskii, *Ocherki*, 32, 43.

[20]Palibin, in *Trudy po prikladnoi botanike*, vol. XVIII, 3 (1927–8), 14.

a pound. This was less than in earlier years because, he claimed, the price of tea had fallen.[21] There was clearly some demand for tea by this time, but it was scarcely an everyday commodity.

It was in the period 1680–1720, roughly corresponding to the period between the treaties of Nerchinsk (1689) and Kyakhta (1727) for Russia, that tea prices fell sufficiently in Western Europe for tea to become a popular drink. In the Dutch East India Company's auctions tea became a commodity of great importance in Western Europe in the first third of the eighteenth century.[22] In the 1670s tea imports from China had often been a few hundred pounds in weight a year, in 1718 for the first time more than half a million pounds were imported.[23]

In the early eighteenth century John Bell experienced the tea consumed on the caravan route to China.

> The hospitable landlady immediately set her kettle on the fire, to make us some tea; the extraordinary cookery of which I cannot omit describing. After placing a large iron-kettle over the fire, she took care to wipe it very clean with a horse's tail, that hung in a corner of the tent for that purpose; then the water was put into it, and soon after, some coarse bohea tea, which is got from China, and a little salt. When near boiling, she took a large brass ladle and tossed the tea, till the liquor turned very brown. It was now taken off the fire, and, after subsiding a little, was poured clear into another vessel. The kettle being wiped clean with the horse's tail, as before, was again set upon the fire. The mistress now prepared a paste, of meal and fresh butter, that hung in a skin near the horse's tail, which was put into the tea-kettle and fried. Upon this paste the tea was again poured; to which was added some good thick cream, taken out of a clean sheep's skin, which hung upon a peg among the other things. The ladle was again employed, for the space of six minutes, when the tea, being removed from the fire, was allowed to stand a while in order to cool. The landlady now took some wooden cups, which held about half a pint each, and served her tea to all the company. The principal advantage of this tea is, that it both satisfies hunger and quenches thirst. I thought it not disagreeable; but should have liked much better had it been prepared in a manner a little more cleanly.[24]

The 'kettle' here, of course, is an open cauldron, not a closed vessel with a spout. Bell called this dish *zaturan* (perhaps meaning Turanian tea) and distinguishes it from the tea drunk in China.[25]

This 'Tatar' (i.e. Mongol) and Kalmyk consumption of tea, usually

[21] Bakhrushin, *Nauchnye trudy*, vol. III, 1, 242. *Istoriya Moskvy*, vol. I, 425.
[22] Glamann, *Dutch–Asiatic Trade*, 212–13, 219, 285.
[23] Chaudhuri, *Trading World*, 538.
[24] John Bell, *A Journey from St Petersburg to Pekin, 1719–22* (1965), 86.
[25] *Ibid.*, 110, 181–2.

brick tea crumbled into milk, boiled, sometimes with added butter and some grain, and eaten with a spoon, does not seem to have influenced Russian diet.[26] The preparation of this thin porridge was common throughout the area of the caravan routes from the Chinese border westwards through Central Asia; its use among pilgrims in Persia continued into modern times.[27] It requires a pot or cauldron rather than a spouted kettle or other water–heating vessel for its preparation. Boiling at the high altitudes of part of the caravan route would take place at a reduced temperature and so not 'stew' the tea.

Trading relations between Russia and China did not develop at all systematically till after the death of Peter the Great, despite earlier imports such as those mentioned by the merchant Mikhail Gusyatni-kov, who had been in China in 1716.[28] In the 1727 convention be-tween Russia and China, a border trading post was designated midway between Kyakhta and another nearby location; Tsurukhaitu, on the Argun, was also established, but never developed. Free settlement at the trading quarter (*sloboda*) at Kyakhta was permitted in 1743. After the establishment of Kyakhta state caravans were despatched to Pekin in 1728, 1731, 1735, 1740, 1745 and 1754.[29] In 1762, however, they were abandoned and merchants were allowed to make their own ar-rangements, provided they paid customs duty.[30]

Customs tariffs of the 1730s already give some details of the varieties of tea being imported into the Russian Empire.[31]

(1) *zhulan*, the best green tea, evidently flavoured with leaves of the shrub *Chloranthus spicatus* (*zhulan*) native to northern China, came in $2\frac{1}{2}$ pud containers of woven bamboo lined with lead and cost 25 bales of nankeen (*kitaika*); others were *monikho* (Chinese for 'jas-mine'), the lowest quality green, with added jasmine flowers, *tsy-tun*, *lonkhovyi* or *khankhua*;

(2) ordinary green which came packeted and loose;

(3) *lugana* (perhaps a corruption of *lamiancha*, the original term for brick tea when it was first made in the tenth century or, perhaps more likely, a corruption of Mongol *nagana*, 'green') a poor qual-ity green, brick tea 'and all sorts of poor' tea;

[26]Dal', *Tolkovyi slovar'*, *s.v. chai*; Staveacre, *Tea*, 5; Chulkov, *Opisanie*, vol. III, ii, 48; Reinbot, *Chai*, 24.

[27]d'Allemagne, *Du Khorassan*, vol. I, 180.

[28]Chulkov, *Opisanie*, vol. III, ii, 81, 85.

[29]Twinings Russian Caravan Tea is available in tins which state that 'in 1735 the Empress Elizabeth established a Caravan Tea Trade between the Far East and Russia'.

[30]Samoilov, *Sbornik*, vol. II, 5–6; Sladkovskii, *Ocheki*, 43.

[31]Chulkov, *Opisanie*, vol. III, ii, 48.

(4) *bui* or *ui* (i.e. Bohea, a name derived from the Wu-i hills in Fujiang province),[32] and *baikhovoi*, black tea which came in large containers and small packets; finally,

(5) *Khaar*, 'stone tea'; this was not really tea but a medicine called *terra katekha*. This may have been *jui-mingzi*, a grass seed which was mixed with *shi jueming*, abalone shell or 'stone'.[33]

The tea trade really started to develop only under Catherine the Great. The import of tea through Kyakhta, however, underwent a development only at the end of the eighteenth century. In the 1770s and 1780s tea was still a secondary item of Russian imports.[34] Before this, in the 1740s and 1750s, there had been at least half a dozen minor interruptions in the trade.

Early in the reign of Catherine the Great there were periods when the trade was seriously interrupted. From 1762 to 1768 Kyakhta ceased to operate; it was closed as a result of differences with the Chinese. Even when, after over six years, the differences had been resolved and relations re-established there were further interruptions: a few days only in 1775, but then a period of over two years, 1778–80. A third long interruption lasted almost seven years from 1785.[35] By this time tea drinking was well enough established in European Russia for this interruption in supply through Kyakhta to have to be made good elsewhere.[36] 'We received tea from the English during the whole time Kyakhta was closed; but Buryats and Kalmyks brought cotton textiles and brick tea secretly for themselves.'[37] Even if at this time tea was re-exported to Russia mainly from England, it also arrived from Amsterdam, Lubeck, Hamburg and elsewhere.[38] According to a contemporary historian of the Dutch East Indies, by the 1760s tea was the largest item of trade from China to Europe, but the amount sent was only known to the merchants involved.[39]

For the nomads of Siberia tea was a food, a necessity; smuggling met their needs when regular trade was broken off. For the westernised

---

[32]Glamann, *Dutch–Asiatic trade*, 214; Needham, *Science and Civilization in China*, vol. I, 71. See also Palibin, in *Trudy po prikladnoi botanike*, vol. XVIII (1927–8), 3, 6, 8, 12.

[33]I am most grateful to Professors Tien Ju-Kang and Owen Lattimore for their comments on these terms.

[34]Sladkovskii, *Ocherki*, 70.

[35]Samoilov, *Sbornik*, vol. II, 8.

[36]Russian and French replaced Chinese silks during 1785–92; Mancall, 'The Kiakhta trade', in *Economic Development*, ed. Cowan, 29.

[37]Korsakov, *Obozrenie*, 71, citing *Zhurnal manufaktury i torgovli*, 9 (1837).

[38]Chulkov, *Opisanie*, vol. VI, ii, 242.

[39]Du Bois, *Vies des gouverneurs généraux* (1763), 25–6, Chaudhuri, *Trading World*, 539, gives total imports of tea from China in 1760 as over 6 million lb.

gentry of European Russia, however, tea was a drink, one of those luxury items which signalled status and alienated them from the mass of eighteenth-century Russians. In European Russia in the last third of the century 'tea was still not a popular necessity and its acquisition was limited'.[40] This was so even though prices were not considered to be very high.[41] It seems possible to go a little further than this.

The import of tea into Russia from China for the period from around 1760 to the late 1790s seemed to have amounted to about 12,000 puds (432 thousand lb) of leaf tea a year; brick tea imports then recorded averaged perhaps 16 or 17 thousand puds (about 600 thousand lb) a year.[42] The importation of crystallised sugar, used with tea fluctuated between about 1.5 and 2.5 thousand puds (54 and 90 thousand lb). This seems to indicate a fairly stable consumption in this period when the samovar was still a rare item of equipment even for gentry households. These amounts, however, were supplemented by any imports from the West. The figures probably mean that, even if consumption was entirely restricted to gentry families, about 1 lb of leaf tea a year and less than $\frac{1}{4}$ lb of sugar was available per person.[43] A Japanese seaman in Russia in the 1780s reported that 'the ordinary people dry strawberry leaves and use them in place of tea. Tea costs from 1 to 5 silver rubles a pound.'[44]

From the late 1790s, however, imports rose sharply; in 1798 leaf tea amounted to more than 21 thousand puds (343,000 kg) and brick to almost 26 thousand (424,000 kg). In part this rise may possibly be accounted for by the interruption in imports from the west during the Napoleonic wars, but the main factor seems likely to have been the spread of the tea drinking habit to wider sectors of the population. At the same time the samovar became somewhat more common-place, though by no means every family had one, even among merchants.

In the nineteenth century there were great changes in the amounts of tea imported and the routes used, and in distribution. Leaf tea imports continued to rise from 70 thousand to about 100 thousand puds (1.6 million kg) a year by 1820; but even more noticeable is the growth of brick tea imports which reached 35 thousand puds (0.6 million kg) in the same year, and this seems to be totally ascribable to the widespread increase in tea drinking among the Siberian and the subject Russian

[40]Korsakov, *Obozrenie*, 88.

[41]Korsakov, *Obozrenie*, 92; Chulkov, *Opisanie*, vol. III, ii, 474.

[42]Mancall, 'The Kiakhta trade', 46, based on Trusevich, *Posol'skie i torgovye snosheniya*, 274–5.

[43]See Appendix for the sources relating to this calculation.

[44]Katsuragawa, *Kratkie vesti*, 208.

population.[45] By this time, evidently, tea drinking was no longer restricted either to medicinal consumption or to the upper classes; the spread of leaf tea consumption, however, seems to have taken much longer. Brick tea, of course, had been mostly consumed in the Trans-Baikal area, and in commenting on the import figures for 1814 Korsakov noted that 'of teas, only the brick was then an item of popular consumption, that is in Siberia and among the Kalmyks and Tatars in Russia. Black tea was then used in Russia only in the circle of high society and a few rich merchants.'[46] This situation continued long, but throughout the nineteenth century tea drinking gradually spread and became more usual among the lower classes. By mid-century more than 300,000 puds (4 5 million kg) of tea a year was being imported. Consumption rose from 0.047 kg per head at the start of the century to 0.2 kg by 1870 and 0.4 by 1880.[47]

Towards the middle of the nineteenth century tea accounted for 95% of the value of goods imported into Russia through Kyakhta; but there was a decline in the years 1848 and 1849, apparently owing to tea also passing across the Sinkiang border and the great growth in contraband trade.[48] At the same period the British carried China tea from Shanghai and other southern ports to Russia by sea. Russian tea might be worse than 'the brick tea unknown in Europe, but even that sells here at a higher price than the very last English or American tea'.[49] The high Russian price was due to the nature of the trade and to transport costs as well as the costlier nature of the quality teas imported. It is estimated that transport costs from China to Western Europe were five-and-a-half times less than on the overland route from Kyakhta to Central Russia.[50] Moreover, the cost within China of transporting tea to Kyakhta was in some cases eight times greater than the cost of taking it to the nearest port.

Only in 1862 was Canton tea permitted to be brought to Russia.[51] In 1880 regular sailings were established between Odessa and Vladivostok; in the mid-1880s this service began to include visits to Canton and Shanghai. This was the origin of Russia's own sea-borne transport of tea. The growth of this trade is shown by Table 6.1.[52] Despite tariffs

[45]Brokgauz–Efron *Entsiklopedicheskii slovar'*, 75 (XXXVIII): 369–70.
[46]Korsakov, *Obozrenie*, 111.
[47]Brokgauz-Efron, 75 (XXXVIII), 370.
[48]Sladkovskii, *Ocherki*, 91–3.
[49]Korsakov, *Obozrenie*, 395.
[50]Sladkovskii, *Ocherki*, 115.
[51]Reinbot, *Chai*, 22.
[52]Sladkovskii, *Ocherki*, 119, citing *Kratkii ocherk vozniknoveniya, razvitiya i tepereshnego sostoyaniya nashikh torgovykh s Kitaem snoshenii cherez Kyakhtu*, 83.

Table 6.1. *China tea imported through Odessa*

	puds ('000)	lb ('000)	tonnes ('000)		puds ('000)	lb ('000)	tonnes ('000)
1885	246.2	8,863.2	4.0	1890	661.8	23,824.8	10.8
1886	380.5	13,698.0	6.2	1891	722.0	25,992.0	11.8
1887	370.3	13,330.0	6.1	1892	471.7	16,981.2	7.7
1888	495.5	17,838.0	8.1	1893	640.7	23,065.2	10.5
1889	511.6	18,417.6	8.4				

designed to favour the Kyakhta trade which were quite effective, the cheaper sea-borne tea, both Russian and West European, was probably the main factor in encouraging the drinking of tea in Russia on a mass scale.

In 1901 1.7 million puds (27.7 million kg) of leaf and 1.5 million puds (24 million kg) of brick tea were imported. By this time the first tea plantations had been started a few years before in the Caucasus.[53]

This enormous increase over the nineteenth century in the amount of tea available in Russia gradually came to provide an alternative to alcoholic drinks. The milder alcoholic drinks, such as beer or kvas, were never a serious challenge to spirits in the nineteenth century.[54] As early as the 1840s, however, some of those concerned to eradicate drunkenness in Russia argued that tea, and coffee, had helped the wealthy in the rest of Europe in this respect. 'Among our merchants and townsfolk tea is, evidently, spreading . . . the beneficient Chinese drink is starting to penetrate into rich settlements in the interior of Russia; the post-horse drivers along the Petersburg–Moscow route drink it almost daily; it is impossible not to rejoice at this . . . If, at some time, beet sugar, now coming into use with such trouble, becomes widely known and spreads everywhere, it would, of course, increase the use of tea and decrease the coarse behaviour of the common people.'[55] Yet there seems to have been no widespread advocacy of tea as a temperance alternative to vodka during the popular movement against drink in 1858–60.[56]

Only by the 1870s had tea drinking become sufficiently widespread among working people for it to be advocated as an alternative to spirits. The temperance movement did what it could, against state

[53]Kozhin, *MIZ*, II, 713f.
[54]See ch. 8.
[55]Gersevanov, *O p'yanstve*, 121–2.
[56]Fedorov, 'Krest'yanskoe trezvennoe dvizhenie 1858–1859', 107–26.

pressure, to encourage tea drinking. Vodka in immoderate quantities resulted in weakness of both bodily and mental powers, but tea had no such ill effects. 'Tea, even taken in considerable quantities, has a moderate stimulus; tea does not weaken the body; its arms and legs remain under control, unlike those of vodka drinkers.'[57] By the fifth glass of vodka a man became quite unfit for work. 'In view of this it was commonsense that tea drinking should be widespread and England was regarded as an exemplar; there the poor, living from day to day, made every effort to keep a few spare coppers to buy an ounce of tea a day.'[58] Doctors, as well as publicists, propagated tea drinking from public platforms, mainly on health grounds, and it was even argued that tea, not spirits, should be distributed to troops in the steppe zone.[59] It was in the late nineteenth century, too, that 'for tea' (*na chai, na chaek*), rather than 'for vodka', became the set expression for a tip.

One particular piece of equipment which has become virtually synonymous with tea drinking in Russia is the samovar; many people believe it is an exclusively Russian item. Zamyatin categorically asserted that 'the icebreaker is as specifically Russian a thing as is the samovar'; he was evidently unable to think of anything more 'Russian'.[60] A recent scholarly work more cautiously states that 'today it is hard to say when and where the first samovar, that "self-heating" apparatus which became a particular symbol of Russian life, was invented'.[61] The term 'samovar' has even established itself in English: antique dealers use it of any heated urn and maybe the word has more exotic appeal than the common-place terms 'urn' or 'vase' that it replaced. The term itself seems to mean 'self-boiler', though this etymology has been challenged; attempts have been made to derive the term from the Turkish *sanabar* ('kettle'), but the view that Turkish *samavar*, Tatar *samaur*, *samuwar* etc. are Russian loans appears more probable and is now generally accepted.[62]

Some people believe that the samovar is of oriental origin and have called attention to Chinese and Korean vessels used for heating food. Such Chinese vessels (called *go-ho*), and the Korean (*sin syol lo*), are used only for cooking at table, not for heating water or preparing tea as

[57]Reinbot, *Chai*, 27.
[58]*Ibid.*, 28.
[59]*Ibid.*, 30–1.
[60]E. Zamyatin, *Mosty*, 9 (1962), 21. I am indebted to G.S. Smith for this reference.
[61]E.A. Ivanova, *Russkie samovary*, 7.
[62]Fasmer, *Etymologicheskii slovar'*, vol. III, 553. Professor A. Tietze has written to me that in the Near East 'the samovar is certainly an importation from the Russian area'.

24 A samovar, dated 1801. The urn design has many eighteenth-century western analogues.

a drink.[63] A Korean example, however, has been called 'of the samovar type', although it appears to be closely similar to other cooking vessels, since it has no tap or spout.[64] It may be noted, however, that such cooking bowls would be suitable for preparing the porridge-like tea consumed with a spoon. Such vessels, however, have a central chimney, bulbous towards the base (to accommodate the fire); this element is the same in samovars.

What Hough called a 'teapot stove', a Chinese vessel with a pierced brass base and a conical hot-air flue ventilating through the lid seems

[63]Ivanova, *Russkie samovary*, 7; Hough, *Collection of Heating and Lighting Utensils in the US National Museum*, 92; *Sakai dai hyakka jiten*, 15, 411. Cp. Ukers, *All about Tea*, vol. II, 398, 446.
[64]Hough, *Collection*, 92 and plate 80, fig. 5, catalogue no. 77054.

25 Toddy seller, 1858. The seller has a kettle heated by a central cylinder, which passes through it, containing a charcoal fire, similar to a samovar. He carries a string of ring pretzels. The hawker carries a board advertising 'Monsieur Julia'.

closer in appearance, and perhaps in function, to English tea tackles (see below, p. 242) and some eighteenth-century Russian utensils.[65] It should be regarded as a charcoal-heated kettle, rather than a teapot, since it was placed immediately over a fire; like both teapots and kettles it was fitted with a spout. It differs from ordinary kettles in that the conical hot-air flue passes through the vessel; it thus resembles a Russian toddy-kettle (*sbitennik*). These are known from the mid-eighteenth century and seem to be among the earliest types of Russian samovars in the broad sense.[66] Their earlier history appears to be at least as obscure as that of the samovar proper. It seems that they were used not only for toddy, though that usage may be taken to hint at a

[65]Hough, *Collection*, 93 and plate 80, fig. 2; catalogue no. 75338.
[66]Ivanova, *Russkie samovary*, 8, 11 and plates 1, 3, 13.

derivation from the Far East where warmed drinks were usual. A mid-eighteenth century example from the Urals has a perforated plate at the base of the spout, and hence was probably a tea kettle.[67] This utensil had no pierced base support to allow air to circulate. The question whether these Russian kettles derive from the Chinese *go-ho* therefore remains open, but it seems at least a possibility. The example quoted was made in the Urals; another, probably from the second half of the eighteenth century, was from Nizhnii Novgorod.[68] It may be noted that Nizhnii Novgorod was the western end of the overland route from China.[69]

Tula, a town 110 miles (177 km) south of Moscow where there had been armaments and other metal works from the sixteenth century, became the centre of the samovar-making industry, though there were other places where samovars were made. Early in the eighteenth century Peter the Great had expanded the metal working industry at Tula; an Imperial Arms Manufactury was established. This accumulation of experience in metal, especially brass, working was the basis used for the first known Tula samovar workshop set up by Ivan Lisitsyn in 1778.[70] Grigorii Lisitsyn of Moscow, probably a relative, was another famous samovar maker.[71] Not earlier than 1776 a merchant called Aleksandr Shmakov had a works in Moscow which produced 'candlesticks and samovars' worth 486 rubles 80 kopek, not a very considerable output.[72] In another report Shmakov is listed as having one of three brass works in Moscow, this had fifteen serf workers.[73] There is a silver samovar, now in the Hermitage, bearing the date 1762 and stamped 'Sibir' in Roman letters; but it has been shown that this was a tea kettle modified in the nineteenth century by adding three feet and replacing the spout by a tap.[74] Evidently such metal items of equipment were valuable. It seems doubtful, then, whether samovars were made in Russia much before the 1770s. The term samovar itself appears to be attested no earlier than this; throughout the eighteenth century the Russian samovar was a comparative rarity.[75] By the turn of the cen-

[67] *Ibid.*, 11–12 and plate 1.
[68] *Ibid.*, plate 3; cp. plate 13.
[69] Reinbot, *Chai*, 5.
[70] *Nauka i zhizn'*, 4 (1967), 94.
[71] Krutikov, 'K istorii tul'skikh kustarnykh promyslov', 12.
[72] Chulkov, *Opisanie*, vol. VI, iii, 654, 658.
[73] *Ibid.*, 711.
[74] Ivanova, *Russkie samovary*, 11. Krutikov, 'K istorii', 6, claimed there were samovars 'of an earlier period, going back approximately to the first quarter of the 18th century'. Unfortunately he gave no details.
[75] The term occurs in *Slovar' Akademii rossiiskoi*, part 1, col. 506, (1789).

26 Peasant dwelling with stove and samovar, late nineteenth century. The sleeping area above the stove is seen on the left; a samovar, with a temporary pipe to carry the smoke into the stove chimney, is on the right.

tury, as tea imports rose sharply, the samovar became somewhat more common-place, though by no means every family had one, even among merchants. In the mid-nineteenth century the samovar was an indicator of wealth in the families of townsfolk and, sometimes, of peasants; a prescriptive Old Believer verse on tea claimed that 'I have been sent from China to the masters, not for the simple, bearded muzhiks'.[76] It was not till the 1870s that it could be said with some truth that 'throughout Russia, particularly in trading towns, not a single man spends a day without drinking tea twice, sometimes three times; and in the countryside those who are better off have come to use the samovar!'[77] Even then Old Believer opposition to tea continued. Samovars were so costly that in the countryside, it appears, some people made their own.[78] As late as 1892 a *zemstvo* report noted that in Elets 'very few drink tea, for the most some of those in industry or

[76]Gersevanov, *Op'yanstve*, 122; Begunov, in *Rukopisnoe nasledie Drevnei Rusi*, 245.
[77]Reinbot, *Chai*, 1. Cp. Korsakov's statement quoted above (p. 235).
[78]Ivanova, *Russkie samovary*, 9.

living in town; and even those only on certain holidays or some particular occasion'.[79]

Tea nowadays seems as typical of England as of Russia, though usually consumed in a somewhat different manner. It was introduced into England about 1645; there was a tea-house in Exchange Alley, London, in 1657. Tea, however, did not become fashionable until well into the seventeenth century; at first, incidentally, it was the custom to infuse the leaves and preserve the resultant liquid in barrels from which it was drawn off, like beer, and warmed as required in the coffee houses.[80]

By the 1670s teapots and, apparently a little later, tea kettles are known; an inventory of Ham House in 1679 includes 'one Indian furnace for tee garnished with silver'.[81] A curious 'tea tackle', consisting of a water container with a small charcoal furnace beneath, is known and has been dated 1710.[82] Possibly the 'Indian furnace' was something like this.

West European silver hot-water urns are known from the early eighteenth century. A Dutch *kraantsjeskan* from The Hague, 1709, has a pierced base 'to allow a good circulation of air for the wax candle or copper charcoal burner which can be placed in the foot'.[83] It has two taps, one on each side of the body. An urn by Christian Waarenberg, Amsterdam, 1717, has three taps.[84] Another silver tea-urn is known by Andele Andeles, Leeuwarden, 1729.[85] There is a magnificent example, which clearly shows a central tube for the charcoal fire and a teapot support on top; this Danish example is by Christian Werum, Copenhagen, 1762.[86]

Water heating utensils identical with the Russian samovar, that is having an outer casing containing the water and fitted with a tap, and a fire box, usually central, or a narrowing tube for charcoal, then, were known in Western Europe by the mid-eighteenth century. It seems at least possible that utensils such as these had served as models for the Russian manufactures of the 1770s and later. Moreover, the West

[79]*Opyt sanitarno-statisticheskago issledovaniya Izvol'skoi volosti, Eletskogo uezda* (1892) 49.

[80]Staveacre, *Tea*, 2–4; Ibbetson, *Tea*, 4–6; Mennell, *Tea*, 9.

[81]Oman, *Caroline Silver*, 57–8.

[82]Leicester City Museum. Illustrated in Ukers, *All about Tea*, vol. II, 403, who gives this date; the Leicester Museum does not confirm this.

[83]Premsela and Hamburger, private communication, 6 January 1978. A similar vessel by Jesaias Engouw, The Hague, 1720, is illustrated in J.W. Frederiks, *Dutch Silver*, part 2, no. 495.

[84]Brunner, *Old Table Silver*, no. 42.

[85]Brunner, *ibid.*, no. 130.

[86]Brunner, *ibid.*, 43 and no. 55.

European urns with three taps have Russian brass equivalents.[87] These are *bul'otki* (i.e. lamp-heated vessels) or *réchaud* of the second half of the nineteenth century. A curious feature is that while the Dutch example of 1717 has tap thumb pieces of a mermaid sounding a cornucopia-like horn, both Russian examples have a cock. The general appearance seems sufficiently close to suggest a modification of the design when copying from the elegant silver original into the more plebeian brass. It is known that the wine-cooler (*fontan*) of urn shape, which was 'a peculiar prototype of the samovar', was found at court and in some houses of Russian nobility as an import from the West in the first decades of the eighteenth century.[88] Prince V.A. Dolgorukii, ambassador to Denmark in 1707–20 had one. It does not seem improbable, therefore, that imports of such silver utensils should continue into the period of Catherine II (1762–96).

According to some authorities, in England

The silver tea-kettle was beginning to go out of favour shortly after 1760. The first indication of a general change in public requirements was the modification of the kettle design to include a ball-handled tap close to the vessel's broad base.[89] The resulting utensil, a heated water container with a tap rather than a spout, is essentially a samovar. Some tea-urns were heated by charcoal in a central tube. Charcoal heaters began to be superseded from 1774, following Wadham's patent, by the solid cylindrical box iron.[90]

Lamp-heated tea-urns, which were not sold until about 1790, appear to have been used for drawing off tea or coffee into cups. Even about this date, however, charcoal-heated urns continued to feature occasionally in manufacturers' pattern books.[91] The types heated by a charcoal fire or a pre-heated iron billet in a central tube usually contained reserves of hot water, but Hughes states that 'contrary to popular notion, tea was not made directly in the teapot but in the tea urn, as proved by several contemporaneous conversation pieces, such as James Northcote's "Dr. Johnson taking tea with Sir Joshua Reynolds" painted in 1783'.[92] The pictorial evidence, however, is by no means as clear as this would suggest. For example, tea-parties painted by Zoffany in the period 1760–90 show both urns and teapots being used. The silver teapot

[87]Ivanova, *Russkie samovary*, plates 96 and 101.
[88]Ivanova, *Russkie samovary*, 13.
[89]Hughes and Hughes, *Three Centuries of English Domestic Silver*, 174. Cp. Hughes, *Antique Sheffield Plate*, 141; Banister, *An introduction*, 280.
[90]Hughes, *Antique Sheffield Plate*, 141.
[91]Boulton & Watt Pattern Book, II, 108, no. 2155; 188, no. 2390.
[92]Hughes, *Antique Sheffield Plate*, 141. Cp. Hughes and Hughes, *Three Centuries of English Domestic Silver*, 175.

depicted in his 'The Auriol family' has been identified and is hall-marked 1785.[93] The silver urn shown in his 'Lord Willoughby de Broke and his family', painted in 1766, still survives; but we do not know whether it contained tea or water. In fact, from early in the eighteenth century it appears that a common way of taking tea was from a small teapot replenished, presumably with water, from a much larger kettle.[94] The metal teapot was sometimes kept warm on a *réchaud* stand.[95] The urn seems most probably to have been used as a reserve of water because most teapots of the period were small; its advantage over the kettle was that it required only the turn of a tap and so relieved the hostess of handling a kettle heavy with boiling water.

In England 'hot water, coffee or tea urns held a place on the side-board of the wealthier classes from about the middle of the 18th century'.[96]

> Now stir the fire, and close the shutters fast,
> Let fall the curtains, wheel the sofa round,
> And, while the bubbling and loud-hissing urn
> Throws up a steamy column, and the cups,
> That cheer but not inebriate, wait on each,
> So let us welcome peaceful evening in.
>
> Cowper, *The Task*, book IV, l.34 (1783)

These hissing urns were, of course, often of silver or silver plated, not, as now, electrolytically, but by the fusion of thin sheets of silver with the base metal, usually copper or brass; this method gave what is known as Old Sheffield plate.

In the 1740s and 1750s one of the categories in Russian tariff sched-ules relating to imports was 'tea and coffee pots, candlesticks, trays, holders and similar small items, tinned and untinned'.[97] If West Euro-pean or English tea-urns as well as tea had been imported into Russia when the Kyakhta trade was interrupted, they would have been liable to duty under this category. It is, therefore, particularly interesting to note that in the 1782 tariff the same category is mentioned (though specified by the additional words 'of red and green copper'), but it is followed by a new item: 'Similar objects and small items, silvered and

[93]Mary Webster, *Johan Zoffany 1783–1810* (National Portrait Gallery, 1977), 75–6.

[94]See, for example: Nicolaas Verkolje (?) (1673–1746), *Two ladies and a gentleman at tea*, *c.* 1715–20; Balthasar Denner (1685–1749), *The Duchess Elisabeth Sophie Marie of Braunschweig-Wolfenbüttel taking tea*; William Hogarth (1697–1764) *The Strode family*, 1738; English School (eighteenth century), *The Carter Family*, *c.* 1740.

[95]Anon, *A Family Taking Tea*, *c.* 1720.

[96]Bradbury, *History*, 359.

[97]Chulkov, *Opisanie*, vol. VI, i, 375 (1744 and 1745); vol. IV, iv, 293 (1757).

gilt or *argent-haché* and applied silver sheet made the same way'.[98] This clearly refers to Old Sheffield plate (the earliest known tea-urn in which is dated 1762) or its French imitations; it suggests that such wares were among the luxury items imported into Russia by the 1780s.[99] In 1790 English plated samovars were on sale in St Petersburg.[100] This is not surprising; a list of works producing beaten silver ware in St Petersburg mentions one works in 1765, three others in 1774, and shows that they were all held by foreigners.[101] Silver plated ware was only produced in Russia in the nineteenth century.[102] Brass and copper urns may have been imported before this, along with tea and also sugar.[103] Numbers of both imported tea-urns and also of domestically produced samovars were probably limited at this time. The memorandum book of an unnamed merchant in 1775, quoted as an example of trade book-keeping, lists his inventory, including such items as a silver teapot, coffee pot and sugar bowl; even half a dozen spoons and a tea strainer are noted. But although this evidently well-to-do merchant in St Petersburg would have been in a position to acquire a samovar, or a tea service from abroad, none is recorded.[104]

It might be objected that the Russians, importing tea from China, were more likely to have imported any tea-making equipment from there as well. In fact, there seems to be no evidence to support this; the material on imports from China has no mention of tea urns or similar utensils. Central Asian tea vessels, such as the tea-jug (*chaidjush*), lack any fire-box.[105] It may be that the zone of brick tea consumption through which the Russian merchants had to pass on their road from China formed a cultural barrier; in that area the tea-making equipment was of quite a different kind and vessels like the Chinese *go-ho* were not required there for the preparation of tea. In fact, though at the moment it is only speculation, the Chinese heating utensils may well be the origin of the Russian samovar, but if so, it seems likely that they made their impact on Russia through other intermediaries: the West Europeans who were trading both in China and in Russia in the seventeenth and eighteenth centuries. Of these, the Dutch seem the most likely to have introduced the charcoal-heated water urn to Russia.

[98]Chulkov, *ibid.*, vol. IV, v, 785.
[99]Bradbury, *History*, 160 (illustration), 360–6.
[100]*Sanktpeterburgskie Vedomosti*, no. 48, 14 June 1790, 791. I am grateful to A.G. Cross for this reference.
[101]Chulkov, *Opisanie*, vol. VI, iii, 671–3.
[102]Lobaneva, *Tr.GIM*, fasc. 17, 6.
[103]Hamilton, *The English Brass and Copper Industries to 1800*, 138, 292.
[104]Chulkov, *Opisanie*, vol. IV, vi, 356.
[105]Westphal-Hellbusch, *Metalgefässe aus Buchare*.

APPENDIX

Tea imports: Korsakov, *Istoriko-statisticheskoe obozrenie torgovykh snoshenii Rossii s Kitaem* (Kazan', 1857), 68; L.M. Samoilov, 'Istoricheskie i statisticheskie issledovaniya o Kyakhtinskoi torgovle', *Sbornik statisticheskikh svedenii o Rossii*, kn.II, SPb., 1854, 3–38.

Gentry numbers: V.I. Kabuzan, *Narodonaselenie Rossii*, 153–4. V.M. Kabuzan, S.N. Troitskii, 'Izmeneniya v chislennost', udel'nom vese i razmeshchenii dvoryanstva v Rossii v 1782–1858gg.', *Istoriya SSSR*, 4 (1971), 153–69. Ya.E. Vodarskii, *Naselenie Rossii v kontse XVII-nachale XVIII veka*, M., 1977.

Unfortunately, the available data is inadequate, so only rough calculations can be made. In 1782 there were an estimated 108,255 male gentry. In 1792, the nearest year for which statistics are available, 246,996 lb (112,000 kg) of black tea was imported via Kyakhta. Assuming there were as many female as male gentry, and dividing the number into the figure for the 1792 tea imports, we obtain an average of 1.2 lb (0.54 kg) per head.

A similar calculation may be made for two years closer together and to the end of the century. In 1795 there were an estimated 362,574 male gentry. In 1797 460,764 lb (209,000 kg) of black tea was imported via Kyakhta. This calculation results in an average of 0.6 lb (0.27 kg) per head.

Gentry family members will have been more numerous than the number of gentry noted in the revisions since only those on the higher levels of the Table of Ranks were hereditary gentry. A proportion of gentry children, therefore, will not have been classed as gentry. On the other hand, there will have been some additional imports of tea from China other than via Kyakhta and also, of course, through European ports.

On the basis of these tentative calculations I assume that perhaps less than 1 lb (0.45 kg) of leaf tea a year was available to members of gentry families in the late eighteenth century.

Date	Gentry ('ooo)		Leaf tea imports	
	males	est. totals	('ooo lb)	lb per person
1700	22–7			
1719		140		
1738	50	140–50		
		100		
1782	108.3			
1792		216	247.0	1.2
1795	362.6			
1797		725	460.8	0.6

Notes:

[a] Vodarskii, (*Naselenie Rossii*) without explanation other than stating that this was the average family size for service people, uses a factor of three to estimate total number of gentry.

[b] The more than threefold increase in gentry numbers between 1782 and 1795 seems unlikely, even allowing for the accretion following from the partitions of Poland.

PART III

****

Rural diets on the eve of change

7

❋❋

The established pattern

INTRODUCTION

Everything said in the earlier chapters makes it clear that the peasant diets had remained essentially unchanged over many centuries. By the nineteenth century it is possible to describe this dietary regime in some detail. The provincial surveys undertaken by the Army General Staff in the 1860s depict a diet overwhelmingly dominated by grain.[1] Cabbages, particularly when pickled in salt, were important, but less so than grain, and other vegetables – onions, beetroot, cucumber, peas and radishes, in particular – were common. Potatoes were a recent, but increasingly important supplement, often supplanting porridges and gruels – by 1907 an English traveller could describe potatoes as one of the four main elements of the Russian peasant diet.[2] Milk and dairy products were important, but not eaten in large quantities; milk, sour cream and cottage cheese were used mainly as seasonings in soups or gruel or they were used for children or the sick. Meat was a rare luxury, often eaten only on feast days. Animal fat was used as a seasoning for soups or gruel (*kasha*) on meat days, but 'fast oils' (*postnye masla*) made from vegetable products – hemp-, flax- or millet-seeds – were used on fast days. Fish was also rare and usually eaten salted or dried, except by those who lived near large rivers. Fruit or berries were collected, but as much for sale as for consumption by those gathering them. This was also true of game and honey, and often of fish as well, and even of much livestock produce. Mushrooms were perhaps the most important of gathered foods, and, like berries, they were often preserved.[3] Honey, the traditional sweetener, and an important preservative, was slowly being ousted by sugar in many areas, but salt re-

---

[1] *Materialy dlya geografii* (25 vols., S.Pb., 1859–68). One of the best single accounts of rural diets in this period is in v. 19, Ryazanskaya guberniya, 397–9.

[2] Kennard, *The Russian Peasant*, 80.

[3] Urals families in the late nineteenth century 'preserved both mushrooms and berries. They collected them in buckets, in particular bilberries which were preserved in ice.' Krupyanskaya and Polishchuk, *Kul'tura*, 140.

mained the most important of all preservatives. Potatoes, sugar, and tea were probably the most important additions to the dietary regime during the nineteenth century.

As in earlier centuries, there existed a clear distinction between the ordinary diet and the festive diet – between the monotonous dishes of most days and the special foods saved for festive occasions. And the festive diet – above all meat, pies and pastries, and liquor – acquired a symbolic importance quite distinct from its purely nutritional role.

Geographical variations existed, of course, but they were not as radical as one might expect, given the size of European Russia. In the Ukraine, beetroot and beetroot soup (*borshch'*) occupied the niche held by cabbage and cabbage soup (*shchii*) in the northern diet; in the northern and central provinces of Russia milk was more common than in the south, but meat was probably more readily available in the less thickly settled steppelands of the Ukraine and south-west; wheat was more common than rye in the south and barley was predominant in the far north; melons, pumpkins, gourds, and many fruits were rare in the central and northern provinces but abundant in the south. However, in its broad essentials, the same dietary regime could be found in most regions of Russia. 'The national dishes of Russian people are the same over the whole of Russia; cabbage soup, gruel, pancakes, and pies [*shchii, kasha, bliny, pirogi*] – you'll find them everywhere.'[4] In Kostroma province, to the north-east of Moscow,

The peasants' food is not in any way different from that of other Great Russian provinces: the same rye bread; the same *kvas*; the same soup made from pickled cabbage, with milk or fat on meat days and groats or nothing extra on fast days; sometime gruel, sometimes milk, cottage cheese, eggs, potato soup, noodles, lightly roasted peas, dried or pickled mushrooms, turnips.[5]

At the other extreme, in Kherson province on the Black Sea, the Ukrainian inhabitants

. . . generally make fresh food each morning and evening. It consists of *borshch'* and dumplings or millet gruel with or without flavourings. Sometimes they cook peas, *salamata* [a liquid gruel], potato, or pumpkin gruel . . . They eat rye bread . . . As seasoning, they use pork fat and meat, sometimes mutton, rarely beef; and also butter, cottage cheese, sour cream and fresh or fermented milk on meat days; on fast days the flavourings are fish and hemp- or flax-seed oil.[6]

[4]Martynov, 'Nekotoryya zametki', 271.
[5]*Materialy*, v. 12, Kostromskaya gub., 32–3.
[6]*Materialy*, v. 24, Khersonskaya gub., 504.

27 A market for berries, Moscow, late nineteenth century.

In this way different foods occupied similar places in a remarkably uniform pattern. And this should not really surprise us, given the basic similarity of agricultural techniques in the whole of European Russia.

Table 7.1 gives some indication of the relative proportions in which different foodstuffs were consumed. The figures are, of course, approximate, and they are not as representative as one would like. The figures in the first two columns represent small samples, one from Mozhaisk district in Moscow province and the second from semi-rural working class families in the same province. And all these figures come from the late nineteenth or early twentieth centuries. Nevertheless, they provide a rough quantitative confirmation of the sort of relationship between different foodstuffs which is suggested by more descriptive sources. And they also suggest the extent to which the dietary patterns of the nineteenth century persisted into the twentieth century, at least in rural areas.

In the rest of this chapter, I will look more closely at the various elements which make up this dietary regime, and the different roles played by different foodstuffs.

GRAIN

In Russia, as in early modern Europe as a whole, the dominance of grain meant, as Braudel puts it, that: 'Eating consists of a lifetime of

Table 7.1. Per capita consumption of different foodstuffs in rural Russia 1880–1960

	1880s (rural)[a]* kg	%	1880s (semi-urban)[b] kg	%	1896–1915[c] kg	%	1940[c] kg	%	1960 kg	%
Grain and grain-based foods	337 / 207	40 / 38	317	57	255	40	160–182	29	149–169	24
Potatoes	185 / 149	22 / 27	91	16	132–42	22	120	20	148	22
Vegetable and fruit	109 / 97	13 / 18	94	17	51–61	9	158	26	81	12
Vegetable oils	4 / 3	(0.5) / (0.5)	6	1	2	(0.3)	2	(0.3)	5	(0.8)
Sugar	/	/	5	(0.9)	3	(0.5)	2	(0.3)	16	2
Meat, lard, poultry,	16	2	23	4	17–19	3	14	2	26	4
Fish	6 / 4	(0.7) / (0.7)	9	2	8–10	1	4	(0.7)	14	2
Milk and dairy produce	183 / 89	22 / 16	7	1	138	22	127	21	205	31
Eggs (1 egg = 50 g)	/	/	/	/	2	(0.3)	2	(0.3)	6	(0.9)
Salt	/	/	/	/	16	3	/	/	/	/
Totals	840 / 549	100.2 / 100.2	552	98.9	636	101.1	600	99.9	660	98.7

Notes: * = Upper figure rich families, lower figure poor families. All figures in this column refer to adults. / = no information available.
[a] Skibnevskii, in Sed'moi gubernskii, 227.
[b] Erisman, Pishchevoe dovol'stvie, 27.
[c] Kerblay, 'Alimentation rurale', 894. Kerblay explains his own calculations in detail on 910–13.

consuming bread, more bread, and still more bread.'[7] In the 1880s, a Moscow doctor listed as one of the main features of Russian peasant diets, their 'extreme monotony. No one has any choice. Everyone, from young to old, must eat the same thing, and eat it day in and day out.' He concluded: 'the food of the peasants is terribly uniform: day in and day out rye bread, potatoes, cabbage; the remaining foods are merely a sort of seasoning for these three'.[8] Proverbs testify clearly to the feeling that a meal without bread was hardly a meal at all: 'while there is bread and water, things are still all right'; 'a meal without bread is not a meal'; 'it's a poor meal that lacks bread'; 'a meal without bread is not worth having'.[9]

In the nineteenth century rye was still by far the most important grain grown in Russia. In the late eighteenth century, rye accounted for about 40% of the area under grain; a century later it still accounted for about 38% of the total area under grain, which in turn was most of the arable land in European Russia.[10] However, it was in the nineteenth century that the dominance of rye began to be challenged for the first time by the more commercial grain, wheat. This change itself marked the penetration of the market into the rural economy, for wheat was a crop grown more for sale than rye, and capitalist agriculture seized on wheat before it tackled the subsistence crop, rye.[11] The challenge of wheat was made possible both by the final colonisation of the rich black soil lands of the south and south-east, and also by the great export drives of the late nineteenth century which provided much of the capital needed for industrialisation.[12] But for most Russians outside the expanding wheat-producing regions to the south, wheat remained a luxury grain. In Moscow province in the 1880s, 'Wheaten bread, made from the cheapest flour, is a rarity used only at great festivals, and even then only in wealthy households.'[13] As a proverb put it: 'Mother rye feeds all alike; but wheat is choosey.'[14]

Other, poorer grains also had an important, if secondary place in the dietary regime. The most important were probably oats (also used for

[7]Braudel, *Capitalism*, 88–9.
[8]Skibnevskii, in *Sed'moi*, 226.
[9]Dal', *Poslovitsy*, 180.
[10]For the eighteenth century, Confino, *Systèmes agraires*, 69; for the nineteenth century, Drobizhev, et al., *Istoricheskaya geografiya*, 209.
[11]*Ibid.*, 206–7. On the growth of the market in grain, see Koval'chenko and Milov, *Agrarnyi rynok*.
[12]Drobizhev, et al., *Istoricheskaya geografiya*, 206–7.
[13]Skibnevskii, in *Sed'moi*, 222.
[14]Dal', *Poslovitsy*, 811.

28 Peasant carts outside a Moscow railway station, late nineteenth century. Such carts were the most widespread means of transport for grain and other provisions during the snow-free period.

fodder), barley, buckwheat and millet.[15] In 1881, rye covered 37% of all sown land (36% was 'winter' rye); wheat 16.5%; oats 20%; barley 7%; buckwheat 5.5%; millet 4.0%. Altogether, about 91.5% of all sown land was under grains of various sorts.[16]

But, particularly in the central region dominated by three-field crop rotation – the heartland of Russian history – rye remained by far the most important subsistence crop.[17] Of this region Confino writes:

It was this cereal which gave life and nourishment to the peasant, as is shown clearly by the name it is given in popular songs: *rzhitsa kormilitsa*, literally, 'rye, provider of mother's milk'. In the peasants' understanding of nature's mysteries and in the nebulous symbols which were attached to the 'mother earth' and which had pagan origins, rye – mother rye [*rozh' matushka*] – seemed to occupy a special place amongst all the other products of the earth's entrails.

[15]'Oats are mainly used for feeding horses. The inhabitants use it in a sort of fool [*kisel'*], and in pancakes – but the amounts are very small compared with the total amount of oats produced.' *Materialy*, v. 9, Kaluzhskaya gub., vol. i, 471. Yanson, when calculating available food reserves in the 1870s, excluded the area under oats, on the grounds that this would support livestock, not people. Yanson, *Statistika*, vol. ii, 310–11.

[16]*Statisticheskii vremennik*, 3rd series, 4.

[17]Confino, *Systèmes agraires*, 26, gives a map of the area dominated by three-field rotations in the nineteenth century.

Confino adds: 'When the peasant said *khleb* [bread, grain], without any adjective, he meant "rye bread" or simply "rye".'[18] One final measure of the significance attached to rye is the fact that it was sown in the winter field – that is in the field which had just been left fallow for a year and which was, therefore, most likely to yield a good crop. Its privileged position in the agricultural routine reflected accurately its central position in the rural dietary regime.

Both relatively and absolutely, the amounts of grain consumed were large by modern standards. The earliest detailed budgetary studies conducted in Russia (in 1853) show clearly the importance of grains. In Orenburg, in the newly colonised south-east beyond the Volga, the family studied by the French sociologist, Le Play, ate a diet of which 60% by weight was derived from grain. A family from the Oka region near Moscow consumed 69% (by weight) of its food as cereals.[19] A survey of thirty-two Moscow working class families in the 1880s found that on average bread contributed about 47% of calories, groats and flour another 25%, and potatoes about 9%. Altogether, grains and potatoes accounted for about 80% of caloric intake.[20] The more careful budgetary studies of the later nineteenth and early twentieth centuries suggest that these proportions are not far out. For example, budgetary studies of thirteen provinces suggest that on average 40% of food consumption by weight was made up of grain products, flour, groats and legumes; while potatoes counted for another 20%.[21] In 1913 84.2% of calories in the average peasant diet came from vegetable matter, 62.8% of them from grains.[22]

So, as Table 7.1 suggests, we can probably assume that grains and potatoes together accounted for 60–80% of food by weight, and perhaps a similar proportion of caloric intake. By any standards, this was a monotonous diet.

In absolute terms, the scattered budgetary evidence suggests normal consumption levels of all grains varying from 250–375 kg a year for the average population and 400–500 kg a year for adults.[23] For comparison, the figures available on West European diets before 1800 almost all fall within the range of about 180–440 kg a year. 'Until the nineteenth century, a ration was not judged satisfactory if it was not

[18]*Ibid.*, 80.
[19]Le Play, *Ouvriers*, vol. II, 74–5, 204–5.
[20]Erisman, *Pishchevoe dovol'stvie*, 30–1. Erisman's survey is based on urban working class families, but their ties with the countryside remained so strong that it seems reasonable to assume that the diets he surveyed were not too dissmilar from rural diets of the time.
[21]*Chayanov, on Peasant Economy*, 129–30.
[22]Kerblay, 'Alimentation rurale', 895–6.
[23]See Table 7.2.

around the level of 700–800 gm a day', that is, about 250–95 kg a year.[24] These figures are extremely rough, but suggest that Russian consumption of grains was not exceptional by the standards of early modern Europe as a whole.

How was grain eaten? In a society in which cereals formed so large a part of the diet, there existed many different ways of preparing them. The bread was normally black rye bread. An English writer, travelling in Russia in the 1840s complained: 'They ferment their bread to the third or acetous degree; the black bread, unlike that of all other countries, is bitter and sour, and as nauseous in the mouth as alum.'[25] Others argued that Russian workers showed sound nutritional judgement in preferring a bread that was well fermented and as heavy as possible; the lactic acid which made bread sour was a vital dietary supplement and its heaviness was also valued.

'Solid' [*prochnyi*] food is food which is both nourishing and slow to digest, which remains in the stomach for a long time, for once your belly is empty you can no longer do heavy work until you eat again.

As black rye bread is the main component of the diet, it is important that the bread should be thick, not light, not doughy, and made well, out of fresh flour. A worker pays great attention to bread. Good bread is the most important thing.[26]

In the village of Viryatino in Tambov province, villagers interviewed by Soviet researchers in the 1950s remembered that the bread was normally baked about once a week, 'sometimes on cabbage leaves'.[27] Bread was baked generally 'from sour dough raised with yeast, kvass, or beer lees . . . [and made] in the *pech'*, usually on a clean hearthstone'.[28] There was generally some ceremonial surrounding the eating of a loaf: 'the [Russian peasant] treated a loaf reverentially, standing it upright on the table and breaking it instead of cutting it'.[29]

Gruel [*kasha*] was a food which allowed of more variations than bread. And its place in the dietary regime was almost as important: 'buckwheat gruel is our mother – and rye bread is our father'; 'a meal without gruel is not a meal'.[30] Gruel was not quite as important as bread, and in some areas it was a semi-luxury, preserved for special

[24]Bennassar and Goy, 'Consommation alimentaire', 420.
[25]*Revelations of Russia*, vol. i, 71.
[26]Engel'gardt, *Iz derevni*, 265.
[27]Kushner, *Viryatino*, 98.
[28]Matossian, 'Peasant Way of Life', 12.
[29]*Ibid.*
[30]Sobolov, *Poslovitsy*, 214; Dal', *Poslovitsy*, 812.

occasions. In Ryazan' province in the 1850s: 'The use of gruel is itself a sign of modest wealth.'[31]

Generally, gruel was made from groats of buckwheat, oats, barley, or millet, and sometimes also included some rye or wheat. But the word *kasha* could also be used to describe the pulp of boiled potatoes or even crushed pumpkin.[32] On the river Oka in 1853, gruel was made from 'millet or buckwheat cooked with milk, butter, and fat or oil, and with salt added. This dish takes many forms depending on the different seasonings and the length of the cooking. It is served either in the form of a hot thick liquid, or as a thick paste.'[33] The English traveller Cochrane, who travelled on a barge from Nizhnii Novgorod to Kazan' in 1820 and ate with the barge's crew (at the start of a walking tour across Siberia!), found that the crew's diet was

... wholesome, although rather new to me, consisting of ... [barley and rye] flour boiled and stewed down with water and oil. He who likes burgoo must relish casha; and it was with extreme pleasure that I received the spoon into my hand, in my proper turn, to partake of this humble fare. This we did three times a day.[34]

Like bread, gruel could be stretched out in bad times; after a hard winter, peasants would harvest a small amount of unripened rye, crush it and boil it to produce 'green kasha'.[35]

The thickness and solidity of gruel was also important to its connoisseurs. Woodcutters, when working particularly hard, picked their food carefully: 'They spared no money on food. Each day they had vodka; and gruel so thick that you could hardly stick a spoon in it, and covered in butter; as well as cabbage soup with plenty of oil.'[36]

More festive than bread and gruel were various pies and pastries, both sweet and savoury (*pirogi*). Making them, like making cabbage soup or bread, was one of the fundamental skills of any peasant woman.

Of all the dishes known in Russia, there is nothing in such general esteem, from the peasant to the prince, as a kind of pâtés which are called *piroghi*. These, at the tables of the great, are served with the soup in the first course. In the streets of Moscau and St. Petersburg they are sold upon stalls. They are well-tasted, but extremely greasy and often full of oil, consisting of minced meat or brains, rolled up in pancakes, which are afterwards fried in butter or oil, and served hot.[37]

[31]*Materialy*, v. 19, Ryazanskaya gub., 397.
[32]Kushner, *Viryatino*, 99.
[33]Le Play, *Ouvriers*, vol. II, 191.
[34]Cochrane, *Narrative*, 104–5.
[35]Engel'gardt, *Iz derevni*, 108.
[36]*Ibid.*, 267.
[37]Clarke, *Travels*, 45.

Today you can still find (greasy) meat pies sold on the streets of Soviet towns. But there were many other forms of pies and pastries: '*pirogi* – tarts stuffed with fish, cottage cheese, berries, cabbage, etc.; *blini* – thin pancakes; and *knyshi* – puff pastries layered with *kaimak* (cream taken from boiled milk).'[38] Proverbs and sayings show clearly how strongly these foods were linked with special occasions: 'a river is beautiful for its banks, a meal for its pies'; 'you can't have a name day without pies'; 'Without pies, there's no Shrovetide'.[39]

LIVESTOCK AND FISH

Nutritionally, animal-based foods are generally reckoned to be a very important part of any dietary regime. Some animal protein is valuable in a healthy diet as most vegetable protein lacks the essential amino-acid, lysine, whose absence can be a contributory factor in tuberculosis, lung infections, dysentery, and typhus. So most students of popular diets have argued, like Maurice Aymard, that the presence of adequate quantities of animal protein is 'a decisive test of the enrichment of diets in the developed countries, a test closely correlated with sanitary improvements, and with an increase in average height'.[40] Most nineteenth-century Russians who interested themselves in rural diets had similar views. The presence, or absence of meat from the peasants' diet was regarded as the clearest measure of the quality of the diet, as a good measure of an improvement or decline in living standards generally, and also as a sensitive indicator of class distinctions.[41] To take just one illustration, in reports of the commission of 1872 into the state of agriculture, one finds time and again the refrain: 'The consumption of meat has not increased and the peasants' food has not improved' (from Moscow province); or 'In some areas the peasants' food has improved and the consumption of meat has increased' (Tver' province).[42]

But we should not accept this judgement without question. Vegetarian diets clearly can be healthy, and the peasants themselves did not take for granted the view that meat was vital nutritionally; or rather, they attributed far more importance to meat fat or vegetable oil, than to meat itself.

---

[38]Matossian, 'Peasant Way of Life', 12.
[39]Dal', *Poslovitsy*, 814.
[40]Aymard, 'Alimentation', 432.
[41]In contemporary Soviet society the availability of meat remains a crucial popular index of living standards.
[42]*Doklad*, Prilozhenie 1, section 1, 225, 228.

All of us [i.e. people of the educated classes] regard meat as an extremely important part of our diet, and regard a diet as poor and unsatisfying if it contains little meat, so we try to eat as much meat as possible. But the peasant, however hard his work, does not attribute as much importance to meat. I do not mean they do not like meat – any peasant prefers cabbage soup which contains a little pork or chicken – I mean only that meat is not reckoned so important from the point of view of work. The peasant attributed far more importance to fat and oil.[43]

Proverbs clearly reflect the great importance attributed to fat and oil: 'The more fat in food the better: "you'll never spoil gruel with butter"; "priest's gruel with a little butter"; "when the gruel's cooked don't spare the butter". A diet is reckoned good if it is fatty, if it has milk, eggs, or butter in it.'[44]

A navvy explained that he avoided eating meat if he had to do really hard work, as it made hard work more difficult; 'he would tire more quickly, and have to rest more than if he had for breakfast a piece of extremely fatty pork, or even just pork fat'.[45]

How little significance is attached to meat is clear from the fact that a working man will always agree to replace it with vodka. Of course, people will say that it is well known that Russians are drunkards, ready to sell their father for a drink. But, forgive me, the same worker will never agree to give up the lactic acid of his normal food, nor will he accept vodka in return for his fat or buckwheat gruel.[46]

And these judgements were not mere matters of taste. They reflected the calculations of people who could tell precisely how much work they could do on any given diet.[47] Further, peasants with some spare cash did *not* immediately rush out to buy more meat. An observer reported from Simbirsk province in the early 1870s that in years of good harvests the demand for overcoats, boots, horses, drink and so on rose greatly, but the demand for meat remained steady.[48] Thus, the amount of meat consumed is not necessarily an adequate measure of the nutritional value of diets, though it may measure a family's wealth. As we will see, meat was reckoned an essential item in the festive diet of the peasantry, and because of this it acquired a symbolic role which

[43]Engel'gardt, *Iz derevni*, 259. Some modern nutritionists also argue that the importance of meat protein has been greatly exaggerated. Tudge, *The Famine Business*, ch. 5.
[44]Engel'gardt, *Iz derveni*, 259.
[45]*Ibid.*, 260.
[46]*Ibid.*, 268.
[47]*Ibid.*, 258.
[48]*Doklad*, 232.

far outweighed its real nutritional value. If you were eating meat, things couldn't be too bad.

Meat and, to a lesser extent, animal fat and dairy products were luxury items in most areas. This was true of pre-industrial Europe as a whole, and the general reason is that food from animal products is more expensive to produce than food in vegetable products, as it has passed through one more chain in the energy cycle, and lost energy on the way. Livestock could require perhaps about ten times as much land as grains in order to supply the same amount of calories.[49] Thus, wherever land was in short supply, preference had to be given to the production of grain rather than of fodder. The problem was particularly acute in the central and northern provinces of European Russia where the prolonged winters meant that cattle were more dependent on fodder, and could be left to graze for shorter periods than in Western Europe. On the other hand, given an agricultural regime in which livestock played a crucial role – as draught animals, and as suppliers of manure – it was impossible to do without livestock altogether. Even the poorest 'horseless' families, for example, had to hire or borrow horses if they were to continue farming their own allotments. The result was that as land became scarce, the amounts of fodder available declined, the quality of livestock declined, and so did the amount of meat in rural diets. But so, eventually, did the quality of grain farming itself if livestock declined so seriously that insufficient manure was available for the arable land. This trap was almost unavoidable given the agricultural methods of pre-industrial Europe, and peasants everywhere had to find their own solutions.

How did this trap affect Russian diets? In general, the amount of cattle per head seems to have declined in Russia in the nineteenth century, so that it is probable that consumption of meat (at least of beef) declined, but this can only be a guess.[50] Certainly, the quality of livestock was not high. Clarke was appalled at the cattle he saw in the spring of 1800: 'such cattle! – blind, lame, old, out of condition, of all sizes and colours, connected by rotten ropes and old cords full of knots and splices'.[51] What he saw was the natural consequences of the fact that most cattle spent the winter in stalls. By spring, the livestock were almost invariably on starvation rations.

The dietary consequence of this age-old conflict between livestock and grain was that meat and animal products were almost invariably

---

[49]Cipolla, *World Population*, 40.

[50]Drobizhev, *et al.*, *Istoricheskaya geografiya*, 221; Koval'chenko, 'K istorii skotovodstva'.

[51]Clarke, *Travels*, 19. In the late nineteenth century, cattle in south Russia weighed 260–330 kg, while in England they often weighed 490–660 kg. Khromov, *Ekonomicheskoe razvitie*, 348.

Table 7.2. *Estimates of per capita consumption of grains and animal-based foods*

Source		Dates	Kg/Person/Year
A. Grains			
Nizhnii Landowner[a]	Adults	1840s	400 (approx.)
	Children	1840s	300
	Average	1840s	345
Voronezh[b]	Adults	1840s	400
Vitebsk[c]	Average	1840s	300
Maress[d]	Adults	1890s	500
	Average	1890s	375
Haxthausen[e]	Adults	1840s	500
	Average	1840s	250
Erisman[f]	Average	1880s	600
Le Play[g]	Orenburg	1850s	600
	Oka River	1850s	650
Chernigov cossacks[h]	Average	1860s	300
Dikhtyar[i]	Average	Early 20th century	210–300
B. Meat			
Le Play, Orenburg[g]		1850s	70.8
Oka River		1850s	35.9
Erisman[f]		1880s	17.0 + 9 of fish
Chernigov cossacks[h]		1860s	10.0 (+ 5 of fish?)
Maress[j]	Average	1890s	23.0
	Voronezh	1890s	17.6
	Mozhaisk (Moscow)	1880s	12.4 (but 12% had none)
	Bogorod (Moscow)	1880s	8.1
Dikhtyar[i] Average		Early 20th century	10.3 poorer families
			19.2 richer families

Notes:
[a] Based on 15 household serfs and families over a two-year period. *Etnograficheskii sbornik*, vol. I, 17.
[b] 'Three chetverts per person is not a lot if you consider that some will be lost in milling, because while working, especially in the fields, a man always eats at least four pounds (*c.* 1.64 kg) of good rye bread and much more of wheaten bread; adolescents and those who do not do hard work eat less than three pounds (*c.* 1.2 kg).' *Etnograficheskii sbornik*, vol. I, 232.
[c] *Ibid.*, 245.
[d] Maress, 'Pishcha narodnykh mass', pt. 2, 11. Based on figures from 17 landowners from all over Russia. This is the average amount consumed by agricultural labourers and their families. The range is from 360–640 kg.
[e] Haxthausen, *Russian Empire*, vol. I, 163.
[f] Erisman, *Pishchevoe dovol'stvie*, 27.
[g] Le Play, *Ouvriers*, vol. II, 74–5, 204–5.
[h] *Materialy dlya geografii*, v. 25, Chernigovskaya gub., 551–2; see Table 9.3.
[i] Dikhtyar, *Vnutrennyaya torgovlya*, 27.
[j] Maress, 'Pishcha narodnykh mass', pt. 2, 60–1.

available, but they were mostly consumed sparingly and treated as semi-luxuries, except in the few areas where livestock farming was a local speciality. The church, as have seen (in ch. 1, p. 10), encouraged this abstinence. Financial pressures, too, often discouraged meat eating, by forcing peasants to sell their livestock rather than eat it. In Ryazan' province in the 1860s, 'Large and small livestock and fowls even, if they are owned in abundance, are not used as food, but reckoned essential for agriculture or for sale so as to acquire cash.'[52] Often during famines, while the price of grain rose, that of meat fell as peasants sold livestock to find the cash to buy grain.[53]

Beef was the most luxurious of animal products, and its consumption was almost invariably confined to the major festivals. For some peasants it was simply never available. A report from Samara province in the 1870s found that about one third of households never had beef, using meat fat instead, and even in Moscow province there were those who never had beef.[54] But such extremes were probably exceptional. In Smolensk province in the 1870s: 'the best a peasant can hope for is plenty of meat on festivals, and perhaps on ordinary days a tiny piece of meat to season other foods, as well as enough milk, eggs, and meat for children, the aged and the sick'.[55] In Tula province in 1872, 'Beef is eaten usually three times a year, at Easter, Christmas, and the patron saint's day of the local church.'[56] Only the very wealthy could afford to slaughter their cattle; most of those who did eat beef at all purchased it at a local market.[57]

Beef, in fact, was an urban luxury, and in the town it was possible to find huge quantities of meat produced and sold by peasants whose own diet was almost entirely vegetarian.[58] The English traveller Parkinson visited the St Petersburg market, held near the Alexander Nevsky monastery, a few days before Christmas, and was surprised to see what must have been a common sight at this time – sledges containing whole frozen pigs, 'stiff and upright as if they were stuffed'.[59] In Moscow, there was an Easter fair, at which the citizens of the town had a chance to buy fresh meat for the first time since the previous autumn:

[52]*Materialy*, v. 19, Ryazanskaya gub., 398–9.
[53]*Chayanov on Peasant Economy*, 171.
[54]*Doklad*, 232; Skibnevskii, 223–5.
[55]Engel'gardt, *Iz derevni*, 269.
[56]*Doklad*, 236.
[57]*Ibid.*, 247, from Mogilev province.
[58]*Ibid.*, 236.
[59]Parkinson, *Tour*, 71.

The night before the famous ceremony of the Resurrection, all the markets
and shops of Moscow are seen filled with flesh, butter, eggs, poultry, pigs, and
every kind of viand. The crowd of purchasers is immense. You hardly meet a
foot-passenger who has not his hands, nay his arms, filled with provisions, or a
single drosky that is not ready to break down beneath their weight.[60]

In the 1880s cattle from the south reached St Petersburg by a long
and complicated route during which their value tripled. They were
sold first at a village market to the 'runner' of a cattle trader or *prasol*.
He in turn fattened them and got them to St Petersburg by train. Here
he sold them to a factor (*kommissioner*), who in turn sold them at cattle
markets in the capital to the slaughterer who then sold the meat to the
retail butchers of the capital.[61] Most of the profits in this trade went to
the middlemen. Peasants who lived near large commercial towns
sometimes consumed more meat than those in remoter districts. Thus,
in the districts of Nizhnii Novgorod province nearer to Nizhnii itself,
with its huge annual market, 'many peasants eat meat almost daily'.[62]
But their situation was unusual; they were beneficiaries of the town's
privileged position in the consumption of meat.

Much more common than beef in the rural diet was the meat of
pigs, sheep, or domestic fowl, and for most peasants this was the only
form in which they did eat meat. A correspondent from Simbirsk
province described what seems to have been the normal pattern:

The consumption of meat is extremely limited, and then it is usually pork.
Before Christmas each peasant will fatten one or two pigs; their meat is eaten
during festivals, and their fat is salted and used as a seasoning for other foods
on festivals. This is all the meat the peasant eats throughout the year; several
suckling pigs and domestic fowl are kept for the children or for the sick.[63]

The presence of meat was one of the delights of church or family
festivals, and each region had its own special feast day variations. In
Kazan' the peasants ate 'beef cooked in fat as well as mutton, pork,
chicken, goose, and pies with gruel, fish or chicken, and also cheese
curd tart (*vatrushka*) or buckwheat pancakes'; in Kostroma feast day
food included 'pies with fillings of gruel; meat, eggs or pancakes;
chicken and noodles; fish baked with eggs; and the favourite food,
roast pork'; in Chernigov 'even the very poorest peasants slaughter a

[60]Clarke, *Travels*, 18.
[61]Bakhtiarov, *Bryukho Peterburga*, 2–16, traces the route in detail.
[62]*Doklad*, 230.
[63]*Ibid.*, 226.

sheep or pigs and suckling pigs for Christmas day, Easter, and, in autumn, St Philip's day'.[64]

Meat fat was often used as a seasoning for gruel or potatoes even on normal days, and indeed meat fat was a much more common food than lean meat. In Borisovsk district of Minsk province 'meat is eaten by the peasants only at great festivals and at baptisms, weddings, and similar occasions. On normal days, the place of meat is taken by pork fat, milk and hemp oil.'[65] But in those areas where even meat fat was a luxury, the difference between meat days and fast days, which had such a precise ecclesiastical meaning, must have lost its nutritional meaning altogether.

In the southern and south-east provinces, where pressure on the land was not as intense as in the central provinces, and where livestock rearing flourished better, meat was more common. In part of Voronezh province in the early 1870s, a correspondent claimed that 'pork fat, mutton, and domestic fowl are very common', but even here such a diet was probably confined to the few very wealthy peasants.[66] More typical of these southern provinces was Kherson province where, in the 1860s, meat fat and even small chunks of pork and mutton were reasonably common as 'seasonings' for other foods on meat days, and even small pieces of beef were sometimes used in this way. But even in the south, there were poorer regions. In Ekaterinoslav province, mutton, pork and fowl were unusual in the diet; and beef was extremely rare, so rare that some peasants regarded its consumption as sinful.[67]

One of the most striking things about the Russian dietary regime, for a West European observer at least, is the relatively small quantity of dairy products consumed. These were semi-luxuries except in areas which specialised in dairy farming. In the far south and south-east, where there was free pasture land, cattle could be raised for their meat. In the northern steppes and the southern parts of the non-steppe Black Earth regions, cattle were used as work animals. On the northern borders of the black soil regions, horses were the work animals and livestock were kept mainly for their manure,

But such livestock can only be profitable if combined with some dairying. The use of livestock for their meat is possible here only under exceptional conditions. As the soils are lighter, the work can be done by horses, and in order to secure the manure necessary to produce grain more cheaply, the

---

[64]*Materialy*, v. 8, Kazanskaya gub., 212–13; v. 12, Kostromskaya gub., 32–3; v. 25, Chernigovskaya gub., 551–2.
[65]*Doklad*, 246.
[66]*Ibid.*, 238.
[67]*Ibid.*, 241.

Table 7.3. *Milk and butter production in the 1870s*

Region	Milk (litres per cap.)	Butter (kg per cap.)
Baltic	139	1.5
N. Provinces	115	1.4
Poland	102	1.1
West	68	0.8
S. non-Steppe	52	0.6
S. Steppe	50	0.5
S.W.	49	0.5
Non-Black Earth	47	0.5
Central Black Earth	42	0.4
E. Steppes	19	0.2
Average	61	1.2

Source: Yanson, *Statistika*, vol. II, 658.

livestock must be put to other uses than in other parts of Russia – above all to dairying . . . In other parts of Russia, of course, both milk and meat are produced from livestock, and sometimes even cheese, but there these products are used by the rural population themselves and only a tiny amount is sold to the towns . . . In the non-black earth provinces we find, on the contrary, that milk is not only an important part of agriculture, but is rapidly growing and that it supplies not merely the home market, but also foreign markets as well.[68]

On average, Yanson estimated, Russia produced 61 litres of milk and 1.23 kg of butter per inhabitant in the 1870s, though he seems to be thinking mainly of milk and butter produced for sale.[69] The regional distribution of milk and butter production is shown in Table 7.3.

This table gives a very rough idea of the relative availability of milk and dairy products in different regions in the 1870s, but it does not tell us how much was consumed by the rural population themselves.

In general, demand for milk and dairy products was clearly more elastic than demand for grain products and, like meat, dairy produce was more readily available in the towns.[70] In the countryside, milk was often not available at all; sometimes it was available, but only in summer as the cows did not have enough to eat in winter. In Orel province in the 1890s, 'Only 2/3 of the people have milk, and then only

[68]Yanson, *Statistika*, vol. II, 642–4.
[69]*Ibid.*, vol. II, 657–8.
[70]Chayanov, *Starobel'sk*, 33.

if they have enough fodder. But in winter, when fodder consists of nothing but rye straw, there is hardly any milk at all.'[71] In Ryazan' province in the 1860s, 'Few milk based foods are used. Milk and sour cream [*smetana*] are used rather as seasoning for cabbage soup and gruel. Sour milk is sometimes used, but cottage cheese [*tvorog*] is made from it, and this, like omelette, is more common on feast days.'[72] Sometimes milk was used regularly, at least in summer, particularly in dairying regions in the north and around the capitals. In such regions milk was regarded as a normal part of the diet, even if its use was confined to summer and it was used chiefly as a flavouring.[73] Where it was available only in small quantities it was used mainly for children, or as a 'whitening' for gruel or cabbage soup. In the form of sour cream or cottage cheese, it was a crucial ingredient of many festival luxuries such as pies. Sometimes, the small quantities available were all earmarked for sale. Thus, in Chernigov province in 1872, 'Milk is a luxury and is used only for sale, and in the food of children.'[74]

Often milk was used for children in ways which did as much harm as good. In Orel province in the 1890s, 'Even three month-old babies are fed, not only on the breast (which often supplies too little milk) but also on pretzels [*krendel'i*], gruel, and black bread. These are sometimes soaked in soured mik (or if there is no milk, in water), then wrapped in a dirty rag and given to the child to suck.'[75] Here is a similar description from Moscow province in the 1870s:

In the vast majority of cases, children start being fed on cow's milk, gruel, ring-shaped rolls [*baranki*] and black bread, from the age of 2 to 3 months, and in summer, during the harvest they start almost from the very first days. They are fed cow's milk with the aid of the familiar 'cow's teat': gruel, black bread, and rolls are first chewed, then twisted in some piece of rag and tied up and stuck in the mouth of the child almost for the whole day.[76]

Butter, like milk, was not rare; but it was a semi-luxury and greatly appreciated when it *was* available, for example, at Shrove-tide, whose Russian name, *Maslyanitsa*, means 'butter-week'.

Like other forms of livestock produce, milk was very often sold by peasants, particularly those near large towns. In St Petersburg, local Finnish villagers all sold their milk in the town. Every morning, those

[71]*Opyt*, 46.
[72]*Materialy*, v. 19, Ryazanskaya gub., 398–9.
[73]See, for example, *Doklad*, 225, 228, 231, 232, 246, 247, for examples from Novgorod, Vladimir, Yaroslav, Kazan', Perm', Minsk, and Mogilev provinces.
[74]*Ibid.*, 240.
[75]*Opyt*, 48.
[76]Skibnevskii, 232–3.

29 Selling live fish, nineteenth century. Fish barks. James Walker's text reads: 'These vessels, which are kept upon the river Neva, as well as upon the Moika and other canals of that river in St. Petersburg, serve the fishmongers at once for dwelling houses, shops, and fishponds: they live in huts or cabins constructed upon the barks. They sell their fish upon the deck, and the whole lower part of the bark is divided into different wells for the keeping of all kinds of fresh-water fish. Naturalists mention upwards of twenty sorts of salmon caught in the Neva; the other fish usually sold are sturgeon, sterlet, sudak, sige, eels, a kind of lamprey, stone perch, a great dainty, red-finned perch of an extraordinary size, rapoushka, smelts, crawfish, carp, tench, and fresh and salted cavia.'

in the suburbs would see two-wheeled Finnish carts passing through with tin churns of milk and wooden buckets of butter. At the height of summer, these would be packed in ice and covered with hay or matting. Generally, they would take them to the Okhtennskii market, where it was sold retail by milk-maids known as the *Okhtyanki*.[77]

The other major animal-based foodstuff in the peasant diet was fish. This, too, was not an essential part of the diet; but it was not uncommon. It was consumed either fresh, in those villages near well-stocked

[77]Bakhtiarov, *Bryukho Peterburga*, 235–6.

rivers, or salted and dried. Fresh fish were usually a locally 'gathered' food; dried and salted fish were purchased and might originate elsewhere.

Fish was perhaps the cheapest form of animal food available for the majority of the population, and for this reason it was increasingly an article of mass consumption in the late nineteenth century.[78] Commercially, fish were divided into two main groups: (1) 'red' or noble fish (*krasnaya ryba*), which included sturgeon and all members of the salmon family; and (2) netted fish (*chastikovaya ryba*), from *chastik*, a fine net.[79]

Fish were marketed in several distinct ways. In the larger towns, and for export, one could find fresh fish or, particularly as the railway network grew in the last forty years of the century, frozen fish. Such fish were intended for an urban and relatively affluent market. As in the past, fresh fish were towed through the Volga river system; live sturgeon were sometimes towed from Astrakhan' as far as St Petersburg, in perforated barges called *prorezi*. In 1843, the German traveller Haxthausen saw a massive sturgeon near Yaroslavl 'placed in a reservoir formed of stakes and planks on the bank of the river. Only a stream like the Volga could contain such a monster; it measured eight or ten feet in length and perhaps as many around the body.'[80] Some fish were transported live in special wagons, but this technique was used only for the more valuable fish, sturgeon and sterlet.[81] In St Petersburg in the 1880s, a live 10 pound sturgeon could cost 50–75 rubles – a 15 pound sturgeon up to 100 rubles. These were mainly used in restaurants. The owners would buy a thousand or more but keep them live in special tanks to which they kept the key.[82]

The trade in frozen fish was even more limited than the trade in live fish, and was aimed mainly at the export market. Perch would be sent from Tsaritsyn or Uralsk to Berlin and Vienna in wooden boxes with handles, packed between layers of straw and ice. A perch which cost 2–3 rubles a pud might fetch 12 rubles abroad.[83] In winter frozen fish were more common, as the techniques involved in catching and freezing them were simple enough to make their sale a common peasant trade. Fish would be kept in tanks in small lakes, and as soon as the first frost came they would be dragged out live and frozen on the ice.[84]

[78] Brokgauz–Efron, vol. 53 (xxvii), 384.
[79] *Ibid.*, 401.
[80] Haxthausen, *Russian Empire*, vol. I, 96.
[81] Brokgauz–Efron, vol. 53 (xxvii), 401.
[82] Bakhtiarov, *Bryukho Peterburga*, 150.
[83] Brokgauz–Efron, vol. 53 (xxvii), 400.
[84] *Ibid.*, 401.

30 Street sellers of birds, game, caviare and toddy, nineteenth century.

The other main luxury product was of course caviare. Here is how it was prepared by the Urals cossacks, who harpooned the sturgeon as they swam up the river Ural from the Caspian sea in early winter.

The roe is placed in a large rectangular sieve called a *grokhotka* [*grokhot'* = sieve or rattle], with holes just big enough to let the grains of roe pass through. Under the sieve they place a barrel of linden wood or a large trough; and these are filled with cold water, strongly salted . . . The roe is squeezed through the sieve, and then, using narrow wooden paddles it is mixed in the brine, and when it is sufficiently salted, it is placed in mat sacks . . . and pressed to squeeze out the water. Then the roe is placed in barrels; this is so called 'pressed caviare', which is made from the stellate sturgeon.

It is an ancient custom that the Ural cossack host sends the fish and caviare from the very first harpooning to the Imperial Court in St. Petersburg. Under Nicholas I the 'present' always arrived in time for the Tsar's name-day, December 6.[85]

Much more common than these luxury products were the various forms of salt or dried fish. It was these that were most familiar to the ordinary people of Russia. Such fish were either dried, or pickled or

[85]Bakhtiarov, *Bryukho Peterburga*, 146.

brined. Caspian roach and perch were the most common dried fish. The fish were generally caught and prepared along the Black Sea, Azov sea and Caspian, and were sold in huge quantities in the Nizhnii market and in Tsaritsyn, mainly for the industrial regions around Moscow.[86] The roach were either salted whole and then dry-cured (*kolodka*), or gutted first before being salted and dried (*karbovka*).[87] Each year as many as 300 million Caspian roach were caught in the Volga and another 60 million in the Ural river.[88]

Salted or 'heavily salted' fish were those salted so heavily that they would keep even without brine. These were usually fish of the sturgeon and salmon families. 'Lightly salted' fish were kept in brine – and this was generally reckoned the most popular form of preserved fish. The most commonly brined fish was herring, generally imported from the North Sea.[89] Pickled herring were the favourite food of the working population of St Petersburg. Here they were sold by fishwomen or 'herring wives' (*seledochnitsy*), who could sell up to 100 herring a day, usually to the poor of the capital 'for whom herrings and potatoes are never absent from the table'.[90]

One can get some idea of the relative importance of the different ways of selling fish from the different types which left Astrakhan' in 1897. Altogether, 8 million puds of fish (*c.* 130 million kg) left Astrakhan' that year: *c.* 76% were salted (dry salted or pickled); *c.* 24% were sent live; *c.* 11% were frozen or packed in ice; *c.* 0.01% were smoked, and smaller amounts were sent in the form of more valuable products such as caviare.[91]

The range, variety, and quantity of fresh fish available to those fortunate enough to live near rivers was impressive;

The fishes caught [in the Don] are much too numerous to be mentioned, as perhaps there is no river in the world which presents a greater variety or one in greater perfection. Among the principal are the beluga, the common sturgeon, the sterlet, sudak, trout, common carp, tench, pike, perch, water-tortoises and crayfish of enormous size, some of which are as large as lobsters. The last are caught in great abundance by sinking small nets about 6 inches in diameter, baited with pieces of salted fish. They sold at the rate of twopence (English) per hundred, and in some seasons of the year the same number may be had for half that sum. The beluga is the largest eatable fish known. In the kidneys of very old ones are sometimes found calculi as large as a man's fist . . .

[86]Brokgauz–Efron, vol. 53 (xxvii), 400–1.
[87]*Ibid.*, 420.
[88]*Ibid.*, 419.
[89]*Ibid.*, 401–2.
[90]Bakhtiarov, *Bryukho Peterburga*, 161.
[91]Brokgauz–Efron, vol. 53 (xxvii), 401.

The lower sort of people keep these calculi as talismans, for the cure of certain disorders.[92]

At the Hay Market in St Petersburg, in winter, there was a row of fishmongers, where you could get an idea of the rich variety of fish available at least to those who lived in the capital.

Here are gathered all the many inhabitants of the countless rivers, lakes and seas of our huge country, beginning with the tiny Beloozero smelt, and ending with Volga sterlet. Wherever you look you see little piles of snow, on the ground, on the shelves, in baskets. Frozen fish are kept in the snow . . . Mounds of perch reach almost to the roof; the fish are laid in horizontal rows. On the shelves there are smoked salmon and silvery salmon with bright red slashes across them. There are barrels of marinaded lamprey with pepper and bay leaves. On the ground there are special tanks with live fish: bass, pike, ruff, eel, and even crabs.[93]

But how much of this abundance reached the majority of the population that lived in the countryside away from the major rivers? The story seems to be similar to that of meat. In the 1860s in Ryazan' province:

Fish is eaten even more rarely [than meat] at places far from the rivers. In general, fish is eaten only during the final days of Shrovetide, on the winter St. Nicholas' day, and at the feast of the Annunciation. In beluga or stellate sturgeon soups it is eaten salted, but the many smaller fish which abound in the rivers and lakes of the province – roach, perch, ruff, gudgeon, ide, carp and sometimes pike or bream – are eaten fresh.[94]

Fish remained the main fast day food – the only source of animal protein during fasts. At a village near Rybinsk, 'On festival days which coincide with fasts, one eats whatever is available, but certainly some fish – fresh if there is any – otherwise salted. Sturgeon is rare, and pike is the favourite fresh fish.'[95] Salt fish, when it was available, was not always healthy. In Ryazan', 'the consumption of salt fish, which is generally brought in as soon as the sled road is passable (about St. Nicholas' day – December 6), often leads to cases of food–poisoning and even death, partly because of its poor quality, and partly because the common people are accustomed to eating it uncooked'.[96]

In Moscow province, similarly, 'The only fish eaten is salt herring. . .

[92]Clarke, *Travels*, 58.
[93]Bakhtiarov, *Bryukho Peterburga*, 200.
[94]*Materialy*, v. 19, Ryazanskaya gub., 398.
[95]*Etnograficheskii sbornik*, vol. I, 78.
[96]*Materialy*, v. 19, Ryazanskaya gub., 398.

fresh fish is extremely rare for there is nowhere to catch it.'[97] In such regions, where almost all the fish consumed was purchased, fish was kept for special occasions. In Orel province in the 1890s, 'Salt fish is eaten on certain occasions such as on major fasts, at Shrovetide and so on.'[98]

However, those who lived near well-stocked streams appear to have eaten much more fresh fish. The Don supplied those who lived in or near Voronezh with

. . . an astonishing quantity of fishes, in the list of which the carp is the most abundant; but they have also tench, sterlet, bream, bleak, trout, lamprey, perch and pike. The last absolutely swarm in their rivers and grow to a prodigious size. The flesh is not on that account coarse, yet it is only the poorer classes of people who eat it.[99]

In the basin of the Oka river, fish stew [*oukha*] was a common dish: 'oukha is a genuine fish soup, seasoned with salt and various condiments; the most popular is made with sterlet, . . . a delicate fish, with yellowish flesh, which is caught in abundance in the nearby river'.[100]

Because the amount and type of fish consumed varied so greatly with local conditions, it is hardly worthwhile attempting to estimate average consumption levels. The rule is that those near-well-stocked rivers generally had access to plenty of fresh fish, though they might sell rather than consume it; those in or near towns could generally get salt or pickled fish; while those in rural areas far from good fishing ate hardly any fish at all, and what they did eat was mainly salted or dried.[101]

GARDEN PRODUCE AND POTATOES

Every peasant household had, besides an allotment of arable land, a small plot of land around the house in which vegetables and fruit could be grown. The produce grown here was an important, though secondary, part of the dietary regime. Vegetables and fruit were not eaten in huge quantities, but they played an important nutritional role, providing significant amounts of vitamin C, and (in the case of beans and peas) vegetable protein, and they are mentioned in almost every general description of rural diets. In a village near Rybinsk in the 1840s,

[97]Skibnevskii, 223.
[98]*Opyt*, 46.
[99]Clarke, *Travels*, 45.
[100]Le Play, *Ouvriers*, vol. II, 491.
[101]See Table 7.1 for some estimates of the quantities of fish consumed.

Gardening is only moderately important and barely covers the limited needs of the peasants. Radishes, carrots, and beetroot, are sown in small quantities; beans and peas are more rare. Small, turnip-like onions are sown and sometimes several *chetveriks* of these are left over for sale at 30 silver kopeks a *chetverik*. There is no garlic. There are sometimes enough potatoes to sell some at 10 silver kopeks a *chetverik*. There are turnips and swedes. There is not much cabbage – sometimes it has to be bought in Mologa, and sometimes, for lack of pickled foods, they have to make do with oatmeal gruel.[102]

In Ryazan' province in the 1860s,

Vegetables are not eaten much as the peasants do not have good vegetable gardens. The potato, which could be an extremely nutritious and tasty part of the peasants' diet is still not common . . . Peas, beetroot, and cucumbers are even less common. Only cabbage is used much and also onions and radishes on fast days. The peasants hardly know of any other vegetables.[103]

Pulses, in particular peas, clearly occupied a minor but nutritionally valuable role as sources of vegetable protein. Vegetables such as cabbages and cucumbers, which could be pickled for winter, were more central. In Moscow, early in the century, the English traveller Parkinson, 'was much amused with the market where they sell mushrooms, saurkraut, salted cucumbers, radishes, parsnips, etc., etc. There are several sledges full of mushrooms which were sold in strings. The cucumbers and saurkraut were in large tubs by which the dealer stood ready with a wooden ladle in his hand to serve out to the purchaser.'[104]

Pickled cabbage (Parkinson's 'saurkraut') was a universal staple in Great Russia. Haxthausen claimed, with some exaggeration, that cabbages were the only vegetable widely used in Russia.[105] In the Oka river region, 'dinner consisted of *shchii* made of cabbage for most of the year, and of *shchii* made of sorrel during the spring'.[106] This cabbage soup was described as a 'mixture of chopped cabbage, barleymeal, and salt, together with a modicum of kvass'.[107] Cabbage soup was often seasoned with meat fat or small chunks of meat. Cabbage soup without any seasoning at all was generally reckoned poor, and was known as 'empty soup'.

Pickled vegetables may have provided a valuable anti-scorbutic.

---

[102]*Etnograficheskii sbornik*, vol. I, 87–8.
[103]*Materialy*, v. 19, Ryazanskaya gub., 398.
[104]Parkinson, *Tour*, 102.
[105]Haxthausen, *Russian Empire*, vol. I, 163.
[106]Le Play, *Ouvriers*, vol. II, 192.
[107]Kennard, *The Russian Peasant*, 80.

Certainly, peasants generally attributed great importance to the presence of something sour in the diet.

For the peasants, something acidic [*kislota*] is an essential part of any diet. Without something sour, a meal is not a meal for a worker. Some acidity is, for a working man, almost more important than meat and he will generally prefer cabbage soup with pork fat to a fresh soup with beef if it has nothing acid in it. The lack of acidity is reflected in the amount of work done, in the health, and even in the mood of the workers. Even maggoty sour cabbage is better than no sour cabbage at all. In supplying the army, the supply of pickled cabbage, of acid food, is a matter of great urgency . . . Soup made of pickled cabbage, cold or hot, is the basic item in peasant diets. If there is no pickled cabbage, then it is replaced with pickled mashed beetroot in *borshch*. If there is neither pickled cabbage nor pickled beetroot, no pickled vegetable at all, as happens sometimes in summer, then cabbage soup is made from fresh vegetables, beetroot, pig-weed, nettles, sorrel – and fermented with sour whey or with the sour leavings after making butter. In desperation, cabbage soup can be fermented with specially prepared sour kvas or replaced with fermented soup containing pickled cucumbers, kvas, fermented dough, biscuits made from sour black bread.[108]

In Moscow province, as we have seen, cabbages and cucumbers were not particularly common; the main garden vegetables were potatoes, turnips, radishes and onions in the 1870s. But this was not typical. In Sebezhsk volost in White Russia, the villagers grew 'beetroot, radish, swede, carrot, horseradish, and cabbage. After potatoes, cabbage and beetroot occupied most space. Very few other vegetables are grown.'[109]

In the Ukraine, beetroot often took the place of cabbage, making *borshch* the national soup of the Ukraine in place of *shchii*. Squashes and melons were in general much more common here than further north. Travelling in the Crimea, Edward Clarke met

. . . several caravans which were principally laden with cucumbers of such immense length and size, that the statement of their dimensions will perhaps not be believed. We measured some that were in length above two feet. There is no article of food so grateful to a Russian as the salted cucumber, and all the inhabitants of the Crimea cultivate the plant for the sake of the pickle they afford. They have varieties of this vegetable unknown in England; among others, one which is snow-white and which attains the astonishing size I have mentioned, without running to seed or losing anything of its crisp and refreshing flavour.[110]

[108]Engel'gardt, *Iz derevni*, 264.
[109]*Etnograficheskii sbornik*, vol. II, 247.
[110]Clarke, *Travels*, 94.

31 Mushroom market in Moscow, late nineteenth century. An autumn scene, probably late autumn, because a sledge can be seen at the left-hand edge of the picture. The box on the sledge supports a pair of scales on which a container of fungi is being weighed.

The Ukrainians also enjoyed more fruit as it was easier to grow in the south and fruit gardens were much more common. It was the large fruit gardens of the south which mainly supplied the needs of St Petersburg later in the century.[111] In Great Russia, fruit were not at all common in the villages. Where they were grown it was often for sale. In Ryazan' province, 'Fruit are grown for sale, but in the northern districts they are extremely rare.' Berries, another valuable source of vitamin C, were equally undervalued as a dietary supplement, partly as a result of financial pressures once again. 'Berries are gathered only for sale, although the children taste them occasionally without seeing if they are ripe or not, with the result that when berries and fruit are ripe there are always many upset stomachs and many cases of diarrhoea.'[112]

Mushrooms, while often preserved and sold, could also be an important supplementary food. In Ryazan', 'Mushrooms are eaten in large quantities – the peasants could hardly get by without them on fast days.'[113] They were particularly valuable in spring, when stocks were

[111]Bakhtiarov, *Bruykho Peterburga*, 91–8 describes how St Petersburg was supplied with fruit.
[112]*Materialy*, v. 19, Ryazanskaya gub., 398.
[113]*Ibid.*

low. In Smolensk province in the spring of 1873, 'The mushrooms are out and things are slightly easier. They are at least a supplement. This year mushrooms appeared early and in exceptional quantities. Of course, you cannot do much work on mushrooms alone, without bread, but you can at least survive until you have bread, or you can use them to stretch out the bread you do have.'[114]

What evidence there is on the amounts of garden produce consumed shows that they were far less important than bread, but they were a basic foodstuff in the sense that they were rarely entirely absent from the diet.

One of the most important garden crops by the late nineteenth century was the potato. As we have seen in (pp. 199–200) the potato had reached Russia in the eighteenth century, but it was not until the nineteenth century that it earned a secure place in the popular diet. The spread of the potato during the century marked a significant change in the basic nature of the Russian diet, a change which caused upheavals in many areas of peasant life. 'It was a revolution which affected much more than diet or agricultural routines.'[115] This change was closely related to the slow erosion of the natural economy, though in rather complex ways, so the potato clearly deserves more space than other garden crops.

Ever since it was first introduced into Europe from South America in the sixteenth century, the potato has been used as a way of cheapening labour. Weight for weight, it is a poorer food than the cereals which were the basis of the European dietary regime.[116] Its cultivation also costs more labour. As Chayanov showed, 'high labor intensive crops usually give a smaller labor payment than do more extensive crops. Therefore, peasant farms turn to intensive crops only when, due to land pressure, they cannot meet their demands to the necessary extent with an optimal labor payment.'[117] So, from the peasant's point of view, the arrival of potatoes meant an increase in the labour expended on subsistence.

From the point of view of the employer, however – and this was true for landlord, entrepreneur, or state – the crop had many advantages. Its cultivation required less land to produce the same amount of calories as grain, so that less land had to be set aside to support the same amount of labour power. And the difference was paid for by the peasant's increased expenditure of labour, or increased 'self-exploita-

---

[114]Engel'gardt, *Iz derevni*, 106.
[115]Confino, *Systèmes agraires*, 305.
[116]Salaman, *The Potato*, 122–3.
[117]*Chayanov, on Peasant Economy*, 115.

tion' in Chayanov's phrase. In this way, the introduction of the potato increased the amount of labour effectively extracted from the peasant by those who made use of the peasant's labour, so that, throughout its history the potato has made possible the cheapening of agricultural labour. As Salaman points out, 'the Spanish conquistadores who first encountered the potato, immediately realised its economic importance, and at once relegated it as food for slaves'.[118] Lenin made the same point in the terminology of Marxian economics, when he argued that the increased area under potatoes in nineteenth-century Russia was 'from the viewpoint of the rural entrepreneur class, the production of relative surplus-value (cheapening of the cost of maintaining labour-power, deterioration of the people's nourishment)'.[119]

The last point is an exaggeration. The potato is in fact an extremely valuable foodstuff nutritionally, containing well-balanced quantities of proteins and carbohydrates, and even significant amounts of vitamin C. For the peasant, the fact that it produced more food energy per hectare made it a natural fallback as the land available diminished during the nineteenth century. This suggests why, traditionally, it has been famines or land shortage which have broken peasant resistance to the growth of a crop which required more work, and was also the object of immense superstitious fear.[120]

In terms of the economy as a whole, the increase in cultivation of the potato meant a growth in agricultural productivity in general. It also accelerated the penetration of market forces into the village, for the potato was of value not merely for consumption but also for industrial processing into alcohol or starch. Lenin could with some justice claim that the rapid spread of the potato in nineteenth-century Russia was a significant measure of the growth of Russian capitalism.[121]

Before the 1840s, there were probably some potatoes sown in all provinces of Russia, but the amounts were tiny and concentrated in the western provinces, and around urban centres. There had been some experiments with using potatoes for distilling (particularly in the Baltic provinces) and for making flour, molasses and starch, but as yet the commercial value of potatoes had not been proved.[122] Where they were sown, they were clearly regarded as a supplement for other foods and not yet as a staple. In Perm', in 1802–3, they were grown only in

[118]Salaman, *The Potato*, 101.
[119]Lenin, *Development of Capitalism*, 257.
[120]Tudge, *The Famine Business*, 39–41; *Chayanov on Peasant Economy*, 115, on the extra labour required to grow potatoes; Salaman, *The Potato*, 541 and ch. 25; and Blum, *End of the Old Order*, 273.
[121]Lenin, *Development of Capitalism*, 257.
[122]Blum, *End of the Old Order*, 275; and Lekhnovich, 'Kul'tury kartofelya', 395–6.

villages around the provincial capital. 'The peasants eat them baked, boiled, and in gruel . . .; they use potato flour to make pies and *sharangi* [a sort of pie], and in the towns they add them to soups, fry them and use potato flour to make *kisel'* [a sort of fool].'[123]

By 1840, no more than 1 million chets were sown.[124] The Ministry of State Domains claimed that potatoes were already common in Moscow, Orel, Tula and Pskov provinces; were quite common in fifteen central and southern provinces; and could occasionally be found in another fifteen provinces in the central Black Earth region, along the Volga and in the north.[125]

During the 1840s, the government, in particular the newly created Ministry of State Domains (which dealt with the affairs of those peasants subordinated to the state rather than to private landlords), began a large-scale attempt to make potatoes a major crop amongst the state peasants who, in 1836, constituted 42% of the peasantry as a whole.[126] Apart from experiments by the Ministry of Royal Domains in 1834, this was the first serious effort since the mid-eighteenth century, and, as before, it was provoked by a series of poor harvests.[127] As the Ministry argued: 'The bad harvests of 1839, 1840 and earlier years provided the motive for government measures aimed at spreading the planting of potatoes, for they are one of the best possible supplements for the people's food.'[128]

In August 1840 the government issued a decree ordering state peasants to plant a certain amount of potatoes on common lands. The decree described the potato as 'a vegetable which is a healthy and nourishing food, and can replace grain as a popular foodstuff in times of poor harvests as it is itself less subject to poor harvests and can also serve as fodder for domestic livestock'.[129] At the same time, the Ministry of State Domains undertook a substantial propaganda campaign:

From the centre countless circulars and memoranda were sent out; from abroad the government ordered information on different varieties of potato; governors were given instructions to cooperate to the full with the reforms; the Holy Synod issued instructions to priests to explain to peasants the value of potatoes; district heads and their assistants exerted pressure on the volost and village authorities; ignoring the opinion of village meetings and ignoring local

[123]Elovskikh, 'Iz tetradei', 131. (Thanks to Stephen Ellis for this reference.)
[124]Pintner, *Economic Policy*, 177.
[125]Druzhinin, *Gosudarstvennye krest'yane*, vol. II, 235.
[126]Tokarev, *Kartofel'nye bunty*, 9.
[127]On previous attempts by the government to spread the cultivation of potatoes, see above, ch. 5, and Tokarev, *Kartofel'nye bunty*, 25–6.
[128]Ministerstvo gos-ykh imushchestv, *Obzor*, vol. III, 112; and Tokarev, *Kartofel'nye bunty*, 24.
[129]Druzhinin, *Gosudarstvennye krest'yane*, vol. II, 53.

conditions, they forced peasants to set aside large plots of land and forced them to plant potatoes.[130]

In addition, the authorities issued 'brief but clear handbooks on the cultivation, storing and use of potatoes'.[131]

The government's actions provoked widespread opposition and in some cases pitched battles against army units sent to enforce the new regulations.[132] There were riots in ten provinces of European Russia (Perm', Vyatka, Orenburg, Kazan', Saratov, Ryazan', Moscow, Vologda, Olonets and Tambov) and in Tobolsk province in Siberia. They were most serious in the Volga and Ural provinces along the eastern border of European Russia. It was here, too, that the Pugachev revolt has been most serious.[133] These areas had not known the fully developed serfdom of the central regions, partly because the nobility had preferred to settle in more fertile areas, and partly because the government had settled small serf-holding gentry along the dangerous southern borders of Muscovy. It was the state peasants of the Volga provinces, the Urals, and the north that still had a precarious independence to defend, and were willing to fight for it.[134]

The hostility of the peasants was directed only in part at the introduction of potatoes. The new regulations interfered with long-established agricultural routines, forced peasants to set aside land of their own which they would have used for rye, and forced them to surrender valuable labour time to grow a new uncertain crop. In areas where the potato was already familiar as a garden crop, it was the extent of the compulsory sowings and the forcible methods used to introduce them that provoked resistance. In some regions the peasants had already had failures with potatoes, and in other regions it was feared that potatoes would reduce the harvest of other crops. Elsewhere, the order to plant potatoes was seen, with some justice, as a sort of compulsory labour, or as a step towards the conversion of state peasants into landlords' serfs or crown serfs, whose condition was, by and large, worse than that of most state peasants. The fact that the original decrees were issued in the form of ministerial circulars was also significant, as it seemed proof to many that the tsar' had not sanctioned them.[135] Religious superstitions probably played some role, particularly where there

---

[130] *Ibid.*, vol. II, 235.
[131] *Ibid.*, vol. II, 53–4.
[132] *Ibid.*, vol. II, 471–3.
[133] Tokarev, *Kartofel'nye bunty*, 4–5.
[134] *Ibid.*, 10, and see also 33–4, for a summary of the causes of the potato riots.
[135] *Ibid.*, 57–9.

were Old Believers who saw the potato as the 'devil's apple'.[136] But there were probably more general reasons for the peasants' violent opposition. The protests were directed against a whole series of reforms undertaken by the new Ministry of State Domains, all of which profoundly affected the peasants' lives, increased their fiscal burden, and increased official interference in their lives. 'The material of peasant discontent was already prepared, and the compulsory sowing of potatoes was sufficient to supply the spark which turned this discontent into open revolt.'[137]

It is worth describing one incident in more detail, to illustrate the way in which the government's interference in an area of peasant life as delicate as that of diet, could provide the spark necessary to fire a large number of accumulated grievances.

The 'potato riots' were most insistent and most widespread in the Urals provinces. In Vyatka province, in May 1842, the peasants of Bykovskii village in Nolinskii district refused to plant potatoes. They tilled the land which was set aside for potatoes, and sowed oats instead. Neighbouring villages also began uprooting the potatoes they had planted and tearing down the fences around the specially allocated potato patches. The peasants believed that the order to plant potatoes was a first step towards making them landlords' serfs and imposing a new religion on them. (They were in fact correct in thinking that there were plans to change their legal status.)[138] In several villages in Vyatka province local government officials were beaten or arrested by the peasants, and peasants began to arm themselves with pikes, axes and scythes. Eventually, up to 100,000 peasants were involved in several districts of the province and the movement acquired a certain degree of organisation, with couriers, special agitators, and the rudiments of a concerted military strategy. Bridges were systematically destroyed to hamper the movements of troops.

On June 13, the governor, Mordvinov, arrived at Bykovskii at the head of 300 troops with 2 cannon, and was faced by a crowd of 600 peasants who refused to move. After some argument, the soldiers fired on the crowd wounding 18, but the peasants still refused to move, insisting that they were all ready to die rather than obey the government's orders. Eventually Mordvinov ordered the soldiers to attack the crowd using their rifle butts, and to bind them, which the troops did, after a long hand-to-hand fight. The leaders were arrested and of the

---

[136]Druzhinin, *Gosudarstvennye krest'yane*, vol. II, 466–7; and Tokarev, *Kartofel'nye bunty*, 6–8.
[137]*Ibid.*, 34, and 21–5; see also Druzhinin, *Gosudarstvennye krest'yane*, vol. II, 474.
[138]Tokarev, *Kartofel'nye bunty*, 53.

rest, 1 in every 8 was whipped. This finally broke the peasants' resistance.[139]

In other villages the resistance was even more stubborn. A month later, in the village of Taranki, Mordvinov led an army detachment against 1,500 peasants. A first volley killed or wounded 30, but the peasants stood firm. Again, he ordered the soldiers to attack using rifle butts, and after a 20 minute battle the soldiers finally bound all the peasants opposing them. But at this point a new crowd of peasants appeared from the nearby woods to help their neighbours. This time the governor ordered a cannon loaded with grape-shot to be aimed at them, and when they refused to stop, he gave the order to fire. Eighteen fell. After a brief battle the new arrivals were also bound. It was found that altogether 8 peasants had been killed and 4 later died of their wounds, while 42 peasants were wounded.[140] This seems to have broken the resistance of the Vyatka peasants. But the stubbornness of the initial resistance is a powerful reminder of the dangers of direct government interference in the agricultural and dietary routines of the peasantry.

By 1843 the government gave up the attempt to spread the forced cultivation of potatoes, and began to use persuasion instead. But in spite of the opposition to it, the reform seems to have marked an important turning point in the introduction of potatoes into Russia. By 1843 the amount of potatoes planted in Russia had increased 5 times, from 1 million chetverts in 1840 to 5.3 million, and this latter figure remained steady for a decade.[141] By 1860 potatoes were well established, not merely as a garden vegetable now, but also as a field crop in a number of provinces.[142] By 1861 potatoes already dominated peasant diets in Vilno province in Lithuania.[143] The General Staff surveys found that potatoes were a regular part of peasant diets in Perm', Kazan', Kostroma, Chernigov, Kherson, and Archangel provinces. For the most part they still remained a novelty, however. In Kostroma, for example, it was generally only the younger peasants who were willing to eat vegetables of which the older generation retained a superstitious fear.[144]

During the second half of the century, plantings of potatoes grew more rapidly than sowings of grains, and they also spread south, as

[139]*Ibid.*, 56–61, and also see 82–91 for documents on the revolts in Vyatka province; Druzhinin, *Gosudarstvennye krest'yane*, vol. II, 471–3.
[140]*Ibid.*, vol. II, 473–4.
[141]Pintner, *Economic Policy*, 177.
[142]Drobizhev, *et al.*, *Istoricheskaya geografiya*, 210.
[143]Confino, *Systèmes agraires*, 478–479.
[144]*Materialy*, v. 12, Kostromskaya gub., 32.

Table 7.4. *Harvest of potatoes 1850–1900*

Decade (average annual harvest)	Gross harvest (mln chetverts)	Per capita (chetverts)
1850s	19.8	0.28
1860s	25.3	0.32
1870s	40.8	0.44
1880s	49.8	0.46
1890s	96.8	0.46

Source: Nifontov, *Zernovoe proizvodstvo*, 183, 266. See also Lenin, *Development of Capitalism*, 256.

population pressures and land shortage increased there, too. In the 1880s, the total area under potatoes was about 2% of the area under grains, but by 1913 it was 4%; in absolute terms the amount of land under potatoes increased from 1.438 million desyatinas in the mid 1880s (*c.* 1.57 million hectares) to 3.107 million desyatinas in 1913 (*c.* 3.39 million hectares), an increase of 216%.[145] While the total output of potatoes in European Russia grew 5 times between 1861 and 1900, that of the major grains only doubled.[146]

Figures for the gross harvests of potatoes in European Russia in the second half of the nineteenth century are given in Table 7.4.

Clearly, after the initial gains during the difficult years of the 1840s, the spread of potatoes was steady but slow until the 1890s. The fact that it spread more rapidly during the 1840s and 1890s, the hardest years of the century, is typical of the potato's history elsewhere in Europe. In the 1890s, the increased growing of potatoes was clearly linked with the 1891 famine, and it kept rising in a period of increasing difficulty for the peasant class as a whole.

By the 1880s most potatoes were grown on peasant land. Of a gross harvest of 49.6 million chetverts in 1884, 36.1 million chetverts (or 73%) came from peasant lands.[147] Relatively, they took up slightly more arable land on peasant than on gentry lands; in the early 1880s, 2.28% of peasant arable was under potatoes, and only 1.72% of the arable land of gentry landowners.[148]

We can assume that almost all of the potatoes produced on landlords' land was used commercially. But we do not really know what

[145]Drobizhev, *et al.*, *Istoricheskaya geografiya*, 209.
[146]Goldsmith, 'Economic Growth', 446.
[147]*Statisticheskii vremennik*, 3rd series, vol. VIII, 130–3.
[148]*Ibid.*, vol. IV, xxxvi–xxxvii.

Table 7.5. *Sowings of potatoes 1891–1900*

Date	Mln chets sown
1881	10.7
1891	13.1
1892	17.1
1893	18.2
1894	19.2
1895	19.5
1896	21.0
1897	22.1
1898	23.0
1899	23.1
1900	23.4

Source: Nifontov, *Zernovoe proizvodstvo*, 225.

proportion of peasant-grown potatoes was consumed directly, and what proportion was either marketed or used in small commerical operations. Some wealthier peasants did grow potatoes commercially. Lenin cites a description in the early 1880s of a peasant-owned starch works with twelve wage workers.

This peasant grows potatoes on his own farm, which he has enlarged by renting land. The crop rotation is seven-field and includes clover. For the farm work he employs from 7 to 8 workers, hired from spring to autumn (from end to end) . . . The pulp is used as cattle feed, and the owner intends to use the waste water for his fields.[149]

But such farms were hardly typical. We can safely assume that most peasant-grown potatoes were produced for consumption at home.

Certainly, what direct evidence is available shows that potatoes had become a very important element in peasant diets by the late nineteenth century in almost all regions of Russia. From the General Staff surveys, one gets the impression that potatoes often entered the peasants' diet in the form of a potato soup (*pokhlebka*). In Moscow province in the 1880s, it seems that potatoes had come to usurp the place once occupied by groats and gruel. 'As buckwheat groats almost always have to be bought, buckwheat gruel is rarely eaten, only on holidays, and even then only amongst the better-off households; potatoes are eaten everyday.'[150] On average, in the better-off households in this

[149]Lenin, *Development of Capitalism*, 302.
[150]Skibnevskii, 222.

Table 7.6. *Average per capita consumption of basic foodstuffs*

Type of food	Grams per person per day
Bread	692
Potatoes	399
Vegetable and Fruit	166
Meat and Fish	73
Salt	44
Sugar	11
Vegetable Oils	6
Eggs	0.1 units

Source: Dikhtyar, *Vnutrennyaya torgovlya*, 30.

district, adults consumed about 330 kg of rye and barley each year, and 190 kg of potatoes, as well as 100 kg of cucumber and sauerkraut and 17 kg of meat. In the poorer households people ate about 200 kg of barley and rye, 150 kg of potatoes, 80 kg of sauerkraut and cucumbers, and no meat.[151] Clearly, in terms of weight, potatoes were already the second most important item in the diet, and this was even truer in poor than in rich households. On average potatoes accounted for about 20% by weight of peasant diets by the early twentieth century.[152] The average figures for consumption, based on budgetary studies of the early twentieth century, are shown in Table 7.6.

It seems that potatoes were no longer a poor peasants' food by the end of the century. On average all groups ate similar amounts, though in relative terms potatoes were probably more important in the diet of poorer peasants.[153] Thus, by the late nineteenth century, potatoes had come to occupy a central place in the dietary regime of the Russian peasant. Here, as in the instance of vodka, the autocratic government played a crucial role in modifying the dietary regime of the Russian peasantry.

The main defect of the dietary regime we have been describing was undoubtedly its unreliability – the danger of sudden shortages of important elements. We will describe these fluctuations in detail, together with the costs they extracted, in chapter 9. But it is equally important

[151] *Ibid.*, 224–5.
[152] Kerblay, 'Alimentation rurale', 894.
[153] Dikhtyar, *Vnutrennyaya torgovlya*, 30.

to note that in its general features, the dietary regime of nineteenth-century Russia was remarkably well-balanced, with its combination of grains and smaller amounts of vegetables, potatoes, meat and fruit. It is the sort of diet to which some modern nutritionists are inclined to look with renewed respect as the inadequacies of modern systems of food production and distribution become increasingly evident.[154]

[154]See, for example, Tudge, *The Famine Business*, particularly chs. 3 and 5.

8

✻✻✻

Tavern and treasury

INTRODUCTION

In pre-industrial Russia, as in Europe as a whole, the absence of pure water meant, as we have seen, that drinks had to be prepared specially. Water from wells, rivers and ponds was never entirely safe. In parts of Dmitrovsk district of Moscow province in the 1870s, frequent attacks of typhus, scarlet fever, dysentery, measles, and other diseases were attributed to the fact that the peasants used

... stagnant pond water. Clothes are washed, and the cattle drink and are even bathed in ponds whose water is a yellowish-brown; in summer, the water is covered with mould, and swarming with myriads of insects of all kinds; in autumn, it is completely foul from standing rainwater, and various types of filth from the streets and courtyards; and the water is putrid even in winter.[1]

Sometimes water came from wells, springs and rivers and could be of good quality, except in the spring when it tended to be dirty.[2] But in general, as Le Play found, 'it is very rare for Russian working people to use water as their ordinary drink. Even those in most straightened circumstances habitually use fermented drinks made at home with rye flour.'[3] Of kvas, it was said, 'Even if it turns your nose aside, at least it's kvass, not water.'[4] Until better wells were dug or modern sanitation was introduced, drinking water would remain an unhealthy and sometimes unpleasant way of slaking one's thirst.

As we have seen, milk was not common and in any case, it could be as unhealthy as water (ch. 7, pp. 266–8). The use of boiled water in tea was less risky, but tea-drinking was still a luxury for most nineteenth-century peasants. (See ch. 6, pp. 241–2.)

Not surprisingly, alcoholic drinks were generally preferred to water or milk. But like most elements of the festive diet, the significance of

---

[1] *Pervyi gubernskii s"ezd*, addendum, 31.
[2] *Materialy*, v. 19, Ryazanskaya gub., 399.
[3] Le Play, *Ouvriers*, vol. II, 177.
[4] Martynov, 'Nekotorye zametki', 273.

Map 2 The provinces of European Russia in the late nineteenth century

alcohol was as much social as nutritional. According to the proverbs: 'you drink and dance for others, but eat and sleep for yourself'; 'without bread you can't work; without vodka you can't dance'.[5] And, roughly speaking, the more alcoholic the drink, the more one danced. Or, to put it more prosaically, the more alcoholic the drink, the greater its social significance, the greater its power to dispel the monotony of daily life and daily diet, the greater, too, its price, and its significance to the Russian economy as a whole.

A peasant saying offers a clear ranking order for drinks: 'no vodka, then drink a little beer; no beer, then drink a little kvas; no kvas, then drink a little water from a small spoon.'[6] The order reflects more than popular preference; it reflects the relative strength, the relative difficulty of production and the relative costs as well. Kvas could be brewed in any household for everyday use, but was barely alcoholic. Beer, ale (*braga*) and mead were usually stronger, but still simple enough to make at home; but their production was expensive enough to confine their use to festive occasions. Vodka was strongest of all, but its production involved distilling and this meant using techniques and equipment which were beyond the resources of peasant households in nineteenth-century Russia.[7] In the nineteenth century, then, vodka was commercially produced and sold to the rural population for cash, which the peasants had to find by selling either their own produce or their own labour. (The word 'vodka' is here used to cover all common drinks based on grain spirits.)

Of these three grades of alcoholic drink, it was the weakest and the strongest – kvas and vodka – which were dominant in nineteenth-century Russia. In this, Russia differed from most other European countries north of the grape. There, beer had for the most part resisted the encroachment of spirits during the early modern period and sometimes (as in England) the tide had actually been reversed; by the nineteenth century, beer was the major drink both for everyday consumption and for festive occasions. But in Russia beer (and mead), the main popular drinks in medieval Russia, never regained the festive territory lost to spirits and failed to capture the more everyday territory occupied by kvas. In the western provinces, for example, real beers were not common for

---

[5] Dal', *Poslovitsy*, 817–18.

[6] *Ibid.*, 818.

[7] I have not come across a single reference to distilling in peasant households in nineteenth-century Russia. If it did occur, it was extremely rare. However, since the temporary introduction of prohibition in 1914, this has ceased to be true. See, for example, Amalrik, *Involuntary Journey*, 173.

Their price makes them inaccessible for those who are not wealthy. The poor classes use large quantities . . . of cheap, weak beer, which in fact has little in common with proper beer. Further, the development of brewing outside the towns has been hampered by the relative cheapness of vodka and the poverty of the rural population; and in the towns by the high excises imposed where the trade was farmed out.[8]

This momentous fact of Russian social history reflects to a large extent the fiscal policies of the Russian government, particularly in the eighteenth and nineteenth centuries.

KVAS

Kvas was a central element in the everyday diet – tasty, cheap and usually hygienic. It was, not surprisingly, the alcoholic drink most commonly encountered by foreign travellers in Great Russia. And it can still be found easily by modern visitors to the Soviet Union, sold in summer on street corners from metal tankers. The English traveller, Parkinson, was introduced to 'the Russian's nectar, quass', by Princess Dashkov, the childhood friend of Catherine the Great. He found it 'a quenchy draught' and reckoned it to be a valuable antidote to scurvy.[9] (The modern visitor will almost certainly agree, at least with the first part of this judgement.) Parkinson moved in high society, but in the ordinary rural household, too, kvas was the main drink: 'If there's bread and kvas, then we have all we need.' The general staff survey of Ryazan' province concluded: 'the main drink is kvas'.[10]

In Great Russia, making kvas was as basic a skill as making bread. The main ingredients were flour and bread, malt and water, though often the malt was left out. There were many different kinds of kvas depending on the type of grain used – barley, rye, wheat, buckwheat, or oats – and the proportions in which they were used. And there were also fruit or berry kvases flavoured with pears, cherries, lemons and other fruit (see p. 74).[11] Usually, the preparation of kvas was extremely rudimentary.

To make it one puts a pailful of water into an earthen vessel, into which one shakes two pounds of barley meal [or rye], half a pound of salt, and some honey, more or less according to the wealth of the family. This is placed in the evening in the oven with a moderate fire and stirred. In the morning, it is left

[8]Korsak, 'Pivovarenie', 24.

[9]Parkinson, *Tour*, 68.

[10]Dal', *Poslovitsy*, 811; *Materialy*, v. 19, Ryazanskaya gub., 399.

[11]In the Ukraine, a drink made of wild apples and pears was extremely popular. Korsak, 'Pivovarenie', 23.

for a time to settle; the clear liquid is poured off and it is ready to drink in a few days.[12]

Like all foodstuffs, kvas varied greatly in quality. In the late 1870s, in villages in Mozhaisk district of Moscow province, the kvas was 'of such poor quality – extremely watery and very sour – that its consumption probably did more harm than good'.[13] In Ryazan' province the local kvas was 'generally pale and insufficiently fermented and often of poor quality, particularly in summer, when it rapidly turns'.[14] In the village of Viryatino in Tambov province, in the late nineteenth century, 'during the winter, [kvas] was prepared as a first course with sauerkraut and horseradish. It was sometimes cooked with peas, particularly during feasts, and during the summer the poor would add bread crumbs and chopped scallions, while the more affluent added cucumbers, onions and eggs.'[15]

Kvas was closely related to beer, but the relationship is complex. It was generally weaker than beer, with about 1.0-2.5% alcohol by volume, as the fermentation of lactic acid during its production inhibited the formation of alcohol.[16] In contrast, commercially produced beers usually had about 3.8% alcohol by volume.[17] In 1863, the government defined as beers grain-based fermented drinks using hops.[18] But in practice the borderline remained unclear. Kvas, for example, was not common in the western provinces and the Ukraine, where its place was taken by beer. This led some writers, including Baron Haxthausen, to detect along the river Dnepr a clear boundary between the kvas- and the beer-consuming parts of the Russian Empire.[19] In fact, much of the beer consumed in the western provinces was closer to kvas than to real beer. Often it was so weak that, 'it does not deserve the name of beer, consisting as it does of something between diluted kvas and a sort of mudy sludge [*burda*], though it is distinguished by its cheapness (from 25–40 kopeks a bucket)'.[20] Like kvas, weak beer of this kind was used not as an intoxicant, but rather as a sort of sauce (*priprava*) for dry food.[21] After 1863, many small breweries in the western provinces began calling their product kvas as a way of avoiding the excise pay-

---

[12]Kennard, *The Russian Peasant*, 80.
[13]Skibnevskii, 231.
[14]*Materialy*, v. 19, Ryazanskaya gub., 399.
[15]Kushner, *Viryatino*, 98.
[16]Brokgauz–Efron, vol. 27 (XIV), 864–5.
[17]Korsak, 'Pivovarenie', 1.
[18]*Ibid.*, 44.
[19]*Ibid.*, 23; Haxthausen, *Russian Empire*, vol. II, 170.
[20]Korsak, 'Pivova enie', 34.
[21]*Ibid.*, 38–40.

able on beer, even though their product was identical to the cheap beers they had made before, except for the use of various herbs instead of hops.[22] Thus, the difference between kvas and weak beer was often merely a matter of fiscal convenience for the brewers.

BEER, ALE AND MEAD

The important distinction was that between the weak, cheap drinks – kvas or cheap beers – which were used on ordinary days, and the stronger and more expensive beers used as intoxicants on festive occasions. But even this distinction was a matter of degree, as Le Play was aware: '[kvas] takes on many different forms, but basically it uses rye flour flavoured with diverse vegetable foods. Sometimes, however, barley – malted and washed – and hops are used. It is then known as *braga*, and is almost identical with the beers of the West'.[23]

However, ale and the stronger beers could get you drunk, and it was this that lent them a wider social meaning. In Ryazan'

On festivals, or for special occasions, ale [*braga*] (a hopped beer) is brewed from a thick broth of malt, various flours and hops. Ale is very nourishing, pleasant to the taste, and extremely healthy. Unfortunately, it is too expensive to be drunk much and when it is drunk it is not so much to quench the thirst as to become intoxicated, as a result of which, it is often harmful because of its immoderate use on feast days.[24]

Measuring the consumption of beer is no easy task, particularly where definitions are so vague. The statistics that are available refer only to commercially brewed beers, which passed through the market, and even these statistics are unreliable. For the period up to 1863 they derive from the records of the liquor farmers. As a result, they were incomplete for the western provinces where the liquor farmers did not monopolise the trade, and they were probably lowered elsewhere, where the farmers had an interest in hiding their illicit profits.

The most careful calculations are based on the immensely detailed account of the liquor trade compiled by the State Council in preparation for the reform of 1863, which abolished the liquor farm.[25] These calculations are very rough and ready, and they refer only to the middle years of the century, but in spite of their limitations, the story they tell is clear enough. In 1863, about 8 million buckets of beer were

[22]*Ibid.*, 45.
[23]Le Play, *Ouvriers*, vol. II, 177.
[24]*Materialy*, v. 19, Ryazanskaya gub., 399.
[25]*Svedeniya*, vol. III, 35–40; Korsak, 'Pivovarenie', 61–5.

Table 8.1 *Per capita consumption of beer in Europe (1850s)*

Russia	1.8 litres
Poland	19.3
UK	50.9
USA and Sonderbund Germany	42.1
Austria	26.7
France	11.6

Source: Korsak, *Pivovarenie*, 34.

produced in commercial breweries throughout the Russian Empire (excluding Poland and Finland). Of these, about 3.1 million were produced in Great Russia; over 2 million in the western provinces; about 2.8 million in the Baltic provinces; and merely 15,000 in Siberia. Assuming that each family of the non-Muslim population brewed beer or *braga* once a year on average, in quantities of about 2 buckets, Korsak calculates that a further 20 million buckets of beer were brewed in the household (about 13.5 million in Great Russia and 6.5 million in the western provinces). This gives a total of about 28 million buckets of beer, which suggests a per capita consumption of about 5.3 litres of beer of all kinds, and about 1.5 litres of commercially produced beer.[26] In comparison, about 11 litres of 40% vodka were consumed per capita in this period, which represents over twice the consumption of beer, and almost 10 times the consumption of commercially produced beers (see Figure 8.1). As vodka was roughly 10 times as strong as beer, this means that about 20 times as much alcohol was consumed in the form of vodka as was consumed in the form of beer of all kinds. Separate calculations from the 1840s (also based on the records of the liquor farmers) tell a similar story. For Russia as a whole, 8 times as much distilled drink was consumed as commercially produced beers (5 times as much in the western provinces, and 15 times as much in Great Russia).[27]

Fiscally, the contrasts are even more striking. In 1863, the excise on beer generated about 1.5 million rubles of revenue, while vodka generated about 120 million rubles, or 80 times as much.[28] These figures provide a clear measure of the relative importance of the two types of

[26]Korsak, 'Pivovarenie', 64–5.

[27]Gersevanov, *O p'yanstve*, 26–7. Today, distilled drinks are more dominant in the Soviet Union than in any other country in the world. In the USSR, on average, every person over 15 consumed 8 litres of absolute alcohol in the form of spirits in the early 1970s. Treml, 'Production and Consumption', 297.

[28]Korsak, 'Pivovarenie', 66.

Table 8.2. *Revenue generated by beer in mid–nineteenth–century Europe*

Country	Total Revenue (mln rubles)	Per capita (kopeks)
Russia	1.5	2.5
UK	7.0	36.8
Austria	5.4	31.6
France	2.5	6.9

Source: Korsak, *Pivovarenie*, 66–8

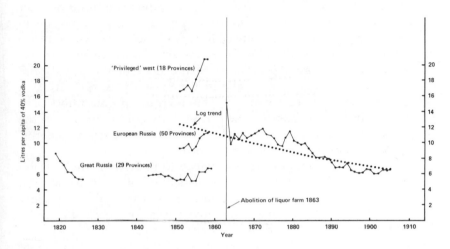

Fig. 8.1 Per capita consumption of vodka (litres) 1819–1905.
(Sources: *Svedeniya*, vol. III, 35–6, for 1819–58; Osipov, *Kazennaya prodazha*, 77, for 1863–7; Dmitriev, *Kriticheskiya issledovaniya*, 68–9, 116, 282, for 1868–1905; population figures from Kabuzan, *Narodonaselenie*, 159–63.)

drink from the government's point of view. The significance of these figures is highlighted by contrasting them with equivalent figures for other European countries. Again, the fiscal contrast is even sharper.

Within Russia, consumption of beer increased the further west one went. It was low in Great Russia, the area covered by the liquor farm (and lowest of all in Siberia). It was higher in the western provinces and the Ukraine, and highest of all in the Baltic provinces and Poland. The figures suggest that per capita consumption of commercially produced beers was about 1.1 litres in Great Russia; and about 1.3 litres in western Russia, though the latter figure is almost certainly too low, as most beer produced in the west bypassed the liquor farmers who provided the government's statistics.[29] As we have seen, consumption in Poland was about 19 litres per capita. Urban areas consumed more than their share, particularly the two metropolitan centres of Moscow and St Petersburg, but even here consumption was low in comparison with the towns of northern Europe. While consumption in St Petersburg was about 40 bottles per capita, in Munich the figure was close to 500 bottles.[30]

The evidence from the area under the liquor farm suggests that there was a decline of about 65% in consumption between 1835 and 1858.[31] There seems to have been a sharp rise in per capita consumption after the 1863 reform. Between 1860 and 1900, per capita consumption may have risen by 300–500%. The official history of the Ministry of Finance argued in 1902 that, 'in the 1860s, beer was drunk only in insignificant amounts and had hardly penetrated to the mass of the population, while nowadays it has become almost the most widespread drink in Russia, especially in the towns'.[32] This increase in consumption of commercially brewed beer was helped by a fivefold reduction in the retail price of beer from 1853–1900, a reflection of the rapid modernisation of the industry after the 1863 reform.[33]

But even these changes were inadequate to undermine the position of vodka, and consumption of beer remained low in comparison with the other beer-drinking countries of northern Europe and remains low to the present. While beer made something of a comeback after 1863, it never seriously challenged the dominance of spirits in Russia.[34] In this qualified sense, Pryzhov, the historian of the Russian drink-shop, was right to talk of the decline of beer. And he was not alone in sensing the huge social implications of this fact. A Pskov landowner argued in 1872 that the problem of drunkenness could have been greatly alleviated by a government willing to discriminate in favour of beer.

Apart from vodka, festivals are celebrated above all in beer, which is used in vast quantities. Poor households brew from 2 to 4 vats [*ushatov*], but those who are slightly wealthier brew up to 10 vats (each of 40 buckets) of beer, which, the thicker it is, the more it is praised. The local people are great lovers of beer, and indeed beer could greatly reduce drunkenness and improve the health of the peasants if the government would permit the sale in villages of tax-free beer.[35]

[29]*Ibid.*, 64–5.
[30]*Ibid.*, 34.
[31]*Svedeniya*, vol. III, 350–1. I have based this calculation on the log trend for 1835 and 1858.
[32]*Ministerstvo finansov*, vol. II, 491.
[33]*Ibid.*
[34]Treml, 'Alcoholism and State Policy', 378.
[35]*Doklad*, 226.

A potential market for beer was apparently there, but it was stifled by the government's fiscal policies. The same argument was developed more systematically by many writers concerned with the growing problem of rural drunkenness, and it became a common-place to argue that the Russian government should follow the English example and try deliberately to replace vodka with beer.[36] The government, however, derived so much revenue from vodka that such proposals were never realistic.

The crucial period, it seems, was the early nineteenth century, and the critical factor was the government's growing reliance on the liquor farm as a collection device. Because of the low level of urbanisation in Russia and the huge distances over which goods had to be transported, commercially produced beers inevitably faced greater competition in Russia than in the rest of northern Europe. The competition was both from above and below. It came, first, from domestically produced drinks such as kvas which, though weaker and of poorer quality, were extremely cheap. At the other extreme, vodka could survive the competition of domestically produced drinks because of its great strength. This made it far more attractive than beer as a festive drink, and also ensured that transportation costs per unit of alcohol were lower. (To lower these costs even further, vodka was usually transported in a highly concentrated form and diluted in the drink-shops just before sale, which, of course, provided vast scope for corruption.) As a result, the vodka trade generated far higher profits than the trade in beer, and the liquor farmers began to regard beer as a dangerous threat to the profits they made through the sale of vodka. Vodka became the liquor farmers' favourite child. Under pressure from the farmers, the government began to regulate the beer trade in ways which both discriminated against beer and increased the influence of the liquor farmers over the trade in beer.

In Great Russia, this process began in the 1780s, when the government forbade the sale of beer outside the drinking houses run by the liquor farmers.[37] Over the next eighty years, the excise on beer steadily rose to a level higher than that in most other European nations.[38] Meanwhile, the liquor farmers secured a stranglehold on both the breweries and the retail outlets, and used their control to discriminate against beer. The government made occasional efforts to defend the interests of the brewers, as in 1807, when it temporarily separated the

[36]See for example, Gersevanov, *O p'yanstve*, and Korsak, 'Pivovarenie'.
[37]Korsak, 'Pivovarenie', 10.
[38]*Ibid.*, 56.

vodka and beer farms, but its attempts were half-hearted and in the long run they proved ineffective. With 30% of its ordinary revenue coming from the liquor farmers in this period, it had little choice but to defend their interests, and that meant protecting the vodka trade.

The details of the process are not important, but one or two examples are illuminating.[39] In 1827, brewers were ordered to brew only high quality beers and the liquor farmers were allowed to brew cheap beers which they used to undermine their rivals. In response to the brewers' complaints, in 1831 brewers were allowed to brew all types of beer, but they had to pay the excise through the liquor farmers. From this time on the liquor farmers began to levy extra, illegal excises, to which the government turned a blind eye. In 1844, some farmers complained that the beer trade was still a threat to their profits, and claimed that they often had to pay brewers not to brew.

Domestic brewing for home consumption was never taxed, but restrictions were imposed on the scale of home brewing, and one liquor farmer proposed in 1845 that peasant households should pay 5 rubles each for the right to brew their own beer. In this case, the government was unimpressed. Such a proposal, it argued, 'would hand over the whole population to the liquor farmers'.[40]

In the western provinces, the liquor farm never gained so powerful a position, and the brewing industry suffered less. One measure of this was the far larger number of breweries in the west. In the late 1850s there were 1,092 breweries here, and only 248 in Great Russia.[41] But even here, spirits were clearly dominant by the early nineteenth century as Figure 8.1 shows.

The history of mead is similar, though more catastrophic. Commercial mead production had never existed as an independent industry. It was always combined with either the brewing of beer, or the manufacture of honey and wax, and it was not easily adapted to large-scale manufacture.

In order to separate wax from honey, many bee-keepers, and even some larger entrepreneurs, build special bath-houses, in which unprocessed honey, still in the honeycomb, is liquified by the heated air and separated from the honeycomb. But hot air alone is incapable of separating all the honey from the comb – attempts to do so produce bad honey and destroy the wax which is of greater value than the honey. So the final separation is done by soaking the

---

[39]The fundamental source is *Svedeniya*, vols I and II. Korsak, 'Pivovarenie', 8–20; and Pryzhov, *Istoriya kabakov*, 306–10, are both based on *Svedeniya*.

[40]Korsak, 'Pivovarenie', 16.

[41]*Svedeniya*, vol. III, 348–9; see Korsak, 'Pivovarenie', 21–7, on brewing in the western provinces.

honeycomb in hot water. As a result, there is a wax-foundry attached to every honey-separator [*medotopnyya bani*]; in which there are cauldrons where the honey-saturated water is boiled together with special ingredients used to purify it. This is how red mead is produced.[42]

Red mead was sold at 25 kopeks a bucket and was extremely popular in the Ukraine. It was

. . . very sweet, pleasant to the taste, and not at all harmful [as the liquor farmers had claimed it was]. As a result, it was often added to bread as a sort of sauce, and when diluted it was used for the preparation of *varenukha*, a popular Ukrainian drink. However, it turns rapidly, and cannot be produced in large quantities or stored for long.[43]

White mead was also made at wax-foundries, but from already purified honey. It was made only in the towns, and, as it cost 60 kopeks to 1 ruble a bucket, was consumed only by the wealthy. Subject to a high excise and with a limited market, the production of white mead could not possibly expand rapidly.[44]

Thus, neither of the meads popular in the Ukraine was in a strong position to withstand the competition of vodka or even of beer. The results are reflected clearly in the scattered figures on consumption. Between 1835 and 1858, commercial production of mead declined by 50%, and hardly any mead was produced at all in Great Russia.[45] By 1890, 80% of commercial production was in the western provinces and Poland.[46] In the period 1835–58, average annual production was about 100,000 buckets, only about 8% of average annual beer production as reported by the liquor farmers.[47] After 1863, mead production, unlike beer production, declined even further. Mead faced growing competition from mineral waters, fruit drinks and grape wines, so that by 1896 total production was down to about 50,000 buckets, or less than 1% of beer production.[48] Domestic mead production declined during the same period as a result of deforestation and the decline of bee-keeping, and the skills of mead-making slowly disappeared.[49]

So it seems that writers such as Korsak and Pryzhov were right in claiming that it was the nineteenth century, and in particular the period

[42]Korsak, 'Pivovarenie', 85.
[43]*Ibid.*, 85–6.
[44]*Ibid.*
[45]*Svedeniya*, vol. III, 350–1. I have used log trend values for 1835 and 1858.
[46]Brokgauz–Efron, vol. 71 (XXXVI), 911.
[47]*Svedeniya*, vol. III, 350–1. These figures do not tally with those of Korsak, who tried to estimate the amounts not recorded by the farmers.
[48]Kovalevskii, *Rossiya*, 373.
[49]Brokgauz–Efron, vol. 71 (XXXVI), 910.

32 A late nineteenth-century pub. On the left gentlemen play billiards in a room illuminated by candles. On the right two members of the lower class, one wearing shoes of woven bast (*lapti*), are about to drink vodka.

of the heyday of the liquor farm before 1863, which saw the final triumph of vodka as the major alcoholic drink of the mass of the Russian people.

VODKA[50]

Vodka is fascinating because it shows more clearly than any other foodstuff the links between social history and political history – the extent to which the life of the Russian state and the life of the Russian village were intertwined. In this section I will deal with the two aspects separately, discussing first the state's involvement in the liquor trade and then the impact of vodka in the life of the village. But the link between the two levels should never be lost to sight. It was the state's thirst for revenue as much as the peasant's thirst for forgetfulness that

[50]In accordance with accepted English usage I am using the word vodka to cover all common drinks based on spirits, whether diluted by water or flavoured. In nineteenth-century Russian usage, the word *vino* was more common, while the word vodka referred usually to the higher grades of spirits.

made vodka so important at both the national and the local levels of Russian life.

Vodka and the state

As we have seen in earlier chapters, the Russian government had discovered as early as the seventeenth century that the trade in spirits provided a large and reliable source of revenue. By the early nineteenth century revenue from liquor was as much as a quarter of all ordinary revenue and its proportion was still rising. On average, throughout the nineteenth century, the revenue from the liquor trade was 30% of ordinary revenue. Sometimes it reached as high as 46% and sometimes it fell as low as 20% (see Figure 8.2).[51]

Until 1840, the liquor revenue was as large as that of all the major direct taxes (the poll-tax, and rent from state peasants) combined. After 1840 it became the major single source of revenue (see Figure 8.3). And as we have seen, it was vodka which contributed by far the greatest amount of this huge income.[52] Partly because of its sheer scale, the trade in spirits had always posed complex political problems for the government. On the one hand, it was a vital source of revenue; on the other hand, excessive consumption of vodka posed a threat to public morals and public order. By the eighteenth century the interests of landlords and merchants were also involved in this tangle. As Bunge, the Minister of Finance, put it in 1887, vodka involved 'financial issues, agriculture, and popular morality'.[53] First came 'financial issues', or rather the state's need for revenue. Second came 'agriculture', or rather the interests of powerful groups who derived a large income from the liquor trade. These included gentry landlords (mainly in the western provinces) for whom distilling was a valuable source of fodder, and a profitable way of using serf labour or (after 1861) cheap peasant labour. They also included, during the first half of the century, the immensely powerful liquor farmers, amongst whom could be found merchants, gentry and government officials.[54] Third (and the order is not accidental) came 'popular morality', the growing problem of drunkenness and alcoholism – the impact made by the liquor trade on the peasantry and workers. This problem had a moral and paternalistic aspect, to be sure, but one which was taken seriously only when

---

[51] As a proportion of *total* revenue (i.e. including extraordinary sources of income) liquor revenue averaged 25% throughout the century.

[52] The fiscal significance of vodka has survived 1917. See Treml, 'Alcoholism', 380.

[53] *Ministerstvo finansov*, vol. II, 382.

[54] *Svedeniya*, vol. III, 61–6 lists the 145 main liquor farmers in 1859–63.

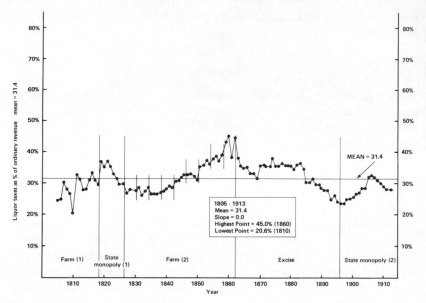

Fig. 8.2 Liquor taxes as proportion of ordinary revenue 1805–1913.
(Sources: Khromov, *Ekonomicheskoe razvitie*, 440–5 and 494–511, based on figures from *Ministerstvo finansov*.)

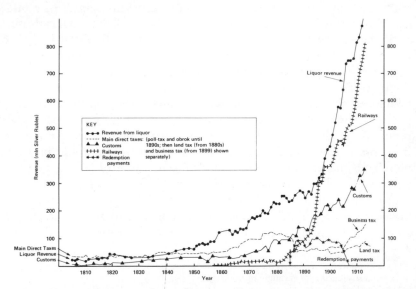

Fig. 8.3 Major sources of government revenue 1805–1913.
(Source: Khromov, *Ekonomicheskoe*, 440–5 and 494–511.)

drunkenness began to seem both a threat to public order and a potential drain on the economy. Two of these pressures favoured the extension of the liquor trade; the third favoured its contraction, so it is hardly surprising to find that, by and large, it was the pressures for expansion that usually won.[55] They reflected, after all, the interests of some of the most influential and wealthy members of the Russian ruling classes.

The dilemma the government faced is evident throughout the century in the contradictory and confused statements it made on the subject of alcohol, such as the following remark made by a Minister of Finance, Count Kankrin, in 1826:

If in recent years drunkenness has declined, this is due above all to changing attitudes, but it is desirable that the moderate consumption of liquor by the simple people should increase, for, given declining exports of grain in a country where agriculture is the major occupation, and there are few towns, excess grain can only be used by distilling it.[56]

The solution favoured both by the government and by many idealistic reformers, was to change the consumption patterns of the peasantry; like the upper classes, they should learn to drink regularly but in small amounts. In this way, total consumption would increase and the problem of drunkenness would diminish. As it turned out, though, the consumption patterns of the Russian peasant were not so malleable; the point of drinking was, after all, to get drunk. So the same dilemmas that haunted Count Kankrin continue to haunt the Soviet government today.

In the nineteenth century the government used three distinct methods for extracting revenue from the liquor trade. Until 1863, the state continued the liquor farm, except for a brief period between 1819 and 1827 when it experimented with a state monopoly. In 1863, the liquor trade was freed, and an excise system was introduced. This survived to the end of the century. But in 1894 Count Witte began introducing a state monopoly, province by province, and by 1902 the state had taken full control over the liquor trade.

[55] *Plus ça change* ... Vladimir Treml writes of the Soviet government that the importance of the turnover tax on alcohol 'is so great that no anti-alcohol measure can be contemplated without considering its impact on tax earnings. And, needless to say, the higher the absolute ruble effect of a planned measure, the more careful the government must be, and the more objections the powerful Ministry of Finance is likely to raise.' Treml, 'Alcoholism', 382. Of course, the Soviet government is by no means alone in drawing a significant amount of revenue from liquor sales.

[56] Cited in *Ministerstvo finansov*, vol. I, 295–6. See p. 315 below, for a similar remark by a later Minister of Finance.

After 1754, as we have seen, liquor distilling became a monopoly of the gentry and the crown, thereby excluding the merchants from an industry in which they had been extremely active. But this may not have been so vast a misfortune for the merchantry. They were not excluded from the retailing of vodka and it was here, under the farming system, that the real fortunes were to be made in the nineteenth century. Retail prices could often be as high as 1,000% of the production costs, and in the late 1850s about 150 liquor farmers earned between them 40–80 million rubles a year. The state's revenue from the trade at this time (that is, the amount paid to the government by the farmers) was about 100 million, and another 40 million went to the landlords who distilled most of the vodka.[57]

With profits like these being made, one is not surprised to find that the trade was extremely corrupt. The vodka (which was officially supposed to contain between 40% and 50% pure alcohol by volume) was watered down sometimes two or three times; the food sold in taverns was powerfully spiced with pepper and salt to increase the thirst of the drinkers; the number of retail outlets and the hours during which they were open were illegally increased; peasants were allowed to offer their own goods as pledges for debts incurred while drinking.[58] In 1819, the government was informed that the liquor farmers of Kaluga and Orel provinces had been using false measures, charged excessive prices, and added jimson weed (*durman*), and 'other poisonous additives' to the liquor they sold. In Perm' province, impurities discovered in vodka included soap, copper and cupric oxide. The last two ingredients were probably dissolved from the copper containers used for distilling.[59]

It was in the 1840s and 1850s that the corruption was at its worst as increasing attempts were made by smugglers to breach the liquor farmers' lucrative monopoly in Great Russia.[60] Smuggling flourished most exotically on the borders of the privileged provinces. Here, cheap vodka was carried across into the central Russian provinces from the 'privileged' west. By the 1840s and 1850s, government anti-smuggling detachments found themselves facing small private armies of smugglers:

---

[57] *Svedeniya*, vol. IV, 278–1, 455–61. On the division of the spoils, see Korsak, 'Vinokurenie', 353, 356, 374, which is based on *Trudy*, vol. I, no. 12, 4.

[58] Druzhinin, *Gosudarstvennye krest'yane*, vol. I, 370. On the internal structure of the liquor farm, see *Svedeniya*, vol. III, 73–128.

[59] Pryzhov, *Istoriya kabakov*, 270. On the subject of adulteration of vodka, see Medvedev, *O khlebnom vine*, and Blosfel'd, 'O p'yanstve'.

[60] *Ministerstvo finansov*, vol. I, 298.

In Kursk, Smolensk and Orel provinces, there appeared whole bands of smugglers, sometimes with 100 men, and these attacked the anti-smuggling detachments and army units ..'. In 1847, on the boundaries of Mogilev and Smolensk provinces [on the border of the liquor farm] a well-armed group of 200 smugglers with 115 carts, attacked an anti-smuggling detachment. Other groups of 35 or 50 men also came to blows with the anti-smuggling detachments, but all these attacks were repulsed.[61]

Right at the border, almost everyone was involved in smuggling.

In 277 villages of Krasna, Roslavl, Elna and Proech'e districts of Smolensk province, almost all the inhabitants are involved in smuggling. They transport the vodka, usually in large groups armed with stakes and rifles, accompanied by vagabonds and army deserters, and not only do they forcibly prevent the anti-smuggling detachments and army units from carrying out their duties, but they even exchange fire with them on occasions, or attack them directly. The passion for smuggling has also had a *terrible influence* [italics in original] on the very guardians of order; in many areas the connivance of the local police is obvious.[62]

The government, of course, while aware of the corruption, had to support the liquor farmers. As one of the most enthusiastic defenders of the system remarked during the reign of Alexander I: 'No other major source of revenue enters the treasury so regularly, punctually, and easily as the revenue from the liquor farm; indeed its regular receipt on a fixed date each month greatly eases the task of finding cash for other expenditures.' He added that the costs of collection were too insignificant to merit attention, and that the system ran better than any other liquor tax in Europe.[63]

Nevertheless, there were costs of at least three different kinds, and they seem to have increased by the middle of the century. First, the huge (and largely invisible) profits made by the liquor farmers were potential revenue lost to the state. Second, the corruption associated with the system affected government officials as well as the agents of the farmers. And third, there was the social cost of increased drunkenness as the farmers, with the tacit support of the government, encouraged the rural population to drink more and more.

Between 1830 and 1860 the government was clearly letting a lot of potential liquor tax revenue slip through its fingers. Liquor tax revenue declined both as a proportion of total revenue (Figure 8.2), and in relation to the trend for the century as a whole (Figure 8.4). (The slight

[61]Pryzhov, *Istoriya kabakov*, 285.

[62]*Ibid.* In 1858 there was even a short (and very bad) novel published on the subject of corruption in the liquor trade: 'The Liquor Farm Affair'. Elagin, 'Otkupnoe delo'.

[63]*Ministerstvo finansov*, vol. I, 110–11, from a report by the Minister of Finance, Golubtsov.

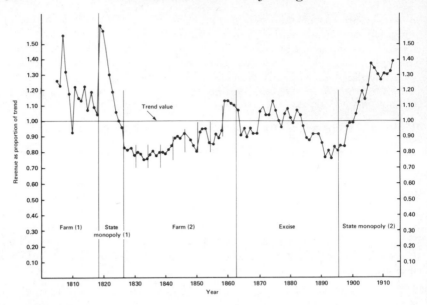

Fig. 8.4 Revenue from liquor taxes as proportion of trend 1805–1913.
(Source: Khromov, *Ekonomicheskoe*, 440–5 and 494–511.)

rise in liquor revenues in the 1850s reflects the boom following the Crimean war, which encouraged the liquor farmers to bid exaggeratedly high prices for the liquor farm at the four-yearly auctions.)

Equally important from the government's point of view, was the fact that the majority of local government officials were paid unofficial salaries by the liquor farmers. To a government committed, since 1856, to fundamental reforms in all areas of Russian life, such a situation was intolerable. K.K. Grot, who was governor of Samara province in the 1850s and became a key figure in the 1863 reform, found that the government lost a significant degree of control over its own officials through this systematic bribery. As long as the government itself paid inadequate salaries:

Provincial and district officials . . . were forced to find lawful or unlawful means of supplementing their salaries. The main supplement of this kind was the regular salary received by all police officials and most government officials of any consequence, from the liquor farmers. As a result, the liquor farmers acquired vast influence over the local authorities and their corrupting influence enabled them to use a vast range of corrupt devices for raising their own profits without fear of punishment.[64]

[64]'K.K. Grot', vol. I, 8.

Table 8.3. *Expenses paid by liquor farmers*

	Provincial Town Rubles	District
To Governor for improving the town and for Kindergartens	3,200	...
To Governor's chancery	1,200	...
Mayor	...	420
Secretary of Police	300	200
Commissaries of Police (3)	720	240
Precinct police officers (6)	360	120
District police captain	600	420
Circuit judge	500	420
Commissaries of rural police (3)	720	540
Permanent assessor	300	240
Secretary of rural police court	300	240
President of Exchequer Court	2,000	...
Councillor for Department of Liquor	600	500
Head clerk and bureau	500	...
Overseer of liquor	600	420
	11,900	3,760

How much money was involved is suggested by the tariff shown in Table 8.3, of 'extraordinary' expenses paid out by the liquor farmers to provincial government officials.[65]

The extent of corruption had been shown clearly during the brief experiment with a state monopoly in the 1820s. To administer the monopoly the government had to hire many ex-employees of the liquor farm, and their methods were naturally passed over to the state officials who now administered the trade in spirits.[66]

It is the duty of a vice-governor to visit the different distilleries and kabaks or gin-shops, to ascertain whether the spirits be adulterated: having already received his bribe from the farmer-general of the province, he of course finds no fault. The latter of these gentlemen then makes his own visit, to examine whether the retailers have not still more adulterated it than was allowed in the first instance: the affirmative is a matter of course, but, on a division of spoils no fault is found. Lastly comes the secretary or clerk of the farmer-general, who finds the spirit still further adulterated and who, having in his hands the

[65] *Svedeniya*, vol. III, 114–115. This information was presumably leaked by a disgruntled official of the liquor farm to the government commission set up to discuss reform.
[66] Kankrin blamed corrupt officials for the failure of the experiment with a state monopoly. *Ministerstvo finansov*, vol. I, 119.

33 Official business round before the holiday, 1858. The non-commissioned officer of police, accompanied by one of his junior ranks, who appears already well-laden, inspects a butcher's shop, his hand lovingly caressing a fat joint, in this popular print. Bribery and, in this case, extortion, were not confined to alcohol.

power of punishment even to the withdrawal of the license, becomes a partici-pator of the last spoils.[67]

Cochrane estimated that the vodka sold in kabaks in 1820 was often doubly or trebly watered down, which was why it was necessary for those who wanted to get drunk to consume huge amounts. The peas-ants themselves had many nicknames for watered-down liquor – s'il-

[67]Cochrane, *Narrative*, 220.

vous-play; French fourteenth class; tsar's madeira; how have I offended you?; thinner than water; cheap; reason for sale; orphan's tears; tongue-untier; don't ask for purity; oh to be drunk!; liquor's auntie; scalds the mouth but leaves you sober.[68]

In 1863, the government avoided these mistakes by hiring totally new (and very well-paid) officials to staff the offices which supervised the collection of the newly introduced excise. In this way, they avoided much of the corruption of the old system.[69]

The third problem was that of what contemporaries called 'drunkenness' [*p'yanstvo*]. We have only approximate figures on per capita consumption for this period, but it seems clear that consumption levels increased, particularly in the 1850s (see Figure 8.1). But the real problem was not so much the absolute quantities consumed – per capita consumption was lower than in most European countries – as the ways in which it was consumed.[70] Instead of drinking small quantities regularly, peasants confined their drinking to a few festive occasions on which they drank to oblivion. But the spread of a cash economy, and the growing number of rural taverns increased the opportunities for getting drunk without any particular ceremonial excuse. Karamzin observed in 1824:

I remember clearly the days of my youth and I remember that in those days it was only on the main annual festivals that the peasants celebrated and got drunk, on either homemade beer or on vodka bought in the towns. Now everyday is a festival, and you find everywhere helpful servants under the royal eagle, ready to relieve peasants of their money, their mind, and their health.[71]

In the western provinces the problem was peculiarly acute. In the absence of the monopolistic practices of the liquor farm, competition kept prices much lower than in Great Russia. In any case, most landlords distilled in order to use up surplus grain and to produce the mash [*barda*] which was much valued as fodder. The same landlords were also allowed to retail vodka so they had a direct interest in establishing drink-shops (known here as *shinki*). Thus, distilleries were much more common in the west (in 1860 there were 723 in 26 provinces of Great Russia, and 4,437 in 16 provinces of the west); and so were drink-shops. In the west, there were 30 for every 10,000 inhabitants as op-

---

[68]Pryzhov, *Istoriya kabakov*, 1, 287, citing Dal', *Poslovitsy*.
[69]'K.K. Grot', vol. 1, 181–6.
[70]At the beginning of the twentieth century, per capita figures for alcohol consumption (in all forms) for different European countries were: France, 18 litres; Switzerland, 14; Russia, 4; Sweden, 3.3; Norway, 2.2. Borodin, *Itogi*, 4.
[71]Pryzhov, *Istoriya kabakov*, 272.

posed to 5 in Great Russia.[72] 'On all small and large roads leading to towns and settlements, on all roads to manufactures, and mills, and even in the woods, in fact anywhere you can reach by road, there are little homes which sell vodka.'[73] When he travelled in Russia in 1843, Baron Haxthausen found that the peasants of White Russia were 'completely demoralised and enervated by the use of brandy'.[74] One of the inspectors who examined the condition of the state peasantry in the late 1830s described the situation in Chernigov province in Dickensian language:

Here the children begin to drink from their earliest years and continue all their life. Their parents give them vodka with bread, and they soon acquire a taste for it and begin to drink it in large quantities. Everyone drinks – the young, the middle-aged, and the old; the men and the women. In the *shinki* there are people of both sexes drinking together with abandon and often forgetting about the children they have left at home with a crust of bread. They drink without regard to place or time, whenever and wherever the opportunity arises. They drink because they are rich, and they drink because of their poverty; they drink in happiness and in sorrow; and always they drink to excess. On feast days all the *shinki* on all the large and small roads and in every village and hamlet are full of drinkers, day and night. And even during work days, these places open early in the morning until late at night and are rarely empty. Those who have ruined themselves through drink will wait whole days in the drinking houses hoping that someone will buy them a drink, and they are rarely disappointed. Many, while on the road, regard it as a matter of honour to visit every drinking house they pass. As a result it is common to see on the roads drunken travellers sleeping in their carts which are pulled by horses who do not know where they are going. Officials, travelling on commandeered horses, say that the horses know all the *shinki* that their owners visit so well that they will automatically turn aside and stop each time they reach one.[75]

Not surprisingly, in the early nineteenth century consumption levels of vodka were also higher in the western provinces than in Great Russia, as Figure 8.1 shows. The scale of the problem was clearly immense: 'From generation to generation the mass of the peasantry became accustomed to the constant consumption of vodka, which tempted them everywhere and on every occasion of communal or private life. Drunkenness became rooted in peasant life; it became an inevitable habit, reinforced by custom, a totally natural phenomenon.'[76]

[72]*Svedeniya*, vol. III, 49–51, 61.
[73]Druzhinin, *Gosudarstvennye krest'yane*, vol. I, 374.
[74]Haxthausen, *The Russian Empire*, vol. I, 68. 'Brandy' continued to be a common translation, strictly of *goryachoe vino*, but usually of any type of vodka.
[75]Druzhinin, *Gosudarstvennye krest'yane*, vol. I, 374.
[76]*Ibid*, vol. I, 373–40.

In Great Russia, within the area of the liquor farm, drink-shops were more common on the land of state peasants, as most private landlords refused to allow them on their land for fear their peasants would all become drunkards (even if the same landlord often distilled surplus grain for sale elsewhere). There were on average 4 drink-shops for every 10,000 male souls on serf lands, and 13 for every 10,000 male souls on state peasant lands. It was in the central industrial region that drink-shops were most common in the 1840s – in Moscow, Pskov, Orel, Tver', Novgorod, and Tula provinces.[77]

Clearly, during this period, it was in the interests not just of the liquor farmers and retailers to increase consumption of alcohol, but also of the landlords and the state itself. The state was not always the most subtle of these groups. In 1823, for example, worried by declining revenue during the brief experiment with a state monopoly, the government made it obligatory for retailers to sell at least as much liquor as the average of the previous three years.[78]

So, while hard evidence is lacking, there is some evidence to suggest that the problem of rural drunkenness grew steadily worse during the period of the liquor farm and that it did so largely as a result of growing pressure to consume hard liquor from the liquor farmers, the state, and many landlords.

By the 1850s the government was no longer willing to tolerate the various defects of the liquor farm and it would probably have abolished it sooner than it did, had it not been for the outbreak of war in 1853.[79] As it was, the Ministry of Finance dragged its heels, fearing a decline in revenue, and was brought round only by a combination of factors in the late 1850s, of which the most important were the liquor riots of 1859 (see below, pp. 325–6), a vigorous press campaign against the liquor farm, and the widespread enthusiasm for reform provoked by the government's decision to abolish serfdom. Ya.I. Rostovtsev, the President of the Editing Commission which prepared the statutes on emancipation, is reputed to have extracted from the tsar', while on his deathbed, a solemn promise 'to place this question [the abolition of the liquor farm] on the agenda immediately after the emancipation of the serfs'.[80] The case for reform was argued vigorously in the State Council by A.P. Zablotskii, who put the moral argument: 'The government cannot and must not lose sight of the effects of the farming system on the moral and economic life of the

[77]*Ibid.*, vol. I, 369, and *Svedeniya*, vol. III, 48–51.
[78]*Ministerstvo finansov*, vol. I, 119, and cf. ch. 4 above.
[79]*Ibid.*, vol. I.
[80]P.P. Semenov, obituary of K.K. Grot, 220.

34 Cartoon on the proposed abolition of the liquor farm, 1859. The bottle of vodka informs the farm that public opinion has decided to do away with him in the name of temperance. The farm, in despair, wanted to utter the well-known saying: *all is lost save honour*, but stumbled on the last word and was unable to say it.

people.'[81] For once, the moral issues seemed to have taken precedence, but in reality little had changed.

The new system abolished the liquor farm and established instead a uniform excise on the production of liquor.[82] Distillers now had to pay the excise, and retailers to pay a licence fee, but apart from this the trade in spirits was freed from almost all forms of government regulation. However, within a few years the government once again began to regulate the trade more carefully.

[81]*Ministerstvo finansov*, vol. I, 514.
[82]*Ibid.*, vol. I, 516–20, for details of the new system.

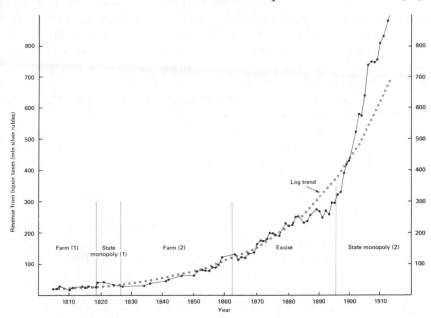

Fig. 8.5 Revenue from liquor taxes (mln silver rubles) 1808–1913.
(Source: Khromov, *Ekonomicheskoe*, 440–5 and 494–511.)

From the fiscal point of view, the reform was an undoubted success. It seems to have allowed the state to garner much revenue which previously was diverted to the liquor farmers, and in this sense the reform can be seen as a way of excluding the merchantry from a share in the huge revenues generated by the liquor trade. As Figures 8.2 and 8.4 and 8.5 show, during the period 1860–85 liquor revenues were usually higher than the trend for the century, and they constituted a larger than average share of government revenue. The new system also seemed for a time to have ended the huge system of corruption associated with the liquor farm.

As a measure against drunkenness the reform was less successful in the early years at least. The reduction in government controls led to the appearance of new, cheaper vodka (rapidly christened 'cheapie' [*deshevka*]) and to an increase in the number of retail outlets, particularly in the areas formerly under the liquor farm.[83] This increase is certainly in part fictitious – outlets which had been illegal before or hidden by

[83]Skarzynski, *L'alcool*, 50; Pryzhov, *Istoriya kabakov*, 317.

the liquor farmers, could now exist legally.[84] But there *was* an increase and, combined with the decline in the price of spirits, this probably led to an increase in consumption. A Smolensk landlord commented in the early 1870s that, 'much vodka is consumed locally as a result of the increase in the number of drinking establishments'.[85]

However, the increase in consumption in the central provinces was eventually counterbalanced by a decline in the western provinces. Here, the introduction of the new excise meant the abolition of the region's 'privileged' status, and the artificially low liquor prices that that entailed. After a year or two, the average consumption levels for the whole of European Russia settled down to about 10–12 litres per capita (see Figure 8.1). However, the government was sufficiently concerned at the initial rise in consumption to reintroduce controls of various kinds. It tried to make drink-shops as unattractive as possible, thereby beginning a process which, by the end of the century, would destroy the *kabak* as a social institution. No food was to be sold; there was to be no furniture except for the bar itself; and drinking houses were to be kept as far as possible from institutions such as churches, schools, courts, or anywhere else where there might be large groups of people.[86] The eventual decline in consumption under the excise system may have been caused in part by such measures, but a more important cause was probably the growing impoverishment of the Russian peasantry as a whole. A third possibility is that the decline was fictitious, reflecting merely the increased skill with which distillers hid from the government the real amounts they were producing.[87]

Thus, apart from an unsteady period at the beginning of the new system, it seems to have achieved the delicate trick of reducing consumption while both increasing government revenue and reducing the amount of corruption. In spite of this, in 1895 the government embarked upon a new reform designed to establish a total state monopoly of the trade in liquor. It was introduced first in four eastern provinces – Perm', Orenburg, Ufa and Samara. By 1902 it had been introduced to all provinces and the excise system had in effect ended.

There were several reasons for introducing the new system, and here I will mention them briefly as the subject of the state monopoly really takes us out of the nineteenth century.[88] The state itself claimed that

---

[84]Pryzhov, *Istoriya kabakov*, 309.

[85]*Doklad*, 277.

[86]Skarzynski, *L'alcool*, 93; Pryzhov, *Istoriya kabakov*, 316.

[87]See Nol'de, *Piteinoe delo*.

[88]On the liquor monopoly, see Fridman, *Vinnaya monopoliya*, and Pechenuk, 'Temperance and Revenue Raising'.

the reform was primarily concerned to tackle the problem of drunkenness. In introducing the reform in 1894, Sergei Witte declared that, 'the reform must be directed, first of all towards increasing popular sobriety, and only then can it concern itself with the interests of the treasury'.[89] And the details of the reform suggest strongly that the government *was* concerned with the social problem of drunkenness. The traditional Russian drink-shop, for example, was in effect abolished, as liquor could no longer be drunk on the premises of the retail outlet. These were also made deliberately sober in tone. The public room was to be bare of furniture, and separated by a grill from the areas occupied by the tavern keeper; pictures of the Emperor and of saints were to be placed on the walls; and customers were to leave as soon as they had completed their purchases.[90] Further, the government was now better able to control the number of retail outlets, and to check adulteration by selling liquor in sealed bottles, and by setting up special laboratories to test quality.[91]

But, as always, fiscal objectives were by no means neglected. In the late 1880s, the Minister of Finance had argued, ingenuously, that private retailers had an interest in encouraging drunkenness. They encouraged 'the fatal passion of the population for excessive consumption of liquor and thereby paralyse the measures taken by the state to reduce drunkenness'. The state, however, derived an income from liquor in ways that did not have such harmful consequences, he continued: 'the main source of government revenue from liquor is not the abnormal consumption ... which is justified by our northern climate and which produces more revenue per soul for the treasury'.[92]

More important, probably, was the growing evidence that once again an unnecessarily large amount of the revenue from the liquor trade was still passing into private hands.[93] One problem was that local cartels of distributors had begun to form, which enforced artificially high retail prices, and as the state taxed at the point of production, these monopoly profits all went into private hands. As the government put it: 'the high prices of liquor adversely affected the flow of government revenue, and placed a heavy burden on the rural population'.[94] Another problem was that distillers became more and more adept at

[89]Borodin, *Itogi*, 6.
[90]Skarzynski, *L'alcool*, 121.
[91]*Ibid.*, 101–2, 119, 171.
[92]*Ministerstvo finansov*, vol. II, 195–6.
[93]*Ibid.*, vol. II, 195.
[94]*Ibid.*, vol. II, 192.

hiding from the government the true quantities they distilled.[95] Whatever the reason, it is clear that from the mid-1880s, the revenue from liquor began to decline both as a proportion of ordinary government revenue, and with respect to the trend for the century as a whole (see Figures 8.2 and 8.5). And whatever the aim of the reform, its most spectacular achievement was to sharply reverse this trend from about 1897 (until the new trend was reversed again with the introduction of total prohibition in 1914). So, once again, a shake-up in the administration of the liquor revenues paid off handsomely in fiscal terms, even if its effects on popular drinking habits are less clear.[96] Presumably this is a reflection of the general principle that tax dodgers take time to find the dodges available in any particular fiscal system.

Vodka and the village

Vodka was the single most important item in the peasantry's festive diet. It was a basic ingredient of all celebrations, of church festivals, family celebrations and so on. It was also a sort of seal on ceremonial – vodka was drunk when a deal was made or a bargain struck. And vodka was used to maintain networks of patronage and to manipulate village politics. It was widely used as a medicine and an anaesthetic, and it could also be quite ruinous.

Because of its overwhelmingly social significance, the purchase of vodka is probably best regarded as a deduction from the household's 'ceremonial' fund rather than its 'subsistence' fund. This is why money often seemed available for vodka even when a family was near starvation. Andrei Zablotskii wrote of a village he visited in the early 1840s that, 'the peasants had no bread, their families had not eaten for days, but the drinking did not diminish according to several of the liquor dealers'.[97]

The connection with ceremonial is mentioned by almost all sources. Thus, in Orel province in the 1890s, a reporter observed that:

Much vodka is drunk, but it is drunk only on festivals or on days of special communal or family events, such as marriages, christenings, leasing of prop-

---

[95]Nol'de, *Piteinoe delo*; and Berezin, *Na sluzhbe zlomu delu*, a fascinating exposé of the methods used by distillers to avoid paying excise, written by an ex-distiller who decided to reveal all.
[96]The impact of the liquor monopoly was debated at length in the years that followed. See e.g. *Ministerstvo finansov*, vol. II, 530–6, and Kovalevskii, *Rossiya*, 921, for the government's side of the argument; and Borodin, *Itogi*, for the views of the increasingly influential temperance movement. The most careful contemporary study is Fridman, *Vinnaya monopoliya*. See also Hutchinson, 'Science, Politics and the Alcohol Problem'.
[97]Zablotskii, *Graf P.D. Kiselev*, vol. IV, 309. On the ceremonial fund, see Wolf, *Peasants*, 7–9.

erty, the hiring of shepherds, services of thanksgiving and so on. On such days vodka is often consumed in huge quantities and the drinkers are reduced to a state of terrible intoxication. Everyone drinks – men, women and even adolescents of 14. On ordinary days when vodka could well be valuable and pleasant, it is not used at all because no one can afford it.[98]

In Perm' province in the 1860s male peasants often consumed up to 25 litres of vodka a year, mostly in huge doses on special occasions: 'The main ones are Easter week, in March or April; the setting out of salt or metal caravans in May; the harvest in July or August; then Christmas, and the Christmas holidays; and the period of village weddings and Shrovetide, that is the end of December, January, and the beginning of February'.[99] Festivals, parties, and the vodka drinking that accompanied them were indeed the major form of entertainment in rural life. They offered a much-needed break from the grinding routine of ordinary life.

[Vodka] is all drunk at a few village festivals, for which each householder prepares with special care, and saves up money, and often sells his last reserves of oats and even, sometimes, of rye as long as he can celebrate the festival 'like a human being' [po liudski]. On these festivals, friends and relatives gather together and often during two or three days the whole crowd moves from one house to another or even one village to another drinking to oblivion. Given the complete absence of other diversions, and the dull monotony of rural life, these festivals are the only diversion from a hard and unattractive world. So the significant consumption of vodka during festivals has . . . primarily a psychological significance, a sort of compensation for the absence of entertainments and the lack of satisfactions in their mental and moral world.[100]

As we have seen, the spread of drink-shops made it possible to drink even on ordinary days. The drink-shops had little need to attract customers with anything more than vodka itself. Engel'gardt described a drink-shop in Smolensk province:

The little drink-shop was in an old, tumbledown little half-rotten hut, shabbier than any poor peasant's hut. The interior was 6 metres long and as many wide. Most of this space was taken up with the stove, a hovel for the owners, a bar, and shelves with crockery, cleaned bottles, balsam – a pleasant and healthy drink – and all sorts of rubbish. This left for the customers a space about 2 metres by 3 metres, with benches along the wall and a small table. Inside the drink-shop was dirty, dark, full of pipe smoke, cold, crowded, and always full. As the saying goes: 'pies not icons make a fine house' [ne krasna

[98]*Opyt*, 49.
[99]*Materialy*, v. 18, Permskaya gub., vol. I, 334–5.
[100]Skibnevskii, 232.

35 Outside a country inn. Two men dance to a balalaika, while the men in the background drink vodka.

izba uglami, a krasna pirogami] – and not only pies, but rather the hospitality of the hosts. The pies were the sort you get in any drink-shop. The liquor was ordinary, green vodka, 'excise' liquor, lower than the official strength, not even proper liquor, but 'bitter sweet vodka' as the label stuck on the barrel proclaimed; there were sardines, bread rolls, and confectioneries at 20 kopeks a pound.[101]

But even in these surroundings, the act of drinking was not devoid of ceremonial. 'Matov filled a small glass with vodka, crossed himself, blew into the glass (to get rid of the devil which sits on top of the vodka), said "Your Health!", drank a bit, and, after filling the glass to the brim, handed it to me with a slight bow.'[102]

Drinking was bound in very closely with the economic life of the village. In Smolensk in the early 1870s: 'If they earn something or sell something, the first thing they do is get drunk.'[103] In Ryazan' in the

[101]Engel'gardt, *Iz derevni*, 232–3.
[102]*Ibid.*, 78–9.
[103]*Doklad*, 226.

1860s: 'Grain liquor is very common in spite of its price, particularly on market days Every sale and purchase is accompanied by a drink in the vodka booth.'[104]

The economic and the festive aspect of vodka were often closely intertwined. This link is shown most clearly in the important village institution of work-parties. The institution existed throughout Slavonic Europe. It was known in Great Russia as *pomochi* (from the root *pomoch'*, to help), in the Ukraine as *toloka*, and as *talaka* in White Russia.[105] A household which had to get an urgent task done, for which it did not have enough labour, would hold a work-party, inviting friends and relatives to help them with their work, in return for a meal and some vodka. In 1853, in Orenburg these were:

> . . . gatherings of a large number of workers, invited by a head of household who has to complete an urgent task, such as the hay harvest, threshing, or the transport of wood for building a house, etc. Those who work are never paid, but a day of *pomoch'* always ends with a large meal and the distribution of aqua vitae, and these prove far more attractive than payment in money.[106]

The logic of the institution is best explained in a conversation that Engel'gardt had with his bailiff, Stepan, in Smolensk province in the 1870s. Engel'gardt wanted to hire some workers to repair a bridge, but he was told he would find it impossible to hire local workers, even for high wages.

> You are doing it like a Petersburger, all for money. You cannot do it that way here.
> But how can I do it?
> Why hire anyone? Simply invite them to work *na toloku*. They will come to work as a favour [*iz chesti*] willingly . . . Of course, you will have to give each of them a glass of vodka.
> But surely it's simpler to work for money? Everything's clearer then.
> Maybe it's simpler for a German, but not for us. It's not 'neighbourly' to take money from you, but everyone will come to work as a favour – take my word for it . . . Just give them a glass of vodka each, and, of course, as the householder you yourself must come and work. It's not even a matter of 'vodka' – they would do it purely as a favour, but vodka makes the work merrier.[107]

A relationship mediated by money was 'German', foreign. It was

---

[104]*Materialy*, v. 19, Ryazanskaya gub., 399.
[105]Pascal, 'L'entr'aide paysanne'. These were the pre-Soviet ancestors of the modern Soviet days of voluntary work, or *subbotniki*; and many of the rituals associated with the *subbotnik* are best explained by reference to that institution's rural ancestry.
[106]Le Play, *Ouvriers*, vol. ii.
[107]Engel'gardt, *Iz derevni*, 78–9.

finished once the money was paid, and left no sense of continuing mutual obligations. But a relationship mediated by food, and above all by vodka, was, because of its very indefiniteness, a relationship which was bound to continue, and in which either side would be prepared to help the other in a crisis, a relationship involving hospitality and mutual aid, a human relationship. Stepan explained:

Your dam breaks, and you immediately try to hire people for cash – that means you do not want to live on neighbourly terms – you want everything on monetary terms, on 'German' terms. Today you want a dam repaired – you pay money. Tomorrow we will want something from you – you will demand money from us. Surely it's better to get on as neighbours – we will help you and you won't harm us.

That the vodka symbolised something more than mere neighbourliness and something closer to rustic insurance, is clear from the fact that poor peasants, with little to offer in return except a meal and some vodka, often had trouble finding friends willing to help them 'as a favour'.

No one works as a favour, *na toloku* or *na pomochi* for a poor peasant. It is a different matter with a noble, on whom the peasant depends for wood, hay, pasture, mushrooms and in case of his cattle damaging the noble's crops – or with a rich peasant from whom one may have to beg some bread in spring . . . Only close relatives go *na toloku* to a poor peasant without demanding wages – other people will go only in order to have the right to ask for help in return.[108]

The institution seems to have worked best in the more rural provinces, where the natural economy of the village could still resist the inroads of the monetary economy.[109] Here people worked hard at a work-party, the entertainment was good, and the atmosphere festive.

In the evening, the householder or his agent invites his neighbours to a work-party, praising the party and promising plenty of vodka and good food. In the morning, at dawn, those invited assemble at his house and, after a substantial drink of vodka and some snacks [*zakuski*], they set to work. Women are invited for cutting and selecting flax, men for mowing and carting manure. Men's work-parties are different from women's only in that the men drink more vodka and do not sing, but chat, and tell stories as they work.[110]

Women's work-parties were generally accompanied by singing and also by half-pagan rituals.[111] When Engel'gardt's cook, Avdotiya, in-

[108]*Ibid.*, 198.
[109]In rural Perm', Pierre Pascal witnessed *pomochi* as late as 1927–8, on the eve of collectivisation.
[110]*Etnograficheskii sbornik*, vol. II, 238.
[111]*Ibid.*, vol. II, 237.

vited neighbouring women to help chop up cabbage or peel beetroot, 'She supplies vodka, bakes pies, makes as fine a meal as she can . . . the best sort of hospitality one could ask. The participants always work excellently, especially the women . . . The work is accompanied with laughter, jokes, songs, gaiety. The work itself is done as a sort of joke . . . It is not even called "working" but "helping".'[112]

But in more industrial provinces the institution seems to have been in decline; it was less common and those who took part seemed more conscious of the wages they were surrendering and therefore more determined to enjoy the party than to help their neighbour. A very full description from a Yaroslav village in the 1840s shows well how monetary calculations began to be applied to the institution with the undermining of the natural economy. In this region, the advantages of holding a day of *pomochi* were becoming dubious, and the institution itself was only resorted to by those in great difficulty.

A good work-party for, say, 50 men, will cost at least 60 paper rubles [*c.* 17 silver]. One must buy at least 2 buckets of vodka, and provide at least 35 buckets of beer, which costs at least 15 rubles; the remaining 24 rubles go on beef, wheaten-flour, bread, and other preparations for the work-party . . . So, each worker costs the householder about 1 ruble 20 k.[113]

And this was in an area where workers could often be hired at 1 ruble a day if one had the time and resources to find them. The quality of the work performed at the work-party was often poor, as most of those involved were far more interested in the party than the work.

Those invited to work-parties are only casual workers, and after a little work, they want to eat and carouse. The local people go to work-parties, it seems, less to help their neighbours than to enjoy themselves and get drunk. And the householders themselves, who need the work done, invite people not to work, but rather by tempting them with their hospitality, with vodka and beer . . . 'Please come and enjoy our hospitality; there will be plenty of vodka, and beer for our guests; only, do us a favour, don't ignore our request; help us with the other Christians we have invited to finish some jobs.'

The result was that little work was done, and the whole event turned into a party, pure and simple. 'I have often seen how during the day, when they should be working, the guests just fool around when the host is absent. Lunch time comes and they sit eating for a long time. Then, perhaps, clouds will appear and rain will either hinder the work,

---

[112]Engel'gardt, *Iz derevni*, 75.
[113]*Etnograficheskii sbornik*, vol. II, 25–7. The author is the village priest; hence the moralistic tone of the description that follows.

or, more often, send them all to their own homes.' But, a success or not, the host is committed to a party and all that entails.

But when it is evening the guests all appear for the party, all dressed up and singing songs. Here, they drink until supper. Songs, dancing, jumping, rowdy conversations, shouts and often fights and arguments are all played out to the tune of the harmonica or balalaika. In short, the place is in uproar, and the hosts would be best off running away. The 'helpers' don't listen to their pleas to calm down. What guests! Then, when many are already half asleep, and some have already slept and woken for the next round, the supper begins. At supper the food and drink is the sort you get only on festivals, and this is what the guests are waiting for. Indeed, if the food and cooking are as good as on festivals, the amounts available are far greater. Nevertheless, the guests spend less time eating and drinking than pouring drink and grovelling on the floor. After supper, the same shouting and noise, the same leaping about, until they all totter and collapse where they stood.

But even this does not end the sufferings of the host. Next morning the householder is obliged to tour the village and offer his hungover guests a hair of the dog, to finish off what was left. Returning home, the host finds the previous day's guests already assembled:

They bow to him and he thanks them for the work they did yesterday, for reaping and mowing, but he says nothing of the dishes and utensils they have broken. He offers them the remains of yesterday's offerings, and the last drops of vodka or beer. Having polished this off, the guests go home and relax as long as they need to, that is, until they have sobered up.

The direct political significance of vodka at village level is most evident from its role in rural elections. Here vodka, or rather the wealth necessary to dispense large quantities of it, was clearly a source of political power – a powerful bribe and a useful device for controlling elections. In state peasant villages in the late 1830s,

For several days before the date appointed for the commune meeting, anyone wishing to secure a significant post, such as commune head, will tour the village with a barrel of vodka, denouncing the previous head, or making promises about what he will do, if he is made head. Finally, the commune gathers together without any sort of order or any clear division into parties, but always with plenty of vodka and rowdiness. The village assessor – an important figure at such gatherings – proposes or gets others to propose one after the other two or three candidates who they are sure the commune will not elect. After three or four hours people slowly drift away and the things quieten down. This is the end of the election. Then the village assessor with five or six others writes the minutes, quite arbitrarily, attributing opinions even to people who were not there. This is all sent to the town and written up in official form.[114]

An account from Vyatka province is even more striking: 'At commune meetings the drink-shop is, so to speak, the arena in which the contesting parties defend their positions . . . Anyone who needs supporters simply buys the meeting a certain quantity of vodka – and that decides the matter.'[115] On the basis of the tours of inspection of the state peasantry of 1836–40, it is clear that this was the general rule in state peasant villages in the early nineteenth century.[116]

What were the effects of vodka drinking on the peasants themselves? Most of the literature available stresses the social, medical and economic damage caused by rural drunkenness. What contemporaries meant by drunkenness was really a continuation into daily life of the habits (and expenditures) customary at festivals. It represented a particularly ruinous confusion of festive with workaday routines, which appalled contemporary moral and social reformers.

There is little doubt that when drunkenness of this kind really seized hold of a village it could do terrible damage.

'The devil take these drink-shops', said peasants of the village of Korobanov in Kostroma province to us. 'But as you go past you somehow go in. Why are there so many of them? If the drink-shop was five verstas away you would not go in so often, particularly in winter; and they are not just huts, but buildings good enough for lords, while our huts arc in ruins. . . ' And indeed, in the middle of the village stood the drink-shop and the outstretched arms of its two-headed eagle seemed to tenderly welcome the ignorant people to its embrace.[117]

Once a peasant started to drink seriously, his decline and that of his family could be swift. Indebtedness generally preceded total ruin. 'Often peasants will sell their hay or their standing grain to an illicit dealer in spirits . . . They [the dealers] find some liquor and then demand repayment just when it is most difficult. The peasant has no money, so he gives up the produce of his hay meadow or field, and even agrees to mow and reap it himself.'[118] Drunkenness was also a moral and spiritual disaster for the family as it often led to family quarrels and even to criminal violence.

There is nothing so vile that the peasant won't do it when drunk. And our people, generally so humble and obedient, are capable of any cruelty or any

[114]Contemporary account, cited in Druzhinin, *Gosudarstvennye krest'yane*, vol. I, 347.
[115]*Ibid.*, vol. I, 348, includes this and other examples.
[116]*Ibid.*
[117]Zablotskii, *Graf P.D. Kiselev*, vol. IV, 309.
[118]*Ibid.*, vol. IV, 311.

frenzy in a moment of drunken violence. Once sobered up, they usually calm down and become as obedient as sheep. But then it is too late, and they become an unfortunate victim not of the spirit of revolt but of that of alcohol. How often do you see father and son fighting as if they were total strangers; when they sober up they come to their senses, but the moral ties are already broken.

The passion for liquor is even more terrible in women. When the women drink, then the family is almost completely destroyed. No one feeds the babies, or cleans them, or worries about the household chores; the drunken women just lie on the floor in the middle of the room half naked and hideous.[119]

Many people simply drank themselves to death – 939 in 1842 (though these were mostly in Moscow), and as many as 1,713 in 1859.[120] There was also a very clear link between vodka and rural crime. A government commission reporting on conditions in Kursk province in the early 1870s was told by a landowner who had acted as a Peace Arbitrator, that 'in the course of 5 years there was not a single criminal case in which vodka and drunkenness did not play a role of some kind'.[121]

The moral, economic and even political damage caused by excessive drinking was evident throughout the century. And, as we have seen, the government itself professed to be at least as interested in controlling drunkenness as it was in raising revenue. But other groups, too, attempted to do something about the problem of drunkenness. By the early twentieth century there was a temperance movement so powerful that it finally persuaded the government to introduce total prohibition on the outbreak of war in 1914. But the peasants themselves were not just simply passive victims of the liquor traders. Many did resist the temptation to drink excessively, and they provided powerful evidence for the temperance argument that connected sobriety with affluence. An example comes from a family of serfs from Moscow province, headed by,

. . . a peasant who was a great drinker. He never had a horse, and spent all his time in the drink-shop. He had a son who grew up, married, and took his father in hand. He never let him go anywhere, repaired everything himself, and, most important of all, does not drink at all. And in two years, from being beggarly, this household has become rich. The young peasant now has four horses, of which the worst is worth 80 rubles. And this is just in two years. There were no other special reasons for this rapid recovery of their fortunes.

---

[119]*Ibid.*

[120]Pryzhov, *Istoriya kabakov*, 319, and see M. Zablotskii, 'O p'yaı .ve', for an analysis of these figures.

[121]*Doklad*, 238.

'Such examples', continues Zablotskii, 'prove that drunkenness is one of the greatest causes of poverty and, consequently, of the lack of education of the people.'[122] One need not accept these conclusions without qualification, but it is clear that for many the drink-shop was a disaster.

There were times when the peasants themselves took action to tackle the problem on a larger scale. The growth of religious dissidence amongst the state peasantry was a sort of temperance movement.

In the state peasant villages there was born an organised form of protest against the universal drunkenness, and this merged with protest against the official church and against the whole system of state administration . . . This protest took the ideological form of religious dissidence. The more independent-minded and active sections of the state peasantry broke all ties with the Orthodox church, took solemn oaths of sobriety, and joined hidden, but widespread organisations.[123]

More spectacular was the 'sobriety movement' of 1859. In 1858, as a protest against excessive liquor prices, a temperance society was formed by the Catholic peasants of Kovno province in Lithuania, and within eight months similar societies had spread through many Russian provinces.[124] Commune gatherings began levying fines and even using corporal punishment on those who drank too much. Elsewhere, whole villages simply took a pledge not to drink. By mid-1859, liquor farmers were pleading with the government to protect their interests, in particular to persuade priests not to give excessive support to this spontaneous temperance movement. The movement was particularly galling to the liquor farmers as, in the 1858 liquor farm auctions, they had bid exceptionally high prices. These payments were, of course, due to the government however much liquor was actually sold, and at least one liquor farmer (from Kovno province) actually went broke. The government, too, was worried, in particular the Ministry of Finance, which informed the Ober-Procurator of the Holy Synod,

. . . that the total prohibition of vodka by the use of religious threats and sworn oaths, which act powerfully on the minds of the simple people, should not be allowed as being opposed not only to the generally accepted view that the moderate use of vodka is beneficial, but also to the agreements on the basis of which the government has surrendered the liquor dues to the liquor farmers.[125]

[122]Zablotskii, *Graf P.D. Kiselev*, vol. IV, 310.
[123]Druzhinin, *Gosudarstvennye krest'yane*, vol. I, 374–5.
[124]On the sobriety movement, see Dobrolyubov, 'Narodnoe delo', and, for a modern account, Fedorov, 'Krest'yanskoe trezvennoe dvizhenie'. See also Pryzhov, *Istoriya kabakov*, 290–2.
[125]Pryzhov, *Istoriya kabakov*, 294–5.

In May 1859, the sobriety movement turned violent as peasants began attacking drink-shops as a protest against excessively high prices. The liquor riots were in some places as violent as the potato riots of the early 1840s, and they provoked equally savage reprisals. It was this outburst of violence that did more than anything else to persuade the government that the liquor farm had to go.[126]

If it is not actually true that the government directly encouraged the Russian peasantry to drink large quantities of hard liquor, its actions nevertheless show clearly how great a financial stake it had in the consumption of vodka. Thus, the government itself was probably the greatest obstacle to any serious temperance movement. And in this sense the extent and nature of drunkenness as a social problem in Russia can be traced back to the fiscal methods adopted by the Russian state since the sixteenth century.

[126]On the liquor riots, see Lur'e, 'Piteinye bunty'.

9

✾✾✾

Good times and bad

I

That the food you ate said a lot about who you were was a truism with which the peasantry themselves were familiar. The food one ate determined or reflected the quality of life in many ways. The quality of the bread alone told you a lot about a family. The amount of vodka doled out at a work-party or a family celebration was a good indication of whether a family was worth cultivating or not. And food, of course, had a lot to do with the level of health and well-being of a family and its capacity to work and to earn. In Chernigov province in the late 1840s, there were districts where land shortage had led to a general undernourishment, so that most villagers were poor and weak, and 'few live to a very old age'.[1] Peasants were acutely aware of the link between diet and capacity for work.

People know *exactly how much you can earn on a particular food, what type of food is necessary for what kind of work*. If, on a diet consisting of cabbage soup, pork and buckwheat gruel with animal fat, you can carry in a certain time, say, a cubic fathom of earth, then if you replace buckwheat gruel with barley gruel you will carry less, say, 7/8 of a cubic fathom, while on potatoes you will carry even less, say 3/4 of a cubic fathom, and so on. This is all perfectly well known to a navvy or a woodchopper, so that, once they know the price of food and the wages available, they can calculate precisely which food is most economical.[2]

The author of this passage, Engel'gardt, was himself a chemist, yet he was convinced that the peasants' nutritional lore was in many respects superior to that of academic nutritionists.

Nor were peasants naive about the political meaning of changes in their diet. Particularly under serfdom, they knew that the poverty of their own diets was in some sense an index of their exploitation. The

---

[1] *Etnograficheskii sbornik*, vol. I, 327.
[2] Engel'gardt, *Iz derevni*, 258. His emphasis.

327

'Lament of a House Serf' asked rhetorically: 'Why should we not be angry at our lords? I think people will soon go mad with anger. The masters sell pure rye to the merchants, but to us they give unwinnowed rye, as if to pigs. The greedy lords eat meat even on fast days, while their serfs get "empty" soup even on meat days.'[3]

Our concern in this chapter will be to try to identify and describe variations in the quality of peasant diets, for these variations were clearly a powerful measure of the rising and declining fortunes of the peasant household. Did the peasants live, on the whole, well or badly? How did people cope when they ran short of food? How good was the diet of a wealthy peasant? What was the real meaning of famine or of affluence in rural Russia?

The importance of these questions is self-evident. But it is only with the nineteenth century that the evidence available makes it worthwhile even posing questions like these. However, the evidence is fragmentary, and many measures of the 'standard of living' are simply not available. It is unrealistic, for example, to try to produce a cost of living index in an economy where so many goods did not pass through the market. But one can analyse the various ways in which living standards changed and try to estimate the range of living standards to be found within the peasantry, as far as these were related to diets. This chapter will be concerned mainly to describe these variations in some detail; it will *not* attempt a thoroughgoing explanation of their causes.

II

First, it is important to establish some general benchmarks against which to measure dietary variations.

It is notoriously hard to agree on objective definitions of nutritional adequacy. What is a 'minimum' consumption level? The number of calories necessary to barely sustain life? Or to sustain a healthy life? But what definition of health will cover all centuries, all cultures, all age groups and all forms of work?

These difficulties, and the crudeness of the available evidence, preclude the use of precise quantitative measures of the nutritional value of peasant diets. But this does not mean one cannot say some valuable things about the quality of these diets, even if one's measures are rough and ready. An important starting point is provided by the measures of adequacy used by a particular society, for, as Marx was well aware: 'Besides the mere physical element, the value of labour is in every

---

[3]Brodskii, 'Krepostnoe pravo', 14.

36 Hunters Row (now Marx Prospect), Moscow, late nineteenth century. A peasant cart stands near a food shop.

country determined by a *traditional standard of life*. It is not merely physical life but it is the satisfaction of certain wants springing from the social conditions in which a people are placed and reared up.'[4]

In assessing reasonable levels of taxation, or in estimating the requirements of famine relief in crises, the Russian government had to devise rough estimates of the food requirements of its population. Given the central role of grain-based foods, it was natural to calculate these amounts as the quantities of grain necessary for an average consumer for a year. The norms adopted by the Russian government in the nineteenth century varied from region to region. They were higher in the more fertile regions, the Central Black Earth region, and the south-east. They were lowest in the non-Black Earth provinces of the west, north, north-west, and Baltic, and also in the provinces of right bank Ukraine. Thus, the norms for Perm' and Orenburg provinces

[4]Marx, *Wages, Price and Profit*, 50.

were 525–650 kg of grain per person per year, while in Mogilev in the less fertile south-west, they dropped as low as 150 kg. Norms also varied with the harvest. In bad years the Provincial Supply Commissions lowered the norms in each region.[5] But in practice, the average norm adopted by the Provincial Supply Commissions in the middle of the century was about 2.25 chetverts of grain per person per year, or about 300 kg a year.[6] This was also the norm adopted by the Ministry of Internal Affairs and the Ministry of State Domains in the early nineteenth century, and it is the norm which the late nineteenth-century writer, Maress, adopted on nutritional grounds.[7] It is worth noting that this norm is similar to those for the Muscovite period.[8]

Assuming that 1 kg of grain will yield about 3,150 calories when milled down to 900 grams, 300 kg a year is the equivalent of about 2,500 calories a day, a figure which compares adequately with the current United Nations estimates of minimum caloric intake.[9] A joint committee of the Food and Agriculture Organisation of the U.N. and the World Health Organisation suggested in 1974 that infants of 1 to 3 require about 1,400 calories a day; adult males about 3,000 calories; and adult females about 2,200 calories a day.[10] So the norms adopted in nineteenth-century Russia are not improbable.

They are, however, 'normal' minima, estimates of what is required under normal conditions. Other estimates of consumption minima were considerably lower. The Russian Central Statistical Committee adopted the lower figure of 220 kg (giving about 1,700 calories a day) in the late nineteenth century, a figure which seems to represent a sort of 'starvation' level, a level of consumption adequate to stop serious biological deterioration, but not reckoned adequate for normal life.[11] These differences reflected not merely disagreements about adequate consumption levels; they reflected different types of minima:

[5]Sivkov, 'Nekotorye itogi', 26; Nifontov, *Zernovoe proizvodstvo*, 139. Military rations (which were designed, of course, not for a demographically average person, but for a healthy adult male) were generally higher than the average figures – three chetverts or more, or about 400 kg. The infantry received in the mid-nineteenth century 1.25 kg of bread a day, 700 g of biscuit, and 100 g of groats for gruel.

[6]The Provincial Food Supply Commissions were created in 1822 and abolished in 1866, when their work was taken over by the newly created zemstva, or elected local councils. Robbins, *Famine in Russia*, 18–20.

[7]Nifontov, *Zernovoe proizvodstvo*, 140; Maress, 'Pishcha noardnykh mass', part 2, 49–50.

[8]For the earlier period see ch. 1, pp. 20–1 and 23, and Smith, *Peasant Farming*, ch. 5.

[9]I have used Colin Clark's estimates in Clark and Haswell, *Subsistence Agriculture*, 58.

[10]Scrimshaw and Young, 'Human Nutrition', 36.

[11]This level comes closer to Colin Clark's estimate of minimum calorific requirements of about 2,000 calories a day. Clark and Haswell, *Subsistence Agriculture*, 17. 230 kg is equivalent to the average annual intake of grains in underdeveloped countries in 1970. George, *How the Other Half Dies*, 24.

The 295 kg norm describes average consumption in years of normal harvests and under normal conditions. The 220 kg norm of the Central Statistical Committee is a minimum level necessary for the population to barely maintain itself in famine years. It is the norm the government adopted during the recent famine of 1891, and as budgetary studies indicate, the 'norm' of very poor peasant families.[12]

In the early stages of the 1891 famine, the Ministry of Internal Affairs opted for a starvation norm of about 150 kg.[13]

Thus, the calculations of the Russian government seem to suggest the existence of two distinct consumption levels – one starting at about 200 kg per year, which is really a famine minimum; and the other at about 300 kg, which is a normal minimum, a level at which a peasantry can keep reproducing itself and paying its taxes year in and year out. Budgetary studies of eighteen provinces in the early twentieth century offer some confirmation for these figures. They give about 300 kg a year as the average consumption for wealthier families, and about 210 kg for poorer families.[14] As we have seen, these figures are not incompatible with the calculations of nutritionists both then and now.

III

Peasant diets varied in ways quite different from those typical in industrial societies today. Where most food was homegrown, the range of foodstuffs available was far narrower, and in this sense peasant diets were monotonous and unchanging by the standards of the industrialised countries today. On the other hand, the precariousness of agricultural production, combined with narrow markets and undeveloped transportation networks, meant that the threat of hunger and even starvation was never far way. Consequently, measured as fluctuations towards or away from some notional 'starvation' level, variations in the quality of peasant diets were really far greater than those we would expect in the industrialised societies today.

It is possible to distinguish between two main types of variation. First come those variations related to the calendar – the regular seasonal variations in diet, the closely related variations imposed by the church, and the less regular annual variations governed mainly by the harvest of different crops, above all grain. Second come what may be called class variations in diet – those variations to be found within the peasantry as a class, variations reflecting the relative wealth or poverty

[12]Chuprov and Postnikov, *Vliyanie urozhaev*, vol. II, 11.
[13]Robbins, *Famine in Russia*, 50.
[14]Dikhtyar, *Vnutrennyaya torgovlya*, 31.

of different sections of the peasantry or different regions. (I am not concerned here with the cultural differences between regions, but with those which indicate relative wealth or poverty.)

These variations share a common pattern, and though the evidence for this will only emerge later, it might be helpful to describe the main features of this pattern now. It is best described not in strictly quantitative terms (we do not have enough evidence for that), but as a sort of ranking order with several distinct levels. There is,

(1) a level of *affluence*, marked by abundance of all foods, regular consumption of livestock products, and the consumption of luxury items such as tea. At this level, a decline in the amount of grain or potatoes consumed marks an *improvement* in the quality of the diet as a whole. (See Tables 9.1 and 9.2.) Then,

(2) there is a level of *adequacy*, in which most of the staple foods are available, although meat is generally something of a luxury, except for the scraps of meat and meat fat used to flavour soups. Such a diet, with adequate quantities of the staple grains and small amounts of animal-based foods and of fresh vegetables or fruits, was probably nutritionally quite adequate. Then,

(3) we can identify a level of *mild difficulty*, when animal foods and fresh vegetables are becoming rare luxuries and even certain staples, such as gruel or cabbage soup and the animal and vegetable oils used to flavour them, are not always available. Poor in animal protein, calcium and vitamin C, such a diet was not fully adequate by modern standards, and was probably particularly hard on the very young. However, it contained just adequate supplies of grain and probably met minimum requirements for calorie intake. Beyond that,

(4) there was a level of clear *inadequacy*, when animal foods became insignificant, and even the quantities and quality of the staple food, bread, began to decline. At this point, total calorie intakes may have approached the nutritional minima. Finally,

(5) *begging*, and then beyond that,

(6) actual *starvation*, should be regarded as distinct stages because those who begged for 'crusts' generally lived in regions capable of protecting them from the ultimate disaster of death by starvation, although they had little protection against the many diseases to which chronic malnutrition made them liable if such conditions persisted.

For all its crudity, this scale may at least help to clarify the sort of variations we are looking for. As we will see, seasonal variations probably accounted for two or three levels on the scale, but harvest varia-

Table 9.1. *Annual consumption of a male worker (vegetable products) Vologda province 1905*

Households (by sown area)	Annual consumption (kg)							Totals			
	Flour			Groats							
	Rye	Wheat	Other	Oats and Barley	Rice and Millet	Peas	Potatoes	Flour	Peas and Groats	Potatoes 'translated' to rye	TOTAL: Grain & potatoes
Desyatinas											
(I) 0.01–1.0	261	40	34	4.8	3.3	2.0	111	335	10	22	367.2
(II) 1.1–2.0	241	53	44	9.3	5.7	1.6	125	338	17	25	379.9
(III) 2.1–3.0	247	58	54	9.5	5.2	2.0	116	358	17	23	398.2
(IV) 3.1–4.0	231	75	75	16.0	5.1	2.1	122	381	23	24	428.7
(V) 4.0 +	218	85	91	20.5	10.5	3.0	112	394	34	22	400.8

Source: N. Korenevskaya, *Byudzhetnye obsledovaniya krest'yanskikh khozyaistv v dorevolyutsionnoi Rossii* (Moscow, 1954), 132. Weights in puds have been converted into kilograms: 1 pud = 16.38 kg.

Table 9.2. *Annual consumption of a male worker (animal-based foods)*
Vologda province 1905

Households (by sown area)		Annual consumption (kg)		Total
		Meat and Fat	Fish	Meat and Fish
Desyatinas				
(I)	0.0–1.0	13.6	9.7	23.3
(II)	1.1–2.0	17.7	8.2	25.9
(III)	2.1–3.0	18.2	7.7	25.9
(IV)	3.1–4.0	25.9	4.9	30.8
(V)	4.1 +	28.7	4.5	33.2

Source: N. Korenevskaya, *Byudzhetnye obsledovaniya krest'yanskikh khozyaistv v dorevo-lyutsionnoi Rossii* (Moscow, 1954), 133. Weights in puds have been converted into kilograms: 1 pud = 16.38 kg.

tions may have counted for more. Average regional differences perhaps covered four notches, while class differences, even in normal times, probably covered all the first five levels. Figure 9.1 attempts to suggest the nature of the seasonal and class variations as measured against this scale. (It goes without saying that this chart *proves* nothing; at best it offers a visual summing-up of the casual descriptive data available.) Each band represents the seasonal variations in quality of the diets of hypothetical households. For a bad harvest one should imagine all diets dropping a notch. For a good harvest they should be raised at least a notch.

How can this scale be related to the two fixed points established already, the starvation and 'adequate' norms for grain consumption? Almost by definition, the starvation minimum must be assumed to be below level five. The higher minimum, however, is harder to place. Probably it should be placed somewhere between levels two and three; but its exact placing varied from province to province. In those provinces where bread was always of poor quality, it may be that even the 'adequate' norm of the local Commission of Supply in the middle of the century drifted downwards to about level four; while in good years, and more productive regions, it may have drifted above level two.

It may clarify the meaning of this scale if it is compared with a particular example. One of the earliest budgets available gives the following information on the diet of a 'poor' cossack family in Chernigov province in the 1860s (see Table 9.3).

Table 9.3. *Annual consumption of a poor Cossack family. Chernigov province 1860s*

Food	Quantity per person per annum		Calories per day	
	Kilograms	%	Total	%
Rye	196.6	54.8	1,314	50
Buckwheat groats	98.3	27.4	937	35
Potatoes	32.8	9.1	73	3
Beetroot	3.3	0.9	4	?
Pumpkins	(12)	?	10	?
Salt	13.1	3.7	?	?
Meat fat	6.6	1.8	162	6
Vodka	19.7 litres	?	?	?
Beef	8.2	2.3	56	2
Totals		100%	2,640 +	99%

Source: *Materialy*, v. 25, Chernigovskaya gub., 551–2.

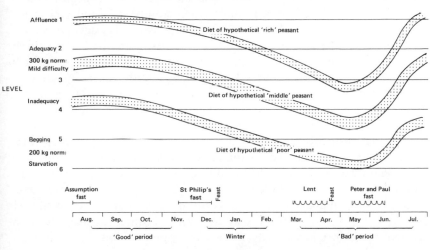

Fig. 9.1 Seasonal and class variations in diet.

The family included a man of 75, too old to work; his son aged 40; a daughter-in-law aged 30; and their two children, a girl of 4 and a boy of 2 years. Regarded as an average diet – averaged, that is, over the whole year – their diet clearly belongs at about level three, the level of mild difficulty. It just meets the 'adequate' norm for consumption of grain (about 300 kg of grain per person per annum), but very little meat is eaten, and even the secondary staples – groats (for gruel), meat fats and beetroot – are consumed in very small amounts. It would be reasonable to assume that this family's diet would decline to about level four or even lower after a bad harvest or during the spring. Equally, in better times, its diet might reach level two. While supplying enough calories, level three is already inadequate nutritionally, and this categorises the average diet of this family as 'poor': it was not a starvation diet, but it did lack certain important elements and one presumes that the family suffered chronic, though mild, malnutrition.

I V

Seasonal variations were the most regular and certain of all variations, and these provide a basic framework for understanding other types of variation. The church calendar with its regular cycle of fasts and festivals, was itself an important constraint on the dietary calendar. But its influence tended, by and large, to reinforce that of seasonal changes. This is clearest in the case of the long spring fasts of Lent, and Peter and Paul, which coincided with periods when supplies of food were running low for most households and abstinence was necessary anyway.[15]

If one ignores the short-term variations associated with the church calendar, it is possible to identify three main dietary seasons which merged into each other and whose precise length in any given year depended on the size of the annual harvest. These were: late summer and autumn, winter and spring, and late spring and early summer. The first period was dominated by the harvest and in a normal year most diets were probably adequate during this period. Vegetables were fresh, there were abundant supplies of newly harvested grain, and berries and mushrooms could be found. Livestock was generally at its fittest, having fed on stubble or hay, so that milk and sometimes fresh meat were available. In those households able to afford to slaughter livestock for food, autumn was the normal time for slaughter. In Moscow province in the early 1880s: 'The peasants' food is most nourishing and varied in the autumn, when all households have grain to spare, and in any case this is the only time when young lambs are slaughtered for food. The largest amounts of food are consumed during harvesting [*stradnaya pora*].'[16] This, in short, was the good period

---

[15]On the influence of the church calendar see above, p. 10, and Kerblay, 'Alimentation rurale', 904.
[16]Skibnevskii, 223.

of the dietary year; food was more abundant, more varied, and more nutritious than at other periods.

The winter diet was characterised by the elimination of fresh foods: fresh meat, dairy products and fresh vegetables all disappeared. Pickled cabbage or beetroot, or cucumbers and salt meat or fish now became the main accompaniments to the inevitable bread.[17] But food was generally available in adequate quantities, even if it was less fresh, less varied, and probably less nutritious than in late summer and autumn.

Spring and early summer was the worst part of the dietary year. The range of foods narrowed and the poorer families began to experience difficulties even in normal years. This natural fast coincided with the religious fasts of Lent and St Peter and Paul, the latter in May and June. In Ryazan', during Peter and Paul, 'the vegetables have not ripened and supplies of pickled cabbage are running out, so that the normal food is kvas with green onions and cucumbers, if these have ripened yet. On top of this, the peasants often do not even have any bread and they have to borrow money, or mill unripened rye.'[18] In Chernigov, 'it is not unusual for a householder, even in the wealthier districts, to have to beg his neighbours for some pickled cabbage from halfway through the winter'. In Vitebsk province, 'In spring and summer, when bread is short, the poor for the most part eat only one food: if there is no cabbage left, they eat soup of sorrel, nettles . . . and other wild herbs.'[19] But most important of all, the quantity and then the quality of bread began to decline. In Smolensk province in the 1870s:

In the autumn, when there is a stock of rye, they eat pure bread, as much as they like, and only a very conscientious peasant eats adulterated bread . . . But then the peasants notice that bread is short. They eat less, not three times a day, but twice and then only once. Then they start adding chaff to the pure flour. If there's money left from selling hemp, they use it to buy bread instead of for taxes. If there's no money, they get by. The head of the household finds work, or borrows . . . When there's no more bread the children and old folk take their knapsacks and go out 'collecting crusts' in the neighbourhood.[20]

By early summer, however, other foods began to appear in the diet and although grain might still be in short supply, the nutritional value of the diet slowly improved. When cattle were able to go out to pasture, some pressure was off grain reserves and it might be possible once again to milk the cows. In Gamayunshchina village in Kaluga province, 'the normal summer food consists of cabbage soup with

[17]*Materialy*, v. 24, Khersonskaya gub., vol. II, 504.
[18]*Materialy*, v. 19, Ryazanskaya gub., 399.
[19]*Etnograficheskii sbornik*, vol. II, 139.
[20]Engel'gardt, *Iz derevni*, 41–3.

chunks of animal fat and buckwheat gruel with milk'; in addition, in this period many wild plants, including mushrooms, 'are a significant addition to the food of our peasants'.[21]

If one compares the high and low points in this cycle, its essential feature stands out clearly: a gradual thinning of the diet, involving the progressive elimination of less essential foods and eventually even the elimination of bread itself, leading in extreme cases to a temporary reliance on gathered foods. This deterioration was experienced as a decline in the quantities available and in the variety and nutritional value of the diet. As we will see, this pattern of change in dietary quality is typical in some degree of other forms of variation as well.

v

The other main form of variation in time arose from variations in the size of the harvest. Of all the different types of variation to which rural diets were subject, this was the most violent, unpredictable and dangerous.

Given the importance of grain in the diet, this variation had an immediate impact on the quality of life for most peasant households. Indeed, in a still weakly monetised economy, it influenced the quality of life more than did changes in price levels. A poor harvest was bad both for those households that were largely self-sufficient (for whom it directly affected the quantities of grain available for consumption), and those which bought most of their food (as it led to rapid increases in the price of grain). Only those fortunate households with surpluses of grain could benefit. A good harvest was, for opposite reasons, favourable for most peasant households (though the rich and the gentry complained about low prices). Finally, price changes combined with stable harvests had little impact on those who were largely self-sufficient, and their impact on other peasants was reduced to the extent that they produced some of their own grain.[22] These rules were, however, being slowly undermined as more and more peasant households were sucked into market relations as sellers or purchasers of grain, and as sellers or purchasers of labour.

In peasant societies in general, the variability of the harvest is probably a better index of living standards than the absolute sizes of the

---

[21] *Materialy*, v. 9, Kaluzhskaya gub., 181.
[22] These 'laws' of peasant economy were analysed as early as the 1890s. See Chuprov and Postnikov, *Vliyanie urozhaev*, vol. I, xiii. More recently, they have been analysed in a different context by Witold Kula, *Economic Theory*. See for example, 110–11.

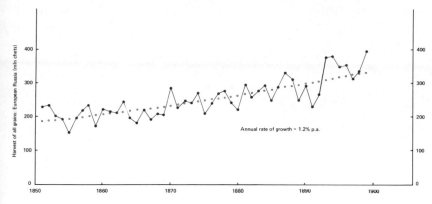

Fig. 9.2 Gross harvests of all grains. European Russia 1851–1899.
(Source: Nifontov, *Zernovoe proizvodstvo*, 117, 183, 267.)

harvest.[23] For those living near the subsistence level, it is far more important to be reasonably sure of getting by, than to aim for a high average standard of living. Thus the analysis of harvest variations should tell us a lot about changing living standards amongst the peasantry.

As it happens, harvest variations are also one of the few factors influencing diet for which we have some reasonably reliable figures. Estimates of the harvest, province by province, were made by provincial governors from the late eighteenth century. Scholars from the mid-nineteenth century tended to assume that these were underestimates, but recent work suggests that this was not true.[24] For the period from 1851 to 1899, a complete series of annual grain harvests for European Russia has been reconstructed (Figures 9.2 and 9.3). As Figure 9.3 shows, the actual harvests ranged from as high as 125% of the trend value to as low as 76%. In other words, variations ranged over 50% of the trend. More precisely (though less vividly) one can say that the standard deviation of values from the trend was equal to 12.6% of the trend values.

What evidence there is suggests that harvest fluctuations were slightly greater in the middle and at the end of the century than in the decades in between. For the first half of the century we have no

[23]Scott, *Moral Economy*, particularly ch. 1.
[24]Nifontov, *Zernovoe proizvodstvo*, 61–2 discusses nineteenth–century estimates, and 35–49 discusses the value of the governors' reports. The government's systematic concern with food supplies went back to the famines of 1721–4. Robbins, *Famine in Russia*, 16.

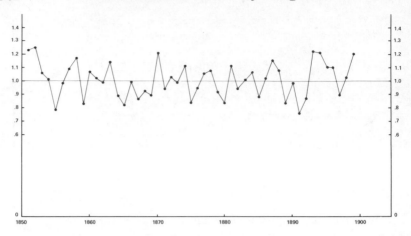

Fig. 9.3 Gross harvests of all grains as proportion of trend. European Russia 1851–1899.

(Source: Nifontov, *Zernovoe*, 117, 183, 267.)

continuous series. But there are indications that variations were greatest in the 1840s and 1850s.[25] For the second half of the century the wildest fluctuations from the trend for the gross harvest come in 1851, 1852, 1855, then 1877, and finally 1891 and 1894 (see Figure 9.3). The standard deviations of annual fluctuations from the trend for each decade are as follows:

1850s	14.06
1860s	12.06
1870s	9.14
1880s	9.27
1890s	14.96

Clearly, harvests were most erratic in the 1840s and 1850s and again in the 1890s.

Both these periods have been seen as times of crisis for the peasantry and for agriculture in general, and both crises have been interpreted as symptoms of wider social crises. But the evidence is by no means unambiguous. Some writers claim that in the earlier period, excessive taxation and growing land-hunger led to a demographic decline in the densely populated provinces which were the heartland of serfdom.[26]

[25]The wildest fluctuations came in 1833 (32% below the average yield for the half century), 1842 and 1843 (both 26% above), 1855 (26% below), and 1839 and 1848 (both 23% below). Dulov, 'Prirodnye usloviya', 44.

[26]Koval'chenko, *Krepostnoe krest'yanstvo*; Perkovskii, 'Krizis demograficheskogo vosproizvodstva'.

Others argue that these claims are exaggerated, and suggest that the demographic evidence can also be interpreted less bleakly.[27] Research on the 1890s has proved equally inconclusive. Some writers claim that the fiscal burden again became intolerable, and exacerbated problems caused by growing land-hunger. As a result, per capita availability of grain and of livestock declined again in the late nineteenth century.[28] Further, arrears of taxation were accumulating steadily and most striking of all is the fact that large-scale famines, which had begun to seem a thing of the past, reappeared in Russia of the 1890s. Yet the most recent calculations of grain balances suggest that the total grain available (in theory) for consumption was not in fact declining, though it remains possible that the grain was increasingly unevenly distributed (see Table 9.4).[29] If variability in harvests were taken as a more general measure of living standards, it would tend to support those who claim that the political crises of 1861 and 1905 were both preceded by a decline in the material security of significant sections of the peasantry.

However, figures for European Russia as a whole tend to underestimate the real impact of local variations in the harvest. Examined province by province the variations are far harsher than the aggregate figures suggest. They are even more erratic if one examines net rather than gross harvests. (The net harvest is the total harvest minus the grain necessary for seed; it represents the grain available for consumption and sale.)

Figure 9.4 shows net harvests in Penza province in the central agricultural region over ten years. As the graph shows, the net harvest for a famine year (1848) was only about 1/20 of the net harvest for the best year of the decade, 1851; but even if one excludes 1848, the lowest year (now 1855) is about 1/5 of the highest year. As the second graph shows, the variations from the trend are far greater than those for European Russia as a whole in this period, as one would expect. These figures are not necessarily typical (as we have seen, harvests in the 1850s were more erratic than for the century as a whole), but they are not entirely exceptional, apart from the inclusion of a famine year, and they do show clearly how wide local variations in the harvest could be.

There were also regional differences in variability. Variations tended to be more violent in the southern black soil provinces. On the one hand the soils were more fertile, but on the other hand hailstorms and

[27]Ryndzyunskii, *Utverzhdenie kapitalizma*, ch. 3; Hoch and Augustine, 'The Tax Censuses'.
[28]Maress, 'Pishcha narodnykh mass', part 2, 54; Yanson, *Statistika*, vol. II, 613.
[29]In Western writings there has been some recent debate on the issue. See Simms, 'The Crisis'; Hamburg, 'The Crisis'; Simms, 'A Rejoinder', 'The Crop Failure of 1891', and 'The Economic Impact of the Russian Famine'.

Table 9.4. *A grain balance 1870–1900*

Consumption	Amounts of grain (mln chets)		
	1870s	1880s	1890s
Rural			
Seed	70.0	72.7	77.2
Household Needs*	149.1	178.6	203.7
Total (Rural)	219.1	251.3	280.9
Outside Agriculture			
Towns*	17.3	22.4	27.1
Army	5.0	5.0	5.6
Distilling	9.0	9.7	10.6
Exports	28.9	43.1	50.8
Total (Urban)	60.2	80.2	94.1
Grand Total Demand	279.3	331.5	375.0
Gross Harvest	257.1	300.8	367.6
Harvest minus Demand	−22.2	−30.7	−7.4

Note: * = Estimates of consumption based on consumption norms (2.25 chets (c. 295 kg) per person of grain and potatoes in towns and rural households in non–Black Earth provinces, and 2.5 (330 kg) in rural households in Black Earth provinces – see pp. 205 and 209) multiplied by total population.
Source: Nifontov, *Zernovoe proizvodstvo,* 214.

droughts often destroyed the harvest. Table 9.5 shows the greater range of variability in the Black Earth provinces of the south. Thus, while in this area 72% of harvests were more than 10% above or below the average figure, in the non–Black Earth provinces of the north only 44% of harvests were outside this range. Similarly, while only 3% of harvests were below 2/3 of the average figure in the north, as many as 12% of harvests fell below this level in the south.

Variations of the kind found in the south posed a serious threat to the continued survival of each household. Tolstoy's son, Sergei, described the characteristic attitudes to such fluctuations in Samara province in 1873:

At that time the Samara steppes were still largely untouched. The rich metre-deep black earth was covered with a thick layer of various grasses . . . I was always amazed at the agriculture of the Samara peasants. All their efforts were directed to sowing as much wheat as possible, either on their land or on leased land. They sowed little rye, and no hemp or oats or vegetables, not even any potatoes. Thus, if the harvest of wheat was poor (and this happened very often, because the harvest depended on the rainfall in May), then they not

Table 9.5. *Harvest fluctuations 1857–66, 1870–6, 1883–9. An 'average'*
harvest is within 10% of the average

Non-Black Earth	% Good harvests	% Average	% Below average	% Below 66% of average
North	25	50	25	4
North-west	25	57	18	6
Mid-Volga/Urals	18	61	21	5
Industrial Centre	20	56	24	—
West	21.5	57.5	21	2
Baltic	25	54	21	3
Average	22	56	22	3
Black Earth				
South Steppes	42	18	40	19
South-west	39	29	32	11
Middle black earth	37	28	35	12
Northern black earth	32	38	30	5
South-Volga/Trans-Volga	40	25	35	15
Average	38	28	34	12

Source: L.N. Maress, 'Proizvodstvo, potreblenie khleba v krest'yanskom khozyaistve',
in Chuprov and Postnikov, eds. *Vliyanie urozhaev*, vol. I, 55–6.

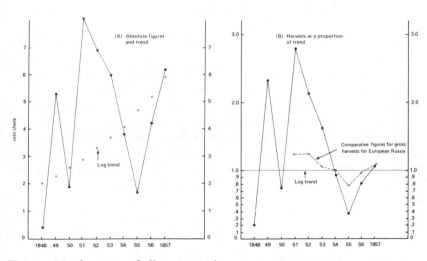

Fig. 9.4 Net harvests of all grains and potatoes. Penza province 1848–1857.
(Source: *Materialy dlya geografii*, v. (2 parts), Penzenskaya gub., ed. A.
Ryabinin (SPB, 1867), i, 432.)

only suffered serious financial loss, but also went hungry. This was not a regulated, systematic agriculture, but a sort of agricultural roulette.[30]

The degree of variability was also related to the technical quality of agriculture, and this inevitably meant that variations were greater on peasants' than on gentry land, that is, on lands which were less well tilled, less well manured, less well irrigated.

It is extremely probable that on peasant lands the harvests, which are always lower than on landlord lands, are also more erratic, deviating both more often and more widely from the average. And in any case, this variability is one-sided: with good conditions both peasants and private landholders benefit, but under poor conditions, the better-cultivated land of the private landholders copes better than peasant lands.[31]

In 1892 in Poltava province, while peasant harvests of rye, spring wheat and oats were below average respectively by 58%, 38% and 43%, harvests on private landholders' lands were down by 52%, 31% and 35%.[32]

This suggests that variability was not merely a matter of chance or climatic accident. It had a lot to do with the techniques of agriculture, the capital invested in it, and in particular the care with which the fertility of the soil was maintained. And this in turn reflected more general economic pressures: in particular, changes in the fiscal burdens on the peasantry. Increasing fiscal pressures towards the middle of the century led to an increase in arable at the expense of pasture land, which meant a decline in livestock numbers, which in turn meant a decline in the amount of manure available. These factors led to the more erratic harvests of the 1840s and 1850s. The case is even clearer for the end of the century, though then the pressures were increasingly commercial as well as fiscal, as peasants were increasingly forced to sell newly harvested grain at low prices in order to pay taxes, and then to repurchase the same grain at high spring prices. 'All this is so common that the practice is the subject of quaintly humorous jests among the peasants. After his manner, when the mujik loads his grain to take to the market, he addresses it: "Don't be sorry, Mother Rye, that my path is city-wards. In spring I will overpay; but I will take thee back!"'[33]

The increased variability of the harvests, particularly in the steppe lands of the south, was caused at least in part by growing land-hunger

---

[30]Cited in Nifontov, *Zernovoe proizvodstvo*, 66–7.
[31]Maress, 'Pishcha narodnykh mass', part 2, 57.
[32]*Ibid.*
[33]Mavor, *Economic History*, vol. II.

and increased fiscal pressures. More crops had to be produced from less land. Yet the poverty of the peasants and the institutional structure of the repartitional commune made it impossible to improve the technical level of peasant agriculture, or even to fertilise the land more thoroughly. All that could be done was to work the land harder, but in the end this was bound to prove self-defeating.

The peasants' efforts to increase their harvests had disastrous consequences. The expansion of tilled land at the expense of fallow rapidly exhausted the soil. By reducing the number of animals, the peasants undermined agriculture at its foundations, eliminating a major source of farm power and depriving the earth of much-needed fertilizers. The destruction of the forests also had dire results. Cutting the trees robbed the land of natural wind-breaks and created conditions which were highly conducive to drought.

By the end of the 1880s the stage was set for tragedy. The over-burdened peasants and their exploited fields could take no more. The ability of the agriculturalists to meet their obligations had reached its limits and arrears on taxes and redemption payments grew steadily . . . Then the land itself began to fail. In 1888, 1889, and 1890, the Volga and central provinces experienced a series of bad harvests which destroyed what little remained of peasant well-being. On the eve of the famine [of 1891] official reports from the countryside indicated that farmers were selling their cows and work animals in order to feed their families.[34]

The problem was compounded by difficulties in the distribution network. Harvest failures in themselves do not necessarily lead to famine. The harvest of 1891 was in fact not much worse than those of 1880 and 1889, and it produced enough grain to feed the whole population. The real problem was how to get grain from the surplus to the deficit areas. In principle, the growth of a railway network in the late nineteenth century ought to have eliminated the risk of local famines. In practice it did not. The railway network was designed to export grain abroad, not to supply the peasants who produced it. As late as August 1891, speculators were frantically exporting grain abroad to take advantage of high prices caused by the famine itself; and when the government tried to reverse the flow of grain, its efforts caused a near breakdown in the operations of the railway network. And, as in all famines, the activities of local speculators and hoarders ensured that many local famines were artificially manufactured.[35]

However, these problems of distribution were rendered more acute by the fact that so many peasants had no reserves to fall back on, and

[34]Robbins, *Famine in Russia*, 10.
[35]*Ibid.*, 59 and ch. 6 on the railways; ch. 1 on the problems caused by rural poverty itself; and pp. 73 and 195 on the activities of speculators.

were therefore totally dependent on famine relief. Ultimately, we return to the fact that the catastrophe of 1891 was made possible by the steady impoverishment of large sections of the peasantry through a combination of inadequate landholding and the excessive taxation exacted in the interests of industrialisation.

What were the consequences of harvest variations for the peasant household? Their main consequence was that even the richer families had at least occasional experiences of temporary malnutrition. And this was a characteristic feature of the dietary regimes of the whole of early modern Europe. These regimes provided 'a calorie intake which was adequate except in periods of famine, which suggests that the majority of the population suffered recurrent cycles of malnutrition and probably suffered from the vitamin deficiences these inevitably cause.'[36]

Harvest fluctuations did not alter the normal dietary regime; they merely distorted the seasonal variations. A good harvest lengthened the good part of the dietary year; it meant that the shortage of bread, which many would have experienced in the spring of a poorer year, was postponed and perhaps avoided altogether. But more grain also meant more livestock and more money, which meant in turn that foods such as vegetables, fruit and livestock produce, which might normally have been sold, now became available for consumption by those who produced them. Thus, a good harvest could affect the whole diet, and a run of good harvests transformed the economic situation of the peasantry. After the good harvest in 1894, observers in Kherson province noted that, 'the peasants are eating pure bread and as much as they like'; 'the peasants' morale is high'; 'the peasants' food has improved significantly, and meat can occasionally be seen, even at the tables of the poor.'[37]

On the other hand, a bad harvest lengthened the bad part of the dietary year. In Smolensk province, a bad year was known by the numbers begging as early as December.[38] In Ryazan' province at the end of the century,

In poor years, some peasants begin to buy immediatey after harvest and by February three-fourths of the peasants are buying. In Mikhailovsky district of this province, the peasants in years of deficient crops, e.g. in 1897, began to buy in August, 16.1% of their households being under the necessity of doing so. By December more than one half were buying.[39]

[36]Bennassar and Goy, 'Contribution', 428.
[37]Pokrovskii, 'Vliyanie', 229.
[38]Engel'gardt, *Iz derevni*, 116.
[39]Mavor, *Economic History*, vol. II, 292.

But buying usually meant that a family had to sell off parts of its capital stock.

Cattle were sold by 23% in order to secure money with which to buy food. These peasants were obliged during that year to sell 35.3% of their cattle. In that year, also, after the cattle, the buildings began to be used up. It became necessary to deroof the houses in order to give the straw to the remaining cattle, while some were wholly utilized either for food for cattle or for fuel.[40]

But the most obvious sign of a bad harvest was the increasing use of various kinds of adulterated bread. A doctor in Kazan' province wrote that, 'usually people start using famine bread at the beginning of spring, some slightly earlier, others slightly later. Last year, 1891, was different *only in that the number of users of famine breads was significantly greater than in* former years.'[41]

In 1891, 'peasants added to their bread potatoes, chaff, goosefoot, hemp dust, leaves, straw, clay, and so on; often they used unwinnowed grain containing large quantities of grass seeds of various kinds . . . In Orel province, these additions made up 30, 40, and even 50% of the weight of the bread.'[42] The surrogate bread of Smolensk province in the 1880s was known as 'husk' [*pushchnoi*] bread.

Husk bread is made from unwinnowed rye, in other words, a mixture of rye and chaff is milled directly into flour and bread is made from this in the usual way. This bread is heavy and doughy and full of tiny needles of chaff. Its taste is not bad – about like ordinary bread. But its nutritional value is, of course, less. But the main drawback is that it is hard to swallow and if you are not used to it you will simply find it impossible to swallow, or if you do swallow it, it leaves an unpleasant sensation in the throat and makes you cough.[43]

Husk bread was extremely hard on the old, the young and the sick, many of whom simply could not digest it.

Similar techniques for padding out food reserves were described in Samara province in 1907 by a correspondent of the London *Times*. Here, the peasants added to their grain

. . . all kinds of eatable but useless ingredients – bran, grass seeds, chaff and even straw. This autumn thousands of persons lived for weeks on acorns, parched and eaten either as porridge or baked into hard black cakes. Often the husks of the acorns were mixed with meal to add to the volume of this awful

[40] *Ibid.*, vol. II, 292.
[41] Stepanovskii, *Golodnyi khleb*, 213.
[42] Maress, 'Pishcha narodnykh mass', part 2, 68.
[43] Engel'gardt, *Iz derevni*, 61. The word *pushchnoi* means 'in its own husk (*s svaiom pusi*)'. *Materialy*, v. 15, Minskaya gub., vol. I, 27.

37 The 1891 famine. Peasants taking thatch from the roofs to feed cattle, 1891.

food. I strongly doubt whether any animal would touch this stuff, which was doled out in small portions even to the weak children.[44]

On the rare occasions when members of the upper classes encountered surrogate breads they were horrified. In September 1891, a government minister wrote in an official circular: 'During a recent tour of the local budgetary institutions, I had to visit seven provinces ravaged by crop failure. Samples of the bread they are eating in these provinces and the products from which this bread is made, lie on my desk and horrify . . . [visitors] to my office.'[45]

The use of adulterated bread as the major foodstuff in times of difficulty was so widespread that it should be regarded as the major strategy for coping with temporary food shortages. In the 1890s, F.K. Stepanovskii of Kazan' University made a special study of the subject. He sent out a detailed questionnaire to doctors in areas nearby where surrogate breads had become common, asking about the extent of their use, their ingredients and nutritional value, methods of preparation, whether they were used even by the young and the sick, and so on. He

[44]Cited in Kennard, *The Russian Peasant*, 37.
[45]Cited in Robbins, *Famine in Russia*, 63.

found evidence of the use either as surrogates or supplements, of straw, birch and elm bark, buckwheat husks, pig-weed, acorns, malt-grains, bran, potatoes, lime leaves, various types of herbs such as gout-wort and cow-parsley, potato plant leaves and lentils.[46] Of these the most common were pig-weed, then acorns and bread supplemented with birch or elm bark, and husks of grain and potato. In some areas a certain percentage of the population always lived on surrogate breads for some of the year. These foods, it should be noted, were not just gathered; they could be bought. Thus, in Tsivil'sk district, pig-weed sold at from 20–70 kopeks a pud, and acorns at 31 kopeks a pud.[47]

The peasants themselves generally disliked surrogate breads and were well aware that they only had limited nutritional value.

All claimed that bread made from pig-weed lacked taste and they usually ate it with hot food. After eating it one was extremely thirsty, and had to drink huge quantities, according to the peasants. As for its nutritional value, judging by the appearance of those who used it, it must be low. The peasants claimed that while eating such bread they had little strength and were rapidly exhausted when working.[48]

The peasants found they could not do the field work necessary to ensure a decent harvest when eating such a diet. They complained of pains in the arms and legs and back, and found that they now took two days to do work which had previously taken only one day.[49]

The use of surrogate breads was itself a sign that things were not entirely hopeless, and regular shortages in the springtime made its use familiar to most households. But how did families cope when things got even worse? In the spring of 1873 in Smolensk province, after a bad harvest,

Some peasants sold any extra cattle they had and bought bread; some contracted to do work, and used the advance to buy bread, some took loans to buy bread until the first crops were harvested; but many had to get by day by day. The muzhik gets hold of a pud of flour somewhere or other, on credit; does a bit of work, sells a lamb, is idle for a bit, works again, then is hungry for a day or two while he rushes all over the place to find some flour.[50]

But when all else failed, there was little choice but to send the other members of the family out 'begging for crusts':

'Begging for crusts' and 'begging' are completely different things. A beggar is

[46]Stepanovskii, *Golodnyi kleb*, 212–13.
[47]Ibid., 214.
[48]Ibid., 217.
[49]Ibid., 221.
[50]Engel'gardt, *Iz derevni*, 106.

a specialist – his job is asking for charity. Usually he has no home, no property, no land, and is continually on the move . . . A beggar is usually crippled,
sick, or incapable of work, too old or too stupid. He is dressed in rags and begs
loudly, even arrogantly. He's not ashamed of his work . . . He rarely goes to
peasants but prefers to beg from merchants and gentry. Those 'begging for
crusts' are quite different. They are local peasants. Offer them work and they
will gladly do it and stop begging. They're dressed like any other peasant
(they sometimes even put on a new overcoat) except for carrying a knapsack
over their shoulders. Some are too ashamed to carry a sack. They turn up, as if
by chance to sit by the fire, and the housewife, if she understands, discreetly
offers something . . . Peasants are usually extremely tactful – they know they
themselves could be doing the same thing . . . A neighbour is ashamed to ask
for a crust – comes into the house, crosses himself and stands silent at the
threshold, and just says, quietly, 'Give me something for the love of God!' No
one notices him; every one carries on as usual, except for the housewife, who
goes to the table, takes a small hunk of bread . . . and hands it to him.[51]

But this was not yet the end of the road. Even worse than begging by
individuals was the starvation of whole regions, for 'Who can give
charity when everyone is begging?'[52] At such times one could see in
Russia the same scenes that famine produced throughout early modern
Europe. In Tula province in the late 1830s:

In famine winters, the situation of the peasants and their families is terrible.
They eat all sorts of revolting things: acorns, tree bark, marsh grass, straw –
everything goes into their food. In addition, they have nothing to buy salt
with; they get dysentery and become bloated and dehydrated. Terrible diseases begin to appear. Milk might help, but they will have already sold their
last cow and so, as they say, there is nothing even to accompany their soul on
its final journey. Women's milk dries up in their breasts, and breast-fed infants
die like flies.[53]

In 1891, in the worst famine of the century, sixteen provinces ran short
of grain. They covered an area of 205 million hectares in a belt from
the Urals to the Ukraine and had a population of 36 million people. At
the height of the famine over 11 million people needed relief supplies
of food, and in spite of a huge relief effort, as many as 400,000 people
died of starvation or starvation-induced diseases.[54]

The direct consequences of such conditions were horrifying. In the
early twentieth century, an English doctor described a household killed
off by famine.

[51]*Ibid.*, 114.
[52]Zablotskii, *Graf P.D. Kiselev*, vol. IV, 301.
[53]*Ibid.*
[54]Robbins, *Famine in Russia*, 61 and 168, and 170–2.

Lying on a mass of straw distributed over a wooden bench lay a wretched, emaciated girl of seventeen years of age, half clad and inexpressibly dirty, the vermin crawling unheeded over her trunk and limbs, while, to my horror, I noticed batches of bloated flies tumbling over one another in their efforts to feed on the sores left bare by the loathsome parasites. Her hectic cheeks and sunken eyes, together with a hacking cough, told their tale: the girl was dying of phthisis, preceded by famine and scurvy. At a slightly higher level, on the stove itself were a baby and a young child of three to four years old, enveloped in loathsome rags, while close up against them were a couple of fowls. On the floor, not three feet from the dying girl, was a young calf lying in a heap of dirty straw commingled with manure, while still more fowls were to be seen perched on points of vantage on the cross-bars of the tiny roof.

This was not all. In another corner of the room was a lad, likewise dying of starvation, the victim of typhus and scurvy – his face drawn and pale, his gums painfully tender, blood oozing from them at the slightest pressure, and his teeth loose in their sockets; unable to eat anything solid, even if it were provided for him; too weak to move, too weak to speak; his legs swollen, angry spots on the skin causing the most intense itching and pain, and a blue-black condition of the skin surface caused by the rupture of superficial blood-vessels. In places the distended skin had burst, leaving large open sores. The boy's breath smelt unbearably, and the best and most charitable thing one could wish him was a speedy release from his sufferings in this world.

Further, in various stages of undress, were to be counted no less than six other human beings – three children with their mother, all in a state of indescribable filth and pitiful emaciation, their hair matted in hopeless entanglement, and cemented by the matter exuding from unsightly sores, evidently of long standing. I questioned the family, and discovered that their breadwinner, the father and husband, had died for his country in Manchuria, and a grateful Government thus attended to the needs of his dying wife and children. Their food was a semi-poisonous kind of weed, ground up with a little rye flour, acorns, and oak bark. Throughout the village the same conditions held.[55]

Conditions such as these illustrate starkly the human costs of the tsarist government's belated industrialisation drive.

VI

The variations in diet that have been described so far were associated with the calendar and affected in some degree all sections of the peasantry. But there were also significant variations in the quality of diets within the peasantry as a class.

---

[55] Kennard, *The Russian Peasant*, 37–40. On famines in the Soviet period, see Wheatcroft, *CREES Discussion Papers*.

The subject of class differentiation within the peasantry is complex, and this is not the place to discuss it in detail. It was posed first during the debates between Populists and Marxists in the 1880s and 1890s about whether Russia was or was not becoming a capitalist society. Broadly speaking, the populists argued that mechanisms such as communal repartition and compulsory purchase of allotment land ensured that the Russian peasantry would remain a relatively homogeneous and stable class. It would not, therefore, split up as the English peasantry had into a large rural proletariat and a small rural bourgeoisie; and Russia would not therefore pass through a capitalist stage of development. The early Russian Marxists argued that differentiation within the peasantry was clearly taking place in spite of legal barriers to the process.[56] For example, although all peasants were forced to buy allotment land, many poorer peasants in fact leased their land to others and lived as wage labourers. In reality they were ceasing to be members of the peasantry and providing the core of a rural proletariat.

What is important to note is that the assumption of homogeneity ensured that the populist pioneers of budgetary studies of the peasantry tended to rely too greatly on average figures. In fact, if you looked for differences of wealth within the peasantry you could soon find them. And this was as true of diets as of other aspects of the peasants' household economy, but it required different, and slightly more subtle statistical approaches.[57]

The types of variation to be found between classes within the peasantry were in many ways similar to the seasonal and annual changes already described. As the quality of diets declined first luxuries vanished, along with animal-based foods and fresh vegetables and fruit. Then supplies of secondary staples such as groats and pickled cabbage became scarce, leaving a diet consisting almost entirely of bread, the least elastic item in the diet. Then the quality of the bread itself declined. And finally, in a crisis, even bread disappeared from the diet leaving real famine conditions.

The diets of richer peasants sometimes included surprising luxuries. The elder of Pestovo village near Velikii Ustyug in Vologda province offered Haxthausen 'an excellent breakfast . . . consisting of pies, veal cutlets, salmon, fruit tarts, waffles, tea, and capital madeira'. Haxthau-

---

[56]For Lenin's view, see *The Development of Capitalism*, in particular ch. 2. For a recent discussion which takes what might be called a neo-populist view, see Shanin, *The Awkward Class*. This has provoked a prolonged debate in the *Journal of Peasant Studies*, beginning with Harrison, 'Chayanov'.

[57]There is a good summary of Lenin's critique of early budgetary studies in Korenevskaya, *Byudzhetnye obsledovaniya*, ch. 3.

sen adds that, 'Our host was rich, but neither he nor his wife had departed from the national customs of the peasants here.'[58]

Diets reflected the whole range of wealth to be found in the village. 'As you eat, so shall you live.'[59] An estate in St Petersburg province in the early nineteenth century classified its peasants into four groups. The first, the rich, 'pay their taxes punctually and carry out their obligations . . . live and dress themselves cleanly and eat very well by peasant standards'. The second group, 'pay their taxes punctually and fulfil their obligations . . . but none have any reserves for a bad time'. The third group were those 'not poor' [*bezbednye*]; 'many of them manage to pay their taxes and fulfil their obligations (the best of them), but in spring and summer they suffer shortages of bread and have to borrow money until autumn from their landlords or from village money lenders'. The fourth group, the poor, never paid their taxes, 'eat only bread and milk, rarely eat gruel, and sometimes do not even have any bread'.[60] In Sebezh district in Vitebsk province in the early 1850s, the ability to survive the year on one's own bread was the clearest sign of wealth. The wealthy peasants were 'those who always have savings of 50 to 100 rubles and live on the previous year's bread right up to the harvest'.[61] In Smolensk, 'the degree of affluence is indicated by the time when a peasant begins to buy bread: before Christmas, before Shrovetide, before Easter, or not until just before the new crop. The later he begins to buy bread, the richer he is.'[62]

The distinction between the diets of rich and poor households appears even more clearly in a description of Kiev province in the early 1850s:

The poor peasants usually eat coarse bread of rye, barley, and sometimes even oat flour, or, instead of bread, *grechanniki*, made of buckwheat flour. Their daily diet includes two dishes – borshch without fat and bread, and gruel; and in addition, occasionally *kulesha* or peas, potatoes, and dumplings of barley, buckwheat, rye, and very rarely wheat flour. Only on holidays, and not always then, do they have meat fat or beef in their borshch, fish or sometimes curd dumplings with cheese, and *lemeshki* made of buckwheat or barley flour with milk or meat fat.[63]

Budgetary studies at the end of the nineteenth century show the same distinctions, only more systematically. Tables 9.1 and 9.2, based on

[58]Haxthausen, *The Russian Empire*, vol. I, 201.
[59]Dal', *Poslovitsy*, 803.
[60]Koval'chenko, *Krepostnoe krest'yanstvo*, 41.
[61]*Etnograficheskii sbornik*, vol. II, 221.
[62]Engel'gardt, *Iz derevni*, 389.
[63]Zhuravskii, *Statisticheskoe opisanie*, vol. I, 287, cited in Govlenko, 'Kommissiya', 22–3.

38 Carpenters taking tea and vodka, late nineteenth century.

surveys of Vologda province in the early twentieth century, show clearly the link between diet and wealth, measured here by the amounts of land held. 'In the diet of poor households the basic position is occupied by bread (mainly from rye flour), potatoes, and other cheap foodstuffs, while in the diet of rich households, wheaten bread is more important, and so are meat and fat, milk, confectionery, and so on.'[64] Budgetary studies suggest three main rules: (1) poorer households relied far more on grain products and richer households had more livestock produce; (2) nevertheless, in absolute terms the rich consumed more grain produce than the poor; and (3) the quality of the food was much better in rich households – wheaten bread, meat, fat, milk and confectionery played a larger role, and in general the diets were more varied.[65]

These sorts of variations could affect whole regions as well as individual households. There were, for example, regions where the whole population was physically stunted by inadequate diets. In parts of Tambov province in the 1880s, adult male workers could only work

[64]Dikhtyar, *Vnutrennyaya torgovlya*, 45.
[65]*Ibid.*

five-and-a-half hours a day on the normal diet, and children were constantly undernourished. A local doctor reported that:

The people are small, weak, sickly, incapable of any prolonged or heavy exertion. There are villages here whose inhabitants are never hired as workers because they are notoriously lethargic and incapable of hard work. The women are pale, ugly, and shapeless; they age very quickly; many of their children are still-born, and miscarriages are even more common. The children are almost all scrofulous and pale, and they are constantly sick.[66]

Such passages provide a cruel illustration of what one might call the law of accumulating disadvantages in peasant society. Poor diets were not merely a reflection of a more general poverty – they could actively contribute to a family's misfortunes, not merely through the physical discomfort they caused, but also by narrowing the possibilities of economic recovery.

VII

Can a survey of rural diets tell us anything about long-term changes in living standards? In principle it ought to in a society in which foodstuffs accounted for so large a part of the family budget, but in practice it is extremely difficult to reach any clear conclusions.

Take, for example, the issue of per capita consumption of grain. Is there any evidence that the average amounts of the staple foodstuff consumed during the century increased or decreased? The problem has long fascinated Russian scholars and government officials, and it has been approached logically enough by the drawing up of grain balances.[67] As we have seen above (pp. 339–41) discussion centred on the possibility that there were two separate periods of crisis, during which the food available per capita actually declined. But in fact these discussions have proved inconclusive. The evidence available is not precise enough to measure changes like this accurately, or to measure the regional and class variations which would be necessary to give the more general figures some meaning.

However, in two respects the study of diets offers indirect support for the claim that the political crises of the middle and end of the century were associated with larger economic and social crises which touched the material life of large sections of the peasantry. First is the

---

[66]Maress, 'Pishcha narodnykh mass', part 1, 67.
[67]For a survey of these efforts see Blum, *Lord and Peasant*, 332–3. For two recent specimens, see Koval'chenko, 'Dinamika urovnya'; and Nifontov, *Zernovoe proizvodstva*, 214. Nifontov's calculations are reproduced in Table 9.4.

evidence that harvests were slightly more erratic in these periods; second is the evidence of a decline in per capita holdings of livestock.[68] Thus, it does seem that for a significant number of peasants, living standards were declining towards the middle and again towards the end of the century. And this suggests in turn that the short-term effect of the 1861 act may have been to temporarily relieve a growing pressure on living standards. But this is all we can conclude about living standards in general in this period, and even this conclusion is tentative. Beyond this, there are a few specific changes in diets that should be noted:

(1) Some new foodstuffs appeared in the nineteenth century and became fairly widespread by its end. Of these, potatoes, tea and sugar were the most important.

(2) Growing monetisation and development of the transport network had a contradictory impact on diets. They may have led to impoverishment of rural diets in the short run, as products such as meat, eggs and honey were increasingly produced or gathered for sale rather than consumption.

(3) On the other hand, there were ways in which rural diets were enriched by contact with the towns. The richer villagers, as we have seen, were generally the first to acquire such urban luxuries as samovars. But migratory workers also exerted a powerful influence on rural diets. Indeed 'from the beginning of the twentieth century, peasant-workers have been the principal agents in the transformation of the dietary habits of the villages'.[69]

(4) For those who moved to the towns, there were important changes not so much in what was eaten, but rather in the relative amounts. The urban population benefited most from improved transportation networks, and it seems that in general town dwellers ate more meat and fish, and drank more tea, vodka and beer.[70]

The really momentous changes were to come in the Soviet period as the population of Russia migrated in increasing numbers to the towns. But even then the eating habits of collective farmers remained conservative, at least well into the 1950s.[71] These, however, are topics which take us beyond the scope of this book.

[68]Yanson, *Statistika*, vol. II, 613; Koval'chenko, 'K istorii skotovodstva'; Koval'chenko, *Krepostnoe krest'yanstvo*, 300.
[69]Kerblay, 'Alimentation rurale', 903.
[70]Krupyanskaya, 'Evolyutsiya', 280.
[71]Kerblay, 'Alimentation rurale', 895.

Conclusion

This eclectic survey of some aspects of food and drink in Russia has, we hope raised a number of themes. Two in particular, deserve comment.

First, we have seen that patterns of eating and drinking cannot be understood apart from their social and economic context. The consumption of food and drink serves a number of ends. Obviously the biological one is the most important; food is essential to maintain life. But even here all is not simple. There may be a physiologically determined minimum calorific intake, but this is dependent on so many variables that it is hard to specify at all narrowly. In addition, there are certain essential elements and vitamins needed for good health, as well as a balance (again, not precisely specified) between different types of food. There are also psychological and cultural aspects of diet. These, however, were constrained by the fairly limited range of crops, animals, fish and so on which were at hand, especially in pre-industrial society. People, both as individuals and as groups in society, have expectations about food, and drink; they have personal fads and fancies, preferences and dislikes; some items are abhorred because of religious (or magical) beliefs, or are attractive because of their social or ritual significance. What may be good and proper food for one person at a particular time, may be bad and wrong for another, or for the same person in a different context; what is acceptable without demur in some social settings may be quite unacceptable in others. Such variations involve changes in time or place, in social location or attitude; in individual mood, in one's health or in the company at, or purposes of, a particular meal.

Considerations such as these are most evident in the attitudes to stimulants. Alcohol, for example, calls forth a great range of reactions from detestation and total prohibition to grateful acceptance as an amelioration of life, or adoration as the blood of Christ; sometimes, of course, the teetotaller is also a devout Christian. Tea has at different times been regarded as a beneficent medicine and as a poison; both, of course, may be true, in some sense.

Eating and drinking also have class and functional implications. On the one hand, certain types of food are regarded as particularly suited to certain categories of population and even to certain types of work. A lavish table with rare dishes, or an ostentatiously frugal one, may be a demonstration of wealth, status, attitude or individual taste. The exercise of individual taste, however, depends on a measure of wealth and also of a developed system of production, storage and distribution. Such developments, on the other hand, involve quite new functions.

A second important theme deserving comment is the distinction between a natural economy characterised by gathering and farming largely for own consumption, and an economy dominated by the market.

In the early period, gathering was probably the main source of supplements to the diet: fungi, fruit, berries, honey and, above all, fish and game. Gathering of foodstuffs, therefore, provided sweetstuffs and much, if not most, of the animal protein consumed. Gathering was also the source of the main condiment and preservative, salt.

The activity of salt winning raises questions about the nature of non-agricultural or 'industrial' development in a society with limited agricultural surpluses. This activity was constrained by the access to and the nature of the raw material. Throughout the early period that material was brine which needed fuel to convert it into salt. The example of the White Sea salt industry shows that the salinity of the brine was of crucial importance, as was the availability of timber for fuel; but it also shows that to feed even a fairly limited number of workers in the relatively severe conditions of the area depended on relative costs between salt sold in the central areas and the grain which had to be acquired there. Surface salt was readily available at the mouth of the Volga once this region was in Russian hands in the late sixteenth century. It did not require considerable fuel inputs for its production; but whether salt was obtained from brine or excavated directly from the ground, it was located in remote areas. Trading it into the more populous regions of the centre involved the development of a transport network and the complexities of a market, storage and finance in a weakly monetised economy. The eighteenth-century developments involved increased exploitation of surface deposits; the problems of the industry had now become very largely those of labour in a society where the labour market, and even the concept of wage labour, was still weakly developed. The growth in the general structure of the economy as a result of the development of river transport and the market resolved the problem of salt supplies in the late eighteenth century.

It is clear that the diet was dominated by grain-based farming for a very long time. It remained so throughout the early period of the diet, into the seventeenth century. Only in that century was there something of a turning point in the slow evolution of Russian diet. Yet even long after that century grain, overwhelmingly rye – the main product of farming – continued to be the most important source of food and drink despite institutional and related changes. Only in the past century have appreciable changes in the structure of the diet become noticeable with a greater variety of foodstuffs available. But such changes did not always result in an improved diet.

The relationship between the natural economy and the market economy affected many aspects of diet. In Russia, this process was largely mediated through the state and its religion. The large number of fast days in the Orthodox calendar may stress the importance of fish in the diet. Yet there is also abundant evidence to show that non-Christian activities linked with the diet continued into the seventeenth century. In fact, we have insufficient evidence for this period to estimate the part played in the diet by either fish or meat. Some material, such as the Assize of Bread in the first half of the seventeenth century, suggests that the growth of market sales of standard and higher quality bread products where there were concentrations of those not mainly living directly off the land (the military and administrators, for example) stimulated state intervention in organising supplies and checking on their quality. Rye bread was everyday fare, but wheaten rolls were a treat. Such preferred food was virtually an urban luxury.

The liquor trade, too, shows how state intervention could influence dietary custom. It was in the middle of this century that the church attempted to assert its authority and restrict access to intoxicating drink largely on moral grounds. There was a spectrum of drinks: the virtually non-fermented materials, such as kvas, were drunk in place of the poor quality water then available; a range of beers and meads, slightly more alcoholic, were used on festive and ritual occasions. In Russia all these drinks might be hopped; this increased their life in cask and probably resulted in a higher alcohol content over time. The virtually non-alcoholic drinks with perhaps less than 2% alcohol may be functionally distinguished from the hopped drinks with perhaps 3–6% alcohol. All these were produced in the home. Spirits came into Russia in the late sixteenth century and rapidly increased in availability in the course of the seventeenth century. The technology involved in producing both distilled spirits and the stronger vodka was not available to everyone and this gave greater opportunities for official control. The state rapidly became concerned to obtain maximum income from the sales of spirits and by the mid-seventeenth century there was a major conflict of interest between the church and the state over this issue. The alternative to alcoholic drinks was the humble kvas. Tea only became generally available in the course of the nineteenth century.

As the Russian Empire grew in size, regional variations in geographical and cultural environment affected diets and contributed to interregional exchanges. In the nineteenth century potatoes became an important item in the diet, yet grain consumption seems to have remained at the levels known from the sixteenth century until the last quarter of the century. There were considerable variations in diet by region and by social situation, and, above all, by harvest size. Nevertheless, we can still detect a basic unity in the diet of different parts of European Russia.

The development of the internal and the international market was not an unmixed blessing. The famine of the 1890s was not avoided although the railway network, the base for increased regular internal trade, a basis for shops rather than intermittent markets, had been established by that time. As the fiscal burden grew in the late nineteenth century, peasants increasingly found they had to sell grain just after the harvest to pay taxes, and then buy it back at higher prices in spring. In this way even peasants who did not produce a surplus were slowly forced onto the market.

The foodstuffs available in towns were more varied and luxurious than those in the countryside. Yet the immediate impact of shops and the growing market on the diet of the mass of the Russian population was by no means straightforward. The market absorbed many less basic items which might have supplemented the grain diet. This was particularly true of gathered items such as berries, honey, or fish, which had added variety to a monotonous basic diet. The market also offered the mass consumer a greater quantity of the items in the basic rural diet, rather than a greater variety of cheap foodstuffs. It offered an improved variety of items mainly to the better off, especially in towns.

However, for some of the population the diet had improved by the twentieth century in that they came to have access to a greater variety of foodstuffs and an increased protein intake. This supplementation of the basic diet of grain products was now based not on gathering, but on farming. Urban tastes had spread to the wider society. But for many Russians the cost of change was high: famines occurred in Russia in the late nineteenth (and in the twentieth) century; drunkenness remained a problem and alcoholism appeared; above all, internal supply remained at risk to the severity of the climate and deficiencies of the market, storage and transport. The Soviet Union still faces these problems.

Bibliography

PRIMARY MATERIALS

Adrianova-Peretts, V.P., *Prazdnik kabatskikh yaryzhek; parodiya-satira, II polo-viny 17v.*, M.-L., 1936.

Akty feodal'nogo zemlevladeniya i khozyaistva XIV–XVI vekov, 3 vols., M., 1951–6.

Akty istoricheskie, 4 vols., SPB, 1841–2.

Akty sobrannye v bibliotekakh i arkhivakh Rossiiskoi imperii arkheografcheskoi ekspeditsieyu, 4 vols., SPB, 1836–8.

Akty sotsial'no-ekonomicheskoi istorii Severo-Vostochnoi Rusi kontsa XIV-nachala XVIv., vols. I–III, M., 1952–64.

Akty yuridicheskie, SPB, 1838.

Barbaro, I., *see* Skrzhinskaya.

Baron, *see* Olearius.

Belyaev, I.S., 'Rospisnoi spisok g. Moskvy 1638g.', *Trudy Moskovskago otdeleniya Russkago voenno-istoricheskago obshchestva*, vol. I, M., 1911, XVIII–XXIII.

[Bochius, J.] Shmid, G., 'Ivan Bokh v Moskve v 1578g.', *Mémoires de l'Académie Impériale des Sciences*, series 8, cl. hist.-phil., vol. V, 1901, no. 3.

Bolotov, A.T., 'Nakaz dlya derevenskago upravitelya', *TrVEO*, SPB, 1770, XVI, 69–230.

Bruin, K. [Bruyns, C. de], *Puteshestvie cherez Moskoviyu*, trans. P.P. Barsov, M., 1873.

Brunschwig [Braunschweig], Hieronymus, *Das neüwe Distilier buoch der rechten kunst von Heronimo Brunschwig ...*, Strasbourg, 1531.

Bussov, K. [Conrad Bussow], *Moskovskaya khronika, 1584–1613gg.*, M.-L., 1961.

Campensis, Albertus [Pighius], *De Moscovia*, Venice, 1543.

Chaev, N.S., 'Severnye gramoty XVv.', *LZAK*, 1927–8, I (XXXV), 1929, 121–64.

Chancellor, R., 'The Booke of the Great and Mighty Emperor of Russia and Duke of Moscovia', in Hakluyt, *The Principall Navigations Voiages and Discoveries of the English Nation*, vol. I, 270–93, London, 1589 (reprint 1965).

Chulkov, M.D., *Istoricheskoe opisanie Rossiiskoi kommertsii*, 7 vols., SPB, 1781–8.

Churchill, A., and J., *A Collection of Voyages and Travels*, 6 vols., London, 1704–32.

Clarke, E.D., *Travels in Russia, Tartary, and Turkey*, Edinburgh, 1839.

Cochrane, J.D., *Narrative of a Pedestrian Journey through Russia and Siberian Tartary ... During the Years 1820–1823*, London, 1824.

[Collins, S.], *The Present State of Russia*, London, 1671.

Contarini, A., *see* Skrzhinskaya.

C[rull], J., *The Antient and Present State of Muscovy*, London, 1698.

Dmytryshyn, B., ed., *Imperial Russia: A Source Book, 1700–1917*, 2nd ed. Hinsdale, Ill., 1974.

Doklad vysochaishee uchrezhdennoi Kommissii dlya issledovaniya nyneshnego polozheniya sel'skago khozyaistva i sel'skoi promyshlennosti v Rossii. Doklad i Zhurnal Kommissii. Prilozheniya I–VII, 5 vols., SPB, 1873.

'Domostroi blagoveshchenskago popa Sil'vestra, soobshch. Dm. Pavlov Golokhvastovym', *Vremennik Imp. Moskovskago OIDR*, I, 1849, section 2, materials, pp. i–iv, 1–116.

[Domostroi] A. Orlov, *Domostroi, izsledovanie*, part 1, M., 1917.

Dopolneniya k aktam istoricheskim, 12 vols., SPB, 1848–75.

Drevnerusskie knyazheskie ustavy XI–XVvv., ed. Ya.N. Shchapov, M., 1976.

Dvinskaya ustavnaya tamozhennaya otkupnaya gramota 1560g., publ. N.S. Chaev, *LZAK*, I (XXXIV), 1926, 199–203.

Engl'gardt, A.N., *Iz derevni: 12 pisem, 1872–87*, M., 1960.

[Ermolai Erazm] V.F. Rzhiga, 'Literaturnaya deyatel'nost' Ermolaya-Erazma', *LZAK*, I (XXXIII), 1926, 103–92.

Etnograficheskii sbornik izd. Imperatorskim Russkim geograficheskim obshchestvom, 6 vols., SPB, 1853–64.

Fletcher, G., *Of the Russe Commonwealth*, 1591, facsimile of Hakluyt Society, first series, vol. XX, Cambridge, Mass., 1966.

Foy de la Neuville, *Rélation curieuse et nouvelle de Moscovie*, La Haye, 1699.

Gerbershtein, see Herberstein.

Gramoty velikogo Novgoroda i Pskova, M.-L., 1949.

Hakluyt, R., *The Principal Navigations, Voyages, Traffiques and Discoveries of the English Nation*, 12 vols., Glasgow, 1903–5.

Haxthausen, A. von, *The Russian Empire: Its People, Institutions, and Resources*, 2 vols., London, 1865.

Herberstein, S. von, *Rerum Muscoviticarum comentarii*, 3 parts, Vienna, 1549.
   Gerbershtein, *Zapiski o Moskovitskikh delakh*, trans. A.I. Malein, SPB, 1908.
   Herberstein, *Description of Moscow and Muscovy, 1557*, ed. B. Picard, London, 1969.
   Notes upon Russia, ed. Major, 2 vols., 1851–2.

Justice, Elizabeth, *A Voyage to Russia*, 2nd ed., London, 1746.

Katsuragawa, Hosyu, *Kratkie vesti*, M., 1978.

Kilburger, *see* Kurts.

Kirilov, I.K., *Tsvetushchee sostoyanie Vserossiiskogo gosudarstva*, M., 1977.

Klenck, K. van, *Historish Vehael of Beschryving van de Voyagie*, Amsterdam, 1677.

Kniga klyuchei i Dolgovaya kniga Iosifo-Volokolamskogo monastyrya XVI veka, ed. M.N. Tikhomirov and A.A. Zimin, M.-L., 1948.

Korb, J.-G., *Diary of an Austrian Secretary of Legation at the Court of Czar Peter the Great*, 2 vols., London, 1863.

Kotošixin, G., *O Rossii v carstvovanie Alekseja Mixajloviča*, text and commentary by A.E. Pennington, Oxford, 1980.

Kovalevskii, E.P., *Puteshestvie v Kitai*, 2 parts, SPB, 1853.

Križanic, Yu., *Politika*, M., 1965.

Kurts, V.G., *Sochinenie Kil'burgera o russkoi torgovle v tsarstvovanie Alekseya Mikhailovicha*, Kiev, 1915. (See also Rodes, J. de.)

Manstein, C.H. von, *Contemporary memoirs of Russia from the Year 1727 to 1744*, 2nd ed., London, 1856.

Margaret, le capitaine, *Estat de l'empire de Russie et Grande Duché de Moscovie*, Paris, 1607.

Maskięwicz, S., *Pamiętniki Samuela i Bogusława Kazimierza Maskiewiczów, wiek XVII*, Wrocław, 1961.

Massa, I., *Skazaniya Massy i Gerkmana o smutnom vremeni v Rossii*, ed. with notes, by E.E. Zamyslovskii, 2 parts, SPB, 1874.

Materialy dlya geografii i statistiki Rossii sobrannye ofitserami general'nago shtaba, 25 vols., SPB, 1859–68.

    v. 8, Kazanskaya gub., ed. M. Laptev, SPB, 1861.

    v. 9, Kaluzhskaya gub., ed. M. Poprotskii, SPB, 1864.

    v. 12, Kostromskaya gub., ed. Ya. Krzhivoblotskii, SPB, 1861.

    v. 15 (2 parts), Minskaya gub., ed. M. Zelenskii, SPB, 1864.

    v. 17 (2 parts), Penzenskaya gub., ed. Ch. Stal', SPB, 1867.

    v. 18 (2 parts), Permskaya gub., ed. Kh. Mozel', SPB, 1864.

    v. 19, Ryazanskaya gub., ed. M. Baranovich, SPB, 1860.

    v. 24 (2 parts), Khersonskaya gub., ed. A. Schmidt, SPB, 1863.

    v. 25, Chernigovskaya gub., ed. M. Domontovich, SPB, 1865.

Michalo Lituanus, *De moribus* trans. S.D. Shestakov, *Arkhiv istoriko-yuridicheskikh svedenii, otnosyashchikhsya do Rossii*, book 2, second half, section 5, i-viii and 1–78.

Morgan, E.D. and C.H. Coote, *Early Voyages and Travels to Russia and Persia*, London, 1866.

Novgorodskaya pervaya letopis' starshego i mladshego izvodov, M.-L., 1950.

Novokomskii, Iovii, [Giovio Paolo, Bishop of Nocera, the Elder] in Gerbershtein, *Zapiski o Moskovitskikh delakh*, 251–75.

Novyi i polnyi rossiiskoi khozyaistvennoi vinokur, M., 1802.

[Olearius], trans. and ed. S.H. Baron, *The Travels of Olearius in Seventeenth-century Russia*, Stanford, 1967.

    Der Welt-beruehmten Adami Olearii Reise Beschreibungen ... nach Musskau und Persien, 4th ed., Hamburg 1969.

Opyt sanitarno-staticheskago issledovaniya Izvol'skoi volosti Eletskogo uezda, Elets, 1892.

Palitsyn, A., 'Skazanie Avraamiya Palitsyna', *RIB*, xiii, SPB, 1892, 473–524.

Bibliography

mqvist, E., Nagre widh Sidste-Kongl. Ambassaden, 1674, Lithographed-facsimile, Stockholm, 1898.

...iyatniki russkogo pravda, 8 fasc., M., 1952–63.

Pamyatniki russkoi pis'mennosti XV–XVIIvv., Ryazanskii krai, ed. S.I. Kotkov, 1978.

Parkinson, J., *A Tour of Russia, Siberia, and the Crimea*, ed. W. Collier, London, 1971.

Paterik Kievskago Pecherskago monastyrya, SPB, 1911.

Perry, J., *The State of Russia under the Present Czar*, London, 1716.

Pervyi gubernskii s''ezd vrachei Moskovskaga zemstva, Avgust 1876 goda, addendum, M., 1877. [*Russian History and Culture*, RHO 8519, University Microfilms International, 1978.]

[Peyerle, G.] trans. in Ustryalov, *Skazaniya*, vol. I, 145–234.

Pimlyco, or, Runne Red-Cap, London, 1609.

Pokrovskii, F.I., 'Puteshestvie v Mongoliyu i Kitai sibirskogo kazaka Ivana Petlina v 1618 goda', *Izv. Otdel. russkago yazyka i slovesnosti imp. Akad. nauk*, vol. XVIII, book 4, SPB, 1914.

Polnoe sobranie russkikh letopisei, SPB, Leningrad, 1841f.

Polnoe sobranie zakonov Rossiiskoi Imperii, First series, 46 vols., SPB, 1830; Second series, 55 vols., SPB, 1830–84.

Pososhkov, I.T., *Kniga o skudosti i bogatstve*, M., 1951.

Povest' vremennykh let, ed. V.P. Adrianova-Peretts, 2 vols., M.-L., 1950.

Pskovskie letopisi, ed. A.N. Nasonov, 2 fascs., M., 1941–55.

Raskhodnaya kniga Patriarshago prikaza kushan'yam, podavavshimsya patriarkhu Adrianu i raznago china litsam s sentyabrya 1698g., ed. A.A. Titov, SPB, 1890.

Razryadnaya kniga 1559–1605gg., M., 1974.

Razryadnaya kniga 1475–1598gg., M., 1966.

Reitenfels, Ya., 'Skazaniya svetleishemu gertsogu Toskanskomu Koz'me tret'emu, o Moskovii', Padua, 1680, *ChtOIDR*, 1905, book 3, x + 1–128, 1906, book 3, 129–228.

Revelations of Russia in 1846 by an English Resident, 3rd ed., 2 vols., London, 1846.

[Rodes, J. de] Kurts, V.G., *Sostoyanie Rossii v 1650–1655gg. po doneseniyam Rodesa*, M., 1915.

Rozhdestvenskii, N.V., 'K istorii bor'by s tserkovnymi bezporyadkami v russkom byta XVIIv.', *ChtOIDR*, 1902, book 2, miscellany, 1–31; text is on 18–31.

[Rubruquis], 'The Journey of William Rubruck to the Eastern Parts of the World 1253–55', *Hakluyt Society*, second series, no. IV, London, 1900.

Ruskiya dostopamyatnosti, OIDR, 3 parts, M., 1815–44.

Sakovich, S.I., *Iz istorii torgovli i promyshlennosti Rossii kontsa XVII veka*, TrGIM, fasc. 30, M., 1956.

Sbornik gramot kollegii ekonomii, 2 vols., Petrograd, 1922–9.

Shcherbatov, M.M., 'Razsuzhdenie o nyneshnem v 1787 godu pochti povsemestnom golode v Rossii, *ChtOIDR*, 1860, book 1, section 2, 81–112.

'Sostoyanie Rossii v razsuzhdenii deneg i khleba, v nachale 1788 goda', *ibid.*, 113–34.

'Statistika v razsuzhdenii Rossii', *ChtOIDR*, 1859, book 3, section 2, 1–96.

Shmurlo, *Izvestiya Dzhiovanni Tedal'di o Rossii vremen Ivana Groznago*, SPB, 1891.

Shumakov, S.A., *Sotnitsy (1537–1597gg.), gramoty i zapiski (1561–1696 gg.)* M., 1902.

Skibnevskii, A.I., report in *Sed'moi gubernskii s"ezd vrachei Moskovskago zemstva*, section 2, 222–33, M., 1884. [*Russian History and Culture*, RHO 8519, University Microfilms International 1978.]

Skrzhinskaya, E. Ch., *Barbaro i Contarini o Rossii, k istorii italo-russkikh svyazei v XVv.*, L., 1971.

Slovar' Akademii Rossiiskoi, 5 parts, SPB, 1789.

Slovar' russkogo yazyka XI–XVIIvv., fasc. 1f, M., 1975f.

Sir Thomas Smithes Voiage and Entertainment in Rushia, London, 1605.

Sobornoe ulozhenie 1649g., ed. M.N. Tikhomoirov and P.P. Epifanov. M., 1961.

Statisticheskii vremennik Rossiisskoi Imperii: 1858–1890, 3rd series, v. 4, SPB, 1884.

[Stoglav] I.A. [i.e. Ierodiakon Agapii = Honcharenko, A.], *Stoglav*, London, 1860.

Kozhanchikov, G.E., ed., *Stoglav*, SPB, 1863.

Svedeniya o piteinykh sborakh, parts 1–5, SPB, 1860.

Tamozhennye knigi Moskovskogo gosudarstva XVII veka, 3 vols., ed. I.I. Yakovlev, M.-L., 1950–1.

Tatishchev, V.N., *Leksikon rossiiskoi istoricheskoi, geografcheskoi, politicheskoi i grazhdanskoi*, in his *Izbrannye proizvedeniya*, L., 1979, 153–327.

Tedaldi, G. *see* Shmurlo.

Trudy kommissii vysochaishe uchrezhdennoi dlya sostavleniya proekta polozhenii ob aktsize s pitei, parts 1–2, SPB, 1861.

Ukaz o khlebnom i kolachnom vesu, 7134g., *Vremennik OIDR*, book 4, 1849, 1–60.

Ulfeld, J., *Hodoeporicon Ruthenicum*, Frankfurt, 1608.

Ustryalov N.G., *Skazaniya sovremennikov o Dmitrii Samozvantse*, 5 vols., SPB, 1831–4.

[Vasmer, M.] Fasmer, M., *Etymologicheskii slovar' russkogo yazyka*, 4 vols., M., 1964–73.

Vernadsky, G., *et al.*, *A Source Book for Russian History from Early Times to 1917*, 3 vols., New Haven, London, 1972.

Veselovskii, S.B., 'O kabakakh i kruzhechnom dvore v 1651g. v Novgorode', *ChtOIDR*, 1907, 1, miscellany, 38–40.

Sem' sborov zaprosnykh i pyatinnykh deneg v pervye gody tsarstvovaniya Mikhaila Fedorovicha, M., 1909.

Vosstanie I. Bolotnikova, dokumenty i materialy, M., 1959.

Yakovlev, A.I., *Namestnich'i, gubnye i zemskie ustavnyya gramoty Moskovskago gosudarstva*, M., 1909.

SECONDARY SOURCES

Alexander, J.T., *Bubonic Plague in Early Modern Russia*, Baltimore and London, 1980.

Alier, J.M., and J.M. Naredo, 'A Marxist Precursor of Energy Economics: Podolinsky', *Journal of Peasant Studies*, IX, 2 (1982), 207–24.

Allemagne, H.-R.d', *Du Khorassan au pays des Backhtiaris*, vols. I–IV, Paris, 1911.

Aluve, K., *Maa-kõrtsid ja hobuposti-jaamad Eestis* (Rural taverns and post-horse stations in Estonia), Tallinn, 1976, with numerous illustrations and summaries in Russian and German.

Amalrik, A., *Involuntary Journey to Siberia*, London, 1970.

Andreev, N.P., Vinogradov, G.S., *Russkie plachi (prichitaniya)*, M., 1937.

Aristov, N.Ya., *Promyshlennost' drevnei Rusi*, SPB, 1866.

Artamof, P., *La Russie historique, monumentale et pittoresque*, 2 vols., Paris, 1865.

Atkinson, T.A., and Walker, J., *A. Picturesque Representation*, vols. I–III, London, 1812.

Aymard, A., 'Pour l'histoire de l'alimentation: quelques remarques de methode', *Annales: E.S.C.*, II–III (1975), 431–42. English version in Forster and Ranum, *Food and Drink in History*, 1–16.

Baddeley, J.F., *Russia, Mongolia, China*, 2 vols., London, 1919.

Bakhrushin, S.V., *Nauchnye trudy*, vols. I–IV. M., 1952–9.

Bakhtiarov, A., *Bryukho Peterburga: obshchestvenno-fiziologicheskie ocherki*, SPB, 1888.

Bakhtin, V.S., Moldavskii, D., *Russkii lubok XVII–XIXvv.*, M., 1962.

Bakhtine, M.M., *L'Oeuvre de François Rabelais*, Paris, 1970.

Baklanova, N.A., 'Yan de-Gron', *Uch. zap. In-ta istorii RANION* (1929), IV, 109–22.

Banister, J., *An Introduction to Old English Silver*, London, 1965.

Baron, S., 'The Origins of Seventeenth Century Moscow's Nemeckaja Sloboda', *California Slavic Studies*, V (1970), 1–17.

Bartlett, R., *Human Capital; the Settlement of Foreigners in Russia, 1762–1804*, Cambridge, 1979.

Bazilevich, K.V., 'Elementy merkantilizma v ekonomicheskoi politike pravitel'stva Alekseya Mikhailovicha (XVIIv.)', *Uch. zapiski MGU*, fasc. 41, history I, 1940, 3–34.

Begunov, Yu.K., 'Stikh-raeshnik o chae', *Rukopisnoe nasledie Drevnei Rusi*, L., 1972, 244–8.

Belkin, A.A., *Russkie skomorokhi*, M., 1975.

Bell, J., *A Journey from St Petersburg to Pekin 1719–22*, ed. J.L. Stevenson, Edinburgh, 1965.

Bennassar, B., and J. Goy, 'Contribution à l'histoire de la consommation alimentaire du XIVe au XIX siècle', *Annales: E.S.C.*, II–III (1975), 402–29.

Berezin, P.V., *Na sluzhbe zlomu delu: Khronika iz zhizni na vinokurennykh zavodakh*, M., 1910.

Bernadskii, V.N., *Novgorod i Novgorodskaya zemlya v XV veke*, M., 1961.

Beskrovnyi, L.G., *Russkaya armiya i flot v XIX veke*, M., 1973.

Bezhkovich, A.S., Zhegalova, S.K., Lebedeva, A.A., and Prosvirkina, S.K., eds., *Khozyaistvo i byt russkikh krest'yan, pamyatniki material'noi kul'tury; opredelitel'*, M., 1959.

Billington, J.H., *The Icon and the Axe; An Interpretative History of Russian Culture*, London, 1966.

Blackwell, W.L., *The Beginnings of Russian Industrialisation. 1800–1860*, Princeton, 1968.

Blosfel'd, Doktor G.A., 'O p'yanstve v sudebno-meditsinskom i mediko-politseiskom otnosheniyakh', *Zapiski po chasti vrachebnykh nauk, izd. pri Imperatorskoi S. Petersburgskoi mediko-khirurgicheskoi Akademii* (1846), book 1, section 1, 140–73, and book 2, section 1, 94–147.

Blum, J., *The End of the Old Order in Rural Europe*, Princeton, 1978.
Lord and Peasant in Russia, Princeton, 1961.

Bobrinskii, A.A., *Narodnyya russkiya izdeliya*, fasc. 7, M., 1913.

Bogoslovskii, M.M., *Oblastnaya reforma Petra Velikago, provintsiya, 1719–1727gg.*, M., 1902.

Bogoyavlenskii, S.K., *Prikazyne sud'i XVII v.*, M.-L., 1946.
Drevnerusskoe vrachevanie v XI–XVII vv., istochniki dlya istorii russkoi meditsiny, M., 1960.

Borodin, D.N., *Itogi vinnoi monopolii i zadachi budushchego*, SPB, 1908. (Russian History and Culture, RHO 8494, University Microfilms International, 1978.)

Bradbury, F., *History of Old Sheffield Plate*, London, 1912.

Braudel, F., *Capitalism and Material Life: 1400–1800*, trans. Miriam Kochan, Glasgow, 1973.

Bridbury, A.R., *England and the Salt Trade in the Later Middle Ages*, Oxford, 1955.

Brodskii, N.L., 'Krepostnoe pravo v narodnoi poezii', in Dzhivelegov, A.K. ed., *Velikaya reforma*, vol. iv, 1–33.

Brokgauz–Efron, *Entsiklopedicheskii slovar'*, 1st ed., xli + ii vols. in 86, SPB, 1890–1904.

Brunner, H., *Old Table Silver; A Handbook for Collectors and Amateurs*, London, 1967.

Buganov, V.I., *Moskovskoe vosstanie 1662g.*, M., 1964.

Bushkovitch, P., *The Merchants of Moscow, 1580–1650*, Cambridge, 1980.

Chaudhuri, K.N., *The Trading World of Asia and the English East-India Company 1660–1760*, Cambridge, 1978.

[Chayanov, A.V.], *A.V. Chayanov on the Theory of Peasant Economy*, ed. D. Thorner, R.E.F. Smith and B. Kerblay, Homewood, Ill., 1966.

Chayanov, A., *Byudzhety krest'yan starobel'skago uezda*, Khar'kov, 1915. [Reprinted in B. Kerblay, ed., *Oeuvres choisies de A.V. Cajanov*, vol. ii, Mouton, 1967.]

Chechulin, N.D., *Ocherki po istorii russkikh finansov v tsarstvovanie Ekateriny II*, SPB, 1906.

Cherepnin, L.V., *Russkie feodal'nye arkhivy XIV–XV vekov*, 2 vols., M., 1948–51.

Chicherov, V.I., *Zimnii period russkogo zemledel'cheskogo kalendarya XVI–XIX vekov; ocherki po istorii narodnykh verovanii* (AN SSSR. TrIE, ns., vol. XL), M., 1957.

Chuprov, A.I., and A.S. Postnikov, eds., *Vliyanie urozhaev i khlebnykh tsen na nekotorye storony Russkago narodnago khozyaistva; sbornik statei*, 2 vols., SPB. 1897.

Cipolla, C.M., *The Economic History of World Population*, 6th ed., London, 1974.

Clark, C., and M. Haswell, *The Economics of Subsistence Agriculture*, 4th ed., London, 1970.

Confino, M., *Systèmes agraires et progrès agricole*, Paris, 1969.

Conrad, H.G., 'Entwicklung der deutschen Bohrtechnik', *Technikgeschichte*, part 38, 1971, 4, 298–316.

Dal', V.I., *Poslovitsy russkogo naroda: sbornik*, M., 1957.

Dal', V., *Tolkovyi slovar' zhivago velikorusskago yazyka*, 4th ed., vols. I–IV, SPB, 1912–14.

Dikhtyar, G.A., *Vnutrennyaya torgovlya v dorevolyutsionnoi Rossii*, M., 1960.

Dit'yatin, I., 'Tsarskii kabak v Moskovskom gosudarstve', *Russkaya mysl'*, 1883, IV, 9, 34–72.

Dmitriev, V.K., *Kriticheskiya issledovaniya o potrebleniya alkogolya v Rossii*, M., 1911.

Dobrolyubov, N.A., 'Narodnoe delo: rasprostranenie obshchestv trezvosti', *Sovremennik*, IX (1859), section 3, 1–36, signed N. T-nov; also in Dobrolyubov, N.A., *Sobranie sochinenii v 9-ti tomakh*, ed. B.I. Bursov, *et al.* (M.-L., 1962), 5, 246–85. See also *Sovremennik* (186), 80, 'Vnutrennee obozrenie', 468–79.

Drobizhev, V.Z., I.D. Koval'chenko, and A.V. Muraviev, eds., *Istoricheskaya geografiya SSSR*, M., 1973.

Drummond, J.C., and A. Wilbraham, *The Englishman's Food: Five Centuries of English Diet*, London, 1939.

Druzhinin, N.M., *Gosudarstvennye krest'yane i reforma P.D. Kiseleva*, 2 vols., M., 1946, 1958.

Du Bois, J.P.I., *Vies des gouverneurs généraux avec l'abrégé de l'histoire des établissemens hollandois aux Indes Orientales*, La Haye, 1763.

Dukes, P., *Catherine the Great and the Russian Nobility*, Cambridge, 1967.

Dulov, A.V., 'Prirodnye usloviya i razvitie proizvoditel'nykh sil Rossii v XVIII-seredine XIX veka', *Voprosy istorii*, I, 1979, 38–53.

Dzhivelegov, A.K., ed., *Velikaya reforma: Russkoe obshchestvo i krest'yanskii vopros v proshlom i nastoyashchem*, 6 vols., M., 1911.

Efimenko, P.S., 'O Yarile, yazycheskom bozhestve vostochnykh slavyan', *Zapiski russkogo Geograficheskogo Obshchestve po otdeleniya etnografii*, II, 77–112.

    Materialy po etnografii russkago naseleniya Arkhangel'skoi gubernii, 2 vols., M., 1877–8.

Elagin, V.N., 'Otkupnoe delo', *Sovremennik*, IX (1858), 'Slovesnost'', nauki, i khudozhestva', 185–264, and X, 'Slovesnost'', 347–426.

Elovskikh, V., 'Iz tetradei arkhivista', *Ural*, XII (1970), 131.

Erisman, F., *Pishchevoi dovol'stvie rabochikh na fabrikakh Moskovskoi gubernii*, M., 1893.

Evdokimov, I., 'Starinnye krasnoborskie pechi', *Izvestiya Vologodskago obshchestva izucheniya Severnogo Kraya*, fasc. 11, 129–31, Vologda, 1915.

Fedorov, V.A., 'Krestyanskoe trezvennoe dvizhenie 1858–1859gg.', in *Revolyutsionnaya situatsiya v Rossii v 1859–1861gg.*, vol. I, M., 1960, 133–48.

Fedotov, G.V. (compiler and ed.), *A Treasury of Russian Spirituality*, New York, 1965.

Forster, E. and R., eds., *European Diet from Pre-Industrial to Modern Times*, New York, 1975.

Food and Drink in History: Selections from the Annales: Economies, Societes, Civilisations, vol. V, Baltimore, 1979.

Frederiks, J.W., *Dutch Silver*, 4 parts, The Hague, 1952–61.

Fridman, M.M., *Vinnaya monopoliya*, 2 vols., SPB, 1914–16.

Galton, D., *Survey of a Thousand Years of Beekeeping in Russia*, London, 1971.

George, S., *How the Other Half Dies*, Penguin, 1977.

[Gersevanov, N.], A.G., *O p'yanstve v Rossii i sredstvakh istrebleniya ego*, Odessa, 1845.

Gilyarovskii, V.A., *Moskva i moskvichi*, M., 1968.

Glamann, K., *Dutch–Asiatic trade, 1620–1740*, Copenhagen, 1958.

Goldsmith, R.W., 'The Economic Growth of Tsarist Russia', *Economic Development and Cultural Change*, IX (1960–1), 441–75.

Golyshev, I., *Atlas risunkov so starinnykh pryanishnykh dosok Vyaznikovskago uezda Vladimirskoi gubernii*, S. Mstera, 1874.

Gomilevskii, V., *Sol'*, SPB, 1881.

Govlenko, V.F., 'Kommissiya dlya opisaniya gubernii Kievskoi uchebnogo kruga', in *Ocherki istorii Russkoi etnografii, folkloristiki i antropologii*, vol. III, ed. R.S. Lipets, M., 1965.

Grinchenko, B.D., *Slovar' ukrainskogo yazyka*, 2 vols., Kiev, 1924.

[Grot, K.K.], *Konstantin Karlovich Grot kak gosudarstvennyi i obshchestvennyi deyatel': Materialy dlya ego biografii i kharakteristiki*, 3 vols., Petrograd, 1915.

Hamburg, G.N., 'The Crisis in Russian Agriculture: A Comment', *Slavic Review*, XXXVII, 3 (1978), 481–6.

Hamilton, H., *The English Brass and Copper Industries to 1800*, London, 1926.

Harrison, M., 'Chayanov and the Economics of Russian Peasantry', *Journal of Peasant Studies*, II, 4 (1975), 389–417.

Hemardinquer, J.-J., ed., *Pour une histoire de l'alimentation*, Cahiers des Annales, no. 28, Paris, 1970.

Hoch, S.L., and W.R. Augustine, 'The Tax Censuses and the Decline of the Serf Population in Imperial Russia', *Slavic Review*, XXXVIII, 3 (1979), 403–25.

Hough, W., *Collection of Heating and Lighting Utensils in the US National Museum*, Washington, 1928.

Hughes, B., and Hughes, T., *Three Centuries of English Domestic Silver, 1500–1820*, London, 1952.
Hughes, G.B., *Antique Sheffield Plate*, London, 1970.
Hutchinson, J.F., 'Science, Politics and the Alcohol Problem in post-1905 Russia', *Slavonic and E. European Review*, LVIII, 2 (1980), 232–54.
Ibbetson, A., *Tea, from Grower to Consumer*, London, 1910.
Istoriya Moskvy v shesti tomakh, 7 vols., M., 1952–9.
Ivanova, E.A., *Russkie samovary*, L., 1971.
Kabuzan, V.I., *Narodonaselenie Rossii v XVIII-pervoi poluvine XIXv.*, M., 1963.
Kafengauz, B.B., *Ocherki vnutrennego rynka Rossii, pervoi poloviny XVIII veka*, M., 1958.
'Khlebnyi rynok v 20–30 kh godakh XVIII stoletiya', *MIZ*, I, M., 1952 [a shortened version of this article is in his *Ocherki*, ch. 5, 232–61].
Kahan, A., 'The Costs of "Westernization" in Russia: The Gentry and the Economy in XVIIIth Century Russia', *Slavic Review*, XXV, 1 (1966), 40–66.
'Natural Calamities and their Effect upon the Food Supply in Russia', *Jahrbücher fur Geschichte Osteuropas*, vol. XVI (1968), 353–77.
Kamentseva, E.I. and N.V. Ustyugov, *Russkaya metrologiya*, M., 1965.
Kapterev, N.F., *Patriarkh Nikon i ego protivniki*, 2nd ed., Sergiev Posad, 1913.
Karamzin, N.M., *Istoriya gosudarstva rossiiskago*, 3rd ed., 12 vols., SPB, 1830–1.
Karger, M.K., 'Zemlyanka-masterskaya kievskogo khudozhnika XIIIv.' *KS*, XI, 1945, 5–15.
Kashtanov, S.M., *Sotsial'no-politicheskaya istoriya Rossii kontsa XV-pervoi poloviny XVI v.*, M., 1967.
Kennard, H.P., *The Russian Peasant*, London, 1907.
Keppen, P.I., 'O potreblenii khleba v Rossii', *ZhMVD*, XXXVI (1840), no. 4, 402–21.
Kerblay, B., 'L'evolution de l'alimentation rurale en Russie, 1896–1960', *Annales: E.S.C.*, Sep.–Oct. (1962), 885–913.
Khoroshkevich, A.L., *Torgovlya Velikogo Novgoroda s Pribaltikoi i zapadnoi Evropoi v XIV–XV vekakh*, M., 1963.
Khozyaistvo i byt, see Bezhkovich.
Khromov, P.A., *Ekonomicheskoe razvitie Rossii v XIX–XXvv.*, M., 1951.
Kirikov, S.V., *Izmeneniya zhivotnogo mira v prirodnykh zonakh SSSR (XIII–XIX, vv.), stepnaya zona i lesostep'*, M., 1960.
Promyslovye zhivotnye, prirodnyaya sreda i chelovek, M., 1966.
Klepikov, S.A., *Lubok*, part 1, 'Byulleten'', Gosudarstvennogo literaturnogo. muzeya, no. 4, M., 1939.
Klyuchevskii, V.O. *Sochineniya*, vols. i–viii, M., 1956–9.
Kolominskii, S. 'Torgovlya sol'yu na Rusi v 16–17v. i obshchee sostoyanie solyanykh promyslov v ukazannyi period vremeni', *Universitetskie izvestiya*, part 12, Kiev, 1912, 1–66.
Kopanev, A.I., *Krest'yanstvo russkogo Severa v XVIv.*, L., 1978.
Korenevskaya, N.N., *Byudzhetnye obsledovaniya krest'yanskikh khozyaistv v dorevolyutsionnoi Rossii*, M., 1954.

Korolev, D.A., *Russkii kvas*, M., 1963.

Korsak, A., 'O vinokurenii', in *Obzor razlichnykh otraslei manufakturnoi promyshlennosti Rossii*, vol. III, SPB, 1865, 215–515.

'Pivovarenie i medovarenie', in *Obzor razlichnykh otraslei manufakturnoi promyshlennosti Rossii*, vol. III, SPB, 1865, 1–97.

Korsak, A.K., *Istoriko-statisticheskoe obozrenie torgovykh snoshenii Rossii s Kitaem*, Kazan', 1857.

Korzhin, A.E., 'K istorii kul'tury chaya v Rossii', *MIZ*, II, M.-L., 1956, 660–705.

Koshcheev, A.K., *Dikorastushchie s"edobnye rasteniya v nashem pitanii*, M., 1980.

Kotlyarevskii, A.A., *O pogrebal'nykh obychayakh yazycheskikh slavyan; izsledovanie*, M., 1868.

Koval'chenko, I.D., 'Dinamika urovnya zemledel'cheskogo proizvodstva Rossii v pervoi polovine XIX v.', *Istoriya SSSR*, vol. I (1959), 53–86.

'K istorii skotovodstva v evropeiskoi Rossii v pervoi polovine XIX v.', *MISKh*, IV, M., 1960, 173–204.

Russkoe krepostnoe krest'yanstvo v pervoi polovine XIX v., M., 1967.

and Milov, L.V., *Vserossiiskiiskii agarnyi rynok XVIII-nachala XX v.*, M., 1974.

Kovaleskii, E.P., *Puteshestvie v Kitai*, 2 parts, SPB, 1853.

Kovalevskii, V.I., *Rossiya v kontse XIX veka*, SPB, 1900.

Krupyanskaya, V.Yu., 'Evolyutsiya semeino-bytovogo uklada rabochikh', in *Rossiiskii proletariat: oblik, bor'ba, gegemoniya*, M., 1970, 271–88.

and N.S. Polishchuk, *Kul'tura i byt rabochikh gornozavodskogo Urala (konets XIX-nachalo XXv)*, M., 1971.

Krutikov, M., 'K istorii tul'skikh kustarnykh promyslov', *Zapiski istoriko-bytovogo otdela Gosudarstvennogo Russkogo muzeya*, fasc. 2, L., 1932, 5–19.

Kula, W., *An Economic Theory of the Feudal System: Towards a Model of the Polish Economy, 1500–1800*, London, 1976.

Kushner, P.N., ed., *The Village of Viryatino*, trans. Sula Benet, New York, 1970.

Kutepov, N.I., *Velikoknyazheskaya i tsarskaya okhota na Rusi s X po XVI vek.*, 4 vols., 1896–1911, vol. I, SPB, 1896; vol. II, *Tsarskaya okhota na Rusi tsarei Mikhaila Feodorovicha i Alekseya Mikhailovicha XVII v.*, SPB, 1898.

Le Donne, J.P., 'Indirect Taxes in Catherine's Russia, I. The Salt Code of 1781', *Jahrbücher fur Geschichte Osteuropas*, XXII (1975), 161–91.

'Indirect Taxes in Catherine's Russia, II. The Liquor Monopoly in Catherine's Russia', *Jahrbücher fur Geschichte Osteuropas*, XXIV (1976), 173–207.

Lekhnovich, V.S., 'K istorii kul'tury kartofelya v Rossii', *MIZ*, II, M.-L., 1956, 258–400.

Lenin, V.I., *The Development of Capitalism in Russia*, M., 1977. 1st ed., SPB, 1899. (*Collected Works*, vol. v.]

Leontovich, F.I., 'Golodovki v Rossii do kontsa proshlogo veka', *Severnyi vestnik*, III (1892), 47–76.

Le Play, P.G.F., *Les ouvriers européens*, 2nd ed., 6 vols., Paris, 1877–9.

Levi-Strauss, C., *Le cru et la cuit*, Paris, 1964.
Levko, O.N., *Vitebskie izraztsy XIV–XVIIIvv.*, Minsk, 1981.
Lewis, I.M., *Ecstatic Religion*, Harmondsworth, 1971.
Linkov, Ya.I., *Ocherki istorii krest'yanskogo dvizheniya v Rossii v 1825–1861gg.*, M., 1952.
Lobaneva, T.A., 'Izdeliya nakladnogo serebra, Moskva XIX vek' (*TrGIM*, fasc. 17), M., 1956.
Lur'e, G., 'Piteinye bunty 1859 goda i P.P. Linkov-Kochkin', *Zven'ya*, vols. III–V, M.-L., 1934, 426–69.
Lyubomirov, P.G., *Ocherki po istorii russkoi promyshlennosti*, M., 1947.
Madariaga, I. de, *Russia in the Age of Catherine the Great*, London, 1981.
Mancall, M., 'The Kiakhta Trade', in *The Economic Development of China and Japan*, ed. C.D. Cowan, London, 1964, 19–48.
Russia and China; their Diplomatic Relations to 1728, Cambridge, Mass., 1971.
Man'kov, A.G., *Tseny i ikh dvizhenie v russkom gosudartsve XVI veka*, M.-L., 1951. Trans. by G.K. Krichevsky as *La Mouvement des prix dans l'Etat russe de XVIe siècle*, Paris, 1957.
Maress, L.N., 'Proizvodstvo, potreblenie khleba v krest'yanskom khozyaistve', in Chuprov and Postnikov, eds., *Vliyanie urozhaev*, vol. I, 1–96.
'Pishcha narodnykh mass v Rossii', *Russkaya Mysl'*, x (1893), pt. 2, 45–67, and XI, pt. 2, 60–75.
Martynov, A.F., 'Nekotoryya zametki o byte vyatskikh krest'yan', *Bratchina*, part I, SPB, 1859.
Marx, K., *Wages, Price and Profit*, M., 1947.
Matossian, Mary, 'The Peasant Way of Life', in S.W. Vucinich, ed., *The Peasant in Nineteenth Century Russia*, Stanford, 1968, 1–40.
Mavor, J., *An Economic History of Russia*, 2 vols., 2nd ed. London and Toronto, 1925.
Medvedev, M., *O khlebnom vine i ego podmesyakh*, SPB, 1863.
Medyntseva, A.A., *Drevnerusskie nadpisi Novgorodskoi Sofiiskogo sobora: XI–XIV veka*, M., 1978.
Mel'gunova, P.E., *et. al.*, *Russkii byt po vospominaniyam sovremennikov XVIII veka*, 2 vols., M., 1914–18.
Mennell, R.O., *Tea, an Historical Sketch*, London, 1926.
Miller, V.F., *Russkaya maslenitsa i zapadnoevropeiskii karnaval*, M., 1884.
Milyukov, P.N., *Gosudarstvennoe khozyaistvo Rossii v pervoi chetverti XVIII stoletiya i reforma Petra Velikago*, SPB, 1892.
Ministerstvo finansov. 1802–1902, 2 vols., SPB, 1904.
Ministerstvo gosudarstvennykh imushchestv, *Obzor deistvii departmenta sel'skago khozyaistva i ocherk sostoyaniya glavnykh otraslei sel'skoi promyshlennosti v Rossii v techenie 10 let, s 1844 po 1854 god*, SPB, 1855.
Multhauf, R.P., *Neptune's Gift; a History of Common Salt*, Baltimore, 1978.
Murzanov, N.A., 'Khlebnye zapasnye magaziny pri Pavle I-m.', *Arkhiv IT v R*, III (1922), 130–3.
Nagel, N., *Kachelöfen des 15. bis 17. Jahrhunderts*, Darmstadt, 1955.
Nares, R., *A Glossary ... on the Works of English authors*, 2 vols., London, 1882.

Nenquin, J.A.E., *Salt* (Dissertationes archaeologicae gandenses, 6), Bruges, 1961.

Nesmeyanov, A.N., and V.M. Belikov, *Pishcha budushchego*, M., 1979.

Neuhoff, J., *Die Gesandtschaft die Ost-Indischen Compagnej*, Amsterdam, 1669.

Nifontov, A.S., *Zernovoe proizvodstvo Rossii vo vtoroi polovine XIX veka*, M., 1974.

Nikitskii, A.I., *Istoriya ekonomicheskago byta Velikago Novgoroda*, M., 1893.

Nol'de, Baron E.F., *Piteinoe delo i aktsiznaya sistema*, 2 vols., SPB, 1882–3.

Ocherki istorii SSSR. Pervaya chetvert' XVIIIv., ed. B.B. Kafengauz, and N.I. Pavlenko, M., 1954.

Ocherki istorii SSSR. Konets XVv.-nachalo XVIIv., ed. A.N. Nasonov, L.V. Cherepnin, A.A. Zimin, M., 1955.

Ocherki istorii SSSR. XVIIv. ed., A.A. Novosel'skii, and N.V. Ustyugov, M., 1955.

Ocherki istorii SSSR. Vtoraya polovina XVIIIv., ed. A.I. Baranovich, B.B. Kafengauz, *et al.*, M., 1956.

Ocherki istorii SSSR. Vtoraya chetvert' XVIIIv., ed. A.I. Baranovich, L.G. Beskrovnyi, E.I. Zaozerskii, and E.I. Indova, M., 1957.

Oman, C., *Caroline Silver, 1625–1688*, London, 1970.

[Osipov, N.O., ed.], *Kazennaya prodazha vina*, SPB, 1900.

Ostroumov, 'Drevnerusskie solevarennye tovarishchestva', *Ustoi*, v (1882), 57–93; VIII, 49–84; IX–X, 127–70.

Ovsyannikov, Yu.M., *Russkie izraztsy*, L., 1968.
    Lubok, M., 1968.

Palibin, I.V., 'Chainoe rastenie', *Trudy po prikladnoi botanike*, XVIII (1927–8), 3, 3–16.

Palmqvist, E., Nagre widh Sidste-Kongl. Ambassaden, 1674, Lithographed-facsimile, Stockholm, 1898.

Pascal, P., *Avvakum et les débuts du raskol; la crise religieuse au 17e siècle en Russie*, Paris, 1938.
    'L'entr'aide paysanne en Russie', *La Revue des Etudes slaves*, XX (1942), 1–4, 82–90; reprinted in P. Pascal, *Civilisation paysanne en Russie: six esquisses*, Lausanne, 1969, 63–73.

Pavlenko, N.I., *Istoriya metallurgiya v Rossii v XVIII veke*, M., 1962.

Pechenuk, V., 'Temperance and Revenue Raising: the Goals of the Russian State Liquor Monopoly, 1894–1914', *New Zealand Slavonic Journal*, 1 (1980), 35–48.

Peretts, V.N., 'Iz starinnoi satiricheskoi literatury o p'yanstve i p'yanitsakh' *Sbornik statei posvyashchennykh S.F. Platonovu*, SPB, 1911, 432–8.

Perkovskii, A.L., 'Krizis demograficheskogo vosproizvodstvo krepostnogo krest'yanstva Rossii v pervoi polovine XIX stoletiya', in A.G. Vishnevskii, ed., *Brachnost'*, 167–190.

Pervushin, S., *Vliyanie urozhaev v svyazi s drugimi ekonomicheskimi faktorami na potreblenie spirtnykh napitkov v Rossii*, M., 1909.

Petrov, P.N., 'Rospis' raskhodov Tsarstva Moskovskago', *ZORSA*, IV, SPB, 1887, 330–51.

Pintner, W., *Russian Economic Policy under Nicholas I*, Ithaca, N.Y., 1967.
Pipes, R., *Russia under the Old Regime*, London, 1974.
Podobedova, *Miniatyury russkikh istoricheskikh rukopisei*, M., 1965.
Pogrebinskii, A.P., *Ocherki istorii finansov dorevolyutsionnoi Rossii*, M., 1954.
Pokhlebkin, V.V., *Natsional'nye kukhni nashikh narodov*, M., 1978.
Pokrovskii, M.N., *Russkaya istoriya s drevneishikh vremen do kontsa XIX stole-tiya*, 4 vols., M., 1933–4.
Pokrovskii, V.I., 'Vliyanie kolebanii urozhaev i khlebnykh tsen na estestven-noe dvizhenie naseleniya', in Chuprov and Postnikov, *Vliyanie*, vol. 1.
Popov, A.N., 'Piry i bratchiny', *Arkhiv istoriko-yuridicheskikh svedenii, otnosya-shchikhsya do Rossii*, book 2, second half, section 41, 19–41, M., 1854.
Preobrazhenskii, A.A., *Ocherki kolonizatsii Zapadnogo Urala v XVII-nachale XVIII v.*, M., 1956.
Prokof'eva, L.S., *Votchinnoe khozyaistvo v XVII veke, po materialiam Spaso-Prilutskogo monastyrya*, M.-L., 1959.
Pronshtein, A.P., *Velikii Novgorod v XVIv.*, Khar'kov, 1957.
and V.Ya. Kiyashko, *Vspomogatel'nye istoricheskie distsipliny*, M., 1973.
Propp, V.Ya., *Russkie agrarnye prazdniki*, L., 1963.
Prozorovskii, D., 'Chai, po starinnym russkim svedeniyam', unpaginated offprint from *Domashnaya beseda*, SPB, 1866.
Prozorovskii, D.I., 'Starinnoe opisanie solevarennogo snaryada', *IAO*, VI, section 1, fasc. 3, SPB, 1868, 233–55.
Pryzhov, I.G., *Istoriya kabakov v Rossii v svyazi s istoriei russkago naroda*, M., 1868.
Ocherki, stat'i, pis'ma, ed. M.S. Al'tman, M., 1934.
Rabinovich, M.G., Latysheva, G.P., *Iz zhizni drevnei Moskvy*, M., 1961.
O drevnei Moskve: Ocherki material'noi kul'tury i byta gorozhan v XIV–XVI vv., M., 1964.
Reinbot, [A.E.] *Chai. Otkuda on idet k nam*, SPB, 1873.
Robbins, R.G., *Famine in Russia, 1891–1892*, New York, 1975.
Rozhkov, N.A., *Sel'skoe khozyaistvo Moskovskoi Rusi v XVI veke*, M., 1899.
Rubinshtein, N.L., *Sel'skoe khozyaistvo Rossii vo vtoroi polovine XVIII v.; istoriko-ekonomicheskii ocherk*, M., 1957.
Rybakov, B.A., *Remeslo drevnei Rusi*, M., 1948.
Ryndzyunskii, P.G., *Utverzhdenie kapitalizma v Rossii*, M., 1978.
Sakharov, I.P., *Skazaniya russkago naroda*, 2 vols., SPB, 1841–9.
Salaman, R.N., *The History and Social Influence of the Potato*, Cambridge, 1949.
Samoilov, 'Istoricheskie i statisticheskie issledovaniya o kyakhtinskoi torgo-vle', *Sbornik statisticheskikh svedenii*, 1854, book 2, 3–38.
Savich, A.A., *Solovetskaya votchina XV–XVII v.*, Perm', 1927.
Schuyler, E., *Peter the Great, Emperor of Russia*, 2 vols., New York, 1884.
Scott, J.C., *Moral Economy of the Peasant Rebellion and Subsistence in Southeast Asia*, Yale U.P., 1976.
Scrimshaw, N.S., and V.R. Young, 'The Requirements of Human Nutri-tion', in *Food and Agriculture: A Scientific American Book*, San Francisco, 1976, 27–40.

Semenov-Tyan-Shanskii, P.P., *Rossiya*, 11 vols., SPB, 1890–1914.

Semenov, P.P., *Geografichesko-statisticheskii slovar' Rossiiskoi imperii*, 5 vols., SPB, 1863–85.

Obituary of K.K. Grot, *Russkaya Starina*, IV (1898), 216–23.

Shanin, T., *The Awkward Class; Political Sociology of Peasantry in a Developing Society: Russia 1910–1925*, Oxford, 1972.

Shchepkin, 'Goloda v Rossii', *Istoricheskii vestnik*, XXIV, 1886, 489–521.

Shmidt, S.O., 'Proekt P.I. Shuvalova 1754 goda', *Istoricheskii arkhiv*, VI (1962), 100–18.

Shunkov, V.I., *Ocherki po istorii kolonizatsii Sibiri*, M., 1946.

Simms, J.Y., Jr., 'The Crisis in Russian Agriculture at the end of the Nineteenth Century: A Different View', *Slavic Review*, XXXVI, 3 (1977), 377–98.

'On Missing the Point: A Rejoinder', *Slavic Review*, XXVII, 3 (1978), 487–90.

'The Crop Failure of 1891: Soil Exhaustion, Technological Backwardness and Russia's "Agrarian Crisis"', *Slavic Review*, XLI, 2 (1982), 236–50.

'The Economic Impact of the Russian Famine of 1891–92', *Slavonic and East European Review*, LX, 1 (1982), 63–74.

Sivkov, K.V., 'Nekotorye itogi zernovogo proizvodstva v Evropeiskoi Rossii na rubezhe XVIII–XIX vv.', in *Ezh AI 1958*, Tallin, 1959, 21–32.

Skarzynski, L., *L'alcool et son histoire en Russie*, Paris, 1902.

Sladkovskii, M.I., *Ocherki ekonomicheskikh otnoshenii SSSR s Kitaem*, M., 1957.

Slovtsov, (Reverend), 'Istoricheskoe i statisticheskoe obozrenie neurozhaev v Rossii', *Sbornik statisticheskikh svedenii o Rossii*, RGO, book 3, SPB, 1858, 465–502.

Smirnov, M., *Nizhegorodskie kazennye kabaki*, Nizhnii Novgorod, 1913.

Smirnov, P.P., *Posadskie lyudi i ikh klassovaya bor'ba v seredine 17 veka*, 2 vols., M., 1948.

Smith, R.E.F., *The Origins of Farming in Russia*, Etudes sur l'economie ct la sociologie des payes slaves, no. 2, Paris, La Haye, 1959.

The Enserfment of the Russian Peasantry, Cambridge, 1968.

Peasant Farming in Muscovy, Cambridge, 1977.

Snegirev, I., *Russkie prostonarodnye prazdniki i suevernye obryady*, fascs. 1–4, SPB, 1837–39.

Sobolov, A., *Narodnye poslovitsy i pogovorki*, M., 1961.

Solov'ev, S.M., *Istoriya Rossii s drevneishikh vremen*, 15 vols., M., 1959–66.

Sreznevskii, I.I., *Materialy dlya slovarya drevnerusskago yazyka*, 3 vols., SPB, 1893–1903.

Staehlin Storcksburg, J. von, *Original Anecdotes of Peter the Great*, London, 1788.

Staveacre, F.W.F., *Tea and Tea Dealing*, London, 1929.

Stepanovskii, F.K., *Materialy dlya izucheniya 'golodnogo khleba'*, Kazan', 1893.

Syroechkovskii, V.E., *Gosti-surozhane* (Izvestiya gos. Akademii istorii i material'noi kul'tury, 127), M.-L., 1935.

Sytin, P.V., *Istoriya planirovki i zastroiki Moskvy* (Trudy Muzeya istorii i rekonstruktsii Moskvy), 2 vols., M., 1950–4.

Tatishchev, V.N., *Istoriya rossiiskaya*, 7 vols., M., 1962–8.

Tereshchenko, A., *Byt russkago naroda: narodnost', zhilishcha, domovodstvo, obraz zhizni, muzyka, svad'by, vremyachislenie, kreshchenie i pr. i pr.*, 7 vols., SPB, 1848.

Tikhomirov, M.N., 'Maloizvestnye letopisnye pamyatniki XVIv.', *IZ*, 10 (1941), 84–94.

Tokarev, S.V., *Krest'yanskie kartofel'nye bunty*, Kirov, 1939.

Tolstoi, D.N., *Istoriya finansovykh uchrezhdenii v Rossii*, SPB, 1848.

Treml, V.G., 'Alcoholism and State Policy in the Soviet Union', in Z.N. Fallenbüchl, ed., *Economic Development in the Soviet Union and Eastern Europe*, vol. II, New York, 1976, 368–98.

Troitskii, S.N., *Finansovaya politika russkogo absolyutizma v XVIII v.*, M., 1966.

Trusevich, Kh., *Posol'skie i torgovye snosheniya Rossii s Kitaem do XIX veka*, M., 1882.

Tudge, C., *The Famine Business*, London, 1977.

Tynurist, I.V., 'Gde vo gusli zvonili?', *Etnograficheskie issledovaniya severo-zapada SSSR*, L., 1977, 16–29.

Ukers, W.H., *All about Tea*, 2 vols., New York, 1935.

Ustyugov, N.V., *Solevarennaya promyshlennost' Soli Kamskoi v XVII veke*, M., 1957.

Van Creveld, M., *Supplying War*, Cambridge, 1977.

Veselovskii, S.B., 'Kabatskaya reforma 1652 goda', *Ezhemesyachnyi zhurnal literatury, nauki i obshchestvennoi zhizni*, IV (1914), 59–66.

Soshnoe pis'mo: issledovanie po istorii kadastra i pososhnago oblozheniya Moskovskago gosudarstva, 2 vols., M., 1915–16.

'K voprosu o sostave i istochnikakh XXV glavy Ulozheniya', *RIZh*, I–II (1917), 27–45.

'O privilegiyakh po sudu otkupshchikov i vernykh sborshchikov', *Trudy po istochnikovedeniyu i istorii Rossii perioda feodalizma*, M., 1978, 120–45.

Vishnevskii, A.G., ed., *Brachnost', rozhdaemost', smertnost' v Rossii i v SSSR*, M., 1977.

Vodarskii, Ya. E., *Naselenie Rossii v kontse XVII–nachale XVIII veka*, M., 1977.

Volkov, M.Ya., *Ocherki istorii promyslov Rossii*, M., 1979.

Voronin, N.N., 'Medvezhii kul't v Verkhnem Povolzh'e v XI veke', Gos. Yaroslavo-Rostovskii istoriko-arkhitekturnyi i khudozhestvennyi muzei-zapovednik, *Kraevedcheskie zapiski*, fasc. 4, Yaroslavl', 1960, 25–93.

Vvedenskii, A.A., *Dom Stroganovykh v XVI–XVIIvv.*, M., 1962.

Webster, Mary, *Johan Zoffany, 1733–1810*, London, 1977.

Wheatcroft, S., article on famines in Soviet period *CREES Discussion Papers*, *SIPS* nos. 1 and 2, Birmingham, 1976; no. 20, 1981; no. 21, 1982.

Wolf, E.R., *Peasants*, Engelwood Cliffs, N.J., 1966.

Yakovtsevskii, V.N., *Kupecheskii kapital v feodal'no-krepostnicheskoi Rossii*, M., 1953.

Yanson, Ya.E., *Sravnitel'naya statistika Rossii i Zapadno-Evropeiskikh gosudarstv*, 2 vols. SPB, 1878.

Yuldashev, M.Yu., *K istorii torgovykh i posad'skikh svyazei Srednei Azii s Rossiei v XVI–XVII vv.*, Tashkent, 1964.

Zabelin, I.E., *Domashnii byt russkikh tsarei v XVI i XVII stoletii*, 4th ed., 2 vols., M., 1862–1915.

Zablotskii-Desyatovskii, A.P., *Graf P.D. Kiselev i ego vremya: materialy dlya istorii imperatorov Aleksandra I, Nikolaya I i Aleksandra II*, 4 vols., SPB, 1882.

Zablotskii-Desyatovskii, M., 'O p'yanstve v Rossii', in [*Ekonomist*], *Prilozheniya k Ekonomicheskomu ukazatelyu*, ed. I.V. Vernadskii (1858), vol. I, book I, 107–50.

Zabylin, M., *Russkii narod; ego obychai, obryady, predaniya, sueveriya i poeziya*, M., 1880.

Zaozerskaya, E.I., *U istokov krupnogo proizvodstva v rosskoi promyshlennosti XVI–XVIIvv., k voprosu o genezise kapitalizma v Rossii*, M., 1970.

Zasurtsev, P.I., 'Postroiki drevnego Novgoroda', *Trudy Novgorodskoi arkheologicheskoi ekspeditsii*, vol. II, *MIA*, 65, M., 1959, 262–98.

Zelenin, D.K., *Russische (Ostslavische) Volkskunde*, Berlin, 1927.

Zertsalov, A.N., *Novyya dannyya o zemskom sobore 1648–1649gg.*, M., 1887.

Zhuravskii, D.P., *Statisticheskoe opisanie Kievskoi gub.*, 3 vols., Kiev, 1852.

Index

(Key references are given in Italic)